ADVANCE PRAISE FOR

Crisis Communication Case Studies on COVID-19

"COVID-19 Communication Case Studies is a remarkably comprehensive and fresh account of how the pandemic crisis took its toll on everyday life in diverse contexts. Each chapter begins with the background needed to frame the study and concludes with findings that offer rich materials for professionals' and students' discussions and springboards for scholarly pursuits. These case studies about crisis and mediated communication are analyzed via an incredibly wide array of theoretical and analytic lenses. They offer poignant reminders of what was happening in restaurants, with sports teams, in families and schools, and well as businesses and other sites during a time when no one knew what would happen next."
—Patrice Buzzanell, University of South Florida and Shanghai Jiaotong University

"A stress test is used in medicine to assess the condition of a patient's heart. Crisis Communication Case Studies on COVID-19: Multidimensional Perspectives and Applications is a stress test for crisis management across multiple levels: individual, organizational, community & regional, and national & international. The best crisis communication research has always been interdisciplinary and this book captures that effectively through the various case studies used to illuminate the various levels of analysis. While much of what we learn about COVID-19 and crises is applicable only in the arena of public health crises, many of the insights presented in Communication Case Studies on COVID-19: Multidimensional Perspectives and Applications have applications to other areas of crisis communication and our understanding of resilience. It is a fascinating read because of its willingness to embrace the complexity of the pandemic."
—Dr. W. Timothy Coombs, Centre for Crisis and Risk Communications and ICA Fellow

Crisis Communication Case Studies on COVID-19

 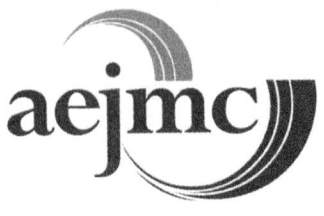

AEJMC—PETER LANG SCHOLARSOURCING SERIES

Vol. 9

Crisis Communication Case Studies on COVID-19

Multidimensional Perspectives and Applications

Edited by
Mildred F. Perreault and Sarah Smith-Frigerio

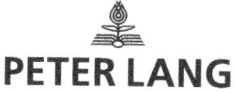

PETER LANG

New York · Berlin · Bruxelles · Chennai · Lausanne · Oxford

Library of Congress Cataloging-in-Publication Data

Names: Perreault, Mildred F., editor. | Smith-Frigerio, Sarah, editor.
Title: Crisis communication case studies on COVID-19 : multidimensional perspectives and applications / edited by Mildred F. Perreault, Sarah Smith-Frigerio.
Description: New York : Peter Lang, [2024] | Series: AEJMC - Peter Lang scholarsourcing series, 2373-6976 ; vol. 9 | Includes bibliographical references and index.
Identifiers: LCCN 2023051701 (print) | LCCN 2023051702 (ebook) | ISBN 9781433192227 (paperback) | ISBN 9781433192234 (pdf) | ISBN 9781433192241 (epub)
Subjects: LCSH: Communication in public health–Case studies. | Communication in crisis management–Case studies. | COVID-19 (Disease) in mass media–Case studies.
Classification: LCC RA423.2 .C76 2024 (print) | LCC RA423.2 (ebook) | DDC 362.101/4–dc23/eng/20240112
LC record available at https://lccn.loc.gov/2023051701
LC ebook record available at https://lccn.loc.gov/2023051702
DOI 10.3726/b18897

Bibliographic information published by the Deutsche Nationalbibliothek.
The German National Library lists this publication in the German
National Bibliography; detailed bibliographic data is available
on the Internet at http://dnb.d-nb.de.

Cover design by Peter Lang Group AG

ISSN 2373-6976 (print) ISSN 2373-6984 (online)
ISBN 9781433192227 (paperback)
ISBN 9781433192234 (ebook)
ISBN 9781433192241 (epub)
DOI 10.3726/b18897

© 2024 Peter Lang Group AG, Lausanne
Published by Peter Lang Publishing Inc., New York, USA
info@peterlang.com—www.peterlang.com

All rights reserved.
All parts of this publication are protected by copyright.
Any utilization outside the strict limits of the copyright law, without the permission of the publisher, is forbidden and liable to prosecution.
This applies in particular to reproductions, translations, microfilming, and storage and processing in electronic retrieval systems.

This publication has been peer reviewed.

CONTENTS

List of Figures	ix
List of Tables	xi
Acknowledgments	xiii
Chapter 1. COVID-19 Communication Case Studies, Where It Began and Why These Studies Matter *Sarah Smith-Frigerio & Mildred Perreault*	1
Chapter 2. When a Pandemic and an "Infodemic" Collide, Uncertainty Prevails: Misinformation & the COVID-19 Crisis *Jennifer Anderson*	13
Chapter 3. #AloneTogether: A Qualitative Content Analysis of a Hashtag Campaign Providing Support through the COVID-19 Mental Health Crisis *Jessica D. Freeman & Jessica Elton*	39

CONTENTS

Chapter 4. "Like Putting Out Fires, While Running on a Treadmill That Was Also on Fire": Working and Parenting in a Pandemic 61
Lauren J. Johnsen & Amnee Elkhalid

Chapter 5. Social Media Mourning: Dealing with Grief and Crisis Response Surrounding COVID-19 79
Jensen Moore

Chapter 6. COVID-19 and Higher Education: Navigating Ambiguity, Constraints, and Misplaced Optimism 99
Anna Valiavska

Chapter 7. Branding, Marketing, PR, and COVID-19 115
Erika J. Schneider

Chapter 8. Advertising as a Form of Public Health Education: An Analysis of the Ad Council and COVID Collaborative's "It's Up to You" Vaccination Awareness Campaign 135
Janelle Applequist & Jeanette Abrahamsen

Chapter 9. Seventeen Weeks: Fan Reactions to the NFL's COVID-19 Protocols during the 2020 Season 153
Virginia S. Harrison, Brandon Boatwright, Carla White, & Kayleigh Jackson

Chapter 10. Coronavirus and Journalism: A Meta-analysis of Early Research on Journalism in the COVID-19 Pandemic 171
Gregory Perreault, Ella Hackett, & Alexis Handler

Chapter 11. Six Feet Apart: A Case Study of Urban and Rural Medical Professionals' and Health Systems' Responses to COVID-19 189
Melanie B. Richards & Ashleigh D. Bunn

Chapter 12. Is There a Difference? Generational Response to COVID and Media Usage 215
Carrie Reif-Stice, Steven Venette, Sarah Smith-Frigerio, Nazanin Bani Amerian, & Joel Iverson

CONTENTS

Chapter 13. Speaking Directly to Indigenous Communities via Social Media: Native Female Politicians Manage Community Information by Addressing Crises within a Pandemic   233
Victoria L. LaPoe, Benjamin R. LaPoe II, Candi S. Carter Olson, Cristina L. Azocar, & Jayne Yerrick

Chapter 14. Coping with a Pandemic Using Social Media: Nurses' Expressions of Individual and Community Resilience on TikTok   259
Sarah Smith-Frigerio & J. Brian Houston

Chapter 15. Political Rhetoric and Crises Communication During a Global Pandemic   275
Joel Lansing Reed & Monique Luisi

Chapter 16. "It spread like Wildfire" and "Flooded Hospitals" Compounding Crisis: Climate, Wildfires, and Hurricanes during the Pandemic   297
Mildred Perreault & Bipulendra Adhikari

Chapter 17. Communicating About COVID-19 and Black Lives Matter: A Case Study of Memes, Twitter & Reddit   321
Mia Moody-Ramirez

Chapter 18. Calling COVID-19 the "Chinese Virus": What Types of #ChineseVirus Messages Get Attention on Facebook Pages?   335
Juan Liu

Chapter 19. Crisis Communication during the COVID-19 Pandemic: A Comparative Perspective from the Online Communication of Public Health Agencies in Italy, Sweden, and the United States   355
Kaila Witkowski, Frederike Albrecht, N. Emel Ganapati, Serena Tagliacozzo, & Derrick Boakye Boadu

Chapter 20. In the End, COVID-19 Goes On and On 379
   Mildred Perreault & Sarah Smith-Frigerio

   Editors 385
   Contributors 387
   Index 393

LIST OF FIGURES

Figure 2.1.	Interpersonal Sources and Trust	22
Figure 2.2.	Percent of People Using Various Media Sources for COVID-19 Information	22
Figure 2.3.	Trust in Social Media for COVID-19 Information	23
Figure 2.4.	Ratings of Trust in Selected Media Sources Based on Political Ideology (on a scale of 1–4)	24
Figure 2.5.	Only 6% of COVID-19 Deaths are Caused by the Virus	25
Figure 2.6.	The Pandemic was Planned	26
Figure 2.7.	Beliefs in Accuracy of Information from Official Health Experts	26
Figure 2.8.	Beliefs in False Statements about COVID-19	27
Figure 2.9.	Beliefs in False Statements about Protective Measures for COVID-19	29
Figure 7.1.	QR Code for Texas Roadhouse Menu	119
Figure 7.2.	Airport Digital Signage	123
Figure 9.1.	Semantic Network for Sept. 8–12 Timeframe	159
Figure 9.2.	Semantic Network for Sept. 28 to Oct. 1 Timeframe	160
Figure 9.3.	Semantic Network for Nov. 19 to Dec. 2 Timeframe	161
Figure 9.4.	Semantic Network for Dec. 30 to Jan. 5 Timeframe	162

Figure 11.1.	Tennessee Urban Health System 1 COVID-19 Social Media Response	198
Figure 11.2.	Tennessee Urban Health System 2 COVID-19 Social Media Response	199
Figure 11.3.	Tennessee Rural Health System COVID-19 Social Media Response	200
Figure 18.1.	Total Interactions among Five Categories of Facebook Posts Containing #ChineseVirus or #ChinaVirus	344
Figure 19.1.	Daily Tweet Country by Country	359

LIST OF TABLES

Table 9.1.	Exemplary Quotes from Thematic Analysis of Twitter Conversation	163
Table 12.1.	Average Discriminating Value for Generations	224
Table 17.1.	Themes in Tweets Containing COVID-19 and Black Lives Matter	326
Table 17.2.	Themes in Memes Containing COVID-19 and Black Lives Matter	329
Table 17.3.	Themes in Reddit Posts Containing COVID-19 and Black Lives Matter	329
Table 18.1.	Hierarchical Regression Predicting the #ChineseVirus Messaging on Facebook	344
Table 19.1.	Coding Scheme in Previous Empirical Studies	360

ACKNOWLEDGMENTS

We wish to express our sincere gratitude to those who supported us throughout the development of this edited volume. At the forefront of this list must be our amazing contributors, who have willingly shared their work and their feedback with us, and with fellow contributors. Thank you for being an integral part of this process.

We also wish to thank the Association for Education in Journalism and Mass Communication, from the members who selected our proposed volume during the 2021 Scholarsourcing competition, to the AEJMC editors who reviewed chapters and provided such wonderful feedback. Specifically, we wish to thank both Dr. Carolyn Bronstein and Dr. Katie Place, personally, for all of their help. This volume would not exist without the support of AEJMC.

We cannot forget to thank Peter Lang Publishing, and especially our editor, Elizabeth Howard, for answering any and all of our publishing questions and being a wonderful coach. You have made the development of this volume an enjoyable experience.

There are several professional groups that contributed to this project as well. We specifically wish to thank the members of the Crisis Communication Educators Facebook group, where so many ideas, including the seeds of this edited volume, began. We also wish to thank the wonderful group of scholars and professionals with the Disaster and Community Crisis Center at the University of Missouri, and in particular the Center's Director, Dr. J. Brian Houston. The training and expertise we developed during our respective times with the DCCC has been invaluable.

Finally, we must be sure to thank our gracious spouses, children, family members, and friends. You have been cheerleaders, sounding boards, kept us fed and well-caffeinated, and so much more. Thank you for supporting us in all of our endeavors.

· 1 ·

COVID-19 COMMUNICATION CASE STUDIES, WHERE IT BEGAN AND WHY THESE STUDIES MATTER

Sarah Smith-Frigerio & Mildred Perreault

Traditionally, crisis communication has found its home in public relations research. This book takes a different approach, building on the premise that crisis communication involves all facets of media and communication. College coursework in crisis communication often focuses on the objectives, strategies, and tactics needed to address a crisis happening at the community, organizational, or individual level. However, the COVID-19 pandemic makes it clear that crisis communication was needed—and happening—at all levels, simultaneously.

Scholars maintain that crises present both challenges and opportunities for multiple publics. In a situation like a pandemic, systems that are already stressed often are pushed beyond a breaking point. Systems and institutions are stressed, individuals experience disaster fatigue, and communities suffer. On the other hand, there is room for either developing or improving community resilience, as well as post-traumatic growth.

That said, scholars have often limited the scope of their studies to a specific level of interaction—individual, community, organizational, or societal—rather than examining the places where these responses intersect and overlap (Houston, 2021). Scholars in media and communication have identified the need to explore a variety of theoretical approaches in order to gain a more comprehensive view of crisis and disaster communication and consider the challenges and inequalities experienced by diverse populations, and the need for social change (Buzzanell & Houston, 2018; Matthews & Thorsen, 2022; Tierney, 2007).

We, like many scholars, experienced the pandemic as an opportunity to rethink the ways our areas of expertise intersect. Even in media and communication scholarship, there is a predisposition to exist in silos—carved out as journalism, public relations, advertising, science, health, or political communication, etc.—as if these fields do not have significant theoretical overlap. The pandemic affirmed how the relationships among these areas build a complex web, or ecology, where the actions of one group directly influence the decisions of another. For example, political pressure impacted the messages created by health departments, which, in turn, affected the way people understood the intensity of the pandemic and threat of the virus, which then changed the actions many took in their daily lives.

Although the pandemic was an unwelcome experience, for the authors contributing to this volume, research on the pandemic was not only a natural progression of their research agendas, but also an opportunity to shine new light on their respective areas of expertise. The pandemic forced us to understand crisis not only as a sudden disruption of daily life and operations, with clearly delineated pre-event, event, and post-event phases, but also as something capable of being a prolonged event that comes in waves, and with the propensity to fundamentally alter individual expectations and organizational goals. It changed the way we interact and engage, work and rest. For many, it communicatively transformed our being and sense of purpose.

These studies use different perspectives and methodologies, as well as situational analyses and foci. *Crisis communication case studies on COVID-19: Multidimensional perspectives and applications* is not only about a virus and its impact on various means of communication. Rather, it represents the ways in which fractures and cracks within our society were also brought to the forefront of our communicative practices. As mentioned above, crisis communication models have relied on a cyclical approach—a phase of preparation, experience of the crisis, recovery and resilience, and planning for the next crisis. That said, the pandemic illustrates that crises can certainly encompass all phases at the same time, with multiple, compounding crises occurring in tandem and competing for resources.

Why Case Studies?

The case studies, or chapters, presented in this volume are snapshots of COVID-19 experiences and topics organized into sections focused on individual, organizational, community and regional, and national and international contexts. Akin to Buzzanell and Houston's (2018) call to advance research into resilience from "different metatheoretical perspectives and communication contexts" (p. 1), we believe the best means to investigate the communicative impacts of the COVID-19 pandemic is to approach it from multiple theoretical perspectives and levels. Case studies are an inclusive and comprehensive way to examine crisis and disaster communication ecologies. Communication ecology approaches seek to understand the complexities and interactions that exist in our lives. People seek out information and interact with information in a variety of ways, but within the constraints of various structures and known options available to them.

Crises do not exist in a vacuum, and we are no sooner past one crisis than another issue or event brings on challenges. For individuals, these events test their character, for organizations they shape their viability and reputation. For example, the use of social media and interpersonal communication is one way to connect to others when you cannot share space, but as social media has become ubiquitous in both professional and personal lives, scholars have recognized the potential shortcomings and challenges of digital communication channels. Many chapters explore the ways in which campaigns situated in the social media realm can lack the tools to address misinformation, political polarization, and provide social support—but can also ensure ways to connect, find critical information and advocate for others. Given this perspective, we ask how social media can empower responses, engage diverse communities, or possibly even dilute crisis response, and crisis communication practices? Social media can be a powerful avenue for activism and engagement and reaches groups traditional media often cannot.

In our research, we have found many scholars evaluate crises at a particular level, and focus on the roles of individuals and audiences, institutions and systems, or communities when discussing topics such as marketing, health campaigns, advertising and engagement. These studies often fail to understand how grassroots efforts contribute to individual and community outcomes. In reality, each community consists of communication practices and processes at multiple levels, with many taking place within the greater ecological environment of a crisis simultaneously. In this volume, we can see how social media, for instance, plays several roles during COVID-19, at multiple levels, and we hope readers will be able to see the intersections of constructs relevant to social media use when reviewing the included cases at various levels within the communication ecology.

Individual

Individuals in crisis often use the knowledge they have gained from previous experiences to inform their responses. Those with prior experiences with natural disasters will, hopefully, be prepared for future ones, and also share their knowledge with those they encounter. Contributors in this section use the perspectives of individuals in the pandemic to inform their scholarship into seeking information, sharing messages, trying to survive without support systems, and coping with hardship, loss, and even death.

- Chapter 2—When a Pandemic and an "Infodemic" Collide, Uncertainty Prevails: Misinformation & the COVID-19 Crisis

In this chapter, Anderson discusses the challenges created as information is distributed. A major finding of this case study is that people who regularly use social media were more likely to believe misinformation around COVID-19 health effects and claims. The author uses Uncertainty Management Theory and the Theory of Motivated Information Management to examine how social media users understood misinformation channels and sources.

- Chapter 3—#AloneTogether: A Qualitative Content Analysis of a Hashtag Campaign Providing Support through the COVID-19 Mental Health Crisis

Freeman and Elton discuss the challenges of social isolation during the COVID-19 pandemic and how people used the #AloneTogether campaign to connect and cope during isolation. Considering how social media has become an increasingly popular channel for disseminating mental health campaigns, given its global reach and cost-effectiveness, this campaign is a great example of the intersection of crisis communication and mental health campaign practices.

- Chapter 4—"Like Putting Out Fires, While Running on a Treadmill That Was Also on Fire": Working and Parenting in a Pandemic

In Chapter 4, Johnsen and Elkhalid discuss the challenges of parents who lost all support systems and were suddenly required to teach, entertain, and protect their children with very limited resources and support structures. By using the ideologies expressed in the work-to-home spillover research, the authors provide a case study of the cognitive blurring of boundaries between work and home responsibilities.

- Chapter 5—Social Media Mourning: Dealing with Grief and Crisis Response Surrounding COVID-19

In this chapter, Moore discusses the challenges of death and grief and how the pandemic heightened those challenges, but also how it created a collective experience beyond family, community, and national boundaries. This case uses the Theory of Social Mourning as a lens to examine the collective experiences of those who lost loved ones during the pandemic.

Organizational

The Crisis Emergency Risk Communication (CERC) framework (Reynolds & Lufty, 2018; Reynolds & Seeger, 2005) has focused on how organizations, specifically the Centers for Disease Control and Prevention and the Federal Emergency Management Agency, should respond to crises and disasters. While the primary purpose of crisis communication and applying this framework is to help organizations overcome crises and disasters, some studies focus exclusively on organizational response, thereby prioritizing—unintentionally—organizational response as the most important response. The cases presented in this section consider this level of response, as well as its shortcomings, constraints, and overlaps with other levels. In this way, the organizational section of this volume mirrors recent research, for example, in healthcare and crisis management which considers how emergency personnel often use dialogue to mediate the actions of others in critical situations—like a pandemic.

Additionally, this section provides a variety of frameworks for understanding the ways in which brand management and audience engagement can differ even when organizations are experiencing the same global crisis.

- Chapter 6—COVID-19 and Higher Education: Navigating Ambiguity, Constraints, and Misplaced Optimism

Valiavska's study examines the specific challenges of those working in higher education during the pandemic. The author examines the demonstrable negative impact on the lives and livelihood of members of historically marginalized communities as a result of the pandemic and how that was augmented on college campuses. The author acknowledged how different narratives emerged in different phases of the pandemic. The chapter also provides an approach to more inclusive practices in future health crises.

- Chapter 7—Brand, Marketing, PR, and COVID-19

In Chapter 7, Schneider examines the ways that specific brands and organizations approached the pandemic. Using the lens of sponsorship, as well as congruence theory, the author presents a case study of digital approaches to marketing, public relations, brand management and other related fields during the COVID-19 Pandemic.

- Chapter 8—Advertising as a Form of Public Health Education: An Analysis of the Ad Council and COVID Collaborative's "It's Up to You" Vaccination Awareness Campaign

Applequist and Abrahamsen examined the "It's Up to You" COVID-19 Vaccine Campaign, which featured an integrated marketing communications approach, employing multiple platforms and materials. The chapter uses the Critical Advertising Studies Paradigm to examine how different types of advertising are a more appropriate fit for crisis and health campaigns.

- Chapter 9—Seventeen Weeks: Fan Reactions to the NFL's COVID-19 Protocols during the 2020 Season

Harrison and colleagues look at the response to COVID-19 by the NFL during the Fall 2020 season in Chapter 9. The authors examine the communications approaches of the NFL by using both Situational Crisis Communication Theory (SCCT) and Image Repair Theory.

Community and Regional

Many crises will impact specific groups, communities, or regions, and all individuals within those communities simultaneously. For instance, crises and disasters can influence the interpersonal relationships of all individuals within a community. That said, there can also be many differences in the experiences of individuals within communities, and public officials must be prepared to communicate effectively with various constituencies without frightening their constituents. This can mean different levels of engagement and varied approaches to these groups. Community leaders must educate without provoking harm whenever acts of terrorism, mass violence, natural or other disasters, and public health emergencies occur.

Additionally, community resilience and crisis planning models can focus on the roles, experiences, and identities held by specific groups. For example, during the pandemic, much emphasis was placed on the roles and experiences of first responders, medical professionals, and journalists. Similarly, the studies within this section examined the roles and experiences of underrepresented racial and ethnic groups, Indigenous communities and others. In the modern era, communities can span beyond geographic borders, and messages are often tailored toward groups with different media preferences, trust, and levels of engagement.

- Chapter 10—Coronavirus and Journalism: A Meta-analysis of Early Research on Journalism in the COVID-19 Pandemic

In this chapter, Perreault and colleagues conducted a meta-analysis of journalism studies research of the COVID-19 published during the early stages of the pandemic in top-tier communication journals. The authors use Bourdieu's Field Theory to understand how journalists thought about their work and how research framed the work of journalists in the pandemic. The study also draws attention to the habits of journalists and how they can inform their actions in future crises.

- Chapter 11—More than Six Feet Apart: A Case Study of Urban and Rural Medical Professionals' Responses to COVID-19

Chapter 11 looks at rural health practices and communication efforts of different hospitals based on their location. Richards and Bunn use the Crisis and Emergency Risk Communication Model (CERC) and a Grounded Theory approach to examine how the practices and challenges of these hospitals were communicated on social media.

- Chapter 12—Is There a Difference? Generational Response to COVID and Media Usage

Reif-Stice and colleagues examine the divides between different generational groups during the pandemic and how they experienced the pandemic differently but also similarly through their media use. Using Uncertainty Management

Theory, the authors identify some specific fragmentations and intersections in the media channels generational groups tapped into when seeking information about the COVID-19 pandemic.

- Chapter 13—Speaking Directly to Indigenous Communities via Social Media: Native Female Politicians' Manage Community Information by Addressing Crises within a Pandemic

La Poe et al. took an in-depth look into how Indigenous communities responded to not only COVID-19, but also persistent external pressures to erase Indigenous heritage, and rising numbers of missing and murdered indigenous women and girls during the pandemic. In particular, the authors conducted an examination of the statements of female Indigenous politicians about their communities' responses to these crises on social media.

- Chapter 14—Coping with a Pandemic Using Social Media: Nurses' Expressions of Individual and Community Resilience on TikTok

In Chapter 14, Smith-Frigerio and Houston examine the use of TikTok as a way in which United States nurses coped with burnout and the increased risks in their jobs during the pandemic. They framed their analysis within the contexts of individual and community resilience to better understand how nurses might contribute to a greater understanding of resilience as a process, as well as crisis communication about the pandemic.

National and International

While COVID-19 spread globally, each nation and government approached their response differently. This section examines national and international perspectives on COVID-19, including efforts to stop the spread of the virus and address additional concerns resulting from how solutions for some could lead to more problems for others. That said, the discussion of the precautions, and the intricacies of messaging often touched on preexisting tensions. In these chapters contributors address political polarization, climate change and natural disaster management, racial injustices, and racism, all from national or international perspectives.

- Chapter 15—Political Rhetoric and Crises Communication During a Global Pandemic

Reed and Luisi argue that, in part, the political rhetoric in the United States around the COVID-19 Pandemic was an extension of other political crises that existed before the pandemic. They recommend ways in which politicians can be effective when communicating about a health crisis and contribute to better understanding and long-term resilience.

- Chapter 16—"It Spread like Wildfire" and "Flooded Hospitals" Compounding Crisis: Climate, Wildfires, and Hurricanes during the Pandemic

In this chapter, Perreault and Adhikari look at a number of natural disasters that took place during the COVID-19 pandemic and how they were covered in several national-level newspapers across multiple countries. The study examined how journalism and the sources in these regions affected by natural disasters directed audiences to information about risk while also discussing or avoiding discussion about COVID-19.

- Chapter 17—Communicating About COVID-19 and Black Lives Matter

Moody-Ramirez's chapter discusses the challenges the COVID-19 pandemic created for the Black Lives Matter (BLM) movement. Using Critical Race Theory (CRT), the author examines how the BLM movement communicated on social media platforms during the COVID-19 pandemic and the recurring themes present in this messaging.

- Chapter 18—Calling COVID-19 the "Chinese Virus": What Types of #ChineseVirus Messages Get Attention on Facebook Pages?

Liu examines how hateful messages around COVID-19 and racist hashtags were used to spread conspiracy theories, as well as criticize people of Chinese or other Asian nations' heritage and descent. The study examined posts and provided suggestions for social media platforms to intervene and combat the rising number of racist and xenophobic posts.

- Chapter 19—Crisis Communication During the COVID-19 Pandemic: A Comparative Perspective from the Online Communication of Public Health Agencies in Italy, Sweden, and the United States

Witkowski and colleagues provide perspective on the United States, Swedish, and Italian governments' approaches to COVID-19, using the ideas presented in Uncertainty Reduction Theory as a lens. The study looks at communication ecologies, objectives, styles, and the leadership of organizations during the COVID-19 Pandemic.

In sum, we hope this volume will be helpful to not only scholars of crisis communication, but also undergraduate and graduate students, scholars in other disciplines, and communication professionals looking for practical applicability to their own crisis and disaster communication messaging. Our chapter contributors have been gracious in not only providing their engaging and insightful research, but by also providing additional resources and discussion questions for each of their chapters. We have included a reference of all resources at the end of the chapters as well as in an appendix at the end of the book.

Personal Note

Seeds of this edited volume were planted long before the pandemic. We (Dr. Mimi Perreault and Dr. Sarah Smith-Frigerio) were both professionally interested in crisis and disaster communication. Dr. Perreault had covered Hurricanes Katrina and Wilma as a journalist in South Florida and had written her master's thesis on journalists' use of technology in covering the 2010 earthquake in Haiti. Dr. Smith-Frigerio coordinated and logistically supported student volunteers working with community partners in Arabi, Louisiana following Hurricane Katrina in 2005.

Yet, we were also personally interested in crisis and disaster communication and response. The Joplin tornado struck mere miles away from Smith-Frigerio's childhood home in 2011, and Perreault had just moved to Missouri around the time of the Joplin tornado. We witnessed, firsthand, how a crisis or disaster, and the ways we communicate about it, can influence every aspect of individual and community life. Then, in early 2020, much of the world learned this lesson as COVID-19 began to spread.

We want to emphasize that it was important to us to create a volume that demonstrated the ubiquitous need for crisis communication in every facet of a prolonged crisis or disaster such as COVID-19. Many of the contributors are emerging scholars who bring fresh and enlightening perspectives, while others have been working in the crisis and disaster communication space for a long time.

It was also important to us to not only include, but highlight, perspectives that have sometimes been missing from crisis communication scholarship, including Indigenous perspectives, conversations around mental health, grief, practices of health and family care, and the mental burden placed on communication practitioners.

As media and communication teacher-scholars representing different academic focus areas, we wanted to create a resource like this for use in our classes in public relations and journalism. To that end, we proposed, and were honored to be awarded a book contract through the AEJMC—Peter Lang Scholarsourcing competition in 2021. It is with the support of the AEJMC membership, the Scholarsourcing editorial board, and Peter Lang Publishing that we are able to share our contributors' invaluable work in this volume.

References

Buzzanell, P.M., & Houston, J.B. (2018). Communication and resilience: Multilevel applications and insights—A Journal of Applied Communication Research forum. *Journal of Applied Communication Research, 46*(1), 1–4. https://doi.org/10.1080/00909882.2017.1412086

Houston, J.B. (2021). COVID-19 communication ecologies: Using interpersonal, organizational, and mediated communication resources to cope with a pandemic. *American Behavioral Scientist, 65*(7), 887–892. https://doi.org/10.1177/0002764221992837

Matthews, J., & Thorsen, E. (2022). Theorising disaster communities: Global dimensions and their local contexts. *The Journal of International Communication, 28*(2), 228–248. https://doi.org/10.1080/13216597.2022.2098164

Reynolds, B., & Seeger, M.W. (2005). Crisis and emergency risk communication as an integrative model. *Journal of Health Communication, 10*(1), 43–55. https://doi.org/10.1080/10810730590904571

Reynolds, B., & Lutfy, C. (2018). *Crisis and emergency risk communication manual.* Center for Disease Control and Prevention. https://emergency.cdc.gov/cerc/manual/index.asp

Tierney, K.J. (2007). From the margins to the mainstream? Disaster research at the crossroads. *Annual Review of Sociology, 33,* 503–525. https://doi.org/10.1146/annurev.soc.33.040406.131743

· 2 ·

WHEN A PANDEMIC AND AN "INFODEMIC" COLLIDE, UNCERTAINTY PREVAILS: MISINFORMATION & THE COVID-19 CRISIS

Jennifer Anderson

> *I (or a friend or family member) know someone who went to get a COVID-19 test, stood in line forever, and gave their contact information to a person who came by with a clipboard. She never ended up getting the test but was told she had tested positive. That's why I don't trust the statistics about how many people have COVID-19.*
>
> —Paraphrase of a story told by students; Summer 2020

The Story of the Fake Positive

I call this the story of the "fake positive," as opposed to a "*false* positive," because it reflects the storytellers' implication that the result of the test was fabricated, whereas a false positive refers to an error in the testing itself. It perplexed me that so many students reported such similar stories that were not consistent with what I knew about COVID-19 testing. When I investigated it, I found that the same type of story was cropping up across the country.

A story from the Fox affiliate in Tampa Bay, FL, in July 2020 is a representative example of some media coverage of these widespread claims of fake positives (Patrick, 2020). The headline reads, "Here's how you might get a 'positive' COVID-19 test result without ever being tested." This headline misleadingly seems to confirm some people's claims of receiving positive results without being tested. But, in the article itself, Patrick puts these rumors to rest, citing the fact that no evidence has been found to confirm these claims. Later in the article, University of South Florida public health professor Dr. Jay Wolfson explains that, rather than positive test results being fabricated, if a person receives positive results without having taken the test, they likely mistakenly received another person's test results. These rare errors are typically quickly corrected; moreover, these errors do not skew the count of people testing positive for COVID-19 because they were not fabricated but instead reported to the wrong person (Patrick, 2020). So, why were so many people, including my students, reporting, and repeating, these false claims?

Misinformation and Disinformation

Unfortunately, information-seeking can lead to finding false information. The story of the fake positive, which rests on unverified and/or misleading information, is an example of misinformation, or possibly disinformation. Many definitions of mis/disinformation exist, but for the purposes of this case study, I have created simple definitions that emphasize the intentionality of sharing false information.

- Misinformation refers to sharing false claims, without the intention to mislead.
- Disinformation refers to intentionally producing and disseminating false information with the intent to mislead.

Misinformation and disinformation are not new; in fact, for close to 30 years, health communication scholars have examined health-related mis/disinformation[1] across a variety of topics including medications, nutrition, cancer, epidemics, vaccines, and vaping (Krishna & Thompson, 2021). However, during the COVID-19 pandemic, we have seen how easily and quickly misinformation can spread (Prieto Curiel & González Ramírez, 2021) with the help of social media. The impact of such misinformation gets amplified when the same stories are shared repeatedly through social media; especially once a story like the "fake positive" gets picked up and misleadingly reported by traditional news outlets. With one click, an article like the one cited above can be shared over social media, where most people will only read the headline which—if misleading—decreases the readers' ability to use the full article text to correct misperceptions caused by that headline (Ecker et al., 2014).

The ubiquity, speed of transmission, and public health impacts of misinformation about COVID-19, have led to the World Health Organization declaring a COVID-19 infodemic:

> An infodemic is too much information, including false or misleading information, in digital and physical environments during a disease outbreak . . . [which] can intensify or lengthen outbreaks when people are unsure about what they need to do to protect their health and the health of people around them. (WHO, 2020, "Infodemic," para. 1)

Notice the role of uncertainty in the development of an infodemic. Uncertainty drives us to find and share information, even when some of that information is likely false.

Uncertainty

Brashers' (2001) Uncertainty Management Theory posits that we feel uncertainty when we are faced with complicated situations without clear-cut answers, when we feel like we don't have enough information, when the information seems inconsistent, and we feel *insecure* about the information we have on the issue—relative to how much we think we should have. Brashers (2001) refers to this insecurity as uncertainty discrepancy, where we perceive that we know less than we think we should about a given issue. COVID-19 is a prime example of the type of situation that would breed uncertainty and create large uncertainty discrepancies—since information about this issue could literally save one's life. The Theory of Motivated Information Management (Afifi & Weiner, 2004) explains that we are motivated to manage information when our uncertainty prompts feelings like anxiety, anger, guilt, or shame. Previous research has illustrated that such emotions drive information-seeking during pandemics (Allen et al., 2014). But when faced with such high stakes (literally life and death) why do so many of us pay attention to, believe, share, and act on misinformation?

The Appeal of Misinformation

Krishna and Thompson (2021) suggest that misinformation serves one or more purposes that demonstrate its utility to a person or group:

1. People who have experienced mistreatment, abuse, or misinformation from public health authorities in the past are already experiencing high

levels of fear or distrust. So, when they find information that confirms their distrust, they are likely to believe it.
2. Misinformation may be the only information available to a person—or the only information they intentionally seek or pay attention to—so believing it serves to alleviate some amount of uncertainty discrepancy.
3. People use misinformation to make decisions, so new (scientifically accurate) information that debunks the misinformation and counters their actions is perceived as ego-threatening and therefore dismissed.

Not only do we sometimes believe misinformation, even if we suspect it might be false, we also then share that information—hence, arriving at an infodemic. But why do we share misinformation? Sometimes, we share information unintentionally, because we lack critical thinking skills or we are unfamiliar with online environments (Laato et al., 2020). For example, we may not think to trace down the source of information to verify its credibility (Kim & Dennis, 2019) or check that other sources are reporting similar information (Laato et al., 2020). However, in an infodemic, seeking further sources to corroborate information may actually lead to more firmly held beliefs in misinformation and even an expanding set of misinformed beliefs. Why? Because the algorithms of social media platforms are designed to feed us content that conforms to our already-held beliefs and preferences (Cinelli et al., 2020), so we are likely to see multiple posts with the same information from seemingly different sources, which confirms our beliefs.

Interestingly, in a study conducted in five sub-Saharan African countries, Madrid-Morales et al. (2021) found that people share misinformation intentionally, but altruistically. That is, they shared information they suspected was false out of a sense of "civic duty ... just in case" (p. 1213). That is, even if they were uncertain about the complete accuracy of the information, they felt enough anxiety about the situation, and anticipated guilt over potentially *not* sharing important information, that they passed the information along.

COVID-19 and Mis/Disinformation

False claims about COVID-19 have been made since the virus was first detected in early 2020 and continued to spring up through late 2021 (Grimes, 2021). Some of the most common claims were (a) COVID-19 was created in a lab in China, (b) COVID-19 was a hoax, or a "plandemic" (Kearney et al., 2020), (c) home remedies (drinking bleach, shining bright lights into the nasal cavity) can cure COVID-19, (d) the COVID-19 test implants a microchip in your brain, (e) the vaccine will implant a microchip in your arm, and (f) the development of the 5G network is causing COVID-19 (Bahja & Safdar, 2020). These claims have been widely debunked by scientists, medical experts, and public health officials (Grimes, 2021). But with declining trust in science and health experts (Latkin et al., 2021), coupled with the lack of health, media, and information literacy (Patil et al., 2021), susceptibility to mis/disinformation about COVID-19 continues, which fuels resistance or refusal to enact protective health measures like masking and vaccination (Bridgman et al., 2020).

Case Study: College Student Beliefs and Behaviors Related to COVID-19

When I launched this case study, in Fall 2020, our university had instituted several protective safety measures to prevent the spread of COVID-19, including the requirement for everyone on campus (faculty, staff, and students) to wear masks. Simultaneously in early September, the Brookings, South Dakota City Council proposed a mask ordinance and held a meeting to hear public comment on it. This was a contentious issue in many places across the United States, but particularly so in South Dakota, where Republican Governor Kristi Noem publicly stated that she opposed government-imposed mask mandates (Groves, 2020). At that city council meeting, I was among the citizens who shared information and evidence in support of the mask ordinance (Anderson, 2020). And while I was at that meeting, I observed vehement opposition to this ordinance based on religious beliefs (God will take care of our health), political beliefs (liberals are using COVID to win the upcoming election), ideological beliefs (requiring masks constitutes government overreach, violating personal freedoms), and even "scientific" "evidence" that was consistently drawn from non-credible sources or completely misinterpreted (Brookings City Council, 2020).

As I stood there listening to the public discourse about this ordinance that echoed the broader public discourse throughout our state, my mind was drawn back to the "fake positive story" I had heard from my students a few weeks earlier. I wondered if students still believed that false information and whether they had come to believe additional pieces of misinformation. And I wondered where students were getting COVID-19 information and how it was affecting them. I left that meeting determined to find out more about our students, their

COVID-19 beliefs and knowledge, and their intentions to enact protective health behaviors, including wearing a mask. So, I conducted a cross-sectional survey study to answer these research questions:

> **RQ1:** What interpersonal and mediated information sources do college students use to learn more about COVID-19?
> **RQ2:** How much do college students trust information about COVID-19 coming from interpersonal and mediated information sources?
> **RQ3:** How accurate is college students' knowledge about COVID-19?
> **RQ4:** What beliefs do college students hold about COVID-19?
> **RQ5:** How do COVID-19 knowledge, beliefs, and protective behaviors vary by information sources?
> **RQ6:** How are COVID-19 knowledge, beliefs, political beliefs, and protective behaviors related to one another?

Method

Sample

The sample for this case study included $N = 416$ students enrolled at South Dakota State University. Ages ranged from 18 to 54, $M = 22.99$ ($SD = 6.23$). Participants predominantly identified as female (66.8%), then male (33.2%), with 1.1% preferring to self-identify or not answer. Most participants identified as heterosexual (93.8%), with 1.9% identifying as homosexual and 2.9% preferring to self-identify as bisexual, asexual, queer, or pansexual. Most participants identified as White or Caucasian (93.5%), with 2.6% identifying as Asian, 1.9% as Black, and 0.7% as Pacific Islander. Additionally, 1.9% of participants identified as Hispanic. Over half of the participants (61.3%) came from rural communities, 27.6% from suburban, and 11.1% from urban. Political-party affiliation was split between Republican (47.4%), Democrat (27.6%), none (15.4%), and other (9.6%).

Sampling

Participants were randomly selected from a list of all undergraduate students enrolled at SDSU in Fall 2020. Participants who completed the survey had the chance to enter a drawing to win one Amazon gift card. To award the incentives, I randomly selected 20 winners from those who entered the drawing and distributed the following: $100 gift card (1 winner), $50 gift card (3 winners), $25 gift card (6 winners), and $10 gift card (10 winners).

Data Collection

All study materials were approved by the Institutional Review Board at South Dakota State University (SDSU). Participants followed a link from their invitation email to an online survey hosted by QuestionPro. Prior to entering the survey, participants provided their age to verify their adult status and provided consent to complete the survey. Participants then completed the measures. At the end of the survey, if they chose to enter the drawing for the incentive, they were directed to a separate survey where they could provide their contact information. All responses on the main survey were anonymous.

Measures

Information Sources

Participants answered questions about interpersonal sources, traditional media sources, social media sources, web-based sources, and public health officials. First, they indicated who they spoke to (most) about COVID-19 from among the following sources: family, friends, medical professionals, other, or no one. Next, participants selected all of the following mediated sources from which they found, saw, or heard COVID-19 information: traditional media, social media, web-based sources, or other.

Trust in Information Sources

Participants answered questions about their trust in interpersonal sources, traditional media sources, social media sources, web-based sources, and public health officials. Participants were asked whether they trusted (yes/no) each interpersonal information source with whom they had spoken. For each mediated information source they selected, through which they were exposed to COVID-19 information, they indicated the extent to which they trusted that source on a 4-point scale (1 = not at all, 2 = somewhat, 3 = quite a bit, 4 = completely). Finally, participants selected all of the sources that they believed provided credible medical information from a list including various news, social media, scientific, medical, governmental, and interpersonal sources.

COVID-19 Knowledge

Participants' COVID-19 knowledge was measured with a 7-item scale using a 5-point Likert-type Likert-scale response (1 = strongly disbelieve, 2 = disbelieve, 3 = not sure, 4 = believe, 5 = strongly believe), where higher scores indicate greater knowledge. Two of the statements (items 1 and 4) were true, and the other five statements were false. The five false items were based on some of the common myths circulating at the time of this case study. Scores on these items were reverse coded.

1. COVID-19 can lead to severe health outcomes, including death.
2. Only people with preexisting conditions (e.g., obesity or old age) are at risk for COVID-19.
3. Only 6% of COVID-19 deaths are actually caused by the virus.
4. COVID-19 is a highly contagious virus.
5. Coronavirus is a coverup for child sex trafficking.
6. COVID-19 is not a serious infection.
7. COVID-19 is a "plandemic" (a planned pandemic).

After removing item 5, the 6-item scale was found to be reliable, α = .831 and unidimensional, χ^2 (9, 415) = 8.69, p = .466, RMSEA = 0.00, CMIN = 0.97, RMR = 0.02.

COVID-19 Beliefs

Participants rated their level of belief in single-item statements about COVID-19 testing and reporting, use of masks or face coverings, President Trump's experience with COVID-19, the relationship between COVID-19 and politics, the (at that time) potential vaccine, COVID-19 and media, and conspiracy theories about COVID-19. All items used the 5-point Likert-type response scale described above.

Political Beliefs

Political beliefs on the spectrum from conservative to liberal were measured with one item, using a 5-point response scale: 1 = very conservative, 2 = somewhat conservative, 3 = in-between conservative and liberal, 4 = somewhat liberal, 5 = very liberal. Participants also had the option to self-describe or select "I do not hold any political beliefs." On average, this sample skewed conservative, M = 2.83 (SD = 1.25). Participants identified as very conservative

(14.4%), somewhat conservative (24.3%), in-between conservative and liberal (23.8%), somewhat liberal (15.6%), and very liberal (11.3%). Additionally, 7.0% reported holding no political beliefs and 2.9% preferred to self-describe, often noting that they vote based on their personal beliefs or values regardless of which party's candidates or policies match those.

COVID-19 Behaviors

Participants indicated the frequency with which they comply with the (then-current) CDC guidelines for COVID-19 safety, including masking, social distancing, handwashing, staying home if sick, isolating, and quarantining. The 5-point Likert-type response scale included the following options: never, once in a while, about half the time, most of the time, and always. Participants could also select "not applicable."

Results

Information Sources (RQ1) and Trust in Information Sources (RQ2)

Interpersonal Information Sources

Participants turned most often to friends to gather information about COVID-19. The next most common interpersonal source for COVID-19 information was family, followed by medical professionals.

An interesting pattern of information-seeking and trust in information sources emerged with this sample: trust is higher among sources that participants speak to less, and vice versa. When you look at the chart below, you can see that people place the most trust in medical professionals, then family, then friends. But, on the flip side (Figure 2.1), people are most likely to be talking to friends, then family, then medical professionals. Bottom line? Participants were least likely to be talking about COVID-19 with the people whose information they trust most. Political ideology did not play a role in who participants chose to talk with, or how much trust they placed in them.

Trust & Mediated Information Sources

Participants used traditional media, social media, and web-based sources fairly equitably, with at least 80% of participants turning to one or more of those

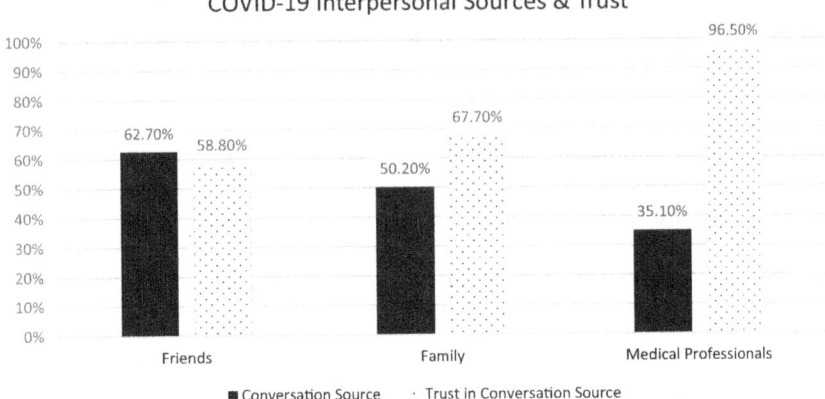

Figure 2.1. Interpersonal Sources and Trust

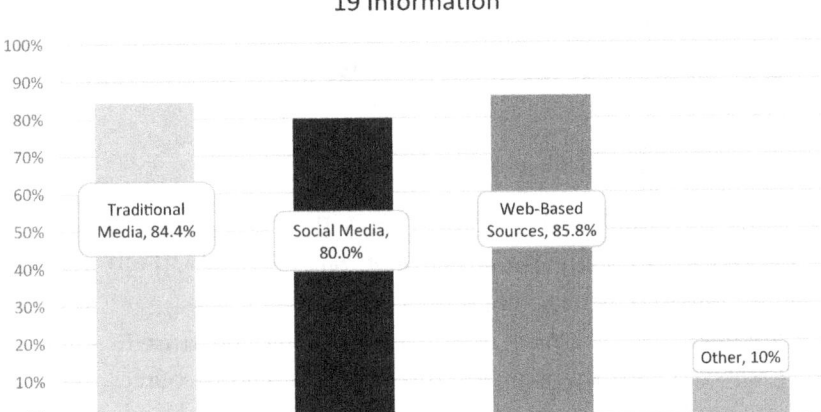

Figure 2.2. Percent of People Using Various Media Sources for COVID-19 Information

sources. About 1 out of 10 participants also turned to "other" sources. A lot of times, participants who selected "other" sources mentioned getting information from the CDC or similar official health organizations—regardless of which platform they used to get it. Liberal participants were more likely than conservative participants to indicate that they turned to "other" sources for information, beyond the choices of traditional, web-based, or social media.

Using a scale of 1 = no trust at all to 4 = complete trust, it turns out that participants have fairly low trust in social, traditional, and web-based media.

Participants had the least trust in social media; the average rating was 1.64. From there, trust increased: for traditional media the average score was 2.15, for web-based sources it was 2.46. Each of those scores falls below the midpoint of the scale, which would be a rating of 2.50. Interestingly, the 10% of participants who used "other" sources placed strong trust in them, with the average score being 3.29 out of 4. That means the only source that produced trust above the midpoint of the scale was "other."

We know that 80% of participants were turning to social media for information about COVID-19, and that it had the lowest trust score compared with other forms of media. The chart below shows even more detail as we look at the proportion of participants from each political ideology who selected each level of trust. Almost half of conservatives said they "do not trust [social media] at all," whereas only a third of liberals said the same. On the other side of the chart, we see that fewer than 1% of participants—regardless of their political ideology—placed complete trust in social media for information about COVID-19.

For traditional media sources and web-based materials, levels of trust followed a normal distribution, meaning that most of the scores were in the middle of the scale—regardless of political ideology. Most participants reported trusting these sources "somewhat" or "quite a bit."

Now let's dive a little deeper into levels of trust for more specific types of media. Trust in information from media sources varied not just by the source, but also by participants' political ideologies. In the chart below, you'll notice a

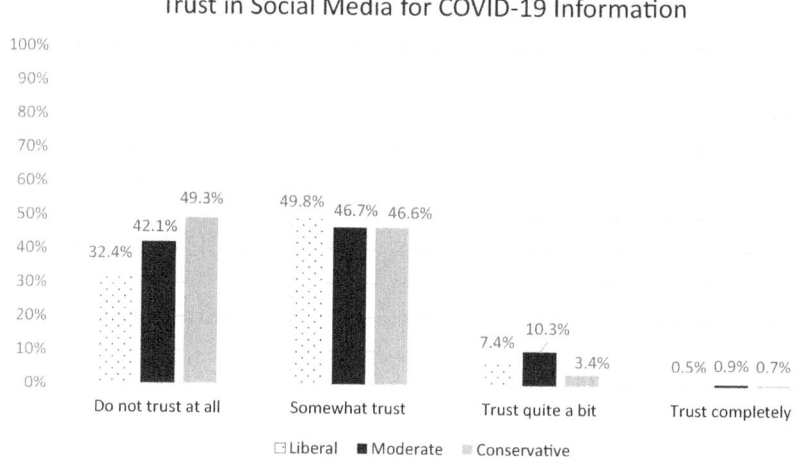

Figure 2.3. Trust in Social Media for COVID-19 Information

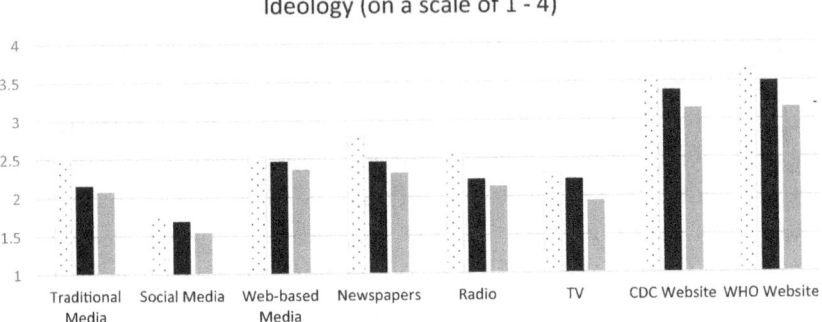

Figure 2.4. Ratings of Trust in Selected Media Sources Based on Political Ideology (on a scale of 1–4)

trend. The more liberal the participant was, the more they trusted traditional, web-based, and social media.

The chart above includes just 8 of the 20 specific media sources where ratings of trust differed significantly based on participants' political ideology. The same pattern emerged for every single source: liberals reported the highest levels of trust, conservatives reported the lowest levels of trust. Moderates, not surprisingly, were in the middle.

Let's put together the information from the previous charts. We can see that levels of trust vary by type of source as well as by political ideology. In general, we see that social media is the least-trusted source, while "other" sources such as the CDC or WHO website are the most trusted sources. This trend holds true regardless of political ideology. However, *within* those sources, there is another trend hidden: trust in each source is highest among liberals, then moderates, then conservatives.

COVID-19 Knowledge (RQ3)

In answer to RQ3, scores on the knowledge scale indicate that participants were mostly familiar with, and confident in their knowledge of, basic information about COVID-19, $M = 3.71$ ($SD = .80$), range = 1.17–5.0. However, findings from two individual items warrant special attention. The most striking item concerns the false claim that only 6% of COVID-19 deaths are caused by the virus itself. Around 2 out of 3 people believed, or were unsure about, that false

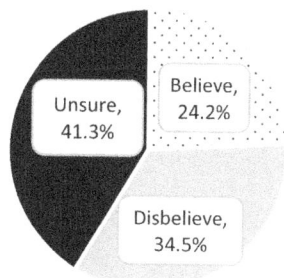

Figure 2.5. Only 6% of COVID-19 Deaths are Caused by the Virus

claim. In fact, more people were unsure about this than were certain it was true *or* false. When it comes to the false claim that pandemic was planned, about 1 out of 3 people believed, or were unsure about, this claim.

COVID-19 Beliefs (RQ4)

Participants' beliefs in COVID-19 misinformation were related to their COVID-19 knowledge. The less they knew about COVID-19, the more misinformation they believed. And, the more that people believed misinformation, the less likely they were to engage in protective COVID-19 behaviors.

Let's look at the breakdown of beliefs related to various claims about COVID-19. In the chart below, you'll see the percent of participants who believed, disbelieved, or were unsure about claims that the CDC and WHO provide accurate information about COVID-19. Close to one-third of participants were *not sure* whether the information from the CDC and/or WHO is accurate. And only a little over half of the participants believed that CDC and/or WHO information about COVID-19 is accurate.

Next, let's take a look at participants' beliefs when it comes to false statements. The chart below shows how these beliefs panned out. The bars labeled with square boxes show the percent of participants who believed a given false statement. More than 1 out of 3 participants believed the false claim that fake positives happen often. See the chart below for more about beliefs in false claims. You can see that for each false claim, between 20% and 50% of participants believed it. That means at least 1 in 5 participants believed one or more false claims about COVID-19. In two cases, false beliefs were actually more

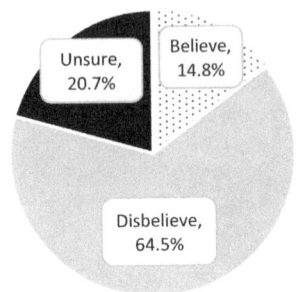

Figure 2.6. The Pandemic was Planned

common than accurate beliefs. About half (50.3%) of participants believed increased testing resulted in more COVID-19 cases, compared with only 28.8% of participants not believing that false claim. Similarly, 41.6% of participants believed that government agencies were lying about the number of COVID-19 cases, compared with only 30.5% of participants who did not believe that false claim.

Notice that beliefs in two related claims provide justification for producing fake positives like those mentioned in my story from the beginning of this chapter. Those claims were that spikes in positive cases were a result of increased testing (believed by about 1 out of every 2 participants) and that fake positives happen often (believed by about 1 out of 4 participants). These claims also produced uncertainty among 20.9% and 36.3% of participants, respectively. No wonder so many of my students relayed stories about false positives!

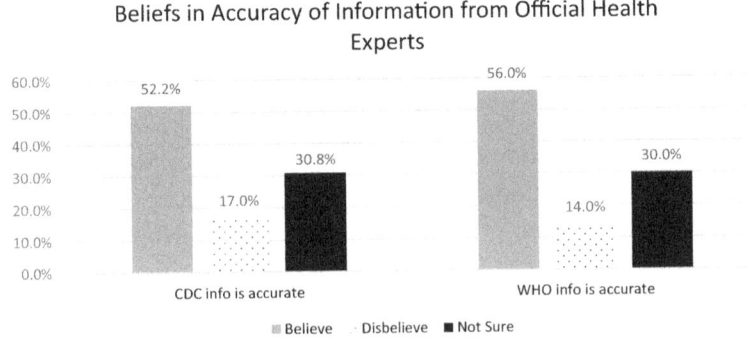

Figure 2.7. Beliefs in Accuracy of Information from Official Health Experts

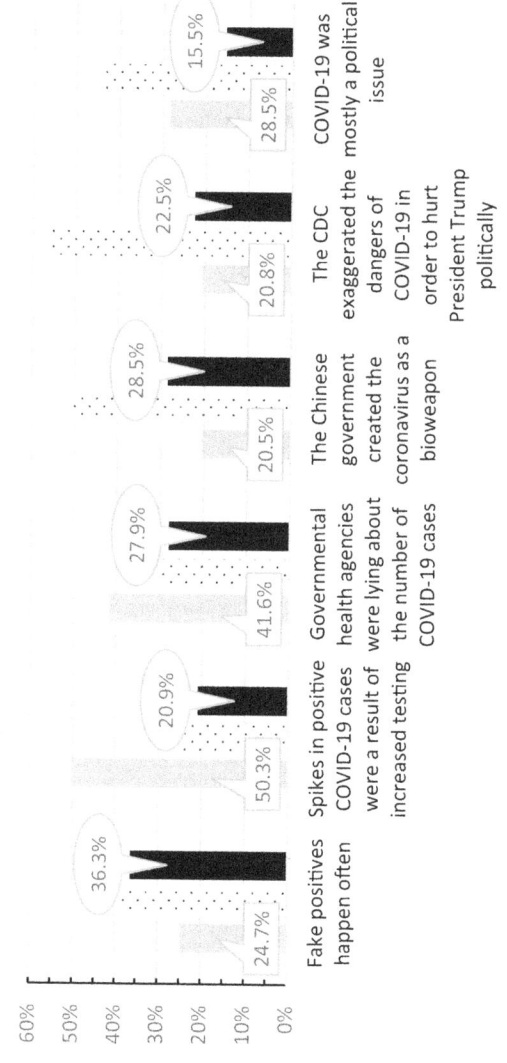

Figure 2.8. Beliefs in False Statements about COVID-19

Now let's turn to participants' uncertainty about these false claims. The bars labeled with circular callouts show the percent of participants who were *unsure* about each claim. For each false claim, you can see that between 15% and 36% of participants were unsure about whether the statement was true or false. That means at least 3 out of 20 participants were uncertain about these false statements. Participants' highest levels of uncertainty centered around COVID-19 testing and reporting of infection rates.

Interestingly, for two claims, there were more people unsure about their truthfulness than there were people who believed them. We see the biggest difference when looking at the belief that China created COVID-19 as a bioweapon: 28.5% of participants were *unsure* if this was true; whereas 20.5% believed this claim. In the second case, 22.5% of people were *unsure* whether the CDC exaggerated the dangers of COVID-19 to hurt President Trump politically; while 20.8% believed this claim.

Uncertainty also surfaced around beliefs about protective health measures such as testing, masking, and vaccination. The chart below illustrates this finding across four false statements about protective measures. For example, more than 1 in 4 participants were *unsure* whether any vaccine would be unsafe and a bigger risk than getting COVID-19 (Figure 2.9). About the same proportion of participants were *unsure* whether such a vaccine would be mandatory for everyone. In addition to uncertainty, beliefs in these false statements ranged from 2% to 21.7% of participants. The most common misbeliefs were that the vaccine would be mandatory for everyone (21.7% of participants believed this) and that wearing cloth masks can cause carbon dioxide poisoning (17.8% of participants believed this).

MISINFORMATION & THE COVID-19 CRISIS   29

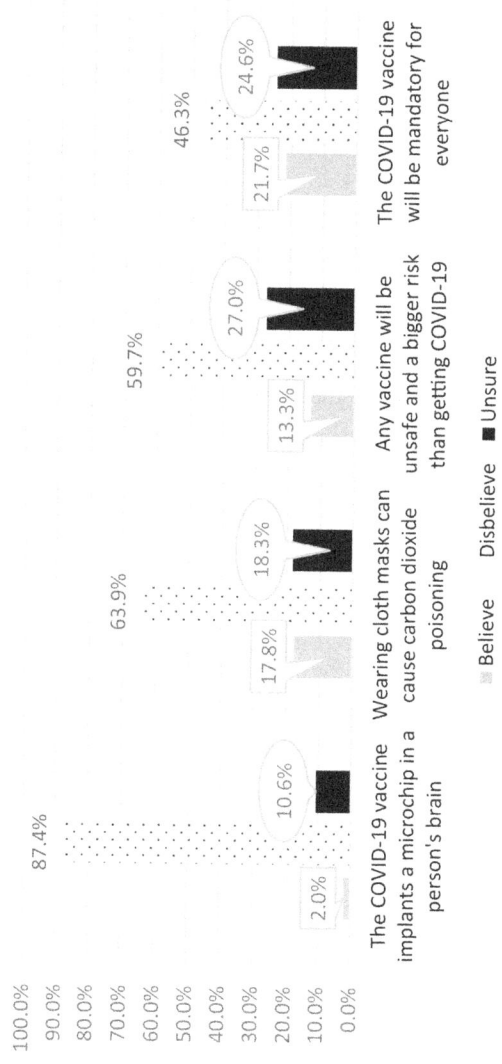

Figure 2.9. Beliefs in False Statements about Protective Measures for COVID-19

Differences by Information Source in COVID-19 Knowledge, Beliefs, and Protective Behaviors (RQ5)

Differences in COVID-19 Knowledge by Information Source

People who turned to social media for COVID-19 information had significantly less knowledge about it than people who used traditional media or web-based information. In fact, knowledge was highest among people who specifically *avoided* social media as a source of information about COVID-19, even compared with people who sought out information through traditional and web-based media.

It turns out participants were right about which interpersonal sources to trust most when it comes to COVID-19 information. Participants who spoke most often with medical professionals had the best knowledge of COVID-19; medical professionals were also the most trusted sources of information. Participants who chose to mostly talk with their friends about COVID-19 had the lowest knowledge levels. Knowledge levels were in the middle for participants who talked most often with their families.

Differences in COVID-19 Beliefs by Information Source

Social media users believed more false claims than any other group. They were more likely to believe that: COVID-19 is a "plandemic," governmental health agencies are lying, COVID-19 is mostly a political issue, some "conspiracy theories" are true, only 6% of COVID-19 deaths are actually caused by COVID-19, COVID-19 will go away after the election in November, the pharmaceutical industry created the COVID-19 virus to boost drug and vaccine sales, and that the Black Lives Matter rallies led to increased transmission of COVID-19. Additionally, participants who turned to traditional media were the most likely to believe the false claim that COVID-19 was a "plandemic."

Participants who spoke with medical professionals or used web-based sources were least likely to believe false claims and more likely to believe accurate claims, respectively. Specifically, participants who spoke with medical professionals were less likely to believe false claims that the COVID-19 test implants a microchip and that COVID-19 was created by the pharmaceutical industry to boost drug and vaccine sales. Participants who used web-based sources for information were significantly more likely to believe that COVID-19 is a highly contagious virus.

Relationships Between Political Beliefs and COVID-19 Knowledge, Beliefs, and Protective Behaviors (RQ6)

It comes as no surprise that the more knowledge a participant has about COVID-19, the less likely they are to believe misinformation about COVID-19. And this knowledge leads to participants enacting protective behaviors, including masking around others outside of the home, masking in public indoor spaces, masking at private social gatherings with people one does not live with, social distancing, handwashing, staying home when sick, and quarantining if tested positive. When knowledge is high, participants were more likely to engage in those behaviors; lower knowledge led to less likelihood of engaging in protective behaviors.

Political beliefs were related to COVID-19 knowledge. Specifically, knowledge was higher among liberal participants than among conservative participants. In fact, the more liberal the participant, the higher their knowledge of COVID-19. Democrats' COVID-19 knowledge was significantly higher than such knowledge among Republicans, non-affiliated participants, and those affiliated with other parties.

Similarly, belief in misinformation rose as participants became more conservative. Compared with Democrats, Republicans were significantly more likely to believe misinformation and significantly less likely to practice protective behaviors.

Discussion

In this case study, I began by wondering what college students knew and believed about COVID-19, where they were getting their information, and how that might relate to their COVID-19 protective behaviors. Overall, the findings indicate that, although COVID-19 knowledge was adequate, belief in misinformation was also prevalent. A unique finding from this study concerns the prevalence of *uncertainty* about both accurate and inaccurate claims about COVID-19. Beyond beliefs in misinformation, high levels of uncertainty also contributed to lower intentions to perform protective COVID-19 behaviors. Although in many ways troubling, the levels of uncertainty seen in this sample provide some hope for increasing vaccine uptake, because they suggest that, rather than focusing solely on addressing misinformation, moving forward, health communication campaigns to increase vaccine uptake can focus on minimizing uncertainty.

The Role of Uncertainty in Knowledge and Beliefs About COVID-19

The findings from this study indicate that, generally, college students' knowledge of COVID-19 was adequate, and students had reasonable confidence in their knowledge. However, when the data are examined more closely, it becomes clear that knowledge and confidence are not consistent across different claims about COVID-19. In other words, students' knowledge about some COVID-19 claims reflected significant uncertainty discrepancy (Brashers, 2001). In one striking example, 26.7% of participants were "not sure" whether COVID-19 was a "pandemic." In another case, 39.7% of participants were "not sure" whether only 6% of the reported COVID-19 deaths were caused by the virus. When it came to beliefs about COVID-19 testing, uncertainty levels were even higher, ranging from 20% to 36% of participants being unsure about every statement—including both true and false statements. For example, about 30% of participants were *not sure* whether COVID-19 reports from the CDC or WHO were accurate.

And, then there's the story of the "fake positive." I found that 36% of college students in this study were not sure whether that situation really happens, and another 26% were certain that it does. No wonder I heard that story so often from my students. Their certainty of belief in this story must be serving some purpose for these students (Krishna & Thompson, 2021), although the specific purpose is not clear. And it's also no wonder that they remain so uncertain about its veracity, because, as I explained above, none of those students could produce any evidence—beyond trusting the person who told them (Kim & Dennis, 2019)—that this type of thing actually happened.

But, what's problematic, from an academic perspective, is that—when presented with a scenario for which no evidence exists, participants did not immediately dismiss that scenario as false or seek additional information to determine its accuracy (Laato et al., 2020). Instead, they hesitated to make a determination about its veracity. Perhaps they wanted to maintain a certain level of uncertainty (Brashers, 2001), not about the claim, but about its source. In other words, they did not want to undermine their trust in that family member or friend by finding out that their story was false. No matter the motivation for maintaining uncertainty, this uncertainty-fueled hesitation was linked to lower intentions to enact every protective health behavior examined in this study from social distancing to planning to get a vaccine. Indeed, this hesitancy-uncertainty cocktail continues to forestall efforts to increase vaccination uptake on a broad scale. And, as Krishna and Thompson (2021) argue, once we have made a decision [such as refusing a vaccine] based on misinformation, exposure to conflicting information is unlikely to affect us, since that information has now become ego-threatening.

The Risks of Uncertainty

Unearthing the prevalence and power of uncertainty in decision-making about COVID-19 helps health communication scholars better understand the barriers for persuasive health messaging. Previous research has provided some detail on the proportions of the population who believe misinformation about COVID-19, which can also be seen in this study. But less research has focused on the substantial parts of the population who are simply unsure. Targeting uncertainty may be the key to persuading the "wait and see" crowd. Because those audiences have not come to conclusions, they should be the most receptive to attitude change (Sherif & Hovland, 1961, Social Judgment Theory). And perhaps the messages need to emphasize the *certainty* with which scientific claims can be believed and *highlight the risks of uncertainty*, or indecision, itself. Still, campaign messaging must be extremely careful to not evoke an ego-threat among people who have taken action—even inaction—based on beliefs in misinformation. Research on functional theory (Knight Lapinski & Boster, 2001) shows that ego-boosting messages can be effective in these situations. For example, "You're a man of action. It's time to step up and do what's right for you and your family. Make sure you and your family are fully vaccinated. Live to fight another day."

A great deal of current messaging, from across the spectrum of COVID-19 beliefs, focuses on the risks associated with getting COVID-19 or with not taking various protective measures (masking, vaccinating). But an approach that focuses on the risks of uncertainty could motivate the uncertain to take action. During a time when we have all been faced with more collective uncertainty than we might have ever experienced or will ever again experience, it could be quite persuasive to appeal to people's uncertainty exhaustion. A vaccination campaign could certainly harness the heightened desire for certainty, using any number of theories related to uncertainty reduction or management, to present vaccines not only as the answer to COVID-19, but as the answer to finally overcoming the uncertainty it has burdened us with. Vaccines could be framed as a "sure bet" for squashing uncertainty. For example, "In these uncertain times, there is one thing we can be sure of: COVID-19 will keep going until we stop it with vaccines."

Uncertainty and Information Sources

It is not only important to know participants' knowledge and beliefs about COVID-19, but also the sources that are informing those beliefs. Participants in this study were getting COVID-19 information from multiple interpersonal and mediated sources. Participants talked most often to family and friends and had the most trust in medical professionals but the least trust in friends. Not surprisingly, perhaps, those who primarily turned to friends for COVID-19 information were more likely to believe misinformation such as COVID-19 not being a serious infection or that COVID-19 is a "plandemic." Participants also turned to traditional media, social media, and web-based information platforms, reporting that they had the lowest trust in social media and highest in web-based information platforms. The lack of trust in social media information among this population should be commended, because the findings also indicate that those who used social media to learn about COVID-19 were more likely to believe in a host of misinformation, such as COVID-19 being a "plandemic" or believing that governmental health agencies were lying about the number of COVID-19 cases.

The least-trusted sources were also the most-used sources for information about COVID-19, and vice versa. This presents a two-pronged challenge for health communication interventions. First, there is a need to spread information more effectively through channels where misinformation has a strong foothold. Especially since, as the results of this study show, belief in (or uncertainty about) one piece of misinformation is significantly related to belief in, or uncertainty about, other misinformation claims, which further reinforces feelings of uncertainty, since there are so many claims about which one cannot be certain (Liu et al., 2021). Second, there is a need to shift information-seeking about health from non-expert interpersonal and mediated communication to credible, expert sources.

Targeting Uncertainty in Ongoing Efforts to Increase COVID-19 Vaccine Uptake

However, in addition to providing more information and working to correct misinformation (Caulfield, in press), another approach could be inviting people to unload their uncertainty by embracing a "sure thing"—vaccination. Information, misinformation, and disinformation are all available and accessible. But their effects are not cut and dry. Information alone does not motivate adoption of recommended behaviors, nor does mis/disinformation always create strong opposition to adopting recommended behaviors. Instead, that combination of accurate and inaccurate information creates an infodemic where information overload (Liu et al., 2021) leaves many in a state of inaction due to uncertainty.

Efforts to increase vaccine uptake must be multi-pronged and multi-staged to be effective for our whole population. I believe that addressing uncertainty, by both highlighting the risks of uncertainty and firmly establishing vaccines as a means for quelching that uncertainty, we could see meaningful gains in vaccine uptake among those paralyzed by uncertainty.

Discussion Questions

1. Have you ever tried to call someone out on sharing misinformation on social media (whether or not it's related to COVID-19)? How did it go? Was it successful? Why or why not? What approach might you take in the future?
2. Have you ever accidentally shared misinformation in person or online? What was your motivation for sharing that information? What happened after you shared it? Did you try to correct any misperceptions that may have arisen from it?
3. Have you, or do you know anyone who has, *intentionally* shared misinformation? What was your motivation for that? Did it serve one of the purposes outlined by Krishna and Thompson (2021) or Madrid-Morales et al. (2021)? If not, what other purpose(s) did it serve?
4. Madrid-Morales et al. (2021) also found that people sometimes intentionally shared misinformation in order to make fun of it, or satirize it, to point out its inaccuracies. What are the potential benefits and drawbacks of this approach to sharing misinformation?
5. How should health communicators respond to the crisis of mis- and disinformation pervading public communication about COVID-19? Where should we start? Building trust in medicine and science? Teaching information literacy? Requiring social media platforms to be more vigilant about removing or blocking misinformation? Other solutions?

Note

1 The term mis/disinformation is used in this chapter for concision. It does not imply the two terms, misinformation and disinformation, are synonymous or interchangeable.

References

Afifi, W.A., & Weiner, J.L. (2004). Toward a theory of motivated information management. *Communication Theory, 14*(2), 167–190. https://doi.org/10.1111/j.1468-2885.2004.tb00310.x

Allen, D.K., Karanasios, S., & Norman, A. (2014). Information sharing and interoperability: The case of major incident management. *European Journal of Information Systems, 23*(4), 418–432. https://doi.org/10.1057/ejis.2013.8

Anderson, J. (2020, Sept. 8). Public comments in favor of a mask ordinance in Brookings, SD [video recording 1:33:33 - 1:35:23]. Brookings City Council Regular Meeting. https://cityofbrookings.granicus.com/MediaPlayer.php?view_id=3&clip_id=695#

Bahja, M., & Safdar, G. (2020). Unlink the link between COVID-19 and 5G networks: An NLP and SNA based approach. *IEEE Access, 8*, 209127–209137. https://doi.org/0.1109/ACCESS.2020.3039168

Brashers, D.E. (2001). Communication and uncertainty management. *Journal of Communication, 51*(3), 477–497. https://doi.org/10.1111/j.1460-2466.2001.tb02892.x

Bridgman, A., Merkley, R., Loewen, P.J., Owen, T., Ruths, D., Teichmann, L., & Zhilin, O. (2020). The causes and consequences of COVID-19 misperceptions: Understanding the role of news and social media. *Harvard Kennedy School Misinformation Review, 1*(3). https://doi.org/10.37016/mr-2020-028

Brookings City Council. (2020, Sept. 8). Brookings City Council Regular Meeting [video recording]. https://cityofbrookings.granicus.com/MediaPlayer.php?view_id=3&clip_id=695#

Cinelli, M., Quattrociocchi, W., Galeazzi, A., Valensise, C.M., Brugnoli, E., Schmidt, A.L., Zola, P., Zollo, F., & Scala, A. (2020). The COVID-19 social media infodemic. *Scientific Reports, 10*(1), 16598. https://doi.org/10.1038/s41598-020-73510-5

Ecker, U.K.H., Lewandowsky, S., Chang, E.P., & Pillai, R. (2014). The effects of subtle misinformation in news headlines. *Journal of Experimental Psychology: Applied, 20*(4), 323–335. https://doi.org/10.1037/xap0000028

Grimes, D.R. (2021). Medical disinformation and the unviable nature of COVID-19 conspiracy theories. *PLoS ONE, 16*(3), Article e0245900. https://doi.org/10.1371/journal.pone.0245900

Groves, S. (2020, Nov. 18). "South Dakota's Noem defends forgoing masks as virus surges". *Associated Press.* https://apnews.com/article/south-dakota-kristi-noem-coronavirus-pandemic-0d58c61ba20c8bf9ba4ee02ef46b1da0

Kearney, M.D., Chiang, S.C., & Massey, P.M. (2020). The Twitter origins and evolution of the COVID-19 "plandemic" conspiracy theory. *Harvard Kennedy School Misinformation Review, 1*(3). https://doi.org/10.37016/mr-2020-42

Kim, A., & Dennis, A.R. (2019). Says who? The effects of presentation format and source rating on fake news in social media. *MIS Quarterly, 43*(3), 1025-1039. https://doi.org/10.25300/MISQ/2019/15188

Knight Lapinski, M., & Boster, F.J. (2001). Modeling the ego-defensive function of attitudes. *Communication Monographs, 68*(3), 314–324. https://doi.org/10.1080/03637750128062

Krishna, A., & Thompson, T.L. (2021). Misinformation about health: A review of health communication and misinformation scholarship. *American Behavioral Scientist, 65*(2), 316–322. https://doi.org/10.1177%2F0002764219878223

Laato, S., Islam, A.K.M.N., Islam, M.N., & Whelan, E. (2020). What drives unverified information sharing and cyberchondria during the COVID-19 pandemic? *European Journal of Information Systems, 29*(3), 288–305. https://doi.org/10.1080/0960085X.2020.1770632

Latkin, C.A., Dayton, L., Strickland, J.C., Colon, B., Rimal, R., & Boodram, B. (2021). An assessment of the rapid decline of trust in US sources of public information about COVID-19. *Journal of Health Communication, 25*(10), 764–773. https://doi.org/10.1080/10810730.2020.1865487

Liu, H., Liu, W., Yoganathan, V., & Osburg, V.-S. (2021). COVID-19 information overload and generation Z's social media discontinuance intention during the pandemic lockdown. *Technological Forecasting and Social Change, 166*, Article 120600. https://doi.org/10.1016/j.techfore.2021.120600

Madrid-Morales, D., Wasserman, H., Gondwe, G., Ndlovu, K., Sikanku, E., Tully, M., Umejei, E., & Uzuegbunam, C. (2021). Motivations for sharing misinformation: A comparative study in six Sub-Saharan African countries. *International Journal of Communication (Online)*, 1200–1220. International Journal of Communication, 15, 1200-1219. http://link.gale.com/apps/doc/A655341695AONE

Patil, U., Kostareva, U., Hadley, M., Manganello, J.A., Okan, O., Dadaczynski, K., Massey, P.M., Agner, J., & Sentell, T. (2021). Health literacy, digital health literacy, and COVID-19 pandemic attitudes and behaviors in U.S. College students: Implications for interventions. *International Journal of Environmental Research in Public Health, 18*(3301), 2–14. https://doi.org/10.3390/ijerph18063301

Patrick, C. (2020, July 24). Here's how you might get a "positive" COVID-19 test result without even being tested. *Fox 13 News—Tampa Bay*. https://www.fox13news.com/news/heres-how-you-might-get-a-positive-covid-19-test-result-without-even-being-tested

Prieto Curiel, R., & González Ramírez, H.G. (2021). Vaccination strategies against COVID-19 and the diffusion of anti-vaccination views. *Nature: Scientific Reports, 11*, Article 6626. https://doi.org/10.1038/s41598-021-85555-1

Sherif, M., & Hovland, C.I. (1961). *Social judgment: Assimilation and contrast effects in communication and attitude change*. Yale University Press.

World Health Organization. (2020). *Infodemic*. https://www.who.int/health-topics/infodemic#tab=tab_1

· 3 ·

#ALONETOGETHER: A QUALITATIVE CONTENT ANALYSIS OF A HASHTAG CAMPAIGN PROVIDING SUPPORT THROUGH THE COVID-19 MENTAL HEALTH CRISIS

Jessica D. Freeman & Jessica Elton

By the time China confirmed its first death from a mysterious new virus on January 11, 2020, it was already spreading across the globe (Bryson Taylor, 2021), and on January 20, 2020, Japan, South Korea, Thailand, and the United States verified their first cases of SARS-CoV-2 (or COVID-19). On February 29, the United States reported its first COVID-19 death (Bryson Taylor, 2021), and less than a month later, all 50 states, the District of Columbia, and four U.S. territories had confirmed cases of COVID-19 (CDC COVID-19 Response Team, 2020). Without any effective vaccines or treatments for this new virus, people in the United States were asked to socially distance and quarantine to impede the spread of COVID-19. By early April 2020, nearly every U.S. state and territory had some sort of stay-at-home orders in place (Moreland et al., 2020). Nearly 93% of U.S. households with school-aged children transitioned to distance learning (Mcelrath, 2020), and in May 2020, about 35% of the workforce reported working from home in the previous four weeks because of the pandemic (U.S. Bureau of Labor Statistics, n.d.). Stay-at-home orders were expected to be in place for a week or two—just long enough to quell the virus.

However, in some U.S. states, counties, and cities, the orders stayed in place for months, exacerbating uncertainty, isolation, and fear.

Prior to the pandemic, social isolation and loneliness were prevalent public health issues, with one study finding that nearly half of its 20,000 participants reported feeling alone sometimes or always (Cigna, 2018). However, during the pandemic, isolation and loneliness were magnified due to social distancing, stay-at-home orders, and uncertainty and fear about the virus (Hwang et al., 2020). This raised concerns regarding a secondary mental health crisis (United Nations, 2020). Early studies documented that social isolation during the pandemic exacerbated mental health conditions, including increased depression, insomnia, stress, anxiety, and fear (Torales et al., 2020). Scholarship has shown social media can be useful in sharing information (de Calheiros Velozo & Stauder, 2018) during a public health crisis, including providing social support, defined as, "the individual feeling valued and cared for by their social network as well as how well the person is embedded into a network of communication and social obligation" (Stephens & Petrie, 2015, p. 735). Thus, some experts suggested using online platforms to provide peer-support networks "for people to share their challenges and resolutions during the outbreak, in turn, fostering comradeship and resilience" (Ho et al., 2020, p. 4).

To facilitate mental wellness during the pandemic, a variety of media, public health, and government entities partnered with the Ad Council, a nonprofit organization that strives to "produce impactful public service engagement campaigns that raise awareness, inspire action and save lives" (Ad Council, n.d., para. 2), to launch the #AloneTogether campaign. The integrated communication campaign utilized media, including the #AloneTogether social media hashtag, to provide mental health support during the pandemic (McAteer, 2020). The study described in this chapter applied qualitative content analysis to investigate discussions of mental health and social support discourse under the #AloneTogether hashtag on Twitter (X). The results offer insights for social support in a social media context as facilitated through a strategic public service campaign, particularly considering the unique circumstances of the mental health crisis during the pandemic.

Literature Review

Social Isolation, COVID-19, and the Mental Health Crisis

Prior to COVID-19, social isolation, the "objective lack of interactions with others or the wider community" (Leigh-Hunt et al., 2017, p. 158), was identified as a public health concern. Studies before the pandemic showed upward-trending social isolation and loneliness within the United States (Leigh-Hunt et al., 2017), attributed to shifting cultural factors, including declining marriage rates, increased childlessness, reduced household sizes, and decreased participation in social groups (Holt-Lunstad, 2018). Social isolation and loneliness have been associated with public health concerns such as increased risk for mortality (Holt-Lunstad et al., 2015). Additionally, level of social activity has been directly linked to mental (Cacioppo & Cacioppo, 2014) and physical health (Uchino, 2006), with wellness benefits related to lower levels of social isolation and increased social connection.

Social distancing orders during the pandemic provided a new context for studying social isolation and loneliness. For example, an October 2020 report showed nearly one-third of U.S. adults had gone between one and three months without interactions outside their home or workplace during the pandemic; more than 70% of U.S. adults agreed that the pandemic made it difficult to connect with friends, and two-thirds reported experiencing social isolation (AARP, 2020). Research also indicated heightened symptoms of anxiety and depressive disorders between April and June 2020 over the same time in the previous year (Czeisler et al., 2020). Moreover, a June 2020 survey revealed that 40.9% of U.S. adults reported suffering from one or more adverse mental or behavioral health conditions, including symptoms of anxiety and depressive disorders, trauma- and stressor-related disorders brought on by the pandemic, and increased substance use as a coping method (Czeisler et al., 2020).

Such factors prompted the United Nations in May 2020 to issue a policy brief warning that in addition to being a physical health crisis, COVID-19 "has the seeds of a major mental health crisis as well, if action is not taken" (United Nations, 2020, p. 2). Indeed, frontline mental health workers have since reported evidence that "this crisis has arrived" (Mulkey, 2021, para. 3). Citing overburdened facilities and practitioner shortages, they noted that more than 18 months after the onset of the pandemic, the mental health system was still unprepared (Mulkey, 2021). To help, experts have suggested alternative community-level interventions promoting social connectedness, supporting those at risk, and utilizing communication strategies and messaging that advance emotional well-being (Czeisler et al., 2020).

The #AloneTogether Campaign

One campaign to answer this call was #AloneTogether, a public service initiative led by the Ad Council in partnership with media companies, including

MTV, Comedy Central, Viacom CBS's Entertainment and Youth Brands, and government institutions, including the Trump Administration, the U.S. Department of Health and Human Services, and the Centers for Disease Control and Prevention (Huesner, 2020). The campaign consisted of phased messaging related to various COVID-focused topics such as masking, modifying holiday plans to reduce the spread, dispelling misinformation, and mental wellness. A mental health arm of the campaign was announced in late March 2020 (Streib, 2020). The campaign also teamed with social media platforms including Facebook, Pinterest, Snapchat, TikTok, and Twitter (X) (Huesner, 2020) to educate audiences on social distancing, provide connection during lockdown, offer support, and highlight mental health resources to combat effects of social isolation (Shorty Awards, n.d.). Brianna Cayo Cotter (as cited in McAteer, 2020), senior vice president of social impact for the Entertainment & Youth brands of Viacom CBS, said of the campaign goals:

> Both for people who are staying home to slow the spread and for frontline workers, it's more important than ever to underscore the message that it's OK to not be OK, and to provide people with actionable tools and resources that help them take care of their emotional well-being. (para. 7)

The idea for the campaign materialized from an effort that was already in progress to unite companies via the Ad Council. Kasha Cacy, a long-time board member for the organization, stated that the Ad Council serves as a hub for competitive entities to work together and that:

> A week or two before COVID struck we got this idea to build a private marketplace where media companies could donate into the Ad Council campaign bucket, but we were moving to get it done at a much slower pace ... When COVID became a real crisis we sped up the effort. (Sullivan, 2020, para. 3)

Companies, public health entities, and media giants—including ABC/Disney, Amazon, Apple, Google, Universal, and WarnerMedia—participated in the cross-industry campaign via adoptions of #AloneTogether assets (Shorty Awards, n.d.; Sullivan, 2020). Utilizing the #AloneTogether hashtag, the multi-channel initiative offered cross-platform public service announcements, a brand-agnostic toolkit, a website, and attempted to connect with fans via social media accounts (Shorty Awards, n.d.). Campaign PSAs encouraging audiences to stay calm and connected aired in the United States and 50 countries around the world (Streib, 2020). ViacomCBS networks also tailored campaign content to accompany traditional programming. For example, Comedy

Central's *The Daily Show with Trevor Noah* introduced a web-based spin-off, *The Daily Social Distancing Show*, which eventually transitioned to a linear format (Streib, 2020).

The digital arm utilized campaign-branded content, including online #MTVUnplugged acoustic performances by musical artists, Comedy Central's web series *My Beautiful Bunker*, and Paramount Network's St. Patrick's Day marathon of the television show *Bar Rescue* on YouTube (Streib, 2020). Google facilitated campaign awareness through advertisements on their search engine and YouTube (Sullivan, 2020). Social media influencers created branded content showcasing the campaign hashtag. Snapchat offered original #AloneTogether custom photo filters, and Twitter (X) generated shareable emojis. The campaign's first week involved more than 500 social posts from partners, which yielded 3 million engagements, 43 million views, and 127 million impressions (Streib, 2020). Data gathered by MTV showed that 51% of people who shared the campaign reported it made them feel like "[W]e are all in this together" (PRWeek, 2020). #AloneTogether received a number of accolades, including winning the PRWeek 2020 Purpose Award in the "Best Collaboration" category (PRWeek, 2020) and the Shorty Social Good Award for "Best Multi-Platform Campaign" (Shorty Awards, n.d.). The campaign also picked up a Shorty award in the "Twitter" category for a collaboration between the Ad Council and Twitter (X) Arthouse, which asked artists to submit creative content showcasing #AloneTogether themes.

Mental Health Discussions and Social Media

The pervasive use of social media makes it a powerful marketing force for companies and brands, something that increased throughout the pandemic (Mason et al., 2021). While #AloneTogether offered a unique take on mental health discussions via traditional and social media through the pandemic, such social media-focused campaigns are not new. In fact, social media is an increasingly popular channel for disseminating mental health campaigns given its global reach and cost-effectiveness. Social media is also distinct from channels, such as television or print, because it allows users to become actively involved (Saha et al., 2019) through posts, reposts, favoriting/liking content, etc. Though health campaign information can be distributed through various social media sites, our study looked specifically at Twitter (X), a microblogging site with more than 300 million users worldwide (Newberry, 2021). Twitter (X) users are limited to 280 words in a post; however, the ability to insert external resource links in "tweets" (i.e., posts) makes the social media platform a hub for discussions on shared interests (Shepherd et al., 2015). Users adopt hashtags in tweets, which elevate a tweet's visibility or popularity, especially if the hashtag is trending (George et al., 2018). Hashtags also facilitate communication and searches focused on mental health topics (Berry et al., 2017).

Although a useful campaign channel, scholarship has found benefits and drawbacks regarding the dissemination of mental health information via Twitter (X). Some research has shown Twitter (X) perpetuated mental health stigmatization (Robinson et al., 2019; Saha et al., 2019). For example, Robinson and colleagues (2019) analyzed tweets that used hashtags of mental health and physical conditions, finding that the mental health condition hashtags were more stigmatized and trivialized than physical conditions. Additionally, in an analysis of Mental Health Awareness Day Twitter (X) hashtags, Saha and colleagues (2019) revealed stigmatizing content was more likely to be retweeted than other content. Some scholars argue Twitter (X) can improve mental health literacy by promoting help-seeking behaviors (Shepherd et al., 2015). Berry and colleagues (2017) found people perceived that Twitter (X) helped combat stigma and raised awareness of mental health issues and provided a space for self-expression, connecting with others, reducing isolation, and sending and receiving support. Our study sought to explore this topic further by examining discourse in tweets using #AloneTogether:

RQ1: How was mental health discussed in tweets under #AloneTogether?

Social Support and Social Media

As noted in the previous section, Twitter (X) may be a useful space for seeking and receiving support (Berry et al., 2017). During COVID-19, as stay-at-home orders restricted access to in-person social support, more people turned to social networking sites, like Twitter (X), as spaces for coping and seeking out social support (Nabity-Grover et al., 2020). Social support describes verbal and nonverbal communication that reduces "uncertainty about the situation, the self, the other, or the relationship, and functions to enhance a perception of personal control in one's experience" (Albrecht & Adelman, 1987, p. 19). The positive impact of social support has been widely documented (Braithwaite et al., 2009), as supportive communication can reduce stress, promote healthy coping, and improve overall well-being (Rains et al., 2015).

Social support involves efforts to alleviate sources of stress or uncertainty (Cutrona & Suhr, 1992) and traditionally is broken into five categories. First, *informational support* involves messages meant to "reduce uncertainty or help make life more predictable for the message recipient" (Braithwaite et al., 2009, p. 133), such as offering suggestions or advice, situation appraisals, teaching, and referrals. Second, *tangible assistance* involves taking "concrete, physical action in support of the recipient" (Braithwaite et al., 2009, p. 135), like providing a loan, expressing one's willingness to help, or direct assistance. Third, *network support* involves messages meant to expand recipients' social networks by facilitating structural connections, companionship, or access to supportive others (Braithwaite et al., 2009). Fourth, *esteem support* describes messages validating "the recipient's self-concept, importance, competence, and rights as a person" (Braithwaite et al., 2009, p. 136). Examples of esteem support include absolving someone of blame and offering compliments or validation to boost a person's esteem. Fifth, *emotional support* involves messages that "express empathy, support the emotional expressions of the recipient, or reciprocate emotion" (Braithwaite et al., 2009, p. 136). Specific types of emotional support include expressing confidentiality or sympathy and providing relational support, prayer, physical affection, and empathy. Recent scholarship has also suggested a sixth category of social support, *directive support*, which mobilizes collective action surrounding societal issues (Hosterman et al., 2018).

Although early studies focused entirely on face-to-face interactions, people increasingly use the internet to seek and provide social support (Rains et al., 2015), which has the capacity to "expand one's social network beyond what would be possible in the face-to-face world (Wright et., al, 2011). Thus, Twitter (X) provides opportunities to observe supportive communication and understand the types of support members provide one another. Our second research question asked:

> RQ2: What forms of social support were offered in tweets under #AloneTogether?

Method

Data Collection and Sample

Tweets were collected between April 1 and July 31, 2020, to capture messages posted throughout the mental health arm of the #AloneTogether campaign.

The launch of the mental health portion of the campaign was first announced in late March, although the specific start date was not reported; thus, we chose April 1 as the beginning date for data collection. April 1 also marks when the vast majority of U.S. states and territories implemented stay-at-home orders and advisories (Moreland, 2020). By early summer, the effects of isolation from social distancing and staying home were becoming more evident to public health professionals (Czeisler et al., 2020). Tweets were collected through July 31, 2020, because the Back-to-School phase of the #AloneTogether campaign ramped up on August 1, 2020, following the mental health phase. In all, 723 publicly available tweets were "scraped" featuring both the #AloneTogether hashtag and the term "mental health." The additional mental health hashtag was included to ensure that only tweets relating specifically to the #AloneTogether mental health initiative were collected. We removed SPAM, redundant tweets, or those with insufficient context to analyze, resulting in a final data set of 644 tweets. A tweet served as the unit of analysis, with themes reflecting presence of each form of discourse captured within each tweet. Themes were not mutually exclusive, given that a single tweet may allow multiple forms of discourse (Tesch, 1990). Exemplars presented here maintain original grammar, spelling, and punctuation to preserve meaning and integrity of the tweets.

Data Analysis

Data analysis involved both conventional qualitative content analysis and directed qualitative content analysis, allowing prior research to ground some themes while also permitting others to emerge inductively (Armat et al., 2018). Applying Hsieh and Shannon's (2005) process, we started by familiarizing ourselves with the data. In addition to the textual body of tweets, we reviewed included memes, photos, videos, links, or GIFs for context. After this, we worked together to form a code frame by conducting a line-by-line review of tweets (Miles & Huberman, 1994). For Research Question 1, which asked how mental health was discussed in the #AloneTogether campaign, the use of conventional qualitative content analysis allowed themes to inductively emerge, yielding five themes: *Commentary on the #AloneTogether Campaign's Approach to Mental Health, Perceptions of Mental Health Issues, First-Person Accounts of Mental Health, Mental Health Conditions,* and *Mental Health Coping.* For Research Question 2, which asked which forms of social support were offered under #AloneTogether, we used directive qualitative content analysis, which involved deductively coding for categories of social support used in previous research (Braithwaite et al., 2009; Hosterman et al., 2018). Specifically, the researchers coded for the aforementioned categories of social support: *Information Support, Tangible Support, Esteem Support, Network Support, Emotional Support,* and *Directive Support.*

Following recommendations by O'Connor and Joffee (2020), after initial establishing of codes, we independently double-coded 10% of the sample (*n* = 70) and ran intercoder reliability measures using Krippendorff's alpha, with initial alphas ranging between .73 and .92. After meeting to refine codes, another intercoder reliability check was performed, showing all variables yielded alphas of at least .93, above what is considered appropriate (Miles & Huberman, 1994; O'Connor & Joffee, 2020). We then independently coded the remainder of the data set (O'Connor & Joffee, 2020).

Results

Research Question 1: Mental Health Discussions Under #AloneTogether

Research Question 1 asked how mental health was discussed in #AloneTogether tweets. Inductive analysis revealed five themes: *Commentary on the #AloneTogether Campaign's Approach to Mental Health, Posters' Perceptions of Mental Health Issues, First-Person Accounts of Mental Health, Mental Health Conditions,* and *Mental Health Coping.*

Commentary on the #AloneTogether Campaign Approach to Mental Health

This theme (*n* = 25) captured tweets that commented on strengths and/or weaknesses of the #AloneTogether campaign. Positive tweets commended the campaign for drawing attention to mental health issues. For example, one tweet expressed gratitude to corporate campaign sponsors "for caring about #emotional #wellness" during a time when so many Americans were struggling. Similarly, another tweet applauded the helpfulness of a campaign advertisement, noting: "As a person that has issues, I found ur #StayCalm #StayConnected #StayActive slogan very useful & to the point. It sounds silly to some but for others, the reminder is useful."

On the other hand, some tweets criticized the campaign, especially the slogan #AloneTogether, which some believed contributed to their sense of isolation or trivialized mental health issues. One tweeted that

> the #AloneTogether hashtag ... it's the worst. "Hi, you're all alone with your thoughts at home. But it's ok; we're all in the same boat." Yeah no, that's a terrible slogan, and it's insensitive to the mental health aspect of the #COVID19 pandemic.

Similarly, another poster explained, "I'm not a fan of #AloneTogether. We're #InThisTogether, but saying we're 'alone' feels negative, even harmful, to me. Many associate 'alone' with 'lonely.'"

Posters' Perceptions of Mental Health Issues

The second emergent theme ($n = 96$) described posters' perceptions of mental health. Posters' tweets demonstrated that mental health was seen as an important issue and emphasized the necessity of caring for psychological well-being. Some tweets highlighted the importance of mental health through additional hashtags like #mentalhealthisimportant or #MentalHealthMatters. Others stated that there was "[t]alk of a second pandemic after this one, a mental health pandemic," so it "was especially important for people look after your mental health in unprecedented times such as these." Tweets also noted the stigmatization of mental health issues. Similar to those noting the importance of mental health, these tweets often used brief hashtags like #destigmatisementalhealth, #breakthestigma, or #changethenarrative. Others called for communities to "come together and fight stigma associated with mental illness." One explained that the way to eliminate stigma "around mental health is talk about it," and that by doing so, "no one struggles in silence."

First-Person Accounts of Mental Health

The next emergent theme ($n = 71$) included personal experiences with mental health through first-person accounts. For example, one poster remarked that he disliked "this quarantine," stating, "I've gotten so much work done but I've also had WAY too much time to just think and get in my own head ... the anxiety is so real I wanna cry." Another lamented, "I cannot express how damaging this Quarantine has been to my mental health." However, some noted that although "Staying at home is making me crazy!" it protected others, so "I'll sacrifice my mental health." Although not as common, others shared humor through first-person accounts, including a post noting, "Not to brag or anything but I totally showered 2day."

Mental Health Conditions

This theme captured tweets that labeled or identified mental health conditions (n = 106), often using hashtags identifying specific mental health conditions or discussions of mental health issues. The range of conditions listed was wide, noting both chronic mental health issues (e.g., depression) and shorter-term effects of staying home (e.g., boredom). The most common conditions that were identified included "depression," "anxiety," and "PTSD." Additional issues included "suicidal thoughts" and "trauma." Some posters noted that these conditions were exacerbated by the pandemic and staying home; however, others simply inserted mental health condition hashtags without context or explanation (e.g., "#depression"). Tweets also noted issues related to mental health conditions, including "boredom," "loneliness," "stress," and "social isolation."

Mental Health Coping

In addition to noting the importance of mental health or identifying specific mental health conditions, tweets in the next emergent theme highlighted tools for coping during the pandemic (n = 367). Most often, posters offered resources or ideas (such as activities) for managing mental health, such as activities for stressed parents staying home with young children to "have fun with the kiddos" and keep them occupied. These tweets included reminders to manage mental health issues and focus on healthy living by engaging in self-care, taking "time to take care of yourself." Acknowledging the potential for media to exacerbate stress or misinformation, tweets recommended people "make sure to use reliable resources and take some time to disconnect from the news." This theme also involved providing links to resources and an acknowledgment that support of various kinds was an important factor in managing mental health.

Research Question 2: Social Support Under #AloneTogether

Research Question 2 asked what forms of social support were offered under #AloneTogether. Posts were coded for occurrences of *Information Support, Tangible Support, Esteem Support, Network Support, Emotional Support,* and *Directive Support*.

Information Support

Information support (n = 473) included *advice, teaching, referral to experts,* and *situations appraisals* (Braithwaite et al., 2009). Examples of *advice* included general suggestions, such as, "Take time to take care of yourself" and "Reach out if you feel alone or know someone who is feeling the same way," and more specific tips for mental health and pandemic lockdown isolation. For example, while one poster advised self-care, stating, "Switch the screen off. Grab a book. Grab a yoga mat," another directed "those stuck inside" to "get creative with *where* you work" and "Create some variation in your workspace for a refreshing change of environment." *Teaching* involved sharing factual or technical information, often through linked articles about mental health. Tweets shared factoids with accompanying articles about research showing that "loneliness can affect you as much as smoking or obesity" and "nature is a natural mood booster, even when enjoyed alone." Others provided *referrals* to expert resources such as companies, mental health providers, and services including helplines, producers of adult coloring books, and journals to alleviate boredom and isolation. Some encouraged use of hotlines to "provide immediate counseling to anyone who needs help in coping with the mental or emotional effects caused by the #CoronavirusPandemic," asking readers to "Call us and let us read you a story to get your mind off of what's troubling you." *Situation appraisals* reassessed or redefined circumstances, namely reframing challenges of the pandemic, such as a poster who stated, "I hope when all is said-and-done with this epidemic, people remember the moments they spent in nature. That when society was crumbling, falling in love with #Earth was a key factor in mental health."

Tangible Support

While the data did not include incidents of *loans, active participation,* or *expressing willingness to help, tangible support* (n = 1) was included via a sole example of *performing a task* (Braithwaite et al., 2009). In an effort to "PayItForward," this poster offered that "If you're an essential worker—hospital, delivery, grocery, mental health, etc—I'd like to buy you lunch for one day next week. I'm picking 1 person."

Esteem Support

Though the data did not feature instances of *relief of blame, esteem support* (n = 10) comprised tweets offering *compliments* and *validation* (Braithwaite et al., 2009). *Compliments* included positive appraisals, such as a post that told readers, "You are brave." *Validation* was present in posts that showed common ground with readers and focused on normalizing their experiences. One such tweet reminded, "It's easy to feel alone & without options," while another stated, "It's normal to feel sad, stressed, confused, scared or angry during a crisis." Similarly, some endorsed the idea that, especially given the unusual circumstances of the pandemic, "It's OK to not be OK."

Network Support

Network support (n = 84) was featured in tweets providing *access, presence,* and *companions* (Braithwaite et al., 2009). Posts involving *access* invited connection to specific social communities, which given the online context, were hosted via links to virtual support groups. A poster offered a link to a "free online support group for people who feel isolated." One directed to Google Meet drop-in rooms, while another linked to a Zoom-based support group and encouraged readers to, "Pass on the link to anyone who is isolated and needs contact and support." *Presence* involved tweets that stressed the existence of supportive listeners. Some broadly offered, "We are here for YOU." Others made more specific propositions, stating, "If you need someone to talk to—I'm here. I'm a good listener, and I do a good line of small talk, if required," and told readers, "I'm here. I got you. I'm not going anywhere." Strongly tied to this, tweets offering *companions* highlighted connections to supportive others. These included tweets stating, "You are not alone," and, "Just because we're serious about stopping the spread of the virus doesn't mean we have to face each day alone—we're in this together."

Emotional Support

Emotional support (n = 52) comprised tweets supporting the emotional state of others (Braithwaite et al., 2009). Though the data did not express *confidentiality* or *sympathy*, it featured *relational* support, *physical affection, understanding/ empathy,* and *prayer*. *Relational* support was characterized by tweets emphasizing closeness and love, such as those stating, "I love you" and "Sending love to everyone." *Physical affection* verbally offered "Distant hugs." Tweets indicating *understanding/empathy* stressed the poster's similarity of experiences with readers, including one stating, "Everyone involved in this project wants you to know we all struggle with mental health issues, whether it's at times or all the time." Others offered understanding, stating, "Isolation is very familiar to us. We completely understand." *Encouragement* provided readers with hope or confidence as they dealt with the pandemic, telling them to "Hang in there," and reminding them "you matter," and that "you are stronger than you think!"

Such tweets also thanked "frontline workers," and provided a "#Shoutout" to all the "coaches, our fellow #therapists, & everyone out there supporting others while dealing with these hard times!" Finally, some posters offered *prayer*, including one that stated they were "Praying for all of the ones struggling with mental health."

Directive Support

Directive support (n = 17) was exemplified in tweets calling for collective action surrounding mental health issues (Hosterman et al., 2018). Mobilization to address mental health issues took many forms, from fundraisers to online content sharing and challenges. One poster incited readers to "Donate now!" and reminded that "Donations go towards more than you think!" such as "Food," "mental health programs," and "keeping families active, etc." Another stated, "Me & my mates are doing a 24 hour stream on Friday to raise awareness & money for @theCALMzone on such an important issue regarding suicide!" Similarly, a tweet highlighting Mental Health Awareness Month asked audiences to "show us how you take care of your emotional well-being" by sharing photos and videos, while another encouraged participation in a "a virtual 5K walk fundraiser" to benefit a mental health organization.

Discussion

The current study sought to understand how the #AloneTogether hashtag was used to discuss mental health and offer social support at the onset of pandemic lockdowns and the related mental health crisis. Results provided insight into how hashtags for health campaigns may be used in practice to foster dialogue and offer assistance in crisis situations.

The first research question asked how mental health was discussed under #AloneTogether, and results underscored well-intentioned efforts to highlight mental health issues alongside struggles to create meaningful and sensitive dialogue. For example, while one subset of tweets normalized mental health discussions, created awareness, and furthered advocacy, another sector focused narrowly upon mental health stigmatization. Tweets involving mental health conditions revealed a similar tension; though discussions denoted various mental health challenges, including anxiety, depression, and social isolation, such conditions were often mentioned in brevity, such as within haphazardly applied hashtags. While these mentions shed light on mental health struggles, they often did not elaborate upon complex issues. For example, #suicidalthoughts is a concerning hashtag; however, when mixed in with other tweets using #AloneTogether and less concerning issues like #boredom, the need to address the seriousness of the former may be diluted or overlooked. The findings echo previous research showing that Twitter (X) campaigns can underplay the seriousness or complexity of mental health issues (Robinson et al., 2019). This may, in part, be a constraint of the platform's 280-character limit or Twitter (X) users' tendency to use trending hashtags to gain visibility/popularity (George et al., 2018). Regardless, the lack of context may trivialize or stereotype mental health issues. This point also relates to tweets about the #AloneTogether campaign's framing of mental health issues—although some Twitter (X) users were grateful for the campaign's efforts to draw attention to this health topic, others felt that the campaign itself exacerbated their feelings of isolation or loneliness, which contradicts the campaign's goals regarding mental health support. Further, a subset of tweets also used the hashtag to share personal mental health accounts, which encapsulated stories relayed in first-person. Research shows that first-person accounts humanize issues and can be powerful persuaders (De Wit et al., 2008), which may reduce stereotyping and stigmatization; however, first-person tweets were in the minority, with the majority offering tools for coping with mental health issues through the pandemic.

Research question two sought to articulate the types of support offered under #AloneTogether. Information far outweighed other forms of support, reflecting previous Twitter-based research, which showed information support predominantly used on Twitter (X) (Hosterman et al., 2018). This was followed by network support, an unsurprising finding given the hashtag theme reminding audiences that they were not alone and part of a bigger community weathering the crisis together. Emotional support was the third most frequently used, likely due, in part, to the campaign focus on mental health and emotion-based topics. We also saw limited evidence of directive support, which mobilized Twitter (X) users around mental health causes. Least used was esteem support, followed by tangible support. Though further research may be needed to account for these results, it could be logically conjectured that Twitter (X) does not foster interpersonal-focused esteem and tangible support, but instead is geared toward microblogging for larger, general audiences.

Though it should be noted that the parameters of this study represent a sliver of communication within a multi-platform campaign, the findings nonetheless provide valuable insight, particularly for practitioners looking to capitalize upon Twitter and its unique features. First, the results illuminate how garnering awareness through a social media hashtag on Twitter (X) is useful in some contexts but limiting in others regarding social support. The results, which show far greater proliferation of information support, indicate that a hashtag-based campaign may prove most efficient in helping people search for a categorized topic, and relatedly, disseminate targeted information. A Twitter (X) hashtag campaign may also be useful in offering network support within an online context, and more general forms of emotional support. However, the platform may not be as appropriate for facilitating intimate types of discussion, such as first-person accounts and connections; similarly, such campaigns may offer minimal esteem and tangible support, which may be better promoted through interpersonal settings.

Secondly, hashtag-based campaigns promoted through user-created content carry both opportunities and challenges. On the one hand, here they allowed organic discussions to emerge surrounding mental health and the pandemic; however, the tradeoff was that the user-driven campaign forewent narrative control that may have been maintained through more structured messaging. Specifically, as we saw through tweeted criticisms of #AloneTogether, user-generated campaigns take on a life of their own and have the potential to backfire.

Finally, the results reveal risks of such Twitter (X)-based campaigns in creating a diluted message. Our data indicated that while mental health issues were brought to the forefront by #AloneTogether, often tweets did so without depth, potentially trivializing a complex topic. Twitter's (X) limited character count particularly narrowed discussions, and a number of tweets used the hashtag in ways that were unconnected to its intended mission. These tweets jumped on the #AloneTogether bandwagon, often promoting products or services at best tangentially related to creating connection and mental health discussion. Although various social media platforms (i.e., Facebook, Instagram, Twitter (X)) may share similar attributes, such as the implementation of hashtags to categorize information, these platforms operate in unique ways based on their distinct tools, features, and modalities that may not be generalized across platforms (Alhabash & Ma, 2017). Further, the uniqueness of these platforms influences the nature of content users share (Waterloo et al., 2018). Given this, our findings provide understanding for how Twitter (X) may be used to foster discussion, but also how its unique features may also be prohibitive.

Practical Implications

In conclusion, practitioners may glean several lessons from #AloneTogether. Specifically, campaign planners for similar causes should clearly articulate mission and goals, especially regarding the types of support they hope to nurture. While Twitter (X) may be an appropriate conduit for certain forms of support—especially information that can be captured in a brief format—it may be less effective in cultivating intimate conversations and more interpersonal forms of support. As a result, practitioners should supplement efforts with a variety of platforms that foster fuller discussions. As with #AloneTogether, multiple forms of social media should be integrated, with thought given to how best to utilize each platform's specific features. For example, while Twitter (X) may be tapped to provide users with brief nuggets of information, other more conversational-oriented platforms may be better suited for fostering in-depth discussions of an issue. Further, following the example set by #AloneTogether, campaign planners may want to consider augmenting social media with other forms of controlled, long-form messaging, including websites and videos that promote the mission. Such multi-channel campaigns carry the benefit of added audience reach, with the potential for various channels to reinforce a message and facilitate behavior change relevant to the campaign mission (Baruch et al., 2021).

Because social media engagement is increasingly preferred by publics and expected by companies and organizations, hashtag campaigns are useful public relations tools (Allagui & Breslow, 2015). Still, it is important to keep in mind that although hashtag campaigns can raise issue or brand awareness, once the public gets a hold of the hashtag, campaign planners may have little control over how it is used. However, as Valentini and Krukeberg (2012) point out, "social media does not exist without users" (p. 6), and it is possible that social media users may employ the hashtag in new and useful ways. As such, campaign planners should thoughtfully implement the use of social media platforms and associated hashtags, with broad expectations for how the public may engage with these outlets while also allowing for the organic nature of social media. Regular monitoring of social media campaigns and rethinking of strategy as the conversation evolves online is encouraged.

Discussion Questions

1. What are your thoughts about the benefits and drawbacks of hashtag campaigns? For which topics (e.g., health, wellness, politics, etc.) do you think hashtag campaigns are best suited?

2. Think about the natural features of various social media platforms (i.e., Twitter (X), Facebook, Instagram, etc.). Do specific platforms lend themselves to certain types of campaign messaging? For example, what type of messaging is best for TikTok versus Facebook?
3. What ethical considerations might researchers using social media data need to take into account? What are some limitations of collecting social media data?

Resources

1. To learn more about the #AloneTogether campaign, check out the #campaign's website: https://www.alonetogether.com/
2. If you would like to learn more about some of the tools we used for this research study, you can find ScrapeHero, the service we used to "scrape" Twitter (X) data, at https://www.scrapehero.com/
3. Also, a great tool for calculating intercoder reliability is ReCal, which you can find here (for free): http://dfreelon.org/utils/recalfront/

References

AARP. (2020, October 6). *The pandemic effect: A social isolation report.* https://connect2affect.org/wp-content/uploads/2020/10/The-Pandemic-Effect-A-Social-Isolation-Report-AARP-Foundation.pdf

Ad Council. (n.d.). *Our history.* https://www.adcouncil.org/our-story/our-history

Albrecht, T.L., & Adelman, M.A. (1987). *Communicating social support.* Sage.

Alhabash, S., & Ma, M. (2017). A tale of four platforms: Motivations and uses of Facebook, Twitter, Instagram, and Snapchat among college students? *Social Media + Society, 3*(1), 1–13. https://doi.org/10.1177/2056305117691544

Allagui, I., & Breslow, H. (2016). Social media for public relations: Lessons from four effective cases. *Public Relations Review, 42*(1), 20–30.

Armat, M., Assarroudi, A., Rad, M., Sharifi, H., & Heydari, A. (2018). Inductive and deductive: Ambiguous labels in qualitative content analysis. *The Qualitative Report, 23*(1), 219–221. https://doi.org/10.46743/2160-3715/2018.2872

Baruch, B., Leenders, E., & Disley, E. (2021). *Supporting parental behavioural change: Multichannel and cross-sector campaigns in Israel.* RAND Corporation. https://www.rand.org/pubs/research_reports/RRA245-10.html

Berry, N., Lobban, F., Belousov, M., Emsley, R., Nenadic, G., & Bucci, S. (2017). #WhyWeTweetMH: Understanding why people use Twitter to discuss mental health problems. *Journal of Medical Internet Research, 19*(4), 1–13. https://doi.org/10.2196/jmir.6173

Braithwaite, D.O., Waldron, V.R., & Finn, J. (2009). Communication of social support in computer-mediated groups for people with disabilities. *Health Communication, 11*(2), 123–151. https://doi.org/10.1207/s15327027hc1102_2

Bryson Taylor, D. (2021, March 17). A timeline of the coronavirus pandemic. *The New York Times.* https://www.nytimes.com/article/coronavirus-timeline.html

Cacioppo, J.T., & Cacioppo, S. (2014). Older adults reporting social isolation or loneliness show poorer cognitive function 4 years later. *Evidence-Based Nursing, 17*(2), 59–60. https://doi.org/10.1136/eb-2013-101379

CDC COVID-19 Response Team. (2020). Geographic differences in COVID-19 cases, deaths, and incidence—United States, February 12–April 7. *Morbidity and Mortality Weekly Reports, 69*, 465–471. https://doi.org/10.15585/mmwr.mm6915e4

Cigna. (2018). *Cigna US Loneliness Index: 20,000 Americans Examining Behaviors Driving Loneliness in the US.* Cigna. https://www.multivu.com/players/English/8294451-cigna-us-loneliness-survey/docs/IndexReport_1524069371598-173525450.pdf

Cutrona, C.E., & Suhr, J.A. (1992). Controllability of stressful events and satisfaction with spouse support behaviors. *Communication Research, 19*, 154–174. https://doi.org/10.1177/009365092019002002

Czeisler, M.É., Lane, R.I., Petrosky, E., Wiley, J.F., Christensen, A., Njai, R., Njai, R., Weaver, M.D., Robins, R., Facer-Childs, E.R., Barger, L.K., Czeisler, C.A., Howard, M.E., & Rajaratnam, S.M.W. (2020). Mental health, substance use, and suicidal ideation during the COVID-19 pandemic—United States, June 24–30, 2020. *Morbidity and Mortality Weekly Report, 69*(32), 1049–1057. https://doi.org/10.15585/mmwr.mm6932a1

de Calheiros Velozo, J., & Stauder, J.E.A. (2018). Exploring social media use as a composite construct to understand its relation to mental health: A pilot study on adolescents. *Children and Youth Services Review, 91*, 398–402. https://doi.org/10.1016/j.childyouth.2018.06.039

De Wit, J.B.F., Das, E., & Vet, R. (2008). What works best: Objective statistics or a personal testimonial? An assessment of the persuasive effects of different types of message evidence on risk perception. *Health Psychology, 27*, 110–115. https://doi.org/10.1037/0278-6133.27.1.110

George, N., Britto, D.R., Krishnan, V., Dass, L.M., Prasant, H.A., & Aravindhan, V. (2018). Assessment of hashtag (#) campaigns aimed at health awareness in social media. *Journal of Education and Health Promotion, 7*, 114. https://doi.org/10.4103/jehp.jehp_37_18

Hsieh, H.F., & Shannon, S.E. (2005). Three approaches to qualitative content analysis. *Qualitative Health Research, 15*(9), 1277–1288. https://doi.org/10.1177/1049732305276687

Ho, C.S., Chee, C.Y., & Ho, R.C. (2020). Mental health strategies to combat the psychological impact of COVID-19 beyond paranoia and panic. *Annals Academy of Medicine, Singapore, 49*(1), 1–6. https://doi.org/10.47102/annals-acadmedsg.202043

Holt-Lunstad, J. (2018). The potential public health relevance of social isolation and loneliness: Prevalence, epidemiology, and risk factors. *Public Policy & Aging Report, 27*(4),127–130. https://doi.org/10.1093/ppar/prx030

Holt-Lunstad, J., Smith, T.B., Baker, M., Harris, T., & Stephenson, D. (2015). Loneliness and social isolation as risk factors for mortality: A meta-analytic review. *Perspectives on Psychological Science, 10*, 227–237. https://doi.org/10.1177/1745691614568352

Hosterman, A. R., Johnson, N. R., Stouffer, R., & Herring, S. (2018). Twitter, social support messages, and the# MeToo movement. *The Journal of Social Media in Society, 7*(2), 69-91. https://www.thejsms.org/index.php/JSMS/article/view/475

Huesner, M. (2020, March 25). *Ad Council joins forces with The White House to launch #AloneTogether campaign.* Campaign U.S. https://www.campaignlive.com/article/ad-council-joins-forces-white-house-launch-alonetogether-campaign/1678313

Hwang, T.J., Rabheru, K., Peisah, C., Reichman, W., & Ikeda, M. (2020). Loneliness and social isolation during the COVID-19 pandemic. *International Psychogeriatrics, 32*, 1217–1220. https://doi.org/10.1017/S1041610220000988

Leigh-Hunt, N., Bagguley, D., Bash, K., Turner, V., Turnbull, S., Valtorta, N., & Caan, W. (2017). An overview of systematic reviews on the public health consequences of social isolation and loneliness. *Public Health, 152*, 157–171. https://doi.org/10.1016/j.puhe.2017.07.035

Mason, A.N., Narcum, J., & Mason, K. (2021). Social media marketing gains importance after Covid-19. *Cogent Business & Management, 8*(1), Article 1870797. https://doi.org/10.1080/23311975.2020.1870797

McAteer, O. (2020, April 23). *#AloneTogether fights crippling loneliness as mental wellness plummets 37%.* PR Week. https://www.prweek.com/article/1681262/alonetogether-fights-crippling-loneliness-mental-wellness-plummets-37

Mcelrath, K. (2020, August 26). *Nearly 93% of households with school-age children report some form of distance learning during COVID-19.* United States Census Bureau. https://www.census.gov/library/stories/2020/08/schooling-during-the-covid-19-pandemic.html

Miles, M.B., & Huberman, A.M. (1994). *Qualitative data analysis: An expanded sourcebook* (2nd ed.). Sage.

Moreland, A., Herlihy, C., Tynan, M.A. Sunshine, G., McCord, R.F., Hilton, C., Poovey, J., Werner, A.K., Jones, C.D., Fulmer, E.B., Gundlapalli, A.V., Strosnider, H., Potvien, A., García, M.C., Honeycutt, S., Baldwin, G., CDC Public Health Law Program, CDC COVID-19 Response Team, & Mitigation Policy Analysis Unit. (2020). Timing of state and territorial COVID-19 stay-at-home orders and changes in population movement—United States, March 1–May 31, 2020. *Morbidity and Mortality Weekly Reports, 69*, 1198–1203. https://dx.doi.org/10.15585/mmwr.mm6935a2

Mulkey, N. (2021, September 16). What the mental health crisis looks like on the ground. *Psychiatric Times.* https://www.psychiatrictimes.com/view/mental-health-crisis-ground-level

Nabity-Grover, T., Cheung, C.M.K., Thatcher, J.B. (2020). Inside out and outside in: How the COVID-19 pandemic affects self-disclosure on social media. *International Journal of Information Management, 55*, Article 102188. https://doi.org/10.1016/j.ijinfomgt.2020.102188

Newberry, C. (2021, February 3). *36 Twitter stats all marketers need to know in 2021. Hootsuite.* https://blog.hootsuite.com/twitter-statistics/#General_Twitter_stats

O'Connor, C., & Joffe, H. (2020). Intercoder reliability in qualitative research: Debates and practical guidelines. *International Journal of Qualitative Methods, 19*, 1–13. https://doi.org/10.1177/1609406919899220

PRWeek. (2020, October 14). *The 2020 Purpose Awards.* https://www.prweek.com/article/1697279/2020-purpose-awards

Rains, S.A., Peterson, E.B., & Wright, K.B. (2015). Communicating social support in computer-mediated contexts: A meta-analytic review of content analyses examining support messages shared online among individuals coping with illness. *Communication Monographs, 82*, 403–430. https://doi.org/10.1080/03637751.2015.1019530

Robinson, P., Turk, D., Jilka, S., & Cella, M. (2019). Measuring attitudes towards mental health using social media: Investigating stigma and trivialization. *Social Psychiatry and Psychiatric Epidemiology, 54*, 51–58. https://doi.org/10.1007/s00127-018-1571-5

Saha, K., Torous, J., Ernala, S.K., Rizuto, C., Stafford, A., & De Choudhury, M. (2019) A computational study of mental health awareness campaigns on social media. *TBM, 9*, 1197–1207. https://doi.org/10.1093/tbm/ibz028

Shepherd, A., Sanders, C., Doyle, M., & Shaw, J. (2015). Using social media for support and feedback by mental health service users: Thematic analysis of a Twitter conversation. *BMC Psychiatry, 15*(29), 1–9. https://doi.org/10.1186/s12888-015-0408-y

Shorty Awards. (n.d.). *From the fifth annual Shorty Social Good Awards, #AloneTogether.* https://shortyawards.com/5th-socialgood/alonetogether#

Stephens, M.H., & Petrie, K.J. (2015). Social support and recovery from disease and medical procedures. In J.D. Wright (Ed.), *International encyclopedia of the social & behavioral sciences* (pp. 735–740). Elsevier.

Streib, L. (2020, April 9). With #AloneTogether, the media industry unites to drive awareness. *CBS.* https://www.viacomcbs.com/news/company-news/with-alonetogether-the-media-industry-unites-to-drive-awareness

Sullivan, L. (2020, April 1). Ad Council COVID-19 #AloneTogether campaign backstory, How dozens of companies collaborated. *Digital News Daily.* https://www.mediapost.com/publications/article/349276/ad-council-covid-19-alonetogether-campaign-backst.html

Tesch, R. (1990). *Qualitative research: Analysis types and software tools.* Routledge Falmer.

Torales, J., O'Higgins, M., Castaldelli-Maia, J.M., & Ventriglio, A. (2020). The outbreak of COVID-19 coronavirus and its impact on global mental health. *International Journal of Social Psychiatry, 66*, 317–320. https://doi.org/10.1177/0020764020915212

Uchino, B.N. (2006). Social support and health: A review of physiological processes potentially underlying links to disease outcomes. *Journal of Behavioral Medicine, 29*(4), 377–387. https://doi:10.1007/s10865-006-9056-5

United Nations. (2020, May 13). *Policy brief: COVID-19 and the need for action on mental health.* https://www.un.org/sites/un2.un.org/files/un_policy_brief-covid_and_mental_health_final.pdf

U.S. Bureau of Labor Statistics. (n.d.). *Supplemental data measuring the effects of the coronavirus (COVID-19) pandemic on the labor market.* https://www.bls.gov/cps/effects-of-the-coronavirus-covid-19-pandemic.htm

Valentini, C., & Kruckeberg, D. (2012). New media versus social media: A conceptualization of their meaning, uses, and implications for public relations. In S. C. Duhé (Ed.), *New media and public relations* (2nd ed., pp. 3–12). New York: Peter Lang.

Waterloo, S.F., Baumgartner, S.E., Peter, J., & Valkenburg, P.M. (2018). Norms of online expressions of emotion: Comparing Facebook, Twitter, Instagram, and WhatsApp. *New Media & Society, 20*(5), 1813–1831. https://doi.org/10.1177/1461444817707349

Wright, K. B., Johnson, A. J., Bernard, D. R., & Averbeck, J. (2011). Computer-mediated social support: Promises and pitfalls for individuals coping with health concerns. In T. L. Thompson, R. Parrott, & J. F. Nussbaum (Eds.), *The Routledge handbook of health communication*, 2nd ed. (pp. 349-362). Routledge.

· 4 ·

"LIKE PUTTING OUT FIRES, WHILE RUNNING ON A TREADMILL THAT WAS ALSO ON FIRE": WORKING AND PARENTING IN A PANDEMIC

Lauren J. Johnsen & Amnee Elkhalid

From suddenly working remotely to managing children's remote school, the COVID-19 pandemic impacted the daily lives of working parents. Parents received increasing attention during the pandemic for various reasons including stressors associated with schools moving to online learning (Misirli & Ergulec, 2021), COVID-19 health concerns (Brooks et al., 2020), or managing work responsibilities in the midst of the pandemic (Cheng et al., 2021). This book chapter stemmed from the heightened attention parents received upon the start of the pandemic, as well as the authors' experiences with parents during the pandemic.

At the start of the COVID-19 pandemic, the first author worked on a project that focused on men's experiences with pregnancy, labor, and delivery. The men interviewed primarily worked from home and in some cases, those who discussed the pandemic were grateful for what they called an "extended paternity leave." The second author worked with an online learning program created in the response to the pandemic. The program was designed to help children improve reading skills with parents as active participants in the learning process. During this experience, challenges related to online learning and COVID-19 were apparent.

The purpose of this chapter is to illuminate the experiences of working parents during the pandemic. This chapter first outlines previous literature that relates to working parents, work flexibility, and the pandemic. Findings highlight the experiences of working parents during the pandemic. Lastly, implications for practitioners and future research are examined.

Working Parents

Compared to prior family dynamics, the modern family is more likely to consist of dual-working or single parents (Coontz, 2000). Shifts in family structures have a direct relationship with employment and work-life balance, which warrants the attention of researchers and employers (Lockwood, 2003). Factors that can impact working parents include gender differences, household income, and household structure (Kim, 2020). For example, working women were more likely to face additional pressures when considering the work–family role balance (Kim, 2020; Lott, 2020). In fact, when compared to fathers, mothers were more likely to provide childcare when employed (Craig & Mullan, 2010). These stressors were only further exacerbated by the COVID-19 pandemic (Barroso & Horowitz, 2021; Igielnik, 2021).

As family dynamics shifted, so too has the modern workplace. Employees now have more flexibility in their workplace dynamics in an attempt to improve employees' work-life balance. There are three types of workplace flexibility: schedule, flexplace, and hour (Hill et al., 2008). Schedule flexibility allows employees to have a choice when they participate in work-related tasks. Flexplace includes employees having a choice in where they engage in work-related tasks (e.g., virtually, at home, coffee shop). Lastly, flexibility allows workers to have a choice in the amount of time they engage in work-related tasks.

Although standard work hours in the United States are typically 40 hours per week, arguments have been made for employees to be able to reduce these standard hours to make more time for family (Barnett & Gareis, 2000). Work flexibility can offer parents an opportunity to be a key influencer with increased involvement in their child's life (e.g., taking their child to the doctor, attending school or sports events; Voydanoff, 2005). Although work flexibility may sound promising to working parents, challenges such as work-to-home spillover often occur.

Work-to-home spillover involves the cognitive blurring of boundaries between work and home responsibilities (Westaby et al., 2016). When work-to-home spillover occurs, individuals can experience emotional exhaustion, stress, and burnout (Liang, 2015). Home-life can also spill over into work-life, such as negative marital interactions spilling over into the workplace; overall, the effects of spillover can have detrimental effects on both families and organizations (Sandberg et al., 2013). Work-to-home spillover is a side effect of work flexibility. Schedule and workplace flexibility could be factors to spillovers because when and where an individual works could blend with home and family life. Such challenges were noted in literature prior to the pandemic (Liang, 2015; Westaby et al., 2016), and with more employees working from home since the start of the pandemic, these problems are likely exacerbated. Overall, being able to wind down and "turn off" from work is important to help avoid burnout and for general individual well-being (e.g., sleep, leisure time quality; Cropley & Millward, 2009). However, turning off from work may prove difficult for individuals who experience work-home or home-work spillover, especially during the pandemic.

COVID-19 and Working Parents

In March 2020, COVID-19 lockdowns changed the daily lives of parents, children, businesses, and schools (Centers for Disease Control, 2021). Parents often rely on family, friends, or external entities for childcare (Emlen, 2010). In fact, the majority of children in the United States receive consistent non-parental childcare (Krogstad, 2015). Consequences of the pandemic included concerns regarding childcare (e.g., availability, expense), online learning, decreases in the job market (Cheng et al., 2021), social isolation, and fear of spreading the virus (Brooks et al., 2020). As such, the pandemic had negative consequences on mental health (Brooks et al., 2020). Cheng et al. (2021) found mental health decline to be more significant among working parents, with childcare and homeschooling being recognized as contributing factors.

At the start of the pandemic, many parents experienced a decrease in support and an increase in parenting responsibilities. Many childcare facilities closed during the COVID-19 shutdown. Further, many individuals rely on older family members, such as grandparents, to care for their children, but were unable to do so due to the elderly population being at a higher risk for contracting the virus (Brown, 2021; Rodríguez et al., 2021). Without childcare facilities, traditional at-school education, or family members available, working parents had to improvise with limited options. With children learning from home and a significant number of jobs moving online, some working parents were simultaneously attending to work and parenting responsibilities (Restubog et al., 2020). Additionally, parents with school-age children may have needed to perform as a mediator for their child's online learning (Misirli & Ergulec, 2021). For those that were required to physically attend work, childcare access and fear of spreading the virus to a family member were significant concerns (Rodríguez et al., 2021). In general, the demands of working parents increased during the pandemic which had consequences on mental health and well-being.

The pandemic not only impacted mental health but also highlighted already existing gender inequalities among working parents (Cheng et al., 2021). Gender inequalities were especially apparent for working mothers during COVID-19 (Barroso & Horowitz, 2021; Igielnik, 2021). Mothers are twice as likely to be caring for children while working, in comparison to fathers (Igielnik, 2021). Mothers were also more likely to experience mental and financial hardships during the pandemic (Cheng et al., 2021). Overall, living during an unprecedented time with abrupt changes, stressors, and uncertainty as it related to home-life, work-life, and health concerns, many parents were left navigating a crisis with reduced or limited resources. Taking this all into consideration, our aim was to understand the impacts of COVID-19 on the lives of working parents, which led us to the following research question:

RQ: What impact did the COVID-19 pandemic have on the work-life balance of working parents?

Method

The purpose of this case study was to describe and interpret the impacts of COVID-19 on working parents. This chapter took an instrumental case study approach in which multiple individuals were surveyed about their experiences with a specific issue or problem (Stake, 1995). Our aim was to understand the challenges and opportunities working parents experienced during the COVID-19 pandemic.

This project utilized an open-ended survey with questions regarding work-life balance before and during the pandemic, the impact of the pandemic on parenting and work-life, as well as challenges and opportunities experienced in both roles. Participants were recruited via researchers' social networks; links to the survey along with a brief description of the project were shared on Twitter (X), Facebook, and LinkedIn. In total, 20 working parents responded to the open-ended survey questions; data were collected in October 2021.

Of the 20 participants that responded, 13 provided demographic information; limitations regarding the sample are discussed later in the chapter. The ages for the 13 participants who reported their demographic information ranged from 26 to 53 years ($M = 39.53$, $SD = 8.56$). Twelve participants identified as a cisgender woman or female, one participation identified as male, all 13 identified as white. Twelve participants identified as Democrat, one identified as Republican. Eleven participants reported obtaining a postgraduate degree, one reported obtaining a bachelor's degree, and one reported having some college but no degree. Participants were asked to identify their household income bracket: $70–79,999 ($n = 1$), $90–99,999 ($n = 3$), $100–149,999 ($n = 2$), and $150,000 or more ($n = 7$). Of note, majority of the participants' income is above the average U.S. household.

Survey answers were downloaded into a spreadsheet and participant answers were organized into two categories: *changes and challenges to work*, and *changes and challenges to parenting*. For this case study the researchers examined individual answers to understand how each of our participants experienced the COVID-19 pandemic. Each participant was treated as a case, as such the first author engaged in a within-case analysis. Each case was then examined in comparison to other cases (i.e., cross-case analysis; Creswell & Poth, 2016). This process involved the first author holistically examining answers to questions within each category to look for general patterns of similarities and differences between each case, while simultaneously analyzing individual responses. Then lessons, or assertions (see Stake, 1995), learned from the data as a whole are discussed to provide a more general understanding of the challenges and opportunities of being a working parent during the COVID-19 pandemic.

Findings

Participants were asked to discuss changes and challenges to their personal and professional lives as a result of the COVID-19 global pandemic. Participants were specifically asked about their parenting life and their work-life. Participant answers are discussed and organized around the two categories: *changes and challenges to work* and *changes and challenges to parenting*.

Changes and Challenges to Work

The biggest change for the majority of participants was moving from an in-person to a remote working environment. About half of the participants worked in higher education, either as a professor, instructor, or administrator. Those participants noted their institutions shut down or moved completely online at the start of the pandemic, though many noted they were transitioning back to in-person classes for the Fall 2021 semester. Many participants working in industry noted they were already remote before the pandemic and stayed remote. One participant noted they already worked from home and other members of their organization worked in an office setting; however, once the pandemic lockdown began their entire team began to work from home instead of in an office. Participants who worked in the health industry (e.g., RN, EMT/public safety officer) noted they worked outside of the home before/during the COVID-19 pandemic and their role did not change in terms of work location. For many participants the job changed modes, but the nature of their job did not change significantly. Two categories of challenges emerged in their work lives as a result of the COVID-19 pandemic: *logistics* and *mental health*.

Logistics

Time emerged as a major challenge for participants, with a specific focus on (lack of) time for work, family, and themselves. Many participants felt they had a good work-life balance before the pandemic, but that was no longer the case once the pandemic began. Other logistics challenges such as issues with Wi-Fi, managing kids at home while trying to complete work, or helping kids with online classes took away time for their own work. Many expressed that having everyone home trying to do their own work proved challenging, as did finding childcare. Most participants said their work-life balance took a significant downturn during the pandemic. Participants felt as if they had to work all the time or did not know when their workday should end to make time for family, household chores, cooking, etc. Some participants discussed changing their own work schedule to accommodate both their children's and their spouse's schedules. One woman commented on her spouse's less flexible work schedule, so she "took the brunt of the childcare while also trying to keep [her] head above water with work"; consequently, she worked when her baby napped or on weekends. Many of the women who were identified in this sample accommodated their own work in order to take on the brunt of childcare (e.g., work early mornings, late evenings).

Some participants felt the pandemic caused specific work challenges. For example, one participant shared, "As an administrator, our job is to put out fires. But the last 18 months was like putting out fires, while running on a treadmill that was also on fire," indicating that problems were more extreme and urgent because of the pandemic. An RN in an emergency department described her workplace as "Apocalyptic." She said, "We didn't have the equipment we needed. We didn't have the know[ledge] we needed. We were afraid of dying ourselves," feeling as if she was ill-equipped to do her job. One college professor said her day-to-day life turned into simultaneously managing hybrid, in-person, and online classes. She felt as if she had no time to keep up with work responsibilities and shared how she "essentially [had] not done any writing for research projects since March 2020." For many people the nature of their work changed, and the majority of their work time was consumed by managing the logistics of a new system. Overall, participants saw drastic changes in their work mode and some functions of their jobs when the pandemic began. At the start of the pandemic, many worked from home for the first time and found it challenging to balance work/family responsibilities in the same location.

Mental Health

Beyond logistical challenges, many participants felt working in a pandemic led to challenges with their mental health. Many participants discussed how working during the pandemic was a draining and emotionally exhausting experience. One participant, an assistant professor, said: "I have had to provide a lot more support to my students than I ever had before. It has been emotionally exhausting." A result of this exhaustion led her to express challenges in completing tasks and a lack of structure to her day-to-day work-life. Some even found it difficult to complete tasks and expressed a lack of motivation. Another university professor said, "This challenge (and those that stemmed from being a working parent) was draining and lonely. Despite reading message after message online from parents having this shared experience, it has always felt isolating and lonely." Even though she knew other people had similar experiences, working from home still felt incredibly isolating.

Another participant who worked in an administrative capacity for a fire academy worked from home for part of the pandemic and expressed having "severe anxiety during this time" and "feeling detached from the world and very lonely." Other participants who worked outside the home felt unsafe being outside of their home, especially early on in the pandemic. They also felt as if they had no life outside of work, for fear of infecting others and feeling as if they could only go to work then go home. One woman who worked as a registered nurse in an emergency department said she and her colleagues were scared they would get COVID from a patient or that they would die. Working during a pandemic mostly negatively impacted participant's mental health. Many felt exhausted or were put in a position to feel constantly worried about their own health and safety while at work. Overall, many participants noted changes and challenges that related to their work-life. Participants noted the consequences these changes had on their mental well-being (e.g., isolation, feeling detached). In addition to navigating work changes and challenges, they also had parenting responsibilities.

Changes and Challenges to Parenting

Participants were asked to discuss their parenting during a pandemic, challenges faced, as well as any positive or negative impacts to their parenting. In general, these participants expressed mostly negative impacts and talked about how difficult it was to parent during a pandemic. Participant challenges also fell into two categories: *logistics* and *mental health*.

Logistics

Navigating the logistics of parenting at home during the pandemic proved challenging for many working parents. Participants often said getting their kids to engage and keep up with schoolwork was the hardest part of online learning. One participant said they were "constantly trying to find a balance between pushing them to stay engaged and just cutting them huge slack for how hard everything was," and a few others mentioned their kids did worse in school while trying to work at home than they had in the past. One participant expressed that their child failed multiple classes despite doing everything she could think of to help them stay engaged. In general, as the pandemic wore on, parents of school-aged children shared how difficult it was to keep their kids focused and motivated.

Many participants expressed how the pandemic disrupted the lives of their children. One participant commented that before the pandemic her children were very outgoing and active, and now she has to "work to get them to leave the house." Another person said they struggled to find "activities to do with [my kids] that were not super repetitive but were also safe." Others said they tried to create "a safe bubble" of people outside of their homes for their children to socialize, but doing so was a challenge. One woman was grateful her child was able to move many of their social activities to online spaces, but in comparison to their normal activity level they now feel like a "hermit." Some parents were more restrictive in socializing outside of the home, and as a result became more lenient with screen time or other activities allowed at home.

A challenge for some parents was disruptions to their kids' day-to-day routines. For example, one participant had two daughters in college who at different points in the pandemic came home unexpectedly. On the other hand, one participant who became a parent in the pandemic found life back to "normal" more challenging; she felt her daughter's life became more disrupted and their schedule was less regular with her daughter in daycare, which also resulted in more exposure to sickness than before. For parents, COVID-19 upended their kids' normal lives, and many found it challenging to navigate the logistics of their children's school and social lives.

For most working parents, the logistics of transitioning to daily life taking place at home proved challenging. Many expressed how there were simply not enough hours in the day for everyone in their house to complete their daily tasks. For many parents, this was the first time they worked from home or had their entire family consistently home at the same time. More often than not working parents spent most of their workday helping their kids complete their schoolwork with little time to do their jobs. The majority of participants who identified as women/mothers reported spending most of their workdays helping children with school rather than their own day jobs. One discussed having to spend more time helping her child with online school because she was too young to be able to engage in virtual school independently. In essence, these working parents prioritized parenting during work hours and had to find time once their spouse was available, or hired outside help, to complete their own work. Over half the participants reported parenting with a spouse, one woman said her mother provided additional childcare, and many said they were able to find some outside childcare though at times it was hard to find. All of these parents were able to pass on childcare responsibility to someone else, at least some of the time.

In general, participants encountered logistical challenges when parenting during the pandemic. In many cases, parents prioritized the needs of their family and children, over their own needs. Many participants discussed how COVID-19 impacted their parenting life and own mental health.

Mental Health

Similar to work-life challenges, most participants discussed the numerous ways parenting in a pandemic had impacted their mental health. Many parents expressed not having any breaks or time apart from their kids. One participant said their work makes them a better parent because "it gives me a way to ground myself and have a mental reset." However, in many cases, the pandemic caused parents to be with their children 24/7, which resulted in having no space or time to complete their own work or have their own life outside of parenting. The lines between work-life and parenting life were blurred, because even while working, they were providing childcare. Many mothers said being with their kids all day, without a break, took a toll on their mental health. For example, participants said, "I'm less happy," expressed being "short-tempered," or "just so irritable." In general, parents expressed negative emotions in response to parenting 24/7 while trying to maintain work responsibility.

Aside from feeling isolated, many parents also felt anxious. These participants felt the lack of a break or space from their kids negatively impacted their mental health, which they worried might negatively impact their ability and capacity to parent their children. One participant commented, "I hope my stress and the world's stress didn't affect [my daughter] negatively." Participants were also concerned about potentially exposing their kids. Some participants expressed feeling more worried about their families being exposed to COVID-19 when a partner worked outside of the house. Others expressed concerns with school districts and state government (e.g., "I don't trust my school board, the district superintendent or the governor to make the right choices for my kids"). Overall, many parents expressed feeling more anxious about the pandemic.

Although many expressed the lack of time away from their kids as a negative, some were grateful to have more time for family. For some, the pandemic led to some positive impacts to their families' overall well-being and helped them grow closer to their kids. One woman shared how "the unexpected time my oldest spent at home" was a positive outcome. Others said they grew closer to their kids during this time. One mom said she was glad to have time with her youngest child, who was leaving for college soon. Many with young children said that the time at home meant more time to enjoy the daily changes in their kids (e.g., "watching a toddler grow this fast is pretty incredible"). Another mom said, "My girls are still little . . . I really enjoyed being able to spend more time with the girls even if it caused me working at times I wouldn't have liked to work." For these parents, they were grateful for more time at home to enjoy their kids and focus on the early milestones, even if it meant sacrificing their own work. Many expressed how increased time with their children, at times, made them feel happier and closer to their kids. More time with family, for some participants, was an unexpected blessing during the pandemic. Some participants also shared positive impacts on their relationship with their partner. For example, one participant said:

> I also think it has pushed my partner and I to talk about our parenting struggles. We've spent more time together and don't have family in town to help us (or many close friends), so we've needed to make some big decisions and have a lot of conversations about being a partnership and dividing labor.

For this participant, the sudden change in their daily routine led to reflecting on and ultimately adjusting how they were handling division of labor and parenting in general, which she was grateful for. This was just one example of the positive impact of the pandemic.

In all, participants reported the challenges that came with managing family responsibilities (e.g., daycare, education). The women who reported their demographics shared challenges that came with being a mother during the pandemic and the ways they adapted their schedules to accommodate their families. Consequently, parents noted a decline in their mental health; however, in some cases, parents noted positive responses to these changes.

Discussion

We surveyed working parents about the impacts of COVID-19 on their work and parenting lives. Surveys were completed in October 2021, about 20 months into the COVID-19 pandemic. Most parents who responded still expressed a general sense of stress and fatigue. Findings highlights changes and challenges to both working and parenting, with a specific focus on logistics and mental health.

Most of the participants who reported their demographics identified as women and speak to the upper-middle class working-parent experience (see Methods section). Many of the participant were in a position to work from home during the pandemic. Previous literature has found that mothers are more likely to take on the brunt of the childcare (Craig & Mullan, 2010; Kim, 2020; Lott, 2020). This was confirmed by the identifiable women in this sample, as almost all of these participants expressed how they took on more childcare responsibilities than the father of their children. Working women often report an unequal distribution of labor in their households (Cheng et al., 2021; Craig & Mullan, 2010; Igielnik, 2021; Kim, 2020; Lott, 2020). Like many working mothers, these women discussed how the pandemic made childcare challenging (Barroso & Horowitz, 2021). In addition, many parents reported not having access to regular childcare during the pandemic. Many parents are increasingly reliant on childcare (Emlen, 2010), and a lack of access to childcare made lockdown challenging.

With changes in education and work modes, many participants found themselves home all day with their spouses and kids. Some working parents had a positive reaction to having more time at home with their kids, but the majority felt they had no balance between their home and work lives. Many parents also had a harder time distinguishing between their parenting, work, and spousal responsibilities; in other words, boundaries between these different roles became more permeable. As a result, participants reported feeling burnt out, stressed, and generally reported negative mental health impacts (Cropley & Millwar, 2009; Liang, 2015; Westaby et al., 2016).

For many participants, familial responsibilities impacted their standard workday during the pandemic, thus shedding light and exacerbating a need to change the standard working hours to better accommodate family life (Barnett & Gareis, 2000). Being able to unwind and "turn off" helps avoid burnout (Liang, 2015), but parents during the majority of the pandemic lockdown expressed difficulty in "turning off" because of increased responsibilities at home, in addition to the stressors of the pandemic. Although the pandemic provided a unique opportunity for families to spend the majority of their time together, many felt overwhelmed being with their kids and partners consistently throughout the day, which impacted their well-being and ability to complete work tasks.

Some participants expressed motivation to help their child with their academic learning during the pandemic, as other studies have found (Nyanamba et al., 2021). However, parents managing their own work responsibilities while simultaneously assisting with childcare and schooling generally led to further burnout and exhaustion. Participants who identified as women also reported working unusual hours (e.g., nights, weekends) to accommodate their partners' and children's schedules. In general, managing childcare, children's learning, and adjusting work schedules in the same environment were factors that blurred the lines between work and home.

Limitations and Future Directions

This case study is not without limitations. One limitation is the number of participants who did not provide demographic information. As such, findings and discussion are recognized within the given context and should be interpreted with this limitation in mind. Our conclusions are based on a small sample of educated (some college to postgraduate degrees), white, working parents, who reported their income as $70,000 or more. In addition, many of our participants reported working in higher education or other industries that allowed the majority to work from home. This limits our findings and conclusion to a specific group of parents. Future research should examine other groups of parents (e.g., different income status, race, education, etc.), as well as men's experiences and parents who were unable to work from home.

Twenty months into the pandemic parents claimed to still feel tired and burnt out. Work-to-home spillovers can have negative consequences on familial relationships (Sandberg et al., 2013); future research should examine management strategies to help working parents cope with work-to-home spillover stressors. Further research could also examine the role of employers; specifically, how employers can better assist their employees balance work and home, especially during times such as the COVID-19 pandemic. Future research should also address the concerns many parents expressed relating to their children's socialization and academic success. These are ongoing issues from the pandemic with lingering consequences, regardless of the reopening of schools and businesses.

Conclusions and Practical Applications

This study focused on how the COVID-19 pandemic impacted the work-life balance of working parents. Findings highlighted the challenges and changes experienced by parents working from home during the pandemic. This study also sheds light on the inequalities that became increasingly prevalent, such as gender inequalities in the workplace (Craig & Mullan, 2010; Kim, 2020; Lott, 2020). Moreover, this study speaks to how childcare and traditional forms of education impact the ways in which society operates. As noted by Misirli and Ergulec (2021), emergency remote teaching during the pandemic was not ideal and in general, remote learning for young children is unrealistic. Emergency online learning for children placed burdens on many parents and lack of childcare significantly impacted parents (Cheng et al., 2021). Lastly, these findings exposed the mental health decline many experienced as a result of the pandemic (e.g., isolation, anxiety; Brooks et al., 2020).

In all, the pandemic highlighted and exacerbated existing issues, but also introduced a new onset of concerns. These findings can benefit employers, organizational leaders, and working parents. Employers and organizational leaders should take time to understand the demands of working parents and gender inequalities in the workplace and at home in an effort to best support their employees. Employers could adjust working hours or provide resources to assist their employees adjust to abrupt changes in work modalities. Further, this case study illuminates some of the issues parents face working from home, and many industries are likely to remain remote (Saad & Wigert, 2021). If some industries continue the practice of remote work, many employees may continue to face these or similar challenges. Therapists and practitioners should use this knowledge to help working parents cope and find strategies to maintain well-being in the midst of uncertainty and stressors that relate to balancing working, parenting, and health concerns. Lastly, working parents may find this information affirming to their experiences and help them recognize they are not alone when facing these challenges.

Discussion Questions

1. How might workplaces help their employees transition to working remotely? How might they help them transition back to working in-person?
2. Should businesses that can remain remote beyond the scope of COVID-19 continue to keep their employees remote? Why or why not?
3. What recommendations would you give for working parents continuing to work remotely beyond the timeframe of the COVID-19 pandemic?
4. These findings support past literature that working mothers disproportionately take on childcare duties. What are the ramifications of this unequal distribution of labor in families? Should workplaces or other systems encourage a more equal distribution of labor in families? If so, how?

Resources

1. Families First: https://www.families-first.org/
2. Centers for Disease Control and Prevention. Coping with Stress: https://www.cdc.gov/mentalhealth/stress-coping/cope-with-stress/index.html

3. Society for Human Resource Management. Accommodating Working Parents During the COVID-19 Pandemic: https://www.shrm.org/resourcesandtools/hr-topics/employee-relations/pages/accommodating-working-parents-during-the-covid-19-pandemic.aspx
4. Option B. How to Support Working Parents During COVID-19: https://optionb.org/articles/how-to-support-working-parents-during-covid-19

References

Barnett, R.C., & Gareis, K.C. (2000). Reduced-hours employment: The relationship between difficulty of trade-offs and quality of life. *Work and Occupations*, 27(2), 168–187. https://doi.org/10.1177%2F0730888400027002003

Barroso, A., & Horowitz, J.M. (2021). *The pandemic has highlighted many challenges for mothers, but they aren't necessarily new*. Pew Research Center. https://www.pewresearch.org/fact-tank/2021/03/17/the-pandemic-has-highlighted-many-challenges-for-mothers-but-they-arent-necessarily-new/

Brooks, S.K., Webster, R.K., Smith, L.E., Woodland, L., Wessely, S., Greenberg, N., & Rubin, G.J. (2020). The psychological impact of quarantine and how to reduce it: Rapid review of the evidence. *The Lancet*, 395, 912–920. https://doi.org/10.1016/S0140-6736(20)30460-8

Brown, V.B. (2021, March 16). The coronavirus means I can't take care of my grandchildren while their partners work. *The Washington Post*. https://www.washingtonpost.com/outlook/2020/03/16/grandparents-child-care-coronavirus/

Centers for Disease Control and Prevention. (2021, September 30). How CDC is making COVID-19 vaccine recommendations. *COVID-19*. https://www.cdc.gov/coronavirus/2019-ncov/vaccines/recommendations-process.html

Coontz, S. (2000). Historical perspectives on family studies. *Journal of Marriage and Family*, 62(2), 283–297. https://doi.org/10.1111/j.1741-3737.2000.00283.x

Cheng, Z., Mendolia, S., Paloyo, A.R., Savage, D.A., & Tani, M. (2021). Working parents, financial insecurity, and child care: Mental health in the time of COVID-19 in the UK. *Review of Economics of the Household*, 19(1), 123–144. https://doi.org/10.1007/s11150-020-09538-3

Craig, L., & Mullan, K. (2010). Parenthood, gender and work–family time in the United States, Australia, Italy, France, and Denmark. *Journal of Marriage and Family*, 72(5), 1344–1361. https://doi.org/10.1111/j.1741-3737.2010.00769.x

Creswell, J. W., & Poth, C. N. (2016). *Qualitative inquiry and research design: Choosing among five approaches*. Sage publications.

Cropley, M., & Millward, L.J. (2009). How do individuals "switch-off" from work during leisure? A qualitative description of the unwinding process in high and low ruminators. *Leisure Studies*, 28, 333–347. https://psycnet.apa.org/doi/10.1080/02614360902951682

Emlen, A. (2010). *Solving the childcare and flexibility puzzle: How working parents make the best feasible choices and what that means for public policy*. Universal-Publishers.

Hill, E.J., Grzywacz, J.G., Allen, S., Blanchard, V.L., Matz-Costa, C., Shulkin, S., & Pitt-Catsouphes, M. (2008). Defining and conceptualizing workplace flexibility. *Community, Work and Family, 11*(2), 149–163. https://doi.org/10.1080/13668800802024678

Igielnik, R. (2021). *A rising share of working parents in the U.S. say it's been difficult to handle childcare during the pandemic.* Pew Research Center. https://www.pewresearch.org/fact-tank/2021/01/26/a-rising-share-of-working-parents-in-the-u-s-say-its-been-difficult-to-handle-child-care-during-the-pandemic/

Kim, J. (2020). Workplace flexibility and parent–child interactions among working parents in the U.S. *Social Indicators Research, 151*(2), 427–469. https://doi.org/10.1007/s11205-018-2032-y

Krogstad, J.M. (2015). *5 facts about American grandparents.* Pew Research Center. https://www.pewresearch.org/fact-tank/2015/09/13/5-facts-about-american-grandparents/

Liang, H. (2015). Are you tired? Spillover and crossover effects of emotional exhaustion on the family domain. *Asian Journal of Social Psychology, 18*(1), 22–32. https://psycnet.apa.org/doi/10.1111/ajsp.12075

Lockwood, N.R. (2003). Work/life balance: Challenges and solutions. *Society for Human Resource Management,* 2–10. http://old.adapt.it/adapt-indice-a-z/wp-content/uploads/2014/06/lockwood_work_life_balance_2003.pdf

Lott, Y. (2020). Does flexibility help employees switch off from work? Flexible working-time arrangements and cognitive work-to-home spillover for women and men in Germany. *Social Indicators Research, 151*(2), 471–494. https://doi.org/10.1007/s11205-018-2031-z

Misirli, O., & Ergulec, F. (2021) Emergency remote teaching during the COVID-19 pandemic: Parents experiences and perspectives. *Education and Information Technology, 26,* 6699–6718. https://doi.org/10.1007/s10639-021-10520-4

Nyanamba, J.M., Liew, J., & Li, D. (2021). Parental burnout and remote learning at home during the COVID-19 pandemic: Parents' motivations for involvement. *School Psychology.* Advance online publication. https://doi.org/10.1037/spq0000483

Restubog, S.L.D., Ocampo, A.C.G., & Wang, L. (2020). Taking control amidst the chaos: Emotion regulation during the COVID-19 pandemic. *Journal of Vocational Behavior, 119,* Article 103440. https://doi.org/10.1016/j.jvb.2020.103440

Rodríguez, P.G., Agapito, B.P.M., Rodríguez, M.S.A., Galdeano, P.A., Rodrigo, M.A., Rodríguez, M.M.F., Olcina, M.J.E., & Sangrador, C.O. (2021). COVID-19: Critical appraisal of the evidence. *Anales de Pediatría (English Edition), 95*(3), 207.e1–207.e13. https://doi.org/10.1016/j.anpede.2021.05.003

Saad, L., & Wigert, B. (2021, October 13). *Remote work persisting and trending permanent.* Gallup. https://news.gallup.com/poll/355907/remote-work-persisting-trending-permanent.aspx

Sandberg, J.G., Harper, J.M., Jeffrey Hill, E., Miller, R.B., Yorgason, J.B., & Day, R.D. (2013). "What happens at home does not necessarily stay at home": The relationship of observed negative couple interaction with physical health, mental health, and work satisfaction. *Journal of Marriage & Family, 75*(4), 808–821. https://psycnet.apa.org/doi/10.1111/jomf.12039

Stake, R. E. (1995). *The art of case study research.* Sage.

Voydanoff, P. (2005). Toward a conceptualization of perceived work–family fit and balance: A demands and resources approach. *Journal of Marriage and Family, 67*(4), 822–836. https://doi.org/10.1111/j.1741-3737.2005.00178.x

Westaby, C., Phillips, J., & Fowler, A. (2016). Spillover and work–family conflict in probation practice: Managing the boundary between work and home life. *European Journal of Probation, 8*(3), 113–127. https://doi.org/10.1177%2F2066220316680370

· 5 ·

SOCIAL MEDIA MOURNING: DEALING WITH GRIEF AND CRISIS RESPONSE SURROUNDING COVID-19

Jensen Moore

The Columbia Journalism School, Craig Newmark Graduate School of Journalism at CUNY, and NYC digital news site, *The City*, teamed up in 2020 to memorialize those in NYC who had died due to COVID-19. The *Missing Them* online memorial's mission is to share stories of the more than 45,000 deaths that have occurred in the city. Mourners can call, text, or email information regarding their deceased loved one to the online memorial. Writers for the site verify the deceased's life details and cause of death and write their online obituary. The memorial's pages can be searched based on name, age, borough, profession (healthcare worker, NYPD, k-12 education, etc.), or event (9/11 survivor) (Missing Them, 2023). Stories about individuals such as John Crowe (age 77), who lived through 9/11 and survived cancer twice before succumbing to COVID-19, are shared on the memorial along with photos and quotes (Nickerson, n.d.).

The memorial is reminiscent of *The New York Times* book *Portraits 9/11/01* (2002) which presented the stories of the individuals lost to the tragedies of September 11, 2001. Yet, it represents something more than a site full of obituaries. It is a new way of grieving that involves the use of digital technologies. And one that is, primarily due to COVID-19, becoming more socially acceptable.

In early 2020, as the United States went into COVID-19 quarantine and implemented strict limits on in-person gatherings, funerals, and other types of death rituals for the deceased—whether the death was due to the virus or any other reason—were suspended throughout the nation (Johnson, 2020; Kramer, 2020; Lozano, 2020; Ward, 2020). In addition to normal national mortality rates, as of the date of this publication more than 1.1 million individuals in the United States and more than 6.9 million global COVID-19-related deaths have occurred (WorldoMeter, n.d.-a, n.d.-b). As we move into "bereavement overload" from the sheer number of COVID-19 deaths and the extended time that COVID-19 has been part of our lives, the need to grieve has become "traumatizing" (Stacey, 2021). "COVID has forced people to confront death while simultaneously upending all the usual ways we process loss, the paradox being that people 'are more aware of death and grieving, yet less available to help others through it'" (Pittsillides & Wallace, 2021, p. 71). In addition, the lack of traditional funeral rituals that help the living move forward from a loved one's death "is a traumatic experience" (Cardoso et al., 2020, p. 1).

The need to mourn deceased loved ones is imperative as COVID-19 protocols have introduced "grief compounding grief" (Ward, 2020) experienced when those in mourning grieve the dead and then grieve that they are unable to mourn in the way they traditionally would have. Lack of ability to mourn properly or "assign meaning to death" (Cardoso et al., 2020, p. 6) can also lead to complicated grief or "long-lasting disorganization that makes it difficult or impede [sic] psychological reorganization and the resumption of life" (Cardoso et al., 2020, p. 2). In addition to grief, isolation during the bereavement process—hinging on the inability to physically console one another—is shown to lead to several different mental health issues including anxiety, depression, and PTSD (Lozano, 2020). (See Chapters 3 and 14 in this book on other mental health issues during COVID-19.) Thus, in order to deal with the constant COVID-19 trauma, grief, and overload, many individuals have begun to replace traditional mourning rituals with social media mourning.

As noted by Pitsillides and Wallace (2021) "during a global pandemic the lack of physical access to ritual practices has left a deep rift, that technology has been expected to fill" (p. 61) ... and as "traditional support structures break down many people turn to social media sites to seek comfort, advice, emotional support and use it as a way to externalize and share lived experiences" (p. 9). Prior to COVID-19 social media mourning via online memorials were used to "augment rather than replace other forms of ritualization, like a funeral" (Pitsillides & Wallace, 2021, p. 64). A pre-COVID-19 study by

Massimi and Baeker (2010) suggested that approximately 65% of individuals used the internet to mourn. However, now "the use of social media as a real time connection through death, can be a way for isolated individuals to take care of themselves and others as 'a network of obligations and services to the soul'" (Pitsillides & Wallace, 2021, p. 68).

How Mourning Influences Social Media Crisis Responses

It is important to understand that in the ongoing crisis of the COVID-19 pandemic, mourning is only one aspect of the crisis communication taking place via social media platforms. As a mass disruption event (MDE), COVID-19 has affected millions of individuals worldwide, leaving many grasping for normalcy. In the last 10–15 years, social media have become the primary means of communication during MDEs (Mirbabaie et al., 2020; Shklovski et al., 2008). Loges (1994) described the three levels of threat experienced during MDEs as follows: (1) conjecture, (2) danger, and (3) personal vulnerability. The latter is especially evident during COVID-19 as the sense of safety enjoyed before the virus has been demolished by mask mandates, vaccinations, and social distancing all designed to simply keep one alive. As noted by Nilsen et al. (2018) "after terror attacks and other disasters, there is a heightened need for communication" (p. 291). Early research by Heverin and Zach (2010) identified five primary types of communication that take place via social media platforms during such disasters: (1) action-related, (2) emotion-related, (3) information-related, (4) opinion-related, and (5) technology-related. The second is of concern in this chapter as Heverin and Zach (2012) described communication of emotions as "talking cure" that "does not add to the collective understanding of crisis . . . Instead, the tweet provides the individual a method for voicing his or her inner thoughts and feelings" (p. 43). Emotional responses such as anger, fear, shock, relief, and grief are commonly shared during crisis social media posts (Heverin & Zach, 2012; Hjorth & Kim, 2011; Palen & Liu, 2007).

A study of convergence behavior in crisis situations showed that rather than avoid crisis areas, individuals instead move toward the crisis (Mirbabaie et al., 2020). The need to make sense of the crisis and gather information outweighs their desire to flee. Crisis managers suggest these convergence behaviors (CB) often result in large amounts of information that do not help with the crisis and impede the ability of officials to act in ways that help those affected. However, since social media remove the geographical and physical boundaries of the crisis, a global community of individuals can take part in the crisis meaning the physical location of the crisis is no longer the convergence location.

Mirababaie et al. (2020) examined crisis convergence behaviors in a digital environment and found that the same convergence behavior archetypes (CBA) exist on social media. These are: (1) the anxious, (2) the curious, (3) the detectives, (4) the exploiters, (5) the fans/supporters, (6) the furious, (7) the helpers, (8) the impassive, (9) the manipulators, (10) the mourners, and (11) the returnees. The mourners archetype "[pays] tribute to victims or people affected by the crisis" (p. 342). Their social network analysis looked at social media crises participants who were information starters (lead the conversation, frequently retweeted), amplifiers (follow the conversation, are constantly retweeting), and transmitters (share information between distinct online communities). The resulting social network graph showed that the mourners were closely linked to the helpers (those trying to share information to aid individuals in crisis) and the manipulators (those using the crisis to seek attention)—basically polar extremes of one another converging on those in mourning. Overall, mourners were predominantly amplifiers who showed the highest impact on the crisis communication by frequently retweeting other emotional messages. Posting their own emotional content allowed them to "amplify *themselves* through emotional contagion" (emphasis in original; Mirbabaie et al., 2020, p. 347). Along with the helpers, mourners were most likely to distribute information to others and take part in conversations. However, they noted mourners' conversations regarding emotions were largely "a high level of noise which can aggravate crisis management efforts" (Mirbabaie et al., p. 347). "Mourners represent a Convergence Behavior type that, while possibly helping users to cope with their feelings of loss and sadness as well as paying tribute to the victims, does not contribute to crisis management in any significant way" (Mirbabaie et al., 2020, p. 351). They suggest crisis management professionals create and promote online memorials on sites like Facebook and divert mourners to these sites to take part in social media mourning so they do not clutter an organization's crisis communication networks.

Social Media Mourning Case: Tweets Surrounding COVID-19 Deaths

In order to examine the social media mourning taking place during COVID-19, Twitter (X) posts openly available to the public were examined using

Twitter's advanced search tool. The terms "COVID" in combination with the following: "mourning," "memorial," "death," "dead," "RIP," "sad," "crying," "thoughts and prayers," and "loss" (Coronavirus was also used in combinations with these terms) were used. Tweets were gathered from March 11, 2020 (when WHO declared COVID-19 a pandemic)—September 1, 2021. Tweets had to specifically refer to the loss of an individual. Tweets from healthcare workers, emergency responders, and similar fields were excluded as there currently is debate about the ethics of sharing patient stories on social media platforms. In addition, news media accounts/stories and headlines about those grieving for COVID-19 deaths were not coded.

The Social Media Mourning (SMM) model developed by Moore, Magee, et al. (2019) was used to organize the tweets. The model suggests those grieving will take part in one or more of the following types of communication: one-way communication (where the individual broadcasts news of the death), two-way communication (where the individual seeks others mourning), and immortality communication (where the individual attempts to continue interacting with the deceased). In addition, tweets were examined for certain issues social media mourners may face when interacting: (1) privacy concerns, (2) grief appropriation, (3) disenfranchisement, (4) grief trolls, and (5) grief tourists.

Sharing news of the death with others in their social media network is the main goal of *one-way SMM communication* (Moore et al., 2014, 2015). This can take place in three different ways: (1) controlling the narrative (deciding who they want to share the death information with and "managing" the type of information shared), (2) permission for dialogue (sharing of emotions online indicating they are ready to talk about the death with others), and (3) evade or acknowledge mourning (taking control of the death communication process by deciding who to respond to) (Moore, Magee, et al., 2019).

Data showed that most mourners used Twitter (X) for controlling the narrative as they simply told the public they had lost someone to COVID-19. "Chris died 2 weeks ago and it has been overwhelming. I couldn't make it his (sic) funeral or burial today but my mom sent me the live stream link. Covid has ruined so many things for a lot of people but I'm grateful for having access to technology to fill the gap." Some shared a few details about why the person would be missed. "RIP Linda (last name redacted for privacy) . . . I'm sad to hear this news. I'm sad I didn't see you over this Covid wild time. Thank you for being an inspiration and always being the light when we saw you. Your spirit was incredible." Another mourner stated, "My mother, and uncle and cousin died of Covid-19. Seeing my mom with it was heartbreaking, and I wasn't able to be with her when she died, and we had a two person funeral. My father and myself."

Many posts did not identify who they were grieving, but offered a general overview of their grief. "Just experience (sic) my family's first covid death . . . that shit is agonizing. Please get vaccinated ;(." Posts were highly descriptive in telling how the individual felt from the loss. "wow, i was just on fb sharing a few posts with funny stuff to cheer relatives up, suddenly i get this im that 2 close cousins just died—kinda feel like i just got hit with a sledgehammer to the face—covid is to blame and you never think it will happen to you. . . RIP fam."

The loss of life was not the only thing many mourners noted, but how they felt moving on after. One mourner noted they felt "bleak as hell—attending a Covid funeral and seeing your uncle, still recovering from Covid himself, sit in his truck (since he can hardly stand) and watch heavy machinery finish burying his wife of 44 years. That's going to stay with me the rest of my life." Another noted the need to stay off social media to grieve without an audience. "RIP my neighbor Ken who passed away from Covid. He didn't get the vaccine and they didn't believe masks worked. His wife told me today on the phone she's taking Ivermectin guess she'll be dead soon too. Taking a few days off Twitter (X) this hit me hard. They were sweet neighbors."

To a lesser extent, Twitter (X) was used to share personal self-expression (i.e., emotional responses) indicating permission for dialogue (Gamba, 2018). "I cried for 3 days for our fallen soldiers and today I am crying even more for the lost (sic) of a dear friend to Covid-19. My God bless her, bless her family and friends who loved her dearly." Another mourner stated, "a close friend lost her brother and her dad to Covid. I have been crying this past hour. let's all please take extra care." Some indicated why the death hit them so hard. "My childhood best friend reached out to me to tell me that her dad just passed away from covid. I hadn't seen that man in years, but here I am crying because I didn't have a dad growing up and that man stepped up treated me like I was his own. This shit fucking blows."

Some mourners noted they could not describe the loss adequately, but still wanted to share how it made them feel. "There are days where my sadness is so overwhelming that I can't even begin to describe it . . . I think that we're all experiencing a lot of the same thing. Covid has brought about a collective sense of sadness, loss and mourning. I really don't think I'll ever be the same." Another mourner stated, "Today hasn't been a great day. My coworkers' son is likely brain dead from COVID. It feels like daggers in the heart every time I say it or type it. Be careful out there, it's not over."

A visible theme once someone shared their emotions was suggesting a call to action asking others to do what they could to avoid death from COVID-19. "My cousin has passed away from covid (sic) after a long, terrible battle during which she also lost her mother. Please keep the family in your thoughts and prayers. And get vaccinated." Another mourner stated, "Sad post: another family friend died from COVID. I'm sad and angry. He was of the mindset that "God would protect him" and refused to wear a mask and take the vaccine. I believe God can do anything, but I also believe He gave us common sense. He created science."

Finally, since sharing grief on social media means the individual has opened the door for comments, it was interesting to see how mourners evaded or acknowledged their grief interactions. In many cases mourners simply did not respond to those commenting. What Fearon (2011) referred to as displays of good intentions (e.g., I'm sorry for your loss) were sometimes liked (with the Twitter (X) heart) by the mourner, but overall were not replied to with words. However, in other cases—especially when the mourner had included a call to action such as wearing a mask, social distancing, or getting vaccinated—mourning turned into an argument. Anger seemed to replace sadness.—"I just lost someone to Covid."—"Sorry for your loss, but did they have underlying health issues?" STOP DOING THIS. The loss of someone's life is NOT the opportunity for you to make yourself feel better about your own chances of dying. What the fuck."

The individual mourner interacting with others who are also mourning creates *two-way SMM communication* (Moore et al., 2014, 2015). This can take place in two different ways: (1) community sharing (communicating with others who are grieving) and (2) relationship formation (creating attachments to others who are grieving) (Moore, Magee, et al., 2019). Community sharing exchanges help mourners feel connected, something necessary during the long periods of isolation associated with COVID-19. Many mourners call others to participate in mourning with them. "PLEASE pray for the family of Captain Mike Stokes. He lost the battle with COVID. He was great police (sic) and a greater man! Our loss is Heaven's gain, but the void is real. He was a GREAT friend!"

Engaging with those who are mourning helps show there are still things to look forward to. One mourner replied to another who had posted about their friend's death, "My Facebook feed is filling up with mourning as death starts to become more regular. Most is Covid but other causes are there, too. Life—and death—goes on. Please seize the day. While life has always been precious, these days it is even more obvious." However, many were depleted by the constant mourning we are experiencing due to COVID-19. When one mourner wrote about all the lives lost to COVID-19, another responded, "There's a collective national mourning at this point. There's a Covid-related death every other day and I'm exhausted. It's funeral after funeral and fundraiser after fundraiser."

On social network platforms it is easy to interact with other mourners and form "mourning communities" which support one another, grieve collectively, and help move forward by sharing stories (Chudzicka-Czupal & Basek, 2019). This was seen in many of the comments to those mourning. "Deepest condolences to you, Alex, and your family. As you have helped put a face to those of us who are mourning the endless tide of covid deaths, we are mourning with you now." Because of the suspension of traditional mourning rituals like funerals, these online mourning communities have become more important than ever (Johnson, 2020; Moore, 2022; Wood, 2020).

Continuing interactions with and remembrance of the deceased are the main goals of *immortality SMM communication* (Moore et al., 2014, 2015). As noted by Bassett (2018), social media platforms "[offer] the opportunity to ensure the dead remain part of our everyday digital lives" (p. 10). Immortality communication can take place in three different ways: (1) continued social actors (mourner continues to insert the deceased into present), (2) eternal remembrance (using digital memorials to remember the deceased), and (3) habitual communication (interacting with or about the deceased on holidays or anniversaries) (Moore, Magee, et al., 2019).

Many of those in mourning used Twitter (X) to speak directly to their loved ones. "Rip uncle David may you Rest In Peace! People covid is real!" Another mourner posted, "I can't believe you are no longer here. Just yesterday you told me you loved me. I will never get to hear it again. I miss you so much. #CovidSucks" Some mourners have used social media to insert their loved ones into daily life, tagging them in photos or situations they are not here to experience. "You didn't get to climb the mountain with me. Covid took you to (sic) soon. But I feel you here with me."

Data showed that when observing someone using social media to mourn, audience members would suggest ways to memorialize or eternally remember those lost to COVID-19. Some of these are offline locations such as the Memorial Wall in London while others are tangible displays of loss such as the COVID Memorial Quilt (https://covidquilt2020.com/) being made by 13-year-old Madeleine Fugate in Los Angeles, CA. In addition to the hundreds of Facebook memorials dedicated to mourning COVID-19 deaths, many states and large cities have begun online memorials for the deceased such as *Faces of COVID* and the *Missing Them* memorial noted in the introduction. Those creating and directing these pages have been active in seeking out and addressing individuals mourning online.

In addition to memorials, some mourners have called for national days of mourning. "Republicans are recalcitrant about acknowledging all the suffering caused by #covid. They know it is connected to criticism of Trump. One hundred thirty-six thousand kids have lost a parent to the disease. Where is the National day of mourning?" Finally, other mourners indicate ways we can keep our loved one's memories alive by fighting COVID-19. "Many know, but maybe not everyone does, buy (sic) less than a year ago, our good friend and moderator; Jala, died from covid complications. I bring this up because it is important that you get vaccinated, and do everything you can to stop covid from spreading." Another noted:

> In the past week, we lost five South Florida law enforcement officers to COVID-19. Their deaths are a painful reminder that the pandemic persists. In fact, for the second year in a row, COVID-19 is the leading cause of death among police officers nationwide. Our thoughts and prayers are with the families of our fallen brothers and sisters. Let us keep their memories alive by doing all we can to prevent further tragedy. Please continue practicing safety precautions and get one of the safe and effective vaccines. We have the power to stop this deadly disease. Let's make it happen.

Finally, as we near almost four years since the WHO declared COVID-19 a worldwide pandemic, we are beginning to see anniversaries of loved ones' deaths. Mourners are using Twitter (X) for habitual communication purposes. "Bill (last name redacted) died in July of 2020, let's get that straight. He was 80 years old and fought covid tooth and nail, but sadly he wasn't able to make it through. He died before we had a vaccine or knew too much about Covid as its (sic) been over a 13 (sic) months since he passed. RIP"

The highly public mourning taking place on social media sites has led to a number of issues as mourners and audiences often don't feel some information is appropriate, or feel the mourning emotions/responses are not appropriate. Thus, in addition to the types of communication shared via SMM, tweets were examined for certain issues social media mourners may face when interacting: (1) privacy concerns (mourners sharing information about the death that family/close friends do not feel is appropriate), (2) grief appropriation (audience members noting that the mourner shouldn't be mourning the person, or their mourning seemed fake), (3) disenfranchisement (audience members suggesting the death does not deserve mourning), (4) grief trolls (audience members who try to disrupt the mourning taking place), and (5) grief tourists (audience members who are not themselves grieving, but try to inject themselves into the death communication taking place).

Sabra (2017) noted that any content that deviates from what the "closest relatives" feel is appropriate results in privacy concerns (p. 37). Members of anti-vax groups who have died from COVID-19 have had much of their lives deconstructed in tweets. Name-calling, stories that frame them in a negative light, and photos that are unpleasant have been attached to "thoughts and prayers" posts. Mourning audiences have noted this trend with disdain. "Can't you see that dancing on the grave of a human being who died of COVID, whose devastated family is mourning the loss—can't you see that diminishes your own humanity?"

Grief appropriation, or claiming another person's grief and acting like you are grieving too, is rampant on social media sites as people get attention from suggesting they are mourning (Sabra, 2017). Comments such as "you don't really know this person, why are you grieving?" and "shut up, you are just seeking attention" are common. Similar to grief appropriation are those called grief tourists. These individuals intentionally frequent social media memorial pages, and look for social media mourning posts so that they can view others' grief. They are interested in why mourning is taking place and their own views on it (Basek & Chudzicka-Czupal, 2016). For example, one audience member asked a mourner, "So please clarify. Did they die of COVID or an underlying medical condition? And may they RIP." Their interest in someone else's death "may result from the primal human need to experience mourning collectively, a need which can no longer be fulfilled offline" (Chudzicka-Czupal & Basek, 2019, p. 3).

In comparison, grief trolls are audience members who try to disrupt a social media mourning by attacking those grieving. As a global pandemic, COVID-19 inherently results in tragic media coverage. Phillips (2015) stated, grief trolls pray on "knee-jerk sympathies" of those mourning a large tragedy that the media sensationalizes (p. 79). One such audience member posted how they trolled those mourning, "I was walking past the 'Covid Memorial Wall' in London and there were people looking at all the messages & hearts. I said: 'Wait till you see the wall for cancer, deaths at home, dementia, heart attacks, strokes, alcohol and suicide. Have a nice day.'"

One of the largest issues, however, facing those using social media to mourn COVID-19 deaths has been disenfranchisement. Disenfranchisement occurs when a loved one passes away and the public attaches a stigma to the cause of death (Sholtis, 2021). In the case of COVID-19 several different factors are at play: (1) idea that COVID-19 is a hoax, (2) idea that people are dying from underlying health issues not associated with COVID-19, (3) idea that COVID-19 is unacceptable as a cause of death, and (4) idea that the person deserved to die from COVID-19 if they didn't mask/socially distance/get vaccinated. One mourner shared that those overseeing funeral rites were pressured not to put COVID-19 as the cause of death so families wouldn't have to face public scrutiny. "When my dad passed in December, the funeral director indicated to me that he was having a rough time. Between the bullying and the expectations to "delete" COVID-19 from the death certificate, the poor guy was close to breaking down." But mostly, mourners are wrestling with the idea that their loved one's death might be perceived as unacceptable, "1,188 COVID-19 deaths and people still think this is a joke or a hoax. My soul is mourning." Another mourner stated, "Unless you've ever had to watch someone you love be lowered into the ground because of this shit, shut the hell up on your conspiracy theories about covid (sic). A year and a half into this shit show of a pandemic and millions of people have died and you people still think it's fake?!?"

It should be noted that immortality communication has been associated with issues such as prolonged grief (constant interaction with the deceased via social media sites that leads to not moving forward from the loss) and second loss (re-experiencing the loss each time the mourner comes into contact with the digital presence left behind by the deceased) that we may not see until COVID-19 is under control and people are able to deal with their losses properly (Moore, 2022).

Importance of Spontaneous Memorials and Mourning Following Disasters

Planned physical memorials have long been used to help those left behind to "honor the dead" while also helping survivors move forward (Veil et al., 2011, p. 166). In comparison, spontaneous memorials often grow from tragedies where "both uncontrolled and public violent deaths ... prompt spontaneous rituals to publicly express individual and collective grief" (Haney et al., 1997). They are informal, quickly created to mourn alongside the tragedy (Doss, 2006), and often "do not conform to traditional mourning practices" (Veil et al., 2011, p. 167). In populations with widespread access to internet technologies, virtual spaces such as cyber shrines, online condolence boards, and Facebook memorial pages are being used as spontaneous memorials (Grider, 2015; Maddrell, 2012; Santino, 2006). Grider (2015) suggested that such memorials "reduce the overwhelming enormity of the catastrophe to a more manageable human scale, thus helping to make the event more comprehensible, especially when the emotions evoked are new and raw" (p. 2). Similarly, Haney et al. (1997) stated, "in a [tragedy] situation where such basic human needs are threatened, spontaneous memorials help minimize the threat by reaffirming that values which promote personal safety and justice are shared by a majority of the community" (p. 165).

Perform a quick search on Facebook using the terms "COVID" and "Memorial" and dozens of different memorial groups and pages show up. There are memorials for each state, for nurses, first responders, health care workers and physicians lost to COVID-19, and individuals who lost their lives to the virus. With its memorial page feature, Facebook has become the premier site for online remembrance (but not online funerals).[1] Social media sites like Facebook have become "the centre of community thought, wishes and reflection" following the death of a loved one (Pitsillides & Wallace, 2021, p. 60). Other spontaneous memorials have been created on websites and promoted on social media. For example, the Wall of Grief (https://www.wallofgrief.org/) memorial lists the names of individuals in India who have died from COVID-19 and is promoted on Twitter (X) and Facebook.

Mini-Case: Wuhan Whistleblower Wailing Wall

One of the most globally recognizable spontaneous memorials belongs to 34-year-old Chinese whistleblower, Dr. Li Weliang, an ophthalmologist at Wuhan Central Hospital who died from COVID-19 on February 7, 2020. At the onset of the virus, Dr. Weliang was told by authorities to stop spreading rumors and was one of eight doctors punished by Chinese police for continuing to speak out. Dr. Weliang's last post on the Chinese social media platform, Sina Weibo, on February 1, 2020, has been forwarded, liked, and shared by millions of people. In it, Dr. Weliang acknowledged that he had a confirmed COVID-19 diagnosis. After a three-week battle, Dr. Weliang succumbed to the virus (BBC News, 2021; Chenkuang, 2020; Yuan, 2020).

Today, Dr. Weilang's Sina Weibo account has become a "wailing wall" where those speaking out about the virus, the government's reaction to it, and how the government continues to censor voices that speak out also hail

Dr. Weliang as a hero (BBC News, 2021; Chenkuang, 2020; Yuan, 2020). Chenkuang (2020) noted: "This [Sina Weibo] is the place where they can express their sadness and helplessness, a virtual gathering place for more than a million people who share similar emotions and want to feel a little less alone" (para. 14). More than four years after his death, The Economist (2023) estimated "every three or four minutes someone adds a comment on his parting words. Posthumously, Wenliang's number of followers has grown into the millions.

Mini-Case: Animal Crossing—New Horizons Memorials

Without realizing it would be used to create spontaneous memorials, in March 2020 Nintendo released their new game, Animal Crossing: New Horizons. In the game, players can do whatever tasks they want on their own island and other players can visit their island and interact with them. Players can design and decorate their island as they like. As noted by Perez (2021), "The game offered a break from the constant uncertainty of the pandemic's earliest days, giving players a routine of small tasks to depend on, and a semblance of social interaction at a time when we were all hunkered down in real life" (para. 1).

One of the additions to the game (not available in other Animal Crossing versions) were stone markers (Western and Zen). With in-person funerals and other death rites impossible due to quarantine restrictions, Animal Crossing players turned to the game to memorialize their deceased, using the stone markers as gravestones (Carpenter, 2020). Players were able to invite other players to their island shrines and memorials to use the game to mourn collectively. The new stones feature inspired several Reddit threads instructing players on how to create their own shrines. Rivera (2021) noted that using the game in this way was expected as "COVID-19 certainly changed the way everyone lives, but it has not taken away people's abilities to mourn and express love for those who have died. Everyone has just become more creative."

Organizations & Mourning During Crisis

Two very different schools of thought exist regarding whether or not an organization should take part in social media mourning. One recent suggestion by public relations professionals is that organizations should refrain from taking part in social media mourning (Cegielski, 2014). Winchel (2019) suggested organizations should "go dark ... so your organization doesn't appear insensitive" (p. 1). In contrast, Hayes et al. (2017) stated organizations that fail to mourn with the public on social media "[risk] being seen as uncaring" (p. 265). They suggested that "organizations [have a] moral or professional obligation to respond to events by which they are not directly impacted" (p. 254). Similarly, Ulmer and Sellnow (2002) indicated "organizations ... have a major stake in the nation's ability to rebound" (p. 362) from tragedies. Ulmer et al. (2010) indicated crises in which the organization is not directly involved in provide opportunities to show organization values, commitment to stakeholders, and focus on the future. Thus, social media mourning is an appropriate way for organizations to show community support and help move those affected by tragedy to move forward. Hayes et al. (2017) posited, "social media have provided an easy, public, and immediate outlet for people and third-party organizations to communally express their emotions, support and grief over tragic events, thereby contributing well to collective healing" (p. 269).

Early research on organization social media mourning by Moore, Pritchard, et al. (2019) indicated that publics wanted organizations to go beyond "thoughts and prayers" and use social media mourning posts to: (1) connect mourners to a larger mourning community, (2) show how communities are coming together to deal with grief, and (3) continue remembering the tragedy years later. Most importantly, organization social media mourning posts should show genuine sympathy for those grieving. For example, South Carolina's public health and environmental protection agency noted on their Twitter (X) on August 11, 2021, that the "DHEC announced that the state has surpassed 10,000 lives lost to COVID-19 in the state. Together, we are mourning these losses, the impact it's had on their loved ones, and working to stop more deaths in the future." They further suggested followers share an image of lit candles to show remembrance of lives lost in the state due to the virus.

A study connecting corporate social responsibility and online grief showed individuals thought organizations that took part in social media mourning were bettering the community, giving back to the community, and that these types of posts should be expected in times of public tragedy (Moore et al., 2020). Their research showed publics preferred organization social media mourning posts that: (1) supported publics, (2) unified publics, (3) contributed to community, (4) showed commemoration, and (5) showed caring (Moore et al., 2020). Furthermore, when individuals perceived organization social media mourning posts as altruistic, informative, and truthful they reported more positive attitudes toward the organization and future behaviors toward the organization (i.e., support that organization, pay more for the organization's goods, encourage others to support the organization, etc.). Hayes et al. (2017) suggested organizational responses should consist of "solidarity," "support," and "sympathy" and be distributed during initial recovery from a tragedy and return to normalcy following the tragedy (p. 267). For example, on August 30, 2021, the Corinth Pirate football program in Wendell, NC, posted thoughts and prayers to everyone mourning a COVID-19 loss. The post ended by calling for positivity and the suggestion that everyone "GetOnBoard" with vaccines and masking thereby supporting returning to a pre-COVID-19 normal.

Conversely, if an organization went further than indicating "thoughts and prayers" and included messages that promoted the organization, encouraged a return to spending, or were seen as a way of taking advantage of the tragedy, the results were opposite. Research by Moore and Stevens (2017) and Moore, Pritchard, et al. (2019) found that many SMM messages posted by organizations were political, patriotic, or commercial in nature—and that publics did not appreciate these messages encroaching on their grief. Furthermore, individuals who indicated skepticism of the organization's social media mourning posts were likely to suggest punitive behaviors such as boycotts (Moore et al., 2020). For example, on August 31, 2021 STR8H cleaning in Patterson, LA, stated: "Our Thoughts and prayers go out to the city's that was impacted by Hurricane Ida. STR8H LLC love to lend a helping hand. Molds thrive in damp, humid, and wet conditions. Call me today to help prevent the bacteria from spreading through your home/business. Covid disinfecting also." Outcry responses from many of STR8H's followers led the organization to apologize for its "inappropriate" tweet.

Conclusion

From the sheer amount of deaths, to the length of time the virus has been depleting the population, to the ways we've had to adjust to new social norms including experiencing grief on our own due to long periods of isolation, COVID-19 has dramatically altered the traditional funeral rites many need to move forward after loss. Social media mourning creates a way for individuals to share grief with others, build community with others mourning COVID-19 losses, and remember our deceased loved ones. Audiences may not want to hear about COVID-19-related deaths, or want to attribute the death to other causes, but that does not diminish the need for those grieving to seek comfort online. In fact, in crisis situations, mourners are the ones who seem to communicate the most—and are most in need of social media outlets like memorial pages for this purpose. Thus, understanding social media mourning is important to crisis communication as at the individual level mourners are dealing with grief, making sense of death, and facing mental health issues if they do not. It is imperative that crisis communicators set up online "spaces" for their grief to take place. At the organization level, there is the opportunity to help those mourning overcome the crisis and move forward. In effect, serving the community by appropriately grieving with them.

Discussion Questions

1. Based on this chapter, what are the future theoretical opportunities and practical challenges that need to be addressed in social media mourning research?
2. Identify some examples of man-made or natural disaster social media mourning posts you have seen from (1) individuals and (2) organizations. What commonalities are present in these messages?
3. What could the effects be for an organization to take part in social media mourning? What could they be if they refrain from doing so?
4. Are some individuals more likely to take part in social media mourning? What could prevent them from taking part?
5. In what ways can organizations help move the country forward during collective grieving situations like COVID-19?

Resources

1. ADEC Distance Education. (2020). *COVID-19 grief, bereavement, and death at a distance international perspectives.* Association for Death Education & Counseling. https://www.youtube.com/watch?v=oltALsn11Wk
2. FEMA. (2020). *COVID-19 best practice information: Alternate funeral arrangements.* FEMA.gov. https://www.fema.gov/sites/default/files/2020-07/fema_covid_bp_alternate-funeral-arrangements.pdf
3. Hoy, W.G., & Harris, H.W. (2020). *Unintended consequences of Covid-19.* Association for Death Education and Counseling. https://cdn.ymaws.com/www.adec.org/resource/resmgr/webinars/2020/unintended_consequences_of_c.pdf
4. Murphy, S. (2020). *Grieving alone and together.* RememberingaLife.com. https://www.rememberingalife.com/covid-19/grief-during-the-pandemic/grieving-alone-and-together-booklet

Note

1 Facebook's feature that prohibits use of copyright music during live-streams makes it so portions of the funeral are muted. If music is used repeatedly, the video will be deleted (National Funeral Directors Association, n.d.).

References

Basek, A., & Chudzicka-Czupała, A. (2016). Modern approach to death and mourning—ethical aspects of mediatization of death. *Społeczeństwo i Edukacja*, 20(1), 375–386.

Bassett, D. (2018). Digital afterlives: From social media platforms to thanabots and beyond. In C. Tandy (Ed.), *Death and anti-death, Vol. 16: 200 years after Frankenstein*. Ria University Press.

BBC News. (2021, February 6). *Li Wenliang: "Wuhan whistleblower" remembered one year on*. https://www.bbc.com/news/world-asia-55963896

Cardoso, E.A., da Silva, B.C., dos Santos, J.H., Loterio, L.D., Accoroni, A.G., & dos Santos, M.A. (2020). The effect of suppressing funeral rituals during the COVID-19 pandemic on bereaved families. *Revista Latino-Americana de Enfermagem*, 28(e3361), 1–9. https://doi.org/10.1590/1518-8345.4519.3361

Carpenter, C. (2020, July 1). *Animal Crossing players are building in-game memorials: "It's kind of like she's living on in the game": Technology has influenced how we grieve*. Polygon. https://www.polygon.com/2020/7/1/21309893/animal-crossing-new-horizons-memorials-nintendo-grief

Cegielski, S. (2014, August 18). *Tragedy is not a PR opportunity*. Ragan's PR Daily. https://www.prdaily.com/tragedy-is-not-a-pr-opportunity/

Chenkuang, H. (2020, March 31). *"Online wailing wall": How Chinese netizens continue to honor Li Wenliang, COVID-19 whistleblower*. SupChina. https://supchina.com/2020/03/31/chinese-netizens-continue-to-honor-li-wenliang-covid-19/

Chudzicka-Czupała, A., & Basek, A. (2019). Reasons why we read blogs and memorial pages of people who lost a child. Life motives of emotional rubberneckers. *Death Studies*, 45(2), 119–130. https://doi.org/10.1080/07481187.2019.1616855

City, The. (2020, June 10). *Here are their names: Remembering the New Yorkers lost to COVID-19*. The City. https://www.thecity.nyc/2020/6/10/21287138/new-yorkers-lost-to-covid-19-missing-them

Doss, E. (2006). Spontaneous memorials and contemporary modes of mourning in America. *Material Religion*, 2(3), 294–318. https://doi.org/10.1080/17432200.2006.11423053

Economist (January 12, 2023). *The cult of Li Wenliang, the doctor who spotted COVID-19*. The Economist. https://www.economist.com/china/2023/01/12/the-cult-of-li-wenliang-the-doctor-who-spotted-covid-19

Fearon, J.C. (2011). *The technology of grief: Social networking sites as modern death ritual* [Doctoral dissertation, Antioch University]. OhioLINK Electronic Theses and Dissertations Center. http://rave.ohiolink.edu/etdc/view?acc_num=antioch1307539596

Gamba, F. (2018). Coping with loss: Mapping digital rituals for the expression of grief. *Health Communication, 33*(1), 78–84. https://doi.org/10.1080/10410236.2016.1242038

Grider, S. (2015). Spontaneous Shrines: A Modern Response to Tragedy and Disaster Update. *New Directions in Folklore, 5*. https://scholarworks.iu.edu/journals/index.php/ndif/article/view/19882

Haney, C.A., Leimer, C., & Lowery, J. (1997). Spontaneous memorialization: Violent death and emerging mourning ritual. *OMEGA-Journal of Death and Dying, 35*(2), 159–171. https://doi.org/10.2190/7U8W-540L-QWX9-1VL6

Hayes, R.A., Waddell, J.C., & Smudde, P.M. (2017). Our thoughts and prayers are with the victims: Explicating the public tragedy as a public relations challenge. *Public Relations Inquiry, 6*(3), 253–274. https://doi.org/10.1177/2046147X16682987

Heverin, T., & Zach, L. (2010). *Microblogging for crisis communication: Examination of Twitter use in response to a 2009 violent crisis in the Seattle-Tacoma, Washington area* [Conference session]. Proceedings of the Seventh International ISCRAM Conference, Seattle, WA, United States.

Heverin, T., & Zach, L. (2012). Use of microblogging for collective sense-making during violent crises: A study of three campus shootings. *Journal of the American Society for Information Science and Technology, 63*(1), 34–47. https://doi.org/10.1002/asi.21685

Hjorth, L., & Him, K.-H.Y. (2011). Good grief: The role of social mobile media in the 3.11 earthquake disaster in Japan. *Digital Creativity, 22*(3), 187–199. https://doi.org/10.1080/14626268.2011.604640

Johnson, K. (2020, March 25). Coronavirus means funerals must wait: "We can't properly bury our dead." *New York Times*. https://www.nytimes.com/2020/03/25/us/coronavirus-funerals.html

Kramer, P.D. (2020, April 2). Burials without funerals, grief without hugs: Coronavirus is changing how we say goodbye. *USA Today*. https://www.usatoday.com/story/news/nation/2020/04/02/funerals-during-coronavirus-pandemic-no-hugs-big-gatherings/5102855002/

Loges, W.E. (1994). Canaries in the coal mine: Perceptions of threat and media system dependency relations. *Communication Research, 21*(1), 5–23. https://doi.org/10.1177/009365094021001002

Lozano, A.V. (2020, April 5). "Awful and beautiful": Saying goodbye to coronavirus victims without a funeral. *NBC News*. https://www.nbcnews.com/news/us-news/awful-beautiful-saying-goodbye-coronavirus-victims-without-funeral-n1175431

Maddrell, A. (2012). Online memorials: The virtual as the new vernacular. *Bereavement Care, 31*(2), 46–54. https://doi.org/10.1080/02682621.2012.710491

Massimi, M., & Baecker, R.N. (2010). *A death in the family: Opportunities for designing technologies for the bereaved* [Conference session]. Proceedings of the SIGCHI Conference on Human Factors in Computing Systems, Atlanta, GA, United States, pp. 1821–1830.

Mirbabaie, M., Bunker, D., Stieglitz, S., & Deubel, A. (2020). Who sets the tone? Determining the impact of convergence behavior archetypes in social media crisis communication. *Information Systems Frontiers, 22*, 339–351. https://doi.org/10.1007/s10796-019-09917-x

Moore, J. (2022). Mourning using social media: The new frontier for death communication. In J. Lipschultz, K. Freberg, & R. Luttrell (Eds.), *The Emerald handbook of computer-mediated communication and social media* (pp. 117–140). Emerald Publishing.

Moore, J., & Stevens, A. (2017, March). *National tragedies as promotion messages: Using remembrance of 9/11 and Hurricane Katrina to influence publics* [Conference presentation]. International Public Relations Research Conference, Orlando, FL, United States.

Moore, J., Magee, S., & Gamreklidze, E. (2014). *Grieving amid the presence of our past(s): How communication technologies are transforming and sometimes challenging the grieving process*. National Communication Association.

Moore, J., Magee, S., & Gamreklidze, E. (2015). *The ghosts in the machine: Toward a theory of social media mourning*. Association for Education in Journalism and Mass Communication.

Moore, J., Magee, S., Gamreklidze, E., & Kowalewski, J. (2019). Social media mourning: Using grounded theory to explore how people grieve on social networking sites. *OMEGA-Journal of Death and Dying, 79*(3), 231–259. https://doi.org/10.1177/0030222817709691

Moore, J., Pritchard, R., & Filak, V. (2019). *Corporate social media mourning: Toward a framework for organizations wishing to sympathize with publics following man-made or natural disasters* [Conference session]. Proceedings of the International Public Relations Research Conference, Orlando, FL, United States.

Moore, J., Pritchard, R., Nicolini, K., & Meux, A. (2020, March). *Corporate mourning: Examining social media spontaneous memorials as corporate social responsibility efforts* [Conference presentation]. International Public Relations Research Conference, Orlando, FL, United States.

National Funeral Directors Association. (n.d.) *Music webcasting licenses Q&A*. https://nfda.org/resources/compliance-legal/music-and-webcasting-licenses/music-webcasting-license-qa#:~:text=Even%20though%20a%20member%20has,user%20from%20using%20the%20system

New York Times, The. (2002). *Portraits 9/11/01*. Times Books, Henry Holt and Company LLC.

Nickerson, S. (n.d.). John Crowe. *The City*. https://projects.thecity.nyc/covid-19-deaths/?_ga=2.124945866.1145818844.1632496522-1864329149.1632496522&memorial=9-11#john-crowe

Nilsen, L.G., Hafstad, G.S., Staksrud, E., & Dyb, G. (2018). Five reasons for using social media among young terror survivors: Results from the Utøya study. *Computers in Human Behavior, 84*, 285–294. https://doi.org/10.1016/j.chb.2018.03.006

Palen, L., & Liu, S.B. (2007). *Citizen communications in crisis* [Conference session]. Proceedings of the SIGCHI Conference on Human Factors in Computing Systems, San Jose, CA, United States.

Perez, N. (2021, August 31). *The best Animal Crossing: New Horizons updates*. Paste Magazine. https://www.pastemagazine.com/games/animal-crossing/best-animal-crossing-new-horizons-updates/

Phillips, W. (2015). *This is why we can't have nice things: Mapping the relationship between online trolling and mainstream culture*. MIT Press.

Pitsillides, S., & Wallace, J. (2021). Physically distant but socially connected: Streaming funerals, memorials and ritual design during COVID-19. In *Death, Grief and Loss in the Context of COVID-19* (pp. 60–76). Routledge.

Rivera, K.P. (2021, January 1). *Changing the way we mourn with animal crossing: New horizons.* Cake. https://www.joincake.com/blog/animal-crossing-memorials/

Sabra, J.B. (2017). "I hate when they do that!" Netiquette in mourning and memorialization among Danish Facebook users. *Journal of Broadcasting & Electronic Media, 61*(1), 24–40. https://doi.org/10.1080/08838151.2016.1273931

Santino, J. (2006). Performative commemoratives: Spontaneous shrines and the public memorialization of death. In J. Santino (Ed.) *Spontaneous shrines and the public memorialization of death* (pp. 5–15). Palgrave Macmillan.

Shklovski, I., Burke, M., Kiesler, S., & Kraut, R. (2008). *Technology adoption and use in the aftermath of Hurricane Katrina in New Orleans* [Conference session]. HCI for Emergencies Workshop Conference on Human Factors in Computing, Chicago, IL, United States.

Sholtis, B. (2021, September 16). *When COVID deaths are dismissed or stigmatized, grief is mixed with shame and anger.* Kaiser Health News. https://www.healthleadersmedia.com/covid-19/when-covid-deaths-are-dismissed-or-stigmatized-grief-mixed-shame-and-anger

Stacey, A. (2021, September 7). *How COVID-19 has changed grieving—and what that means for our mental health.* Psycom. https://www.psycom.net/coronavirus-grief

Ulmer, R.R., & Sellnow, T.L. (2002). Crisis management and the discourse of renewal: Understanding the potential for positive outcomes of crisis. *Public Relations Review, 28*(4), 361–365. https://doi.org/10.1016/S0363-8111(02)00165-0

Ulmer, R.R., Sellnow, T.L., & Seeger, M.W. (2010). Considering the future of crisis communication research: Understanding the opportunities inherent to crisis events through the discourse of renewal. In *The Handbook of Crisis Communication*. Routledge.

Veil, S.R., Sellnow, T.L., & Heald, M. (2011). Memorializing crisis: The Oklahoma City National Memorial as renewal discourse. *Journal of Applied Communication Research, 39*(2), 164–183. https://doi.org/10.1080/00909882.2011.557390

Ward, A. (2020, April 7). *How coronavirus is changing the ways we grieve and mourn the dead.* Vox. https://www.vox.com/2020/4/7/21202788/funerals-during-coronavirus-burials-mourning

Winchel, B. (2019, July 29). *Tasteless PR tactics after the Gilroy shooting.* Ragan's PR Daily. https://www.prdaily.com/tasteless-pr-tactics-after-the-gilroy-shooting-top-pr-tools-and-google-honors-ada-with-giveaway/

Wood, M. (2020). *Finding ways to mourn online as the Corona Virus keeps us apart: Some people are using new tools to express their grief, including those in Nintendo's Animal Crossing.* Marketplace. https://www.marketplace.org/shows/marketplace-tech/covid-19-online-funerals-digital-cemeteries-memorials-mourning-loss/

WorldoMeter. (n.d.-a). *Corona Virus—United States.* https://www.worldometers.info/coronavirus/country/us/

WorldoMeter. (n.d.-b) *Corona Virus—World.* https://www.worldometers.info/coronavirus/

Yuan, L. (2020, April 13). How thousands in China gently mourn a Coronavirus whistleblower. *The New York Times.* https://www.nytimes.com/interactive/2020/04/13/technology/coronavirus-doctor-whistleblower-weibo.html?fbclid=IwAR1AaIVy4cy6FWeiLftEV9Ji0VH-VhPaqTkrLgkPUCpWYbjnKc4FegloHHmc

· 6 ·

COVID-19 AND HIGHER EDUCATION: NAVIGATING AMBIGUITY, CONSTRAINTS, AND MISPLACED OPTIMISM

Anna Valiavska

When the news of COVID-19 reached the shores of the United States, higher education institutions faced many uncertainties. Many universities were ultimately forced to suspend in-person operations and faced numerous questions that demanded urgent answers. How will universities keep the students and faculty safe? What happens to the jobs of front-facing staff (Bauman, 2021)? How can universities continue serving their educational missions under conditions of digital access inequity (Galperin et al., 2020; McMurtrie, 2020)? How can educational institutions manage these new circumstances? (Hubler, 2020)? What messages should leaders send to aid retention, bolster identification, and, ultimately, ensure organizational survival (Yue, 2021)? What are the racial equity implications of reopening campuses (Harper, 2020)? Improper management of the organizational crisis could damage the organizational image and threaten organizational functioning (Coombs, 2015). Yet, university officials hoped that if they handled the crisis successfully, their institutions would be able to pursue growth and implement important and timely cultural changes (Bechler, 2004).

Universities' responses to COVID-19 can shed light on organizational practices during a long-lasting crisis. As we consider organizational responses to the crisis, it is important to note that no organization exists in a vacuum.

Organizations and their communicative practices are impacted by a variety of factors including geographical realities, political influences, size, organizational goals, institutional goals, and others. To better understand how these factors may play a role in organizational internal communication practices, I analyze publicly available communication artifacts from two universities: one large public university located in a Republican-leaning state in the Midwest and a small private university located in the Pacific Northwest (that I call Midwest U and PNW U, respectively). These two organizations experienced political polarization that shaped this pandemic response differently because of their size, location, and funding. I use these pseudonyms because while the universities described here are unique, the challenges they have experienced and the communication strategies they have utilized are not dissimilar to many other educational institutions.

Universities can serve as valuable sites to examine communication practices and as benchmarks for best practices around safety for the surrounding communities. However, universities often receive ire and criticism for their responses. The politically polarized news landscape prevalent throughout the COVID-19 pandemic invited public and media scrutiny of university practices around in-person learning environments, mask use, and vaccination requirements (e.g., Belkin, 2021). The general public (often comprised of taxpayers and members of the communities in which universities are located) had strong opinions about the safety practices of the universities. The students educated in the institutions of higher education are socialized to organizational norms and values. In the case of COVID-19, the students are socialized to see organizational responses that could perpetrate political divisions and inequality in access. University administrators are responsible for protecting the organizational reputation and attracting new students, donors, faculty, staff, and maintaining the support of local legislators. These numerous and often conflicting responsibilities university administrators have make any publicly available response complex.

To analyze how these organizations responded to the COVID-19 crisis, I use primary texts (i.e., official university response messaging) to the COVID-19 pandemic from January 2020 to October 2021. I analyze these texts to understand the rhetorical moves these organizations made to frame the crisis and, ultimately, navigate renewal. Then, I critically analyze the texts through a narrative framework to reveal the nature of the stories these two universities were telling. Finally, I discuss the implications of this critique and suggest more effective approaches for universities handling a public health crisis.

From Crisis to Renewal

A global pandemic led to a series of organizational crises that were answered by a vast variety of responses. An organizational crisis is a "specific, *unexpected*, and *non-routine* event or series of events that create high levels of *uncertainty* and *threaten* or are perceived to threaten an organization's high priority goals" (emphasis in original; Ulmer et al., 2007, p. 7). Yet, a crisis can also have positive outcomes, including accelerating the solutions to pestering problems, engaging in organizational change, creating heroes, and discovering new competitive advantages (Seeger & Ulmer, 2002).

Organizations respond through practical and physical actions and by using discourse to frame their role in a crisis (Ulmer et al., 2007). Both actions and discourse reflect and reinforce organizational ideology and values. In evaluating organizational responses, "perceptions are more important than reality" (Benoit, 1997, p. 178). Furthermore, different publics will have different, and likely conflicting, views of the organizational response to a crisis. In responding to crises, organizations typically utilize the rhetoric of *apologia*, a defense focused on "compelling counter descriptions of organizational outcomes" (Hearit, 1995, p. 188); the assumptions of organizational wrongdoing did not arise for the two universities analyzed here during the pandemic that impacted the globe. In instances where the need for apologia does not arise, organizations still communicate to help constituents engage in sense-making around the crisis as a way of framing the event and its aftermath (Weick, 1988). This renewal and rebuilding discourse can help organizations and their stakeholders endure the crisis successfully (Seeger & Ulmer, 2002).

The discourse of renewal allows organizations to learn from a crisis and begin looking forward. The discourse of renewal has four key features. First, it is prospective in that it looks ahead at future goals and possible opportunities. Seeger and Ulmer (2002) argue that this future focus allows for both senses of loss and opportunities for renewal. Second, the discourse of renewal shifts conversations from a focus on blame to a focus on support and rebuilding. Third, the responses are provisional and instinctive rather than strategic and are driven by the values organizational leaders hold. Subsequent research developed a reliable way to measure discourse of renewal that focuses on "engagement with the community and stakeholders, prospective foci on learning and growing, efficient communication that is provisional and genuine, and an emphasis on organizational culture and values" (Xu, 2018, p. 117).

Overall, there are a few lessons learned, or best practices, when it comes to organizational communication in the aftermath of a crisis. Rapid response is beneficial, as it allows the organization to shape the narrative and engage in two-way communication via social media. Organizations are advised to select an appropriate, skilled, and culturally aware spokesperson to communicate with the public (Bauman, 2011). Finally, organizations are advised to cater to diverse audiences instead of a "one size fits all" message (Marsen, 2020).

In this case study, I analyze the responses of two universities to the COVID-19 pandemic. In my analysis, I am guided by the following question:

> R1: What communication strategies did the two universities use during the different stages of COVID-19, specifically to frame organizational crisis response, and organizational renewal?

Method

To analyze the responses PNW U and Midwest U had to the pandemic, I collected all publicly available press releases and publicly released emails for the two organizations between January 2020 and October 2021. I filtered out any press releases and emails that did not address COVID-19 or the organizational response to the pandemic. I chose to concentrate on the publicly available communication artifacts as they represent the voice with which the universities were communicating. In total, I collected and analyzed 89 communication artifacts from PNW U and 97 communication artifacts from Midwest U. To collect the artifacts, I searched through the university websites and cataloged them by date.

Narrative Analysis

A narrative analysis reveals how an organization is shaping a response to a crisis. A narrative sets the scene, determines key characters, and lays out the plot. In crafting a narrative, the author cues the audience to a particular perspective by framing the story through a set of strategic choices. Narratives function to "ideologically produce, maintain, and reproduce" the dominant power structures (Mumby, 1987, p. 113). This case study will utilize a critical narrative analysis to understand how Midwest U and PNW U framed their responses and trace the rhetorical devices used to craft these narratives. The questions included: what was included, what was left out, whose voices were audible, whose were silent, and what interests were served.

Findings

University Responses in Anticipating COVID-19

Universities are complex organizations that were not prepared to navigate the multitude of logistical and communication challenges posed by the pandemic. Largely, universities do not include pandemic preparation in their strategic plans (Govindarajan & Srivastava, 2020), which may explain the limited communication the two universities engaged in early in the pandemic. In addressing a crisis before it occurs, organizations send messages aimed at anticipating a crisis, avoiding crisis, and managing relationships with the audiences through the crisis.

The universities I selected for this study have access to different sizes and scales of resources, which may have influenced their responses. Midwest U, a large research university, issued early warnings to the campus community about a new coronavirus, a respiratory illness that was first identified in Wuhan, China. In four emails over January 28–31, the campus was informed that "the immediate health risk to the American public is considered low at this time, but it is important that we as a university community remain vigilant." The initial email, sent by a head officer in student affairs, signaled that the members of the university leadership team were aware of the possible risks. The early timing of this email (relative to the course of the pandemic in the United States) may have built legitimacy for the organization. Organizations that send strategic messages preparing their audiences for how to perceive and understand a crisis can navigate the crisis with more success (Waymer & Heath, 2007).

PNW U is a small private campus that did not issue the early warnings. The first mention of COVID-19 occurred on March 6 after the first known death COVID-related death in the region. This email was four sentences long and included the detail that the university has not yet received any guidance from the State Department of Health. The following day, another email notified students that classes would be held virtually the following week so that "over the coming week campus leadership, faculty and staff will work together to consider and develop alternate plans for course delivery to finish the spring semester should that become necessary." These emails portray both urgency and lack of preparedness. Many organizations struggled to assess the unfolding situation and predict the appropriate course of action.

News reports about COVID-19 had been growing in urgency before known cases started appearing in the United States, yet the universities did not seem prepared. The lack of preparedness at PNW U may be explained by how the university leadership framed the mission of the university. In an email sent later in the day on March 6, the president of PNW U wrote: "As a residential campus, the university never truly closes. We may need to modify or suspend normal operations, which could include delivering class content electronically, increasing telecommuting, or reducing the presence of non-essential personnel on campus." The COVID-19 pandemic upended what it meant to be a residential campus. This email points to the issue of organizational identity—the university could not engage in actions that redefine what the organization had positioned itself as until the orders to close the campus were issued by the governor. By not engaging in any messaging about COVID-19 until there were known cases in the county where the university was located, PNW U missed essential opportunities to manage and maintain relationships with key publics like faculty and staff. We live in a highly news-saturated environment and the reports about the possible threats of COVID-19 were already well disseminated. The public was able to see images of empty cities and masked people coming from abroad, thus not having clear organizational messaging about the impending pandemic was a missed opportunity.

Crisis Contagion on a College Campus

As news of COVID-19 reaching the United States became well known, all universities were faced with a similar set of dilemmas. The swift spread of COVID-19 resulted in a crisis contagion, the phenomena of crisis moving "over from one organization to another" (Laufer & Wang, 2018, p. 17). An example of crisis contagion can be seen in the events that impacted the airline industry in April 2017. When one airline received public scrutiny for forcefully removing a paid passenger due to overbooking, the issue of overbooking became an industry-wide problem. The crisis contagion resulted in events that created major negative consequences for many universities. Next, I outline a few ways crisis expanded and discuss the communication strategies the universities used to mitigate the crisis.

Financial Uncertainty and Strategic Ambiguity

Universities experienced specific, material, budgetary consequences of the COVID-19 pandemic. In the spring of 2021, many institutions of higher education announced they were forced to lay off faculty and staff, as previous budget reductions proved inadequate to rein in the damages done by drops in enrollment and mounting spending on health and safety measures (Nietzel, 2021). The universities in this case study experienced similar challenges, but used different approaches to communicate those challenges to faculty and staff. Traditional approaches to crisis communication favor clear and consistent messaging, where clarity is ensured when "stakeholders are able to understand what is said" (Coombs, 2015, p. 85). This allows publics to feel reassured and for the organization to maintain credibility. However, emergent research suggests that *strategic ambiguity*, or the use of language in intentionally ambiguous ways, can enhance trust, restore normality, and allow the communicator to keep modifying the message as new information emerges (Johansson & Nord, 2018). Here I examine how PNW U and Midwest U communicatively navigated tightening budgets.

As early as April 2020, PNW U started signaling to the campus community that the financial consequences of COVID-19 would be felt on campus. An email containing the following was sent to faculty and staff:

> As discussed during the April 1 faculty meeting town hall for staff and faculty, we currently estimate that revenues will be $10 to $11 million short of budget this year [. . .] We are working diligently to secure expense savings to balance the operating budget for this fiscal year and to reduce costs for next year, including:
>
> We have reduced facilities maintenance, halted capital projects, deferred equipment purchases, and temporarily shifted some staff responsibilities.
>
> We have suspended discretionary spending and will realize other savings from reductions in travel, events, utilities, and other items.
>
> We have taken steps to receive funding available to higher education institutions from the Education Stabilization Fund established by the federal CARES Act.
>
> [. . .] We have suspended searches for 25 vacant staff positions and we also are now suspending most in-process searches for visiting assistant professors.
>
> We continue to assess additional actions necessary before the end of the fiscal year on June 30 to achieve a balanced budget, and know that one of the most pressing areas of concern is whether the university will be able to continue to pay staff members past May 15 in the event they are unable to work due to our extended modified operations.
>
> Our goal is to do everything we can to support and retain our talented staff and faculty members [. . .] To this end, the president, provost, and vice presidents have

> communicated to our Board of Trustees leadership their willingness to take temporary reductions in their compensation as one of several strategies that may be needed to reduce expenses.

This email balances clarity and ambiguity in ways that allow the organization to be flexible with the changing environment and for the organizational members to have some certainty about their roles. This communication signals that layoffs are possible. The idea of "support and retain our talented staff and faculty members in alignment with our resources" is intentionally ambiguous. It is not clear what support of organizational members and alignment of resources entail. Similarly, it is not clear how much of a financial impact reduction in compensation for the top executives would produce. The message also lays out clear steps that the organization is taking to manage the budgetary constraints.

Midwest U sent out similar messages that balance strategic ambiguity and certainty. The ambiguous messages include:

> While the exact toll is not yet known, it is clear our major sources of funding will remain under stress and uncertainty for the short-term and into the future. [...] We must plan for severe financial challenges for the next 60–90 days, with forward-looking realism about potential longer-term impacts. [...] We have asked many other senior leaders and administrators throughout our universities to take 10 percent salary cuts for the same upcoming time. We know we will be overwhelmed by the participation of our dedicated leaders.

The last statement involves the strategy of *bolstering* or shifting focus to positive values and attributions. This university also discussed cost-cutting strategies: "Contingency plans for an average of up to 15% cuts must be quickly created, requiring several options to be considered, including layoffs, unpaid leaves, restructuring, strict cost containment, and other measures." These cost-cutting strategies are both ambiguous "other measures" and involve negative material consequences. This university has experienced budget cuts and restructuring in the past, yet the rhetoric is using the *act/essence distinction strategy* (Hearit, 1995) to argue that this set of cuts is not typical of the record of the organization. Here, the act/essence distinction strategy (Hearit, 1995) includes organizations differentiating between the act that they engaged in and the meaning, or the essence of the act.

Students represent another audience that was impacted by budgetary changes. In an email about remote learning, PNW U announced that "[f]ull-time Fall 2020 undergraduate tuition will be reduced to the amount charged in Fall 2019," and financial aid packages would remain the same. Additionally, the university notified the students that it had received funding as part of the Higher Education Emergency Relief Fund II (HEERF II) and that the students were permitted to apply for the funding. It is notable that both universities in this case study focused largely on strategies that would maintain student enrollment and retention. The strategies to ensure staff and faculty retention were not as readily articulated. During a crisis, an organization must consider the competing needs of multiple audiences. The stakeholders and employees need to be reassured of the financial viability of the organization, and the employees also need to be reassured of their health and safety.

In discussing their budget priorities, Midwest U sent similar messages by issuing a list of priorities that included the following: "Ensure our students receive a high-quality education. Support retention and recruitment of our students." Faculty and staff are not mentioned on that list of priorities. It is the case that many universities were in a financial bind. However, rhetoric can be effective even where the material means are not available. By leaving faculty and staff off the list of priorities, the universities neglected the needs of one of their primary publics.

Campus Policies and State Mandates

State politics impacted the way COVID was handled by these two university campuses. These state policies were reflected in the physical and rhetorical actions of both organizations. PNW U is located in a blue state (Democratically controlled) that was quick to issue stay-at-home mandates, masking orders, and mandate closures of public education facilities. When the vaccines became publicly available, the governor created vaccine distribution strategies that included designating campuses as vaccine sites. This was reflected in the rhetoric that PNW U used to discuss campus closures, various degrees of reopening, and vaccination availability and requirements. For example, PNW U shared that "We offer first and second doses of the Moderna COVID-19 vaccine for participants who are 18 or older." Additionally, PNW U offered flexible work accommodations and hybrid class options for faculty and staff. In the spring of 2021, PNW U welcomed a small percentage of students back to campus and allowed faculty to opt into in-person, hybrid, or online-only classes. With this change, faculty who opted into hybrid or in-person teaching were required to undergo regular weekly testing that was free and available in the middle of campus. All communication artifacts that announced these updates referred to the state, county, and CDC guidelines and support. For example, the announcement about the Fall 2020 work plan included the following: "Faculty and staff members will be approved to work on campus in alignment with [State's] Safe Start plan and Governor [...] Fall 2020 Proclamation." The university positions itself in close alignment with the state by stating: "The University has established expectations that help reduce COVID-19 risks on campus. These expectations were developed from guidance by the [State] public health officials and the CDC, as well as the [...] State Department of Labor and Industries and Division of Occupational Safety and Health." This aligning can be indicative of the university and the state falling in line ideologically. A progressive liberal arts university is likely to share political views with a blue state legislature.

Midwest U is located in a historically Republican state, and COVID-19 policies and practices reflected that ideology. The university returned to on-campus operations including in-person teaching in Fall 2020, as the state was slow to implement many COVID-19 safety protocols. Despite rising COVID-19 case numbers in the fall of 2020, the university issued the following: "Based on your diligent efforts, guidance from our public health officials, and the data we have been tracking, *we will continue our in-person and hybrid classes after the Thanksgiving break*" (emphasis in original). The university worked hard to be in line with the state guidelines.

"Transition to Pre-pandemic Days"

Residential universities need students to attend in-person classes and live in residence halls. Both PNW U and Midwest U issued statements that aimed to evoke excitement about the return to in-person learning and campus functioning. Here, I analyze the narratives both universities engage with regarding the return to campus.

Midwest U framed the return to in-person activity in terms that attempted to erase the existing COVID-19 risks and place responsibility for staff safety on the individual, and not on the organization that was mandating specific behavioral and safety practices. A statement issued by Midwest U's Human Resources officer in early May of 2021 reads: "As more of our university community is vaccinated against COVID-19, our lives begin to transition to pre-pandemic days." The statement went on to say that the county where the university is located has achieved a 44% single-dose vaccination rate and that vaccinations continue to be encouraged. This statement proceeded to call faculty and staff to return to work in 10 days. The statement also acknowledged that the return was occurring "at a time when guidelines are shifting," thus, faculty and staff should monitor the campus COVID-19 dashboard to "stay up to date with latest safety expectations on campus." Midwest U framed the return as that of "pre-pandemic days" instead of "post-pandemic life" attempts to create a reality in which the pandemic and its immense toll on lives and livelihood do not seem to count. Further, the move to "pre-pandemic" days is based on relatively low vaccination levels that are cited in the same document. The narrative through-line in this statement positions organizational members as ultimately responsible for their own safety.

PNW U framed the return to in-person operations as a long-awaited joyful occasion. The president of PNW U sent the following email in the summer of 2021:

> It's hard to imagine that fall is just around the corner and we are on the cusp—at long last!—of welcoming everyone back to campus. Thank you for your good, selfless, and heroic efforts [. . .] Over the past year, some of us have continued to work on campus, while others have been working remotely to help de-densify the campus and keep everyone who must be on campus safe. With appropriate health and safety protocols in place, including the vaccination requirement announced last week, we can look forward to being back in the community together in the coming weeks.

This narrative included direct references to the challenges experienced over the previous academic year, the steps taken to overcome those challenges (vaccination requirements and health protocols), and the disruptions in campus life. The email framed the pandemic as an ongoing issue. This is an example of a more successful renewal message. Specifically, this email is able to acknowledge both the struggle that underscored the COVID-19 pandemic on this campus, and the organizational values ("selfless, and heroic efforts" and being a "community together") that can lead to a new normalcy.

Now that I have discussed the identified communication strategies, I want to discuss what was omitted. Neither of the universities acknowledged specific losses in their rhetoric. The pandemic had a demonstrably negative impact on the lives and livelihood of members of historically marginalized communities (Kantamneni, 2020). Students, faculty, and staff experienced death, loss, and significant disruptions to their lives, work, and education. The back-to-campus messages did not do much to acknowledge those losses. Moreover, I could not locate any messages that identified remembrance events or memorials. The lack of such events suggests that the universities have some room to improve in their discourse of renewal. Meaningful acknowledgment of loss and remembrance can give the organizational members a functional script for how to process the crisis events and how to move forward.

Discussion

Expanding the Definition of Crisis

This chapter has discussed a multitude of events that can be examined through the lens of crisis communication and the discourse of renewal. In examining those events, it becomes clear that the conceptualization of what a crisis "is" was expanded by COVID-19. Currently, there are numerous definitions of a crisis (Heath, 2010). While "nearly every conference paper and article implicitly or explicitly treats crisis from the standpoint of the organization" (Kent, 2010, p. 705), disaster literature views crisis as "a phase of disorder in the development of a person, an organization, a community, an ecosystem, a business sector, or a polity" (Boin et al., 2017, p. 5). The concept of crisis contagion discussed above can help extend the definition of crisis to encompass the wide range of disruptions and threats organizations had to navigate in the expanded COVID-19 timeline. However, additional theorizing work is needed to consider what communication practices are most effective during a long-lasting series of crisis events.

Focus on Renewal

Previous research has focused on communal coping in an aftermath of a crisis. The COVID-19 pandemic created conditions where organizations and their members juggled multiple roles and positionalities. It is typical for catastrophes to result in us viewing those who were impacted as both victims who require support and those in power to provide such support (Pennebaker & Harber, 1993). However, the long-lasting nature of COVID-19 and lack of discernable closure or completion of this event created further confusion for organizations and their members.

In my analysis of the narratives that both organizations put forth, I demonstrated how both organizations largely focused on the future without accounting for the damage and loss experienced by the university communities during the pandemic. While Midwest U specifically labeled their process as "renewal," the organization did not engage in renewal discourses. While the discourse of renewal is future-oriented, it also must be provisional (Seeger & Ulmer, 2002).

The universities in this case study did not demonstrate learning from the past, instead the rhetoric portrayed a rushed call to get back to normal. Without an explicit and meaningful acknowledgment of loss and grief, the organizational leaders are unable to offer a single coherent shared meaning to motivate renewal. Both organizations acknowledge the hard work accomplished by the organizational members, but that work does not seem meaningful without a clear narrative that focused on the need for reconstruction. Instead, the framing of back to normal or back to pre-pandemic may invalidate the sacrifices made by staff and faculty.

An alternative narrative could include a discussion of reconstruction and creating communal spaces (through artwork, public statements, moments of silence) to process and experience grief. These symbolic, discursive, and material steps can help the organizational members (re)gain trust in leadership and create their own scripts of how to move forward from a (hopefully) once-in-a-lifetime pandemic.

Discussion Questions

1. If you were in a top leadership position at a university, what resources, knowledge, and tools would you need to make decisions about a developing health crisis?
2. This chapter discussed how two universities handled the discourse of renewal. What other messages could the universities take to more effectively facilitate renewal? Practice by creating a few messages.
3. How did you feel about your school's response to COVID-19? What messages worked well? What was missing in the response?
4. Make a list of the possible audiences universities have in managing this crisis. What were the needs of these audiences?

References

Bauman, D.C. (2011). Evaluating ethical approaches to crisis leadership: Insights from unintentional harm research. *Journal of Business Ethics*, 98, 281–295. https://doi.org/10.1007/s10551-010-0549-3

Bauman, D. (2021, April 19). Here's who was hit hardest by higher ed's pandemic-driven job losses. *Chronicle of Higher Education*. https://www.chronicle.com/article/heres-who-was-hit-hardest-by-higher-eds-pandemic-driven-job-losses

Bechler, C. (2004). Reframing the organizational exigency: Taking a new approach in crisis research. In D.P. Millar & R.L. Heath (Eds.), *Responding to crisis: A rhetorical approach to crisis communication* (pp. 63–74). Routledge.

Beklin, D. (2021). Covid-19 precautions prompt backlash on college campuses. *WSJ.* https://www.wsj.com/articles/covid-19-precautions-prompt-backlash-on-college-campuses-11634376600

Benoit, W.L. (1997). Image repair discourse and crisis communication. *Public Relations Review, 23*(2), 177–186. https://doi.org/10.1016/S0363-8111(97)90023-0

Boin, A., Hart, P., Stern, E., & Sundelius, B. (2017). *The politics of crisis management: Public leadership under pressure.* Cambridge University Press.

Coombs, W.T. (2015). *Ongoing crisis communication: Planning, managing, and responding* (4th ed.). Sage.

Galperin, H., Wyatt, K., & Le, T. (2020). *COVID-19 and the distance learning gap.* University of Southern California, Annenberg Research Network on International Communication. https://arnicusc.org/wp-content/uploads/2020/04/Policy-Brief-5-final.pdf

Govindarajan, V., & Srivastava, A. (2020). What the shift to virtual learning could mean for the future of higher ed. *Harvard Business Review, 31*(1), 3–8.

Harper, S.R. (2020). COVID-19 and the racial equity implications of reopening college and university campuses. *American Journal of Education, 127*(1), 153–162. https://doi.org/10.1086/711095

Hearit, K.M. (1995). "Mistakes were made": Organizations, apologia, and crises of social legitimacy. *Communication Studies, 46*(1–2), 1–17. https://doi.org/10.1080/10510979509368435

Heath, R. (2010). Crisis communication: Defining the beast and de-marginalizing key publics. In W. Coombs & S. Holladay (Eds.), *The handbook of crisis communication* (pp. 1–14). Wiley-Blackwell.

Hubler, S. (2020, June 25). College calendars in the pandemic: No fall break and home by Thanksgiving. *New York Times.* https://nyti.ms/3ivo5w7

Johansson, C., & Nord, L. (2018). The simple truth: Ambiguity works. Discursive strategies by Swedish public authorities during the 2008 financial crisis. *International Journal of Business Communication, 55*(2), 220–236. https://doi.org/10.1177/2329488417710439

Kantamneni, N. (2020). The impact of the COVID-19 pandemic on marginalized populations in the United States: A research agenda. *Journal of Vocational Behavior, 119,* Article 103439. https://doi.org/10.1016/j.jvb.2020.103439

Kent, M. (2010). What is a public relations "crisis"? Refocusing crisis research. In W. Coombs and S. Holladay (Eds.), *The handbook of crisis communication* (pp. 705–712). Wiley-Blackwell.

Laufer, D., & Wang, Y. (2018). Guilty by association: The risk of crisis contagion. *Business Horizons, 61*(2), 173–179. https://doi.org/10.1016/j.bushor.2017.09.005

Marsen, S. (2020). Navigating crisis: The role of communication in organizational crisis. *International Journal of Business Communication, 57*(2), 163–175. https://doi.org/10.1177/2329488419882981

McMurtrie, B. (2020, April 6). Students without laptops, instructors without internet: How struggling colleges move online during COVID-19. *Chronicle of Higher Education.* https://www.chronicle.com/article/Students-Without-Laptops/248436

Mumby, D. K. (1987). The political function of narrative in organizations. *Communications Monographs, 54*(2), 113–127.

Nietlel, M. (2021, January 23). Pandemic still wreaking havoc on university budgets, personnel: New actions by Marquette, William Paterson, and Kansas Board of Regents. *Forbes.* https://www.forbes.com/sites/michaeltnietzel/2021/01/23/pandemic-continues-wreaking-havoc-on-budgets-and-personnel-marquette-william-paterson-and-kansas-board-of-regents-the-latest-examples/?sh=41adb6ef3a43

Pennebaker, J.W., & Harber, K.D. (1993). A social stage model of collective coping: The Loma Prieta earthquake and the Persian Gulf War. *Journal of Social Issues, 49*(4), 125–145. https://doi.org/10.1111/j.1540-4560.1993.tb01184.x

Seeger, M., & Ulmer, R. (2002). A post-crisis discourse of renewal: The cases of Malden Mills and Cole Hardwoods. *Journal of Applied Communication Research, 30*(2), 126–142. https://doi.org/10.1080/00909880216578

Ulmer, R.R., Seeger, M.W., & Sellnow, T.L. (2007). Post-crisis communication and renewal: Expanding the parameters of post-crisis discourse. *Public Relations Review, 33*(2), 130–134. https://doi.org/10.1016/j.pubrev.2006.11.015

Waymer, D., & Heath, R.L. (2007). Emergent agents: The forgotten publics in crisis communication and issues management research. *Journal of Applied Communication Research, 35*(1), 88–108. https://doi.org/10.1080/00909880601065730

Weick, K.E. (1988). Enacted sensemaking in crisis situations. *Journal of Management Studies, 25*(4), 305–317. https://doi.org/10.1111/j.1467-6486.1988.tb00039.x

Xu, S. (2018). Discourse of renewal: Developing multiple-item measurement and analyzing effects on relationships. *Public Relations Review, 44*(1), 108–119. https://doi.org/10.1016/j.pubrev.2017.09.005

Yue, C.A. (2021). Navigating change in the era of COVID-19: The role of top leaders' charismatic rhetoric and employees' organizational identification. *Public Relations Review, 47*(5), 102–118. https://doi.org/10.1016/j.pubrev.2021.102118

· 7 ·

BRANDING, MARKETING, PR, AND COVID-19

Erika J. Schneider

As the pandemic created a universal issue, it disrupted the daily lives of people around the world, and companies faced critical moments for adapting to consumer needs. What initially was thought of as a mysterious, distant threat quickly became a public health emergency as infections and death tolls quickly rose. Restrictions on international travel and quarantine requirements for travel from at-risk areas were initiated. As cases climbed, it was soon realized that the threat was underestimated and no longer impacted a few industries, but became an undeniably complex, global crisis. From changing the way consumers shopped to the way employees worked, the pandemic touched every company and left a scar on the early 2020s. Lockdown orders extended from weeks to months, and the companies that survived were led by leaders learning how to reprioritize and operate within the pandemic. The prolonged state of crisis required companies to think beyond quick fixes and learn sustainable ways to create and maintain relationships with stakeholders. Driven by technological innovation, integrated marketing communication (IMC) is regarded as a process of strategically coordinated messaging to build relationships between a consumer and an organization (Kitchen & Burgmann, 2010; Schultz & Schultz, 1998). As organizations relied on digital communication during the pandemic, effective IMC goals emerged from the combined, synergistic efforts of public relations and marketing approaches.

Public relations is a discipline and profession of making informed decisions for the public's best interest and communicating the information to generate meaningful engagement (Allert, 1999; Solis & Breakenridge, 2009). The way an organization communicates affects public perception and how relationships are developed and maintained. A *brand* is a powerful, strategic projection that connects an organization's identity and public perceptions (Kapferer, 2002; Oswald & Oswald, 2012). A brand represents a company by means of its name, color, symbol, and other identifiers that position an organization in society. While convenience, habit, price, and availability may all be factors involved in how customers make purchase decisions, other considerations, such as the purpose of the brand, have started to come into mind. As the issues customers care about continue to play a larger role in intentions to support an organization, brands have the opportunity and responsibility to represent their societal contributions. Arief and Pangestu's (2021) application of the model of empathic communication shares insight on how brands can implement digital and integrated communication to enhance brand reputation. When a brand expresses authentic advocacy, for instance, corporate responsibility may strengthen the brand association and increase the quality of customer perceptions.

The pandemic created an opportunity for companies to acknowledge the new needs of stakeholders and adapt to higher expectations of safety. Many developed creative ways to earn credibility by publicly communicating how they facilitated an experience that protects the health of customers and employees, not despite the pandemic but with respect to it. Mahmud et al. (2021) studied ways companies supported customers with resources during the pandemic and found that around 92% of sampled companies integrated COVID-19 initiatives addressing the pandemic-related needs of customers. In the entertainment industry, for example, Hasbro launched "Bring Home the Fun," a program to provide at-home activities for families that may have been sheltering in place. The strategic and creative ways companies positioned their brands, directed marketing, and engaged in PR efforts during the pandemic earned appreciation from the public and enabled companies to develop durable relationships with customers.

When close contact was realized as a mode of COVID-19 transmission, businesses that relied on serving customers in enclosed spaces suffered. If social distancing measures could not be maintained, restaurant owners were faced with the decision of closing their doors or finding ways to reduce the risk of transmission to maintain healthy environments. For instance, companies were required to follow government regulations that included measures such as reducing indoor capacities and ensuring customer parties maintained a 6-foot distance apart, which decreased the number of customers served and reduced overall profits. The National Restaurant Association estimated that during the first six months of the pandemic, at least 100,000 restaurants were closed for a long period of time or permanently (Sink, 2020). Datassential, a food industry research and insights firm, confirmed that over 10% of food establishments in operation since the onset of the pandemic permanently closed as of March 2021 (PR Newswire, 2021). The decline in sales revenue during the pandemic affected all business types, including franchises and chains of all cuisines. Datassential's CEO Jack Li says:

> This last year has been one of the toughest the restaurant industry has ever faced. But the good news is that the rate of closures is slowing, and the future is bright for those restaurants who have learned to adapt to the host of new challenges facing them in our new normal. (Morris, 2021, para. 4)

So, the question remains: How do companies adapt? The following textual analysis of primary and secondary documents assessed how two organizations, from the restaurant and airline industries, respectively, engaged stakeholders through new media to build relationships using aspects of integrated marketing communication. The analysis involved using rich descriptions with examples of how the organizations integrated PR and marketing efforts from their physical locations to digital environments (Tate & Happ, 2018). To understand how two companies from different industries utilized integrated communication, specifically PR and marketing digital integrations, campaign materials, such as social media posts, content from mobile applications, and website landing pages produced by the two companies, were collected from March 2020 to November 2021 during the COVID-19 pandemic. To more fully explore the phenomenon, observations of existing data was also used to derive an analysis of how the two organizations successfully developed PR and marketing digital integrations during the pandemic.

Analysis

Roadhouse in the House

At the onset of the pandemic, Texas Roadhouse, a U.S. steakhouse chain, closed dining rooms but remained available for to-go orders. Before the pandemic, Texas Roadhouse reported that less than 10% of total orders were to-go

(Simmons, 2020). Since more guests sought out a dining room experience pre-pandemic, there was little investment in "to-go" or "carry-out" systems. As the pandemic limited and eliminated dine-in experiences, the chain reflected on new ways to reach their communities and quickly improved take-out capabilities in just two weeks. On social media, they created a "Roadhouse in the House" Facebook Group to connect with customers outside of physical restaurants and re-launched a Pinterest account to share famous restaurant recipes, such as a signature margarita and sangria recipes, to encourage customers to recreate experiences at home (Kitterman, 2020). They hosted farmer's markets and created new menu items, such as ready-to-grill steaks, for purchase on an app or online, and, if desired, directly placed into trunks or backseats of customers' vehicles (Kitterman, 2020; Simmons, 2020). In communicating these changes, they commissioned special Curbside Pickup signs, upgraded a smartphone application, enabled new forms of contactless payments, partnered with delivery apps like Grubhub, and installed to-go windows to help make the to-go experience more convenient for carry-out customers (Ruggless, 2021). In May 2020, Travis Doster, Texas Roadhouse Vice President of Communications, shared how an AI-based approach to social media helped them through the crisis in an interview with PR Daily (Kitterman, 2020).

Social Listening and Monitoring

Social listening allows organizations to gauge public opinion and identify issues and trends that emerge from organic conversations online (Schweidel & Moe, 2014). By responding to online evaluations, Texas Roadhouse was able to execute strategies directly addressing the interests of customers. In addition to listening, social monitoring, or systematically evaluating metrics, allowed the organization to assess which initiatives were considered a success through a variety of measures (Barger et al., 2016; Li et al., 2021). By listening and monitoring stakeholder perceptions on social media, organizations can better understand opportunities to make more informed decisions based on public data. With social listening tools and creating partnerships that informed social media strategies, Texas Roadhouse was able to better understand how to serve customers:

> Using a custom-built AI tool, we can identify how our specific content decisions are impacting specific types of consumer engagement. Would you believe posts about fresh-baked bread make more people comment about our curbside pickup? These insights feed into higher-quality content, customized by platform and produced at

the speed of social. The results have been great, including two posts that reached 1 million people organically in two days. (Kitterman, 2020, para. 10)

Digital Adaptations

Texas Roadhouse, like many other restaurants, created digital adaptations, such as QR codes (Figure 7.1), to limit physical touch on high-contact surfaces (Texas Roadhouse, 2020b). A QR code allowed patrons to access a digital menu, without touching a physical, reusable menu and, in some cases, allowed patrons to even pay the bill without touching a pen or receipt. QR codes, short for Quick Response, are the black-and-write matrix barcode invented by Masahiro Hara in 1994 to improve manufacturing (NYU Dispatch, 2021). Although a few restaurants integrated QR codes into their restaurants before the pandemic, they quickly became integral to the contactless customer experience. QR codes on table tents or secured onto tables allowed customers to use their smartphones to scan the squares and access menus without concern of unsanitary reusable, physical menus. With most of the world's population having access to mobile internet, many restaurants integrated digital technology, like QR codes, into marketing plans to provide a safe and efficient customer experience. *Marketing* is paid communication that is controlled, promoted, and directed at a specific goal, such as sponsored content and advertisements. Incorporating QR codes and other scannable content on marketing materials may increase the visibility of products and services offered while decreasing risks of contamination during the pandemic. It also provides an accessible option as smartphone users may simply aim their cameras at the code to be immediately redirected to marketing materials.

Figure 7.1. QR Code for Texas Roadhouse Menu

The introduction of AI tools in restaurants also reinvented ways for restaurants to operate by elevating customer and employee safety. Miso Robotics, for instance, developed Flippy, an automated system for commercial fryers that enables social distancing needs and decreases human contact (Miso Robotics, 2021). This technology helped fulfill kitchen and staff roles that were abandoned, as the U.S. Labor Department reported that 2.9% of the workforce quit in August 2021, with about 892,000 workers (about 32%) leaving their jobs in restaurants, bars, and hotels (Rugaber, 2021). With safety concerns from customers and staff, Flippy and other AI tools like contactless payment methods and hand scanners that identify if hands need to be more thoroughly washed, were integrated into over 32,000 businesses by October 2021, including Buffalo Wild Wings, SONIC Drive-In, and White Castle. A Latin restaurant in Dallas, La Duni, went as far as using robots provided by American Robotech to greet customers and take food to tables when the owner could not find employees to fill positions during the pandemic (Johnson & Williams, 2021). The La Duni robots, which served as hostesses and food runners, were affectionately named and featured on the restaurant's social media platforms, attracting intrigued customers. In a similar concept, robot-assisted restaurant technology like Spyce also attracted curious customers seeking contact-free food options (Heater, 2021). As companies communicated these inventive adaptations, the bridges connecting virtual and physical worlds improved the guest experience amid the struggle of safely staffing and operating during the pandemic.

Integrated Marketing Communications

Texas Roadhouse was previously self-described as having a "dinner-only" concept, usually opening only after 4 p.m. on weekdays, but shifted to opening at noon to give employees more opportunities to work during the lunch hours (KMTV, 2020). These updated hours and other resources became available on the company's website, along with a landing page that created a "virtual roadhouse hub" with sections for kids, adults, and families to access activities, like a tutorial on line dancing (Doe-Anderson, 2021). In addition to more traditional methods of reaching customers, they found new ways to drive online conversations through channels like Animal Crossing, where users could wear a branded t-shirt and cactus blossom hat, Facebook 360, which provided users with a Roadhouse kitchen scene to explore, a Snapchat lens, and themed backgrounds on Zoom, which were platforms with heavy traffic during the pandemic. By consistently communicating a central message on *social media*, or platforms for sharing information and creating meaning through one-way or two-way communication, they engaged with audiences with preferences and reliance on specific platforms.

Creating yet another touchpoint with customers, they launched the Spotify playlist "Texas Roadhouse Jukebox Jams," to share songs typically played through their iconic restaurant jukeboxes, as conveyed in a Tweet (2020c): @texasroadhouse "Our jukeboxes may be paused, but the music doesn't stop. That's why we created a Spotify playlist that features our ENTIRE jukebox playlist." By engaging users in these efforts, the brand developed a positive sentiment that created meaningful and creative ways to listen and respond to current and potential customers. "We chose early on to treat the crisis as a stimulus for positive change," said Doster. "By reframing the disruption as an impetus to explore new things—new ways of serving our employees and customers—we freed our entire team to channel energies and expand creativity."

On Facebook in April 2020, they shared a rendition of "On the Road Again," featuring Willie Nelson dedicating the song and a message about Texas Roadhouse's commitment to helping serve the communities safely (Texas Roadhouse, 2020a). As an effective PR effort, this video earned media coverage and shares on social media, which garnered over 14k "Likes" and nearly 6,500 shares. To support their communities, Texas Roadhouse also reached out to frontline workers with home-cooked meals and delivered comfort food to the front doors of people who couldn't get to grocery stores or simply needed a break (Shvedsky, 2020). When CEO Kent Taylor chose to forego his salary and bonus, directing $1,050,000 to employees, other company executives followed suit, making headlines for their generosity.

Founded in 1993 and based in Kentucky, Texas Roadhouse had more than 630 restaurants in 2021, with plans to open more doors than close in the future. When pandemic restrictions were lifted, to-go sales continued strong, and curbside and drive-up options helped the restaurant not only recover, but outperform pre-pandemic sales in the first quarter of 2021 (Cawthon, 2021). As a company from one of the hardest-hit industries, Texas Roadhouse used digital PR and marketing efforts in IMC campaigns to embrace the changes that were necessary to address the needs of employees and customers, as well as the company's survival. By reprioritizing and understanding how the online interactions translated to offline behaviors, the casual dining chain developed trust by supporting existing relationships and recruiting new customers through their strategic and engaging integrated communications. Adaptations to physical points of contact, from automated systems and robots to digitized menus, helped brands sustain the relationships cultivated in a post-pandemic era.

Turbulent Times for Airlines

Another sector that relied on in-person interactions and faced a revenue loss in the billions is the airline industry. During the time of travel advisories, traffic decreased both on the ground and in the skies. How does an airline encourage flying when it is a health risk? Beyond contactless check-ins and plexiglass partitions, one company made a comeback through digital PR and marketing efforts that focused on the company's mission to serve customers safely.

The 2020 International Air Transport World Air Transport statistics reported a record-high decline in air passengers transported since statistics started being tracked around 1950 (IATA, 2021). In 2020, 1.8 billion passengers flew compared to the 4.5 billion in 2019, which is a 60.2% decrease. International passenger demand decreased by 75.6% compared to 2019, and domestic demand dropped by 48.8%.

At the start of the pandemic, there were many unknowns about transmission, and many may have been alarmed at the thought of squeezing into the middle seat next to strangers on an airplane. Although travel, in general, may have increased the risk of transmission, most airlines instituted distancing guidelines and sanitation protocols that reduced the risk. Travel anxiety persisted as passengers had lingering questions about the effectiveness of the measures. In 2020, data consultants analyzed over 900 million conversations related to COVID-19 and air travel on Twitter (X), news, and other online platforms (Sillers, 2020). They found strong, negative sentiment from passengers, with one-third of comments relating to concerns about how travelers can protect themselves and communicating frustration about the lack of information. Without clearly communicated protocols, passengers lack the information needed to trust an airline and travel with confidence in the airline facilitating a safe experience. As another example of social listening, organizations can sense how the public perceives a situation in real time by paying attention to publicly available data online.

Branding Airlines During the Pandemic

A *brand* is a powerful, strategic projection that connects an organization's identity and public perceptions (Hatch & Schultz, 2002; Kapferer, 2002; Oswald & Oswald, 2012). Marty Neumeier from The Brand Gap adds that branding is "the process of connecting good strategy with good creativity" (Bynder, 2021). A brand represents the experience of a company by means of its name, color, symbol, and other identifiers that position an organization. American Airlines

Group Inc. was formed in 2013 with 350 destinations offered in more than 50 countries as of 2021 (American Airlines, n.d.). American Airlines' recognizable brand, represented by a blue, red, and white logo, coined the "Flight Symbol," which represents both a bird and a wing. During the pandemic, this Flight Symbol reappeared across the company's owned channels and in a 40-second video featured across social media platforms, on banner ads, in email efforts, and on digital screens at airports (Christie, 2020). Although stretched across platforms, the message remained consistent, justifying why it must continue to serve passengers, such as in the cases of supporting essential workers flying to provide care or deliver necessary equipment. When the airline returned to boarding planes at full capacity, selling the middle seat, many customers voiced their concerns, even igniting a #BoycottAmericanAirlines hashtag and creating conversations about business standards (Aten, 2020).

Although they made justifications for capacities, such as low fares and abiding by a set of protocols, they also adopted new policies, such as no change fees when customers changed or rescheduled flights. Every image on AA's website marketing materials included images of people wearing masks to portray brand images that were consistent with the in-flight customer experience. In a Mediacom interview with Dana Lawrence, Managing Director of Global Brand Marketing for American Airlines, Lawrence adds, "Sometimes the best ideas can come out of adversity. This past year was a testament to that. We were forced to think differently . . . It gave us the opportunity for so much innovation." As the airline regained passenger confidence and with recommended individual

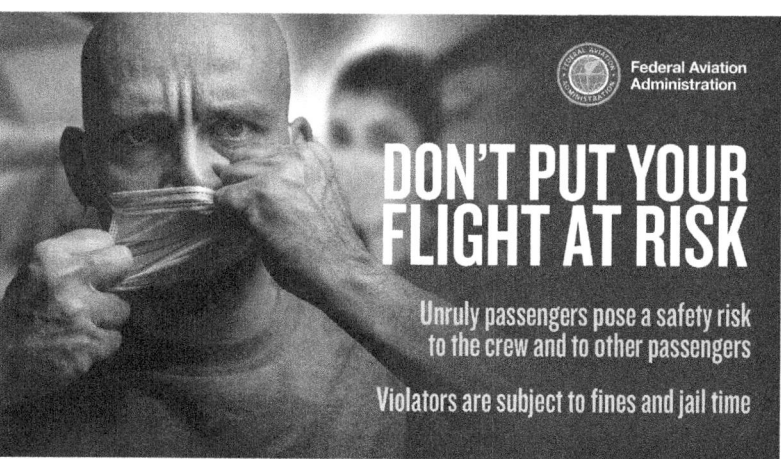

Figure 7.2. Airport Digital Signage

safety measures (e.g., vaccinations), the airline saw a surge in demand (Josephs, 2021). In fact, American Airlines was the top airline internationally ranked by total scheduled passenger-kilometers flown in 2020 (IATA, 2021). Continuing recovery into 2021, American flew more than 44 million passengers in the second quarter, which was over five times higher than the year prior and involved a positive cash flow to finally reverse a negative trend (Shivdas, 2021).

PR and Evolving Crises

By May 2021, most U.S. airlines adopted similar COVID-19 guidelines (e.g., no change fees, free cancellations, sanitation sprays prior to boarding, distancing, disinfectant wipes offered upon boarding, etc.). With an even playing field where all commercial airlines felt the impact of the pandemic, the ways airlines communicated through PR and marketing campaigns that positioned some more favorably than others. In April 2020, Delta Air Lines, another major U.S. airline, successfully initiated three campaigns, despite carrying the same name as a COVID-19 variant. Interestingly, Delta CEO Ed Bastian intentionally acknowledged the variant as the B.1.617.2 variant, rather than its common name (i.e., Delta), possibly out of fear of brand associations or misunderstandings (Delta, 2021a). First, Delta representatives created partnerships to manufacture face shields for hospital workers, quickly delivering 2,000 shields to medical workers in New York and 4,000 for Atlanta-area hospitals (Warpinski, 2020). With fewer flights and an excess of perishable and non-perishable food typically served in flights, they were able to provide more than 200,000 pounds of food to hospitals, community food banks, and other organizations like the Georgia Food & Resource Center and Missouri's Carthage Crisis Center (Peraza, 2020). A few days after this announcement, a Delta news release shared a campaign to support volunteer medical professionals. Delta provided free round-trip flights to Georgia, Louisiana, and Michigan, for eligible volunteers to assist hospitals in areas hardest hit by the virus (Delta, 2020). With this consistent stream of action, it became evident that Delta was invested in addressing the issue from multiple angles and their statements toward customer safety were taken seriously. Had the statements been purely for display, with little actual investment into addressing the issue, the campaign may have been interpreted as brand opportunism, or a brand's intent to capitalize on an issue or use messaging to exploit it (Mundel & Yang, 2021). If Delta's campaigns were perceived as self-serving or disingenuous toward the cause, they might have experienced backlash in forms such as negative attitudes or intentions to disengage with the brand.

The pandemic accelerated the rate of companies aligning their brand with technological advancements that provide a more efficient customer experience. Just as restaurants integrated technology to limit contact with customers, Delta also invested in technology to reduce the risk for travelers. During the pandemic, they rolled out biometric terminals that utilized facial recognition technology programs through partnerships with TSA (Delta, 2021b). After rigorous testing modeled after similar programs created in 2018, Delta allowed travelers to voluntarily scan their digital identity verified by facial recognition technology rather than handing over their identification at security. With the technological investment dating back to 2018, it enabled Delta to be among the first to roll out technology that addresses customer safety relevant to the initial crisis and following variants. These initiatives not only sped up wait times, but they responded to concerns about virus transmission by minimizing contact points. Shortly after its release, officials stated intentions to expand the technology across security checks and airports in its network. Bill Lentsch, Delta's Chief Customer Experience Officer, adds:

> When it comes to pulling forward the future of Delta's customer experience, we think big, start small and scale fast, letting innovation lead the way as we continuously listen to customer feedback. The COVID-19 pandemic has only deepened the importance of providing a touchless experience for our customers. (Delta, 2001b, para. 4)

Amid mask mandates, Delta provided signage throughout the customer touchpoints and advertisements showing safety measures to reiterate protocols, such as cleaning protocols and the types of acceptable masks. Materials from Delta's Global Cleanliness Organization shared the company's innovations in sanitization through partnerships with credible health organizations, such as Mayo Clinic. A website link to an example of material promoted can be found under "External Resources" at the end of this chapter.

Delta utilized *marketing*, or paid communication that is promoted and directed at a specific goal, to intentionally push messages to attract potential customers (Bird, 2004; Smith, 2020). Delta invited passengers back into the sky through advertisements that promoted the ways employees were dedicated to providing a clean, safe aircraft. Even with these expectations set for passengers prior to boarding, Delta flight attendants reported facing many instances of hostility. The Federal Aviation Administration reported an increase in unruly passengers, with 3,580 mask-related incidents reported from January to October 2021 (FAA, 2021). In September 2021, Delta reported having more than 1,600 people on a "no-fly" list with more than 600 names submitted to the

FAA in 2021 (Delta, 2021c). As alcohol consumption was suspected in many of the instances, major airlines were quick to ban sales of alcoholic beverages onboard, such as Southwest and American Airlines implementing a ban until 2022 (Mack, 2021).

Despite the concerns of the unknowns related to the virus and on-flight transmission, many relied on traveling by plane to quickly access destinations they may not be able to reach otherwise. Whether it was for business or pleasure, many passengers boarded planes with some degree of confidence in airlines facilitating a safe experience. For instance, the measures that Delta Air Lines put into place during the pandemic addressed instructional information and support that enabled the company to express how its brand was dedicated to customer safety. Customers connected with each other and the brand in new spaces, such as a room on Clubhouse, posts on Facebook, videos on YouTube, conversations through a smartphone app, and on the @DeltaAssist Twitter (X) page, which was the first airline Twitter (X) account created for customer support. Delta's early investment in serving customers and in-flight accommodations like contactless experiences during the pandemic may have helped the airline secure a COVID-19 Airline Excellence Award in Skytrax's (2021) airline rankings, which were based on 13.42 million customer survey responses. In an industry that took a major hit when there was no longer a need for travel during "stay-at-home" orders, airlines across the globe continued to find inventive ways to prioritize the customer experience (Figure 7.2). Not only did airlines invent words like "deplane," but they reinvented how to safely travel across nations and continents during a global pandemic. Take this chapter as evidence. It was drafted from seat 15C on a cross-country Delta Air Lines flight during the pandemic.

Creating Durable Relationships

Virtually every industry was affected during the COVID-19 pandemic, creating obstacles between organizations and their publics. With distancing and stay-at-home orders, organizations could not research customers with in-store experiences and traditional platforms for communicating messages, such as billboards and radio ads that might expose customers to messages during travel. In acknowledging these limitations, organizations explored ways to position their brand, direct marketing online, and engaged in PR efforts that were meaningful and relevant to stakeholders. Perceptions of a brand are important to monitor because when positive, companies benefit by cultivating positive relationships with customers, and when negative, stakeholders may express negative responses, such as negative word-of-mouth behaviors amplified on social media (Huang et al., 2020; Schneider et al., 2021). Organizations utilized blogs, website landing pages, smartphone applications, social media, and other platforms to attract potential customers and engage with existing relationships. It is no doubt that the pandemic stimulated inventive ways to create real, digital connections to respond to rapidly evolving situations. Organizations became aware of how their marketing and PR efforts resonated with stakeholders and many devoted resources to provide intentional, informed decisions to strategically navigate emerging issues.

Although brands were quick to adapt during the pandemic, many realized new ways to reach and satisfy stakeholder needs and intend to continue efforts initially created in response to COVID-19. Bynder's (2020) State of Branding Report includes survey insight from 301 creative, marketing, and brand professionals. They found that out of respondents surveyed, 36% had increased their output of marketing campaigns since the COVID-19 outbreak and 53% saw the development of new messaging, content, and campaigns in direct response to COVID-19 as their highest branding-related priority at the onset of the pandemic. Marketing and PR professionals were faced with new challenges in their roles, and the effective campaigns noted in this chapter illustrate how many professionals used their expertise to adapt digitally driven brand strategies for organizational survival.

Recommendations for Future Research

It is evident that investing in ways to benefit the public is an effective way to design and coordinate PR campaigns and promote efforts with marketing. During COVID-19, however, there was an abundance of pandemic messaging. It may be important to question if this wave of messaging, although driven by good intentions to address concerns, creates negative affect. Could these communicative efforts cause customers inundated with messages surrounding the same issue to feel anxious, fearful, or, worse, apathetic toward the concern? An abundance of pandemic-related news and widespread media coverage has been thought to lead to psychological problems like anxiety (e.g., Teng et al., 2020), and future research could assess how marketing and PR are used to seriously convey efforts without overwhelming the public.

Future research could also assess circumstances in which brands appear disingenuous in their efforts, such as by partaking in perceived brand opportunism. Earlier in the chapter, for instance, it was noted how some brands understood how to align with pandemic-related efforts. In instances where the brand and issue are inconsistent, or when an organization appears to be capitalizing on an issue, they may lose the trust of customers (Mundel & Yang, 2021). These instances should be investigated to share how it is not only important for brands to engage with issues their stakeholders care about, but how they should communicate the engagement to promote meaningful change. Congruence theory may be one lens to understand how the perceived congruence, such as the relevance and fit with the issue, leads to attitudes and behaviors in support of or against the organization (Jagre et al., 2001). Applications of corporate social responsibility, for instance, find that stakeholders may perceive the brand more credible when campaigns "fit" with the brand (Cha et al., 2016). Additionally, there are other concepts within PR and marketing that may be used to evaluate the effectiveness of an IMC campaign. The present analysis captured how the organizations faced unique circumstances within their respective industries during the onset of the pandemic. Future research may assess other cases and also recognize how brands evolved with the passage of time during the pandemic.

Key Terms

Brand: A powerful, strategic projection that connects an organization's identity and public perceptions. A brand represents the experience of a company by means of its name, color, symbol, and other identifiers that position an organization.

Marketing: Paid communication controlled, promoted, and directed at a specific goal, such as attracting potential customers. Marketing involves using sponsored content and advertisements and techniques to promote a good or service.

Public relations: A discipline and profession involved with organizational process of making informed decisions for the public's best interest and communicating the information that generates meaningful engagement. The ways an organization communicates affects public perception and how relationships are developed and maintained. Publics are constituents that are affected by and have the ability to affect an organization with relationships, such as customers and employees.

Social media: Platforms for sharing information and creating meaning through one-way or two-way communication. As internet-based applications, such as Facebook and Twitter (X), they enable users to create and exchange messages and develop networks.

Discussion Questions

1. Based on the readings, in what ways did Texas Roadhouse effectively direct their public relations efforts to engage with potential and current customers? In brands that you follow, how have you seen a company prioritize its stakeholders through a PR campaign?
2. Based on the readings, in what ways did the airlines effectively position their brands, but ineffectively respond to their publics? In brands that you follow, how have you seen companies ineffectively position their brand?
3. How can social listening and monitoring be used to inform strategies for marketing and public relations efforts?
4. If you were hypothetically asked to communicate a new law or regulation that you anticipate customers to push back on, how could you position your branding, marketing, and PR efforts to address the challenges?

Resources

1. Delta Air Lines. (2020, August 24). *Watch how Delta ensures cleaner surfaces across travel journey.* https://news.delta.com/watch-how-delta-ensures-cleaner-surfaces-across-travel-journey
2. Forbes. (2020, August 31). *Lessons from the early days of "covid-branding."* https://www.forbes.com/sites/davidhessekiel/2020/08/31/lessons-from-the-early-days-of-covid-branding/?sh=25bf1a835c15

References

Allert, J.R. (1999). Ethics in communication: The role of public relations. In S.K. Chakraborty & S.R. Chatterjee (Eds.), *Applied ethics in management* (pp. 187–203). Springer. https://doi.org/10.1007/978-3-642-60151-4_12

American Airlines. (n.d.). *American Airlines Group.* https://www.aa.com/i18n/customer-service/about-us/american-airlines-group.jsp

Arief, N.N., & Pangestu, A.B. (2021). Perception and sentiment analysis on empathic brand initiative during the COVID-19 pandemic: Indonesia perspective. *Journal of Creative Communications.* https://doi.org/10.1177/09732586211031164

Aten, J. (2020, June 28). *United and American Airlines are making customers angry with this change.* Inc. https://www.inc.com/jason-aten/united-american-airlines-are-making-customers-angry-with-this-change.html

Barger, V., Peltier, J.W., & Schultz, D.E. (2016). Social media and consumer engagement: A review and research agenda. *Journal of Research in Interactive Marketing, 10*(4), 268–287. https://doi.org/10.1108/JRIM-06-2016-0065

Bird, S. (2004). *Marketing communications.* Juta and Company.

Bynder. (2020). *The state of branding report: COVID-19 edition.* https://www.bynder.com/en/state-of-branding/2020-covid-19/

Bynder. (2021). *The state of branding report: 2021 edition.* https://www.bynder.com/en/state-of-branding/2021/

Cawthon, H. (2021, April 30). *"We know the recipe to succeed." New Texas Roadhouse CEO on Taylor's legacy.* Louisville Business First. https://www.bizjournals.com/louisville/news/2021/04/30/texas-roadhouse-q1-earnings-2021.html

Cha, M.-K., Yi, Y., & Bagozzi, R.P. (2016). Effects of customer participation in corporate social responsibility (CSR) programs on the CSR-brand fit and brand loyalty. *Cornell Hospitality Quarterly, 57*(3), 235–249. https://doi.org/10.1177/1938965515620679

Christie, D. (2020, April 27). American Airlines' ad signals return to brand-building. *Marketing Dive.* https://www.marketingdive.com/news/american-airlines-ad-signals-return-to-brand-building/576787/

Delta. (2020, March 27). *Supporting the front lines: Medical volunteers can book free Delta flights to Georgia, Louisiana, Michigan.* Delta News Hub. https://news.delta.com/supporting-front-lines-medical-volunteers-can-book-free-delta-flights-georgia-louisiana-michigan

Delta. (2021a, August 25). *Bastian memo to employees outlines COVID vaccine updates.* Delta News Hub. https://news.delta.com/bastian-memo-employees-outlines-covid-vaccine-updates

Delta. (2021b, January 29). *Delta launches first domestic digital identity test in U.S., providing touchless curb-to-gate experience.* Delta News Hub. https://news.delta.com/delta-launches-first-domestic-digital-identity-test-us-providing-touchless-curb-gate-experience

Delta. (2021c, September 23). *Memos reflect Delta's commitment to employee and passenger safety.* Delta News Hub. https://news.delta.com/memos-reflect-deltas-commitment-employee-and-passenger-safety

Doe-Anderson. (2021). *Roadhouse in the house.* Texas Roadhouse. https://www.doeanderson.com/our-work/texas-roadhouse-restaurant-brand-awareness

FAA. (2021, October 25). *Unruly passengers.* United States Department of Transportation: Federal Aviation Administration. https://www.faa.gov/data_research/passengers_cargo/unruly_passengers/

Hatch, M.J., & Schultz, M. (2002). The dynamics of organizational identity. *Human Relations*, 55(8), 989–1018. https://doi.org/10.1177/0018726702055008181

Heater, B. (2021, August 25). *Salad chain Sweetgreen buys kitchen robotics startup Spyce*. TechCrunch. https://techcrunch.com/2021/08/25/salad-chain-sweetgreen-buys-kitchen-robotics-startup-spyce/

Huang, L., Wang, M., Chen, Z., Deng, B., & Huang, W. (2020). Brand image and customer loyalty: Transmitting roles of cognitive and affective brand trust. *Social Behavior and Personality: An International Journal*, 48(5), 1–12. https://doi.org/10.2224/sbp.9069

IATA. (2021, August 3). *Airline industry statistics confirm 2020 was worst year on record*. Pressroom. https://www.iata.org/en/pressroom/pr/2021-08-03-01/

Jagre, E., Watson, J.J., & Watson, J.G. (2001). Sponsorship and congruity theory: A theoretical framework for explaining consumer attitude and recall of event sponsorship. In M.C. Gilly & J. Meyers-Levy (Eds.), *Advances in consumer research*. Association for Consumer Research. https://www.acrwebsite.org/volumes/8544/volumes/v28/NA-28

Johnson, L.M., & Williams, D. (2021, September 8). *They will even sing "Happy Birthday." Robots are picking up unwanted jobs at a Latin restaurant in Texas*. CNN Business. https://www.cnn.com/2021/09/07/business/dallas-restaurant-employs-robots-trnd/index.html

Josephs, L. (2021, July 15). *American Airlines cancels flight attendants' voluntary leaves, plans to hire 800 to meet travel demand*. CNBC. https://www.cnbc.com/2021/07/15/american-airlines-calls-flight-attendants-back-to-work-will-hire-to-meet-demand.html

Kapferer, J.N. (2002). Corporate brand and organizational identity. In B. Moingeon & G. Soenen (Eds.), *Corporate and organizational identities: Integrating strategy, marketing, communication and organizational perspectives* (pp. 175–194). Routledge.

Kitchen, P.J., & Burgmann, I. (2010). Integrated marketing communication. In J. Sheth (Ed.), *Wiley international encyclopedia of marketing*. Wiley. https://doi.org/10.1002/9781444316568.wiem04001

Kitterman, T. (2020, May 29). *How Texas Roadhouse envisions purpose during COVID-19*. PR Daily. https://www.prdaily.com/how-texas-roadhouse-envisions-purpose-during-covid-19/

KMTV. (2020, March 19). *Restaurants adapt to restrictions amid coronavirus*. KMTV News Now. https://www.3newsnow.com/news/coronavirus/restaurants-adapt-to-restrictions-amid-coronavirus

Li, F., Larimo, J., & Leonidou, L.C. (2021). Social media marketing strategy: Definition, conceptualization, taxonomy, validation, and future agenda. *Journal of the Academy of Marketing Science*, 49, 51–70 https://doi.org/10.1007/s11747-020-00733-3

Mack, Z. (2021, September 13). *Major airlines are banning this one thing on all flights*. Best Life. https://bestlifeonline.com/news-airlines-banning-alcohol/?utm_source=morning_brew

Mahmud, A., Ding, D., & Hasan, M.M. (2021). Corporate social responsibility: Business responses to coronavirus (COVID-19) pandemic. *SAGE Open*, 11(1). https://doi.org/10.1177/2158244020988710

Miso Robotics. (2021). *To develop, pilot, and undertake a beta rollout for Miso Robotics' Flippy for White Castle's North American restaurants*. Meet Flippy. https://invest.misorobotics.com/?utm_source=rgamisolandingpage&utm_medium=partmb1017&utm_campaign=partmb10178&tnames=partmb1017

Morris, C. (2021, April 1). *Pandemic killed off 10% of U.S. restaurants. Food trucks among the hardest hit, report finds*. Fortune. https://fortune.com/2021/04/01/restaurants-closed-2020-pandemic-100000-jobs-lost-how-many-have-closed-us-covid-pandemic-stimulus-unemployment/

Mundel, J., & Yang, J. (2021). Consumer engagement with brands' COVID-19 messaging on social media: The role of perceived brand–social issue fit and brand opportunism. *Journal of Interactive Advertising*, 1–18. https://doi.org/10.1080/15252019.2021.1958274

NYU Dispatch. (2021). *Origin of QR codes and why they're on the rise*. https://wp.nyu.edu/dispatch/origin-of-qr-codes-and-why-theyre-on-the-rise/

Oswald, L.R., & Oswald, L. (2012). *Marketing semiotics: Signs, strategies, and brand value*. Oxford University Press.

Peraza, S. (2020, April 17). *Delta has 200,000 pounds of food we can't use. So we're giving it to people in need*. Delta News Hub. https://news.delta.com/delta-has-200000-pounds-food-we-cant-use-so-were-giving-it-people-need

PR Newswire. (2021, March 29). *Datassential: 10% of all U.S. restaurants have closed permanently since the pandemic began*. Cision PR Newswire. https://www.prnewswire.com/news-releases/datassential-10-of-all-us-restaurants-have-closed-permanently-since-the-pandemic-began-301257197.html

Rugaber, C. (2021, October 12). *Americans quit their jobs at a record pace in August*. AP News. https://apnews.com/article/business-459c0884721a213985cdf0185a1176f8?utm_source=morning_brew&utm_medium=newsletter&utm_campaign=mb

Ruggless, R. (2021, February 19). *Texas Roadhouse sees pandemic strengthening to-go sales*. Nation's Restaurant News. https://www.nrn.com/casual-dining/texas-roadhouse-sees-pandemic-strengthening-go-sales

Schneider, E.J., Boman, C.D., & Akin, H. (2021). The amplified crisis: Assessing negative social amplification and source of a crisis response. *Communication Reports*, 34(3), 165–178. https://doi.org/10.1080/08934215.2021.1966064

Schultz, D.E., & Schultz, H.F. (1998). Transitioning marketing communication into the twenty-first century. *Journal of Marketing Communications*, 4(1), 9–26. https://doi.org/10.1080/135272698345852

Schweidel, D.A., & Moe, W.W. (2014). Listening in on social media: A joint model of sentiment and venue format choice. *Journal of Marketing Research*, 51(4), 387–402. https://doi.org/10.1509/jmr.12.0424

Shivdas, S. (2021, July 13). *American Airlines forecasts first positive cash flow since pandemic began*. Reuters. https://www.reuters.com/business/aerospace-defense/american-airlines-sees-adjusted-net-loss-up-12-bln-second-quarter-2021-07-13/

Shvedsky, L. (2020, March 29). *Texas Roadhouse CEO giving up his salary and bonus to pay workers during coronavirus outbreak*. Upworthy. https://www.upworthy.com/coronavirus-texas-roadhouse-ceo-gives-up-salary

Sillers, P. (2020, May 22). *Here's how Covid-19 could change the way we fly*. CNN Travel. https://www.cnn.com/travel/article/air-travel-future-covid-19/index.html

Simmons, S. (2020, May 2). *Safety at "Steak": Restaurants adapt to COVID-19 restrictions.* Tri-state Livestock News. https://www.tsln.com/news/safety-at-steak-restaurants-adapt-to-covid-19-restrictions/

Sink, V. (2020, September 14). *100,000 restaurants closed six months into pandemic.* National Restaurant Association. https://restaurant.org/news/pressroom/press-releases/100000-restaurants-closed-six-months-into-pandemic

Skytrax. (2021, September 27). *2021 World Airline Awards methodology.* https://www.worldairlineawards.com/awards-methodology/

Smith, R.D. (2020). *Strategic planning for public relations.* Routledge.

Solis, B., & Breakenridge, D.K. (2009). *Putting the public back in public relations: How social media is reinventing the aging business of PR.* Ft Press.

Tate, J.A., & Happ, M.B. (2018). Qualitative secondary analysis: A case exemplar. *Journal of Pediatric Health Care, 32*(3), 308–312. https://doi.org/10.1016/j.pedhc.2017.09.007

Teng, Z., Wei, Z., Qiu, Y., Tan, Y., Chen, J., Tang, H., Wu, H., Wu, R., & Huang, J. (2020). Psychological status and fatigue of frontline staff two months after the COVID-19 pandemic outbreak in China: A cross-sectional study. *Journal of Affective Disorders, 275*(1), 247–252. https://doi.org/10.1016/j.jad.2020.06.032

Texas Roadhouse. (2020a, April 3). *Thank you to our friend Willie Nelson for the beautiful rendition of "On the Road Again" and his kind words . . .* [Facebook post]. Facebook. https://m.facebook.com/texasroadhouse/posts/10158326889504228?comment_id=10158329182604228

Texas Roadhouse. (2020b, July 6). *As we re-open our dining room, guest safety remains a top priority. That's why we're happy to introduce contactless menus . . .* [Facebook post]. Facebook.https://m.facebook.com/texasroadhouse/photos/a.403736404227/10158645860964228/?type=3&source=48&__tn__=EH-R

Texas Roadhouse [@texasroadhouse]. (2020c, April 5). *Our jukeboxes may be paused, but the music doesn't stop. That's why we created a Spotify playlist that features our . . .* [Tweet]. Twitter. https://twitter.com/texasroadhouse/status/1246852601263484929?lang=en

Warpinski, J. (2020, April 2). *Delta Flight Products to manufacture personal protective equipment to help healthcare workers.* Delta News Hub. https://news.delta.com/delta-flight-products-manufacture-personal-protective-equipment-help-healthcare-workers

· 8 ·

ADVERTISING AS A FORM OF PUBLIC HEALTH EDUCATION: AN ANALYSIS OF THE AD COUNCIL AND COVID COLLABORATIVE'S "IT'S UP TO YOU" VACCINATION AWARENESS CAMPAIGN

Janelle Applequist & Jeanette Abrahamsen

The campaign features every major sports league you can think of (the NFL, NHL, NBA, WNBA, MLB, NWSL, MLS, NASCAR, PGA, WWE), Willie Nelson, Elmo and all of his friends on Sesame Street, the Pope, former Presidents Barack Obama, Bill Clinton, and George W. Bush, Viola Davis, Simone Biles, Family Guy, and Dr. Anthony Fauci. Those are just a few of the recognizable names, organizations, and television shows that provided their likeness for the "It's Up to You" advertising campaign, launched in February 2021, aimed at helping to build trust with Americans who may be hesitant about getting the COVID-19 vaccine (Harvard, 2021). The campaign was launched by the Ad Council and the COVID Collaborative in conjunction with the Centers for Disease Control and Prevention (CDC). The Ad Council is a nonprofit advertising group responsible for launching many of the pro-social ads we know and love, including Smokey the Bear, Friends Don't Let Friends Drive Drunk, and Love Has no Labels (Ad Council, 2021). The COVID Collaborative is a combination of the nation's leading experts in health, education, and economics aimed at helping to stop the spread of COVID-19 through accurate information (COVID Collaborative, 2021).

"It's Up to You" features an integrated marketing communications approach, meaning that multiple platforms and materials have been integrated, including television, billboards, bus shelters, social media, print publications, as well as ads specifically created to target opinion leaders such as doctors, pharmacists, and church leaders (Harvard, 2021). The campaign includes broadcast ads in English and Spanish to reach more individuals, with website information featuring seven languages (Stobbe, 2021). Another important consideration made by the campaign is its attention to materials tailored to Black and Hispanic populations, where COVID-19 vaccination hesitancy is of significant and understandable concern (Ad Council, 2021; Kricorian & Turner, 2021).

The campaign is continuing to run through 2021, with no end date in sight, and cost $52 million. It was funded entirely by donations for labor, resources, and ad space (Stobbe, 2021). Apple, Facebook, Walmart, Amazon, Google, Verizon, NBCUniversal, Walgreens, and CVS are just a few of the corporate entities that provided leading contributions to the initiative (Ad Council, 2021). The Ad Council notes on its website that it did not receive any funding from pharmaceutical companies or political organizations for the COVID-19 Vaccine Education Initiative, but that it does receive "annual operating general support" from these entities (Ad Council, 2021).

On its surface, or in the traditional sense, a promotion from the "It's Up to You" campaign would be classified as a public service announcement, because it is meant to raise awareness about an important public health issue (Penn State, 2017). Upon further investigation, however, once you consider the corporate ties mentioned above, the campaign becomes classified as advertising because of its ties to paid, mediated content—even if in the form of a donation. While the ends certainly justify the means in this case (to get individuals vaccinated and to eradicate COVID-19), it is important to acknowledge that the corporations associated with this campaign are still benefiting from the cause-related marketing, or corporate social responsibility, associated with it. It benefits a brand to be able to say that they donated to a worthwhile cause, meaning that their public image can be seen in an improved light by their customers—in addition to the tax write-off they receive in exchange for their donations.

Methods

Case Study

This chapter uses two methods to achieve its goal of analyzing the "It's Up to You" advertising campaign. First, the case study method provides a detailed examination of one event (the ad campaign), in an effort to further understand a real-life event within its context (Mitchell, 1983; Yin, 1994). It is important that case study research rely upon multiple sources of evidence in order to ensure that a robust, holistic picture of the situation is being presented. As such, this chapter will utilize three sources of data from the campaign—broadcast ads, the primary campaign website, and social media posts. In order to analyze these advertisements and campaign materials, a second method is necessary.

Textual Analysis

Textual analysis is a methodology that permits for critically analyzing how a text may be understood via various message cues (Allen, 2017). A more straightforward way to think of a textual analysis would be to look at a media artifact and ask yourself, "what is the meaning of this text?" (Allen, 2017). In this case, a "text" can be any piece of media or culture, whether it be a book, film, song, or in the case of this chapter, an advertisement. A textual analysis permits for a deeper investigation into the ways in which individual texts use format, setting, characters, and the presentation of problems and solutions to sell particular ideas to audiences (Applequist, 2020; Gitlin, 1979; Centers for Disease Control and Prevention, 2021). While each ad was analyzed individually, the results are presented in a collective format in an effort to identify the overall themes apparent in the texts themselves, with examples presented in an effort to showcase our findings.

We positioned this chapter from the lens of the critical advertising studies (CAS) paradigm, which examines the role advertising plays in society. Stemming from critical theory, CAS permits for the broader analysis of the role the media and advertising play in influencing audiences, while allowing for consideration of the ideological consequences of promotional messaging (Ewen, 1976; Jhally, 1987; Williamson, 1978). CAS allows for the investigation of meaning-making practices inherent in the advertising industry, where ads act as significant cultural messages that help to establish social norms and elevate brands beyond the material functions of the products they promote (Applequist, 2016; Williams, 1980). Therefore, an important component of CAS involves analyzing the thematic nature of advertising messaging in an effort to understand what ideologies are being perpetuated to audiences. Thus, it could be argued that CAS is similar to more foundational theories such as framing, agenda setting, or traditional persuasion literature, where media are used to influence audiences in particular ways. CAS, however, often takes a more in-depth approach toward this investigation, meriting the need for the textual analysis method utilized in this study.

We followed Stern's postmodern literary framework for conducting a textual analysis, which involves the systematic identification and analysis of individual elements of the ads, followed by a deeper investigation of the meaning embedded in those elements, keeping in mind the deconstruction of any sociological meanings that may be present (Stern, 1996). This approach blends well with CAS, as it relies upon postmodern interpretations that account for language and rhetoric used in advertisements in addition to cultural assumptions and contextual cues (Stern, 1996). Therefore, this relates to the case study methodology by allowing for particular moments in time to be analyzed via triangulation, with a fuller interpretation investigating how different aspects of a text may be interpreted according to social contexts and cultural underpinnings of persuasion (Stern, 1996).

Our focus was on identifying the overall thematic content of the "It's Up to You" advertising campaign, while permitting for a deeper visual semiotic analysis of the linguistic, denotative, and connotative levels that could be identified from the campaign's elements (Barthes, 1972; Fowles, 1996). Linguistic elements are associated with written words, denotative meanings are attached to photographs, images, or symbols, and connotative meanings are linked with "imagined communication" that produce consistent ideas that can be linked to the campaign's overall elements (Fowles, 1996, p. 169).

We first engaged in an independent process of identifying themes we saw present in accordance with the frameworks outlined by Stern (1996) above, also using Fowles' 23-item list as a guiding framework for our analyses (1996). Both authors independently coded the entire dataset, first engaging in data immersion and creating memos of our initial impressions. Next, we created independent initial themes as they arose to help guide our processes. We then came together to compare our findings to determine consistency. Overall themes were very similar, and both authors merged their coding categories to reflect the iterative process of the textual analysis process. This is the point at which individual coding disagreements were resolved.

In total, the campaign's primary website, 51 broadcast ads from the Ad Council's YouTube playlist, and 125 social media posts associated with the campaign were collected and analyzed. Data were collected and analyzed in September and October of 2021, representing a particular snapshot in time during the pandemic.

Findings

Evaluation of the "It's Up to You" Advertising Campaign

Website

Upon visiting the campaign's primary website, it is clear that a two-pronged approach is being utilized. The primary theme being emphasized on the website is that of scientifically backed information that puts the consumer in the driver's seat for finding out more information (It's Up to You, 2021). The secondary theme, depicted visually, is one the emotional benefits that will result from being vaccinated (relationships with loved ones, keeping others safe, etc.).

The website rhetorically positions its focus on information in an empowering way for the viewer, posing a series of questions on the homepage where one can seek answers at their own pace. For those who are already vaccine hesitant, this strategy is sound. In advertising efforts aimed at attempting to mitigate risk (e.g., drinking alcohol, smoking cigarettes, wearing seatbelts), it is common for a "boomerang effect" to take place, whereby messaging runs the risk of coming off as judgmental, threatening, or infringing on one's personal freedoms—if and when it does, the ad runs the risk of making a consumer even more unlikely to change their behavior (Ringold, 2002). By posing the information in question-prompt formats, the messaging comes off as inviting and less threatening. The website banner reads: "[H]ave questions about COVID-19 vaccines? Here's where to start." A ticker below shows the number of people in the United States who received their first dose of the vaccine. As one scrolls down the homepage, the questions are posed in easy-to-understand, straightforward terms that are visually appealing (e.g., "How do the vaccines protect me?" "How do we know they're safe?" "What are the benefits of getting vaccinated?"). The clean lines, limited amount of text, and crisp colors all correspond with Rosen and Purinton's (2004) Website Preference Scale (WSPS), which identifies dimensions of effective website design that lead to higher chances of revisits.

There is one mention of a "hear from healthcare providers" at the bottom of the page, but the emphasis on the information is simplicity. The Ad Council and COVID Collaborative gathered all information for the website and campaign materials from physicians and leading industry experts, but the design of the website was clearly done with consumers in mind.

Visually, the website is free of clutter and relies on the campaign's yellow and white color scheme to maintain its brand consistency. This was a positive decision, as the website is organized in a way that does not overwhelm an individual. It is important to remember that someone visiting this website may be in an emotional state, grappling with the idea of getting vaccinated against their better judgment, which often raises many social, cultural, and political issues. As such, bringing a lot of "clutter" into the mix would only deter someone away from focusing on the most important element of the equation—scientifically backed information. Therefore, the design of the website and its elements are sound, as previous research shows that simplicity in design is an important factor in this form of media persuasion (Rosen & Purinton, 2004).

There are two visual images included on the website. One is featured in the banner and depicts an older white gentleman hugging another individual. The other is a thumbnail of a broadcast ad, featured on the bottom of the webpage, and features a young Black girl blowing out her birthday candles. The use of both images serves as a useful reminder to website visitors that there is more at stake than simply our own health—but our relationships with others as well. Thus, the website's use of positive imagery is well-executed. However, if the campaign's intention was to focus on vaccine-hesitant communities, it stands to reason that an image of an African American or Hispanic individual or individuals should have been used in the banner. Representation matters and this was classified as a missed opportunity to say the least. Media have historically either underrepresented minority populations, or stereotyped individuals in ways that further normalize existing systems of oppression (Kido Lopez, 2020). In instances where minority characters are featured, it is often the case that these representations are "plastic," depicting flattened, artificial caricatures of people rather than multifaceted, culturally specific humans with complex traits (Warner, 2017).

Finally, one of the best aspects of the website was its "action step" available to visitors, whereby they could enter their zip code and find their closest vaccination site. This addition allowed for advertising to extend beyond the act of informing during a pandemic, but enacting change.

Broadcast Ads

The broadcast ads, housed on YouTube, represented the data with the greatest emotional, humanistic elements out of our overall dataset (Ad Council YouTube Channel, 2021). In total, 51 ads were analyzed, with 13 of the ads being classified as strictly informational, 6 categorized as purely emotional, and the majority (32) using a combination of emotional and informational elements.

Emotional appeals are those that are based on images and video, and rely on the use of feelings or emotions to get audiences to relate to the message being conveyed (Gray et al., 2012; Wilson & Wolf, 2009). Informational appeals use rational arguments that are based on facts (Aaker & Norris, 1982).

Ads that were purely informational all used an infographic style. These ads were simplistic and focused on various topics such as the need to rethink traveling, the importance of washing your hands for 20 seconds at a time, and the necessity of wearing a mask.

The emotional ads were understandably more poignant, featuring notable appearances from celebrities. One sub-campaign featuring Viola Davis, Stephen A. Smith, Simone Biles, and others, showcases the stars discussing how even though there is so much against the Black community, they choose to protect themselves, their families, and their communities by wearing masks. These ads use powerful imagery from the Black Lives Matter movement during the opening segments to reiterate the significant challenges still being faced by communities of color while addressing how the coronavirus is a significant concern for African Americans. Here, the message is not one of science or vaccination, but based on emotion and the need to protect one's community.

The "we're all in this together" sentiment was a common theme in the emotional element category, which was well highlighted in another sub-campaign titled "Mask Up America." In one of the ads, a series of simplistic visuals features individuals of all races and ages wearing masks. The narrator says, "[s]how some respect. Some you give a damn. Show the world how it's done. Show that when your community needed you most, you showed up. Mask up, America." The use of background music assists in making the message more poignant.

The most common theme to emerge from the broadcast ads was the use of the combination emotional/informational tactic. The most frequent way this was conveyed was through the narrative that by doing the right things (social distancing/wearing a mask/getting vaccinated), we will soon be able to be together with our loved ones and do the things we were once doing. These choices were always framed as positive steps in the right direction, meaning, what one would gain as a result of doing the right thing. Thus, getting vaccinated, wearing a mask, social distancing, etc. were framed in a positive light, rather than focusing on the negatives that one might associate with having to perform those behaviors.

For example, an ad aimed at children and parents featuring Sesame Street characters discussed the challenges that come with the transition to virtual learning. At first, Elmo stresses the importance of wearing his mask to protect his friends while he will be at school. When his dad informs him that he will not be going to school that day, but learning online instead, Elmo expresses confusion. He removes his mask, and Elmo's dad addresses the camera and reminds parents at home that this can be a difficult time for everyone and reminds them to take deep breaths. The ad ends with the slogan that we're "caring for each other because we are all in this together."

Another example of the emotional/information appeal was the ad featuring Pope Francis, the Archbishops of the United States and Peru, and the Cardinals of Mexico, Honduras, Brazil, and El Salvador. This spot features each religious figure discussing the scientific reliability of the vaccine while addressing that getting vaccinated is an act of love, again addressing the overarching message that we are all in this together.

Another ad featuring former Presidents Obama, Clinton, and Bush highlight the importance and efficacy of the vaccine while showcasing their personal sides, having them reflect on what they are most looking forward to "getting back to" post-COVID-19. Getting to visit with Michelle's mom, getting back to work, and finally getting to attend a Texas Rangers game allow the audience to connect with each of the former Chiefs of Staff.

The use of celebrities and cultural icons is a common occurrence in these ads. Athletes, overall sports organizations, television shows, children's programs, influencers, and the like are featured in the ads, but could not be fully contextualized due to space limitations in this chapter. It is clear in our analysis that the use of the cultural icons was a strategic choice in this campaign—the ads that feature recognizable figures have a certain heir of gravitas that captures your attention in a more profound way. This notion is supported by one study that found that Tom Hanks' disclosure of his positive COVID-19 test in 2020 resulted in increased non-celebrity perceptions of susceptibility to the virus, showing the ways in which celebrity advocacy of public health issues may help to guide individual decision-making (Cohen, 2020).

One ad titled "Back in the Game" features vignettes of sports events around the United States (Serena Williams winning a match, a Terrible Towel waving in the air, fans cheering during an NFL game) as Willie Nelson softly sang "I'll be seeing you"—as the screen fades to black, the on-screen text reads "the COVID-19 vaccines are here. We'll see you soon." Even while analyzing these ads, it was hard to watch the ad and not become emotional as you reflect on the past two years and all that everyone has endured. This makes sense when taking into account the wealth of advertising research that has been conducted showing the integral role emotions play in human information processing and persuasion/behavior (Kover, 1995; Poels & Dewitte, 2019; Vakratsas & Ambler, 1999; Zajonc, 1980).

For all of the glitz and glamor that professional sports and celebrities bring to the table, there is nothing more powerful than authentic, human connection. The most influential ad to be analyzed from this dataset was titled "Do it for Me," and was featured in long- and short-forms. Classified as an informational and emotional appeal in our analysis, the ad featured a series of authentic conversations between friends and family whose opinions differed on the COVID-19 vaccine, but ultimately resulted in one party wanting the other to understand that their rationale for wanting the other to get it was because they cared about them. It featured elements of scientific information, but did rely more heavily on emotional appeal. The ad represented what we feel to be an excellent example of the ways in which advertising can start a conversation about important, and sometimes very difficult, societal issues. In this case, advertising can also serve as a form of public education during a time when it is desperately needed.

Social Media

Social media is a powerful tool to reach mass audiences with important information about COVID-19. It can be particularly powerful when amplified by celebrity voices with huge social media followings. Unfortunately, the "It's Up to You" campaign failed to use strategic techniques that would have helped them get their message in front of more people. Our study looked at the campaign's use of YouTube, Facebook, and Instagram. Several overarching missed opportunities stood out across all platforms. Some issues include a lack of consistent naming, keywords, and hashtags. Our study first approached the analysis of the social media strategy by identifying challenges the public may face when searching for more information related to the campaign.

The It's Up to You campaign is housed on the Get Vaccine Answers website. The website does not link to social media in the footer or menu. This makes it harder for people to find and share the campaign on social media. While the words "It's Up to You" are displayed in an image, the words are not written anywhere on the homepage or the about page. This lack of keyword integration across platforms hurts the campaign's credibility and searchability because it fails to capitalize on search engine optimization.

The hashtag #itsuptoyou was used in more than 183,000 Instagram posts. While we did not find posts with that hashtag associated with the Ad Council campaign, we did find the hashtag used in several unrelated accounts. This suggests the campaign slogan was not unique enough to be used as an effective hashtag. Inadvertently sending people to unaffiliated accounts makes it hard for the Ad Council to control the narrative and ensure accuracy. It can be particularly risky for the Ad Council if people perceive unaffiliated campaigns as accurate sources of information.

The hashtag #getvaccineanswers resulted in 103 Instagram posts. None of the posts came from the Ad Council Instagram account. Seven of the posts were published by the News Media Alliance. The account has less than 900 followers. The body of the posts says they partnered with the Ad Council. Twenty-six of the posts that featured the #getvaccineanswers hashtag were published by the We Are Greater Than COVID account. The account has just over 600 followers. The account pushes users to get more information about the vaccine on greaterthancovid.org. Seventeen of the posts containing the #getvaccineanswers hashtag used the "It's Up To You" band-aid logo. However, none were tied to the Ad Council Instagram account.

The Ad Council Instagram account first posted about the campaign on February 25, 2021. From then until October 27, 2021, the Ad Council Instagram account published 23 posts related to the COVID-19 vaccine. None of the posts included a hashtag despite the fact that social media leaders like Hootsuite stress that hashtags are important for expanding audience reach (Newberry, 2021). Texts in post descriptions were not consistent. Some of the posts included a push to getvaccineanswers.org. Some did not. Some used the words "It's Up To You." Others did not. Some posts included "COVID Collaborative." The use of the campaign's keywords appears arbitrary. Of their 23 Instagram posts, 87% were video. Hubspot and Mention's 2021 Instagram Engagement Report found that video content is the best way to generate engagement (Hubspot/Mention, 2021).

An Instagram account named Get Vaccine Answers exists on Instagram. While it appears to be run by the Ad Council, it only has 90 followers and 11 posts despite the first post being published in February of 2021. The account thumbnail features the It's Up to You band-aid logo in gray, not yellow. Six of the posts feature the It's Up to You logo in the post thumbnail. All videos and photos are related to the vaccine. This fragmented and inconsistent messaging is not ideal when your goal is to reach a mass audience that is already skeptical of your message.

The Ad Council published its first Facebook post about the campaign on February 25, 2021. They published 42 posts about the campaign from then until October 27, 2021. Of those, only eight included hashtags. #GetVaccineAnswers was used only once. #ItsUpToYou was not used at all. However, the Spanish version of the hashtag, #DeTiDepende, was used twice. Twenty-three of the posts were videos totaling more than 750,000 views. The most viewed video promoted the #VaxLive concert. The words "It's Up to You" and getvaccineanswers.org were only displayed in the video at the very end. #VaxLive was the only hashtag in the post description. This suggests the Ad Council missed an opportunity to raise awareness about the campaign since more than 423,000 people watched the video.

The Ad Council's YouTube channel has a playlist called "COVID-19 Vaccine Education Effort." The playlist is not featured on the YouTube channel's homepage. Featuring the playlist more prominently would make it easier to find videos about the campaign. The playlist title includes the keywords "COVID" and "vaccine" but the words "It's Up To You" are not included in the playlist title nor can the words be found anywhere in the 58 video titles. Some prominent videos in the campaign were not added to the playlist despite having been uploaded to the YouTube account. Some other missed opportunities on YouTube include failing to use keywords in video titles. For example, the video series that featured Pope Francis was titled "Unity Across the Americas | COVID-19 Vaccine Education Series." Using his name in the title would have increased the likelihood that people who are interested in the Pope would find this video series in YouTube's recommendation sections. The Ad Council could have also increased reach by adding other notable names in video titles like President Barack Obama. The Ad Council could have better optimized their videos for search. Despite not using the campaign name consistently on YouTube, video descriptions did include the Get Vaccine Answers website URL.

Considering the amount of money that went into this campaign, the Ad Council's failure to properly use social media to disseminate information couldn't have come at a worse time. According to a 2021 Mintel study, 36% of social media users said their social media use increased during the pandemic (Poekling, 2021). Social media users reported seeking compassion over confrontation, so the Ad Council's content strategy was on point with consumer sentiment. While the Ad Council created content that people wanted and needed, they could have done a better job of making their content easier to find. Their reach and impact could have been stronger had they done a better job of using consistent branding, keywords, and hashtags.

Discussion

Our case study conducted a textual analysis of the advertisements and promotional elements used in the "It's Up to You" campaign aimed at addressing COVID-19 vaccine hesitancy. Overall, our results found that there is a combination of informational/emotional appeals being used across the advertisements. The majority of all ads have a positive tone, highlighting the benefits to be derived from certain behaviors rather than focusing on what someone has to "give up" or "focusing on the negative." This aligns with previous research on gain- and loss-framed messaging in health communication, which has been shown to impact people's decision-making on important issues (Kahneman, 2003). Gain-framed messages emphasize positive outcomes that can result from a behavior, whereas loss-framed messages focus on negative consequences that could result from not adopting a behavior (Rothman & Salovey, 1997). The "It's Up to You" campaign used gain-framed messaging because it focused on themes that emphasized how "we're all in this together," needing to stay safe so that we can reunite with our loved ones, and doing what's scientifically sound so that we can get back to the activities we have missed so much. A loss-framed campaign would have used more fear-based tactics highlighting things such as "if you don't get the vaccine you could die," or "not wearing a mask puts your loved ones at risk of death from COVID-19." Recent research related to gain- and loss-framed messages focused specifically on COVID-19 messages has shown that gain-framed messages increase individuals' intention to adopt self-care behaviors (Gantiva et al., 2021). Research has also found that emotional messages related to COVID-19 risk are found to be more empowering for individuals when compared to informational messages (Koinig, 2021). Thus, the Ad Council and COVID Collaborative's approach is sound based on research. Our analyses found that their tactics are appropriate as well—the blend of scientific information and emotional tone is appropriate, with every ad leading audience members back to their website where they can get more information on COVID-19 and the vaccine, yet most being focused on an emotional pull. One critique of the overall campaign, however, is its lack of representation. Public relations materials provided to the media promoting the campaign upon its creation touted that it was aimed at addressing vaccine hesitancy in African American and Hispanic communities, yet our analyses did not see adequate representation of these populations in the characters utilized in the ads. Instead, the character choice that stood out most was the celebrity/pop culture icon.

While the use of celebrities and pop culture icons certainly gets someone's attention via advertising, more research is needed to understand the extent to which celebrity endorsements of vaccination and COVID-19 behaviors (e.g., masking, social distancing) have an impact on changing people's behaviors. Previous research has shown mixed results regarding the use of celebrity endorsements being used to change someone's behavior regarding an important issue. For example, following Katie Couric's on-air colonoscopy on the "Today" show 21 years ago, colon cancer screening rates skyrocketed in the United States for the next nine months (Cram et al., 2003). Similar to the "Katie Couric effect," the "Angelina Jolie effect" occurred in 2013. Following Jolie's op-ed in the New York Times disclosing she had undergone a double mastectomy upon learning she carried the BRCA1 gene, there was a significant increase in the amount of genetic testing women received for the BRCA gene (Liede et al., 2018). Conversely, research has found that individuals closest to us (e.g., our friends, family, etc.) influence our health behaviors to a greater extent than celebrities (Simoni et al., 2011). It is important to note that it depends greatly on the individual consuming an ad and the celebrity endorsing a particular message—meaning that there is no "perfect approach" for using celebrities during public health crises.

Overall, advertising can serve as a vehicle for helping to save lives during public health crises and preventing the spread of disease. The COVID-19 pandemic has provided an important opportunity for analyses, with the "It's Up to You" campaign being an example of how to use advertising for positive social change. While the campaign's website and broadcast ads provide sufficient use of scientifically validated information and strong emotional tones, our findings illuminate an opportunity for the social media promotion to be more fully developed. Advertising is no longer a one-channel medium, but rather an integrated communications process that incorporates multiple platforms and channels working in tandem with one another. Therefore, more thoroughly incorporating social media into its existing campaign would benefit "It's Up to You" by helping to achieve its goals of awareness and ultimately saving more lives through increased vaccination rates. While this campaign remained strong in its use of broadcast and web channels, its largest opportunity for traction was the social media route. Yet, this is where it failed to adequately target and engage audiences. One of the most crucial aspects of advertising, particularly during a health crisis, involves properly targeting your audience and effectively utilizing your communication channels. This case study provides an important analysis of positive and negative examples for future advertisers to consider.

Key Terms

Emotional appeals in advertising are those that are based on images and video, and rely on the use of feelings or emotions to get audiences to relate to the message being conveyed (Gray et al., 2012; Wilson & Wolf, 2009).

Example used in the "It's Up to You" campaign—an ad titled "Grandma" showed a grandma reuniting with her daughter and grandchildren after they had received the COVID-19 vaccine. They cried happy tears after not being able to see each other for the past year and half due to the pandemic.

Informational appeals in advertising are those that use rational arguments that are based on facts (Aaker & Norris, 1982).

Example used in the "It's Up to You" campaign—an ad featuring an infographic discussed the importance of washing your hands for 20 seconds at a time to combat the spread of germs.

Gain-framed messages in advertising emphasize positive outcomes that can result from a behavior (Rothman & Salovey, 1997).

An example of how this could be conveyed in advertising—"By getting vaccinated for COVID-19, you will be able to get back to the things you love to do, and you will also be helping to protect your friends and family by keeping yourself safe"

Loss-framed messages in advertising focus on negative consequences that could result from not adopting a behavior (Rothman & Salovey, 1997).

An example of how this could be conveyed in advertising—"If you don't get the COVID-19 vaccine, you could be responsible for killing other people if you contract the virus and end up infecting others"

Discussion Questions

1. If you were in charge of putting together an advertisement for "It's Up to You," and needed to use a celebrity endorsement, can you think of a celebrity that would be well-received by all audiences? Who is a celebrity that would be considered non-controversial, likable by all, and could get the point across without being seen as "political?"
2. Effective advertising is a multi-channel endeavor. Besides a website, YouTube channel, and social media, what other platforms/channels

would you incorporate into the "It's Up to You" campaign to help reach its target market(s)? Explain your reasoning.
3. We reviewed that the "It's Up to You" campaign utilized information and emotional appeals in its messaging. What other types of appeals do you think could be effective for the campaign? Think creatively.

Resources

1. The Ad Council: https://www.adcouncil.org/?gclid=CjwKCAjwtfqKBh-BoEiwAZuesiAs8FSxrmqu6qbgfDHqti0w3x9UOsuiuQEyMoA1vIQAozBYkpSsBRBoCTx8QAvD_BwE
2. Our favorite ad from the "It's Up to You" campaign ("Do it For Me"): https://www.youtube.com/watch?v=l0ApApElLuU
3. YouTube playlist for all "It's Up to You" ads: https://www.youtube.com/channel/UClwkBPKzW8h_rfZWuG_kWjw
4. The COVID Collaborative: https://www.covidcollaborative.us/
5. Get Vaccine Answers (Primary Campaign Website): https://getvaccineanswers.org/

References

Aaker, D.A., & Norris, D. (1982). Characteristics of TV commercials perceived as informative. *Journal of Advertising Research, 22*(2), 61–70.
Ad Council. (2021). *Our history.* https://www.adcouncil.org/our-story/our-history
Ad Council YouTube Channel. (2021). *Playlist.* https://www.youtube.com/adcouncil
Allen, M. (2017). *The sage encyclopedia of communication research methods* (Vols. 1–4). Sage. https://doi.org/10.4135/9781483381411
Applequist, J. (2016). *Broadcast pharmaceutical advertising in the United States: Prime time pill pushers.* Lexington.
Applequist, J. (2020). The introduction of the medicinal partner in direct-to-consumer advertising: Viagra's contribution to pharmaceutical fetishism and patient-as-consumer discourse in healthcare. *Qualitative Research in Medicine & Healthcare, 2,* 265–276. https://doi.org/10.4081/qrmh.2018.7646
Barthes, R. (1972). *Mythologies.* The Noonday Press.
Centers for Disease Control and Prevention. (2021, September 17). *COVID data tracker.* https://covid.cdc.gov/covid-data-tracker/#vaccinations_vacc-total-admin-rate-total

Cohen, E.L. (2020). Stars—they're sick like us! The effects of a celebrity exemplar on COVID-19-related risk cognitions, emotions, and preventative behavioral intentions. *Science Communication*, 42(5), 724–741. https://doi.org/10.1177/1075547020960465

COVID Collaborative. (2021). *The collaborative*. https://www.covidcollaborative.us/

Cram, P., Fendrick, A.M., Inadomi, J., Cowen, M.E., Carpenter, D., & Bijan, S. (2003). The impact of a celebrity promotion campaign on the use of colon cancer screening: The Katie Couric effect. *Archives of Internal Medicine*, 163(13), 1601–1605. https://doi.org/10.1001/archinte.163.13.1601

Ewen, S. (1976). *Captains of Consciousness*. McGraw-Hill.

Fowles, J. (1996). *Advertising and Popular Culture*. Sage.

Gantiva, C., Jiménez-Leal, W., Urriago-Rayo, J. (2021). Framing messages to deal with the COVID-19 crisis: The role of loss/gain frames and content. *Frontiers in Psychology*, 12. https://doi.org/10.3389/fpsyg.2021.568212

Gitlin, T. (1979). Prime time ideology: The hegemonic process in television entertainment. *Social Problems*, 26(3), 251–266. https://doi.org/10.2307/800451

Gray, L., MacDonald, C., Mackie, B., Paton, D., Johnston, D., & Baker, M.G. (2012). Community responses to communication campaigns for influenza A (H1N1): A focus group study. *BMC Public Health*, 12, Article 205. https://doi.org/10.1186/1471-2458-12-205

Harvard. T.H. Chan School of Public Health. (2021). *Ad campaign aims to convince Americans to get COVID-19 vaccines*. https://www.hsph.harvard.edu/news/hsph-in-the-news/ad-campaign-aims-to-convince-americans-to-get-covid-19-vaccines/

Hubspot/Mention. (2021). *Instagram engagement report*. https://mention.com/pardot-2/files/Instagram_Engagement_Report_2021.pdf

It's Up to You. (2021). *Ad Council/COVID Collaborative*. https://getvaccineanswers.org/

Jhally, S. (1987). *Codes of advertising: Fetishism and the political economy of meaning in the consumer society*. Saint Martin's.

Kahneman, D. (2003). A perspective on judgment and choice: Mapping bounded rationality. *American Psychologist*, 58, 697–720. https://doi.org/10.1037/0003-066X.58.9.697

Kido Lopez, L. (2020). *Race and media: Critical approaches*. New York University Press.

Koinig, I. (2021). On the influence of message/audience specifics and message appeal type on message empowerment: The Austrian case of COVID-19 health risk messages. *Health Communication*, 1–12. https://doi.org/10.1080/10410236.2021.1913822

Kover, A.J. (1995). Copywriters' implicit theories of communication: An exploration. *Journal of Consumer Research*, 21(4), 596–611. https://doi.org/10.1086/209421

Kricorian, K., & Turner, K. (2021). COVID-19 vaccine acceptance and beliefs among black and hispanic americans. *PLoS ONE*, 16(8), Article e0256122. https://doi.org/10.1371/journal.pone.0256122

Liede, A., Cai, M., Fiddler Crouter, T., Niepel, D., Callaghan, F., & Gareth Evans, D. (2018). Risk-reducing mastectomy rates in the US: A closer examination of the Angelina Jolie effect. *Breast Cancer Research & Treatment*, 171(2), 435–442. https://doi.org/10.1007/s10549-018-4824-9

Mitchell, J.C. (1983). Case and situation analysis. *The Sociological Review*, 31(2), 187–211. https://doi.org/10.1111/j.1467-954X.1983.tb00387.x

Newberry, C. (2021, July 19). *2021 Instagram hashtag guide: How to get more reach.* Hootsuite. https://blog.hootsuite.com/instagram-hashtags/#Why_use_Instagram_hashtags

Penn State. Teaching and Learning with Technology. (2017). *Public service announcement.* https://mediacommons.psu.edu/2017/02/14/public-service-announcement/#:~:text=A%20PSA%20

Poekling, J. (2021, May). Social media trends—US, May 2021 [Industry Report]. Mintel. https://www.mintel.com/

Poels, K., & Dewitte, S. (2019). The role of emotions in advertising: A call to action. *Journal of Advertising, 48*(1), 81–90. https://doi.org/10.1080/00913367.2019.1579688

Ringold, D.J. (2002). Boomerang effects in response to public health interventions: Some unintended consequences in the alcoholic beverage market. *Journal of Consumer Policy, 25*(1), 27–63. https://doi.org/10.1023/A:1014588126336

Rosen, D.E., & Purinton, E. (2004). Website design: Viewing the web as a cognitive landscape. *Journal of Business Research, 57*(7), 787–794. https://doi.org/10.1016/S0148-2963(02)00353-3

Rothman, A.J., & Salovey, P. (1997). Shaping perceptions to motivate healthy behavior: The role of message framing. *Psychological Bulletin, 121*, 3–19. https://doi.org/10.1037/0033-2909.121.1.3

Simoni, J.M., Franks, J.C., Lehavot, K., & Yard, S.S. (2011). Peer interventions to promote health: Conceptual considerations. *American Journal of Orthopsychiatry, 81*(3), 351–359. https://doi.org/10.1111/j.1939-0025.2011.01103.x

Stern, B. (1996). Textual analysis in advertising research: Construction and deconstruction of meanings. *Journal of Advertising, 25*(3), 61–73. https://doi.org/10.1080/00913367.1996.10673507

Stobbe, M. (2021, February 25). *Ad campaign launches to build public trust in COVID-19 shots.* ABC News.

Vakratsas, D., & Ambler, T. (1999). How advertising works: What do we really know? *Journal of Marketing, 63*(1), 26–43. https://doi.org/10.2307/1251999

Warner, K.J. (2017). In the time of plastic representation. *Film Quarterly, 71*(2), 32–37. https://doi.org/10.1525/fq.2017.71.2.32

Williams, R. (1980). *Problems in materialism and culture: Selected essays.* Verso.

Williamson, J. (1978). *Decoding advertisements.* Marion Boyers.

Wilson, E.A., & Wolf, M.S. (2009). Working memory and the design of health materials: A cognitive factors perspective. *Patient Education and Counseling, 74*(3), 318–322. https://doi.org/10.1016/j.pec.2008.11.005

Yin, R.K. (1994). *Case study research design and methods: Applied social research and methods series* (2nd ed.). Sage.

Zajonc, R.B. (1980). Feeling and thinking: Preferences need no inferences. *American Psychologist, 35*(2), 151–175. https://doi.org/10.1037/0003-066X.35.2.151

· 9 ·

SEVENTEEN WEEKS: FAN REACTIONS TO THE NFL'S COVID-19 PROTOCOLS DURING THE 2020 SEASON

Virginia S. Harrison, Brandon Boatwright, Carla White, & Kayleigh Jackson

On March 11, 2020, professional sports in the United States were forever altered when the first athlete tested positive for COVID-19 (Curtis, 2020). After practice on March 9, Utah Jazz forward Rudy Gobert made light of the virus during a routine weekly press conference, touching reporters' microphones and recorders sitting in front of him before leaving the room. Two days later, he appeared on the Jazz' injury report with "illness," sending shockwaves through pro sports when the National Basketball Association (NBA) became the first major American sports league to suspend play. By the following day, Major League Soccer (MLS), the National Hockey League (NHL), Major League Baseball (MLB), and college athletic departments had also suspended play indefinitely.

Following a four-month pause, the NBA decided to resume its regular season after introducing their "bubble" method, a sole venue in which participating teams competed under strict COVID-19 guidelines including restricted travel for all players and staff, bans on non-essential personnel, additional isolation procedures, and continuous testing protocols (Vaudreuil et al., 2021). While many stakeholders and fans rejoiced, others questioned whether the continuation of professional sports was appropriate during a global pandemic. Following the guidelines introduced by the NBA, additional organizations set out to create their own versions of the bubble structure (Young, 2021). Some bubbles were more successful than others in curbing the spread of the virus. For example, Major League Baseball (MLB) Commissioner, Rob Manfred, received notable backlash from fans following the surge of players who tested positive for COVID-19 throughout the season even after implementing additional procedures (Young, 2021). The return of professional baseball amid COVID-19 left an impression of unfairness for players who were concerned for their health and safety despite the league's efforts to utilize bubble sites (Apstein, 2020).

The National Football League (NFL) created headlines when they became the first professional league to proceed with their 2020 season without implementing any type of bubble format (Rapoport & Pelissero, 2020). According to the NFL, owners and players had discussed the idea but the sheer volume of players who would have been required to isolate would have simply been too large to accommodate in a single facility (Battista, 2021). While the season contained a multitude of outbreaks, the NFL's In-Season Advisory Committee was adamant that the schedule should not be altered unless absolutely necessary. Even in the case of players testing positive, they believed that most COVID-19 cases were self-inflicted due to failure to follow off-the-field guidelines and protocols. Regardless of whether a star player was out due to illness, the game was still to be played (Battista, 2021). Despite criticism and concern, the NFL ultimately accepted that it would function at the mercy of the pandemic but would continue its season while functioning as close to regular operations as possible.

This chapter investigates fan responses to the NFL's management of the COVID-19 pandemic throughout the 2020 season from a crisis communication standpoint. A semantic network analysis of fan responses on the social media platform Twitter (X) has been divided into four timeframes, each coinciding with different games during the 2020 season to highlight emerging, continuing, and changing trends in the conversation. The first analysis centered on the season's opening game between the Houston Texans and the Kansas City Chiefs on September 10, 2020, where 16,000 socially distanced fans were in attendance (Battista, 2021). The second analysis will represent the fourth week of the season, when four Tennessee Titans players and five members on their staff tested positive for COVID-19 (Battista, 2021). The third analysis will represent the largest outbreak of COVID-19 during the 2020 NFL season when 12 players from the Baltimore Ravens, including quarterback Lamar Jackson, tested positive during the twelfth week of the season (Hensley, 2020). The final analysis through the seventeenth week of the season will address the

Cleveland Browns head coach, Kevin Stefanski, testing positive alongside four other members of the organization ahead of the team's opening-round playoff game (Beaton, 2021). Using both quantitative and qualitative methods, this chapter will present a picture of fan reactions to the NFL's daring policy to orchestrate a "normal" season during the pandemic and what this means for sports crisis communication in the post-pandemic era.

Literature Review

Crisis Communication Theory and Organizational Strategies

Situational Crisis Communication Theory (SCCT) is the dominant crisis-related paradigm in public relations literature today. Emerging from corporate apologia and image repair theory, the SCCT described strategic responses that corporations could employ to emerge from a crisis depending on the type of crisis that was encountered (Coombs, 2006). The SCCT identifies three types of crisis (victim, accidental, or preventable), which dictate the type of crisis response strategy (primary strategies: attack the accuser, denial, scapegoat, excuse, justification, compensation, apology, and secondary strategies: reminder, ingratiation, and victimage) that is used to preserve an organization's reputation and ensure positive stakeholder intentions (Coombs, 2007). Because all crises represent a threat to corporate reputation and thus the viability of the organization, understanding how a corporation could emerge from a crisis and resume business was critical to early studies of SCCT (Coombs, 2007). Repeatedly, studies have shown that these repair strategies build positive relationships and favorable attitudes toward a company after a crisis (e.g., Haigh & Brubaker, 2010; Liu & Ni, 2021). Beyond the corporate context, crisis repair strategies can be used to protect organizational reputation and stakeholder relationships for nonprofits (Vafeiadis et al., 2020) and sports organizations (Harker, 2021; Harrison & Erlichman, 2022). More recent literature has introduced the concept of empathy into the crisis communication framework, expanding the understanding of image repair to be mutually constructed rather than organization-focused preservation (Du Plessis, 2018; Ulmer et al., 2007).

Additionally, crisis communication has been examined in an online context. Specifically, disinformation online can create an informational crisis for organizations on social media, and repair strategies enacted online can restore stakeholder relationships (Kim & Park, 2017; Vafeiadis et al., 2019). Additionally, social media allows stakeholders to respond to crises by forming communities and relaying information to individuals outside of the organization's control (Austin et al., 2012; Pyle et al., 2019), and Twitter (X) can be effective for this outreach (Lim & Brown-Devlin, 2021). Social media provides a platform for organizations and these communities to engage in dialogue and exchange meaningful discourse, leading to the renewal process after a crisis (Du Plessis, 2018). Importantly, these perspectives introduce the agency of the communities affected by the crisis to play a role in the response.

Crisis Communication and Sports Fans

The NFL's COVID-19 response strategy offers scholars an opportunity to address the role that fans play in crisis situations. Based on Coombs' (2007) crisis typology, research has found that fans participate in all types of repair strategies following allegations against organizations (Brown & Billings, 2013) and athletes (Brown, 2016) with whom they are identified. Additionally, it has been noted that identification can act as a buffer for organizations in crisis and prompt more successful outcomes (Guo et al., 2020; Harker, 2021; Lim & Brown-Devlin, 2021). Fans with high levels of brand loyalty, positive previous experiences, and high levels of commitment are likely to be especially useful to sports organizations during crisis situations, which highlights the importance of relationship management on behalf of the organization with their fans (Lim & Brown-Devlin, 2021). Fans often utilize social media, especially Twitter (X), in crisis situations to cope because of its impact on their identity (Brown & Billings, 2013; Guo et al., 2020). Engagement through social media has provided fans with access to public platforms that can either hinder an organization's reputation repair strategy or facilitate meaningful contributions toward crisis management or resolution (Brown & Billings, 2013; Guo et al., 2020).

This research takes a longitudinal approach to fan responses in crisis situations by exploring how NFL fans engage in communication related to the COVID-19 pandemic and the uncertainty of the season's completion by examining conversation around significant events during the NFL season. We take both a quantitative and qualitative approach to better understand these conversations with the following questions in mind:

> RQ1: How does the conversation about the NFL and the COVID-19 crisis change over the course of the 2020 NFL season?
> RQ2: How did fans respond to the NFL's handling of the COVID-19 crisis during the 2020 NFL season online?

Method

Data Collection

Data for this study was collected using a third-party social media analytics platform (Sprinklr) to harvest publicly available tweets that contained the terms "NFL" and "COVID" from four prominent time periods during the 2020 NFL Season. Twitter (X) was chosen for analysis because it is a popular platform among sports fans and commonly used to discuss sport-related issues (Brown & Billings, 2013). In our study, the first time period spanned September 8–12, 2020, surrounding the first game with fans of the 2020 season. The Kansas City Chiefs opened the season by welcoming the Houston Texans to Arrowhead Stadium in Kansas City with fans in attendance at reduced capacity. A total of 19,511 tweets were harvested during this period. The second time frame was from September 28 to October 4, 2020. This window encompassed a larger COVID-19 outbreak across the league preceding Week 4 games. During this span, the Tennessee Titans placed several players on the COVID-19 inactive list and the NFL announced the Titans' game against the Pittsburgh Steelers would be postponed. A total of 27,985 tweets were harvested during this timeframe. The third time frame included tweets from November 19 to December 2, 2020. This period encompassed the largest league-wide outbreak during the 2020 NFL season with multiple teams placing players on the COVID-19 inactive list. A total of 100,606 tweets were harvested during this period. Finally, the fourth window spanned the first round of the NFL playoffs from December 30, 2020 through January 5, 2021. A total of 17,746 tweets were collected during this period. In all, we harvested 165,848 tweets across these four periods of time.

Data Analysis

Phase 1: Semantic Network Analysis. To answer our first research question we employed semantic network analysis which Doerfel (1998) defines as "the use of network analytic techniques on paired associations based on shared meaning as opposed to paired associations of behavioral or perceived communication links" (p. 16). In other words, semantic network analysis allows us to visually map the relationships between words used in a particular context. By focusing on the structural properties of the conversation, semantic networks offer valuable insight into how users use certain words and to what extent those words are related to each other. We conducted a semantic network analysis for each of the four timeframes outlined in the data collection section by first removing stop words (e.g., *a*, *the*, *of*, etc.) from each dataset and subsequently analyzing each dataset using WordStat 8. Specifically, for each dataset, we sought to identify the associated terms used with "NFL" and "COVID" in order to identify the "structured semantic representations of associated contextual and cultural information" (Schultz et al., 2012, p. 99) related to the 2020 NFL season.

Phase 2: Thematic Analysis. To answer our second research question asking how fans responded to the NFL's handling of the COVID-19 crisis during the 2020 season, we used qualitative thematic analysis (Braun & Clarke, 2006) to examine the ways that fans discussed the four COVID-related events targeted in our case study. Thematic analysis is a process for "identifying, analysing and reporting patterns (themes) within data" (Braun & Clarke, 2006, p. 79). To do this, we focused on keywords related to the pandemic appearing in our semantic network analyses in RQ1. We then applied discourse analysis to the *keywords in context* provided by WordStat, which displayed the text of the tweets with those keywords. We focused our analysis on keywords relating to NFL policies related to the COVID-19 crisis. The authors discussed the initial findings together and came to an agreement on 1–2 key themes present in each time period, which are described below.

Results

RQ1: Semantic Network Analysis

As events of the 2020 NFL season transpired, our first research question sought to evaluate the manner in which conversation on Twitter (X) changed over time. Each of the four timeframes were analyzed to visually map out the words associated with "NFL" and "COVID." Figure 9.1 shows the semantic network from the September 8–12 timeframe. Perhaps the most significant structural component of the network is the association between the NFL, COVID, and the word "fraud." Two primary clusters of closely associated words stem from this relationship. One cluster contains the words "Josh," "Bellamy," and "arrested." The other contains "player," "charged," "relief," and "scheme." Although this timeframe included the first game of the NFL season with fans in attendance, there was relatively little conversation around the matchup on the field. Instead, users more widely discussed the federal charges brought against a former player for allegedly participating in a scheme to fraudulently

FAN REACTIONS TO THE NFL'S COVID-19 PROTOCOLS

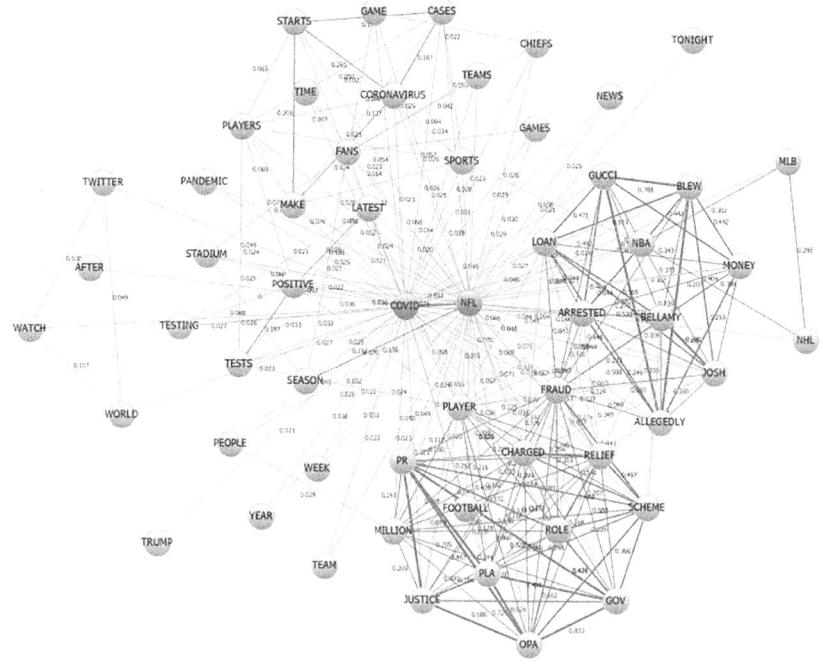

Figure 9.1. Semantic Network for Sept. 8–12 Timeframe

collect Payroll Protection Program loans provided by the U.S. Government for COVID-19 relief.

As the season progressed and the league experienced its first postponement linked to a COVID-19 outbreak, the online conversation began to shift. Figure 9.2 shows the semantic network from the September 28 to October 1 timeframe. After Tennessee Titans players and staff tested positive for the virus, league officials announced the team's scheduled game against the Pittsburgh Steelers would be postponed until later in the season. The semantic network illustrates how prominent this conversation was on Twitter (X) during this timeframe. Words like "Titans," "Steelers," "game," and "positive" were closely associated with "NFL" and "COVID."

Figure 9.3 offers an overview of the Twitter (X) conversation during the November 19 to December 2 timeframe. This period marked the largest outbreak among teams during the season, and it is worth noting that the semantic network for this timeframe is more decentralized than that of the second timeframe. In other words, fewer users are talking about the same subject

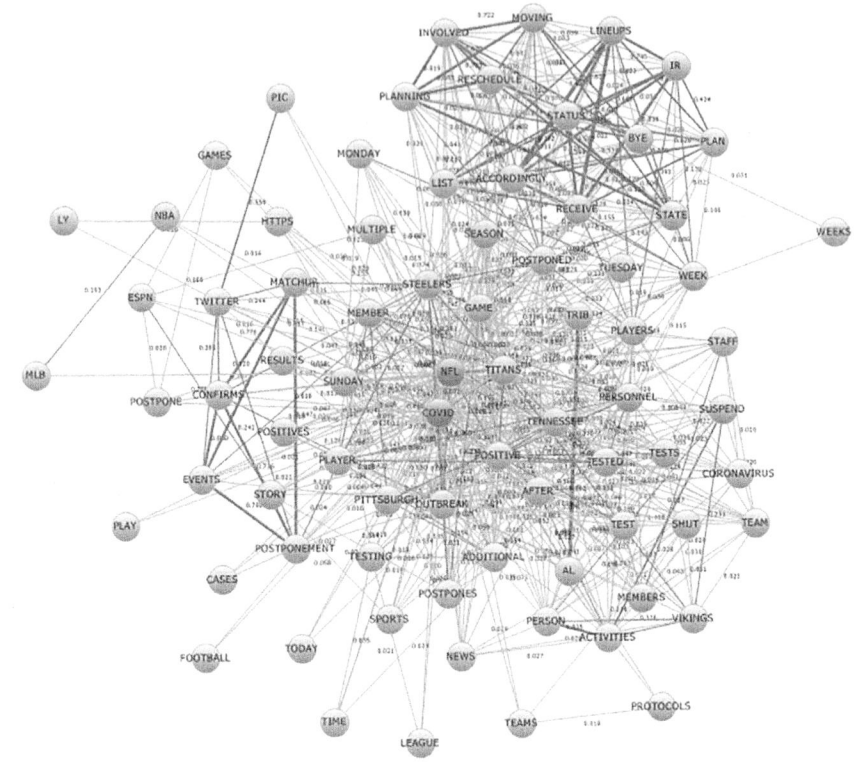

Figure 9.2. Semantic Network for Sept. 28 to Oct. 1 Timeframe

here. Whereas in the previous timeframe, one topic was dominant (i.e., the Titans-Steelers postponement), conversation during this period did not revolve around any one subject. Instead, users appeared to focus on words associated with the league's handling of COVID (e.g., "handling," "rules," "protocols," and "issues"); specific teams (e.g., "Ravens," "Broncos," and "Patriots"); and players (e.g., "Lamar," "Jackson," and "QBs").

Finally, Figure 9.4 shows the semantic network of the December 30 to January 5 timeframe. Once again, the network appears to be more decentralized than earlier in the season. The conversation around the "NFL" and "COVID" has been expanded to encompass a number of topics. Of course, it's important to keep context in mind when evaluating the network: this timeframe marks the beginning of the NFL Playoffs. Participating teams (e.g., "BuffaloBills," "Browns," and "Steelers"), coaches (e.g., "coach," "Stefanski"), and players (e.g., "players," "Fitzpatrick") are frequently discussed. Interestingly, though, various

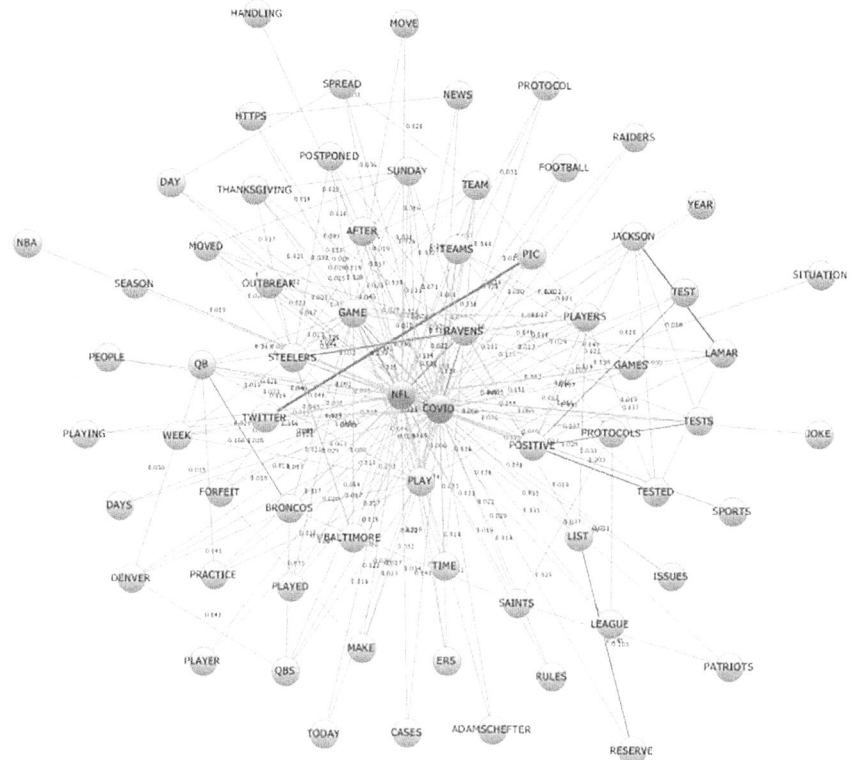

Figure 9.3. Semantic Network for Nov. 19 to Dec. 2 Timeframe

policy terms (e.g., "bubble," "protocol") and authority figures (e.g., "NYGovCuomo") are also mentioned in association with the "NFL" and "COVID."

RQ2: Thematic Analysis

Our second research question asked how fans responded to the NFL's handling of the 2020 NFL season online. Our thematic analysis allowed us to elaborate on the conversation at each time point. Mirroring the network analysis, the conversation during time 1 (the opening game of the 2020 season) was centered on Josh Bellamy's fraud arrest, and thus we focused on the term "fraud." Most of the conversation centered around sharing headlines about the incident from news sources, including blogs like TMZ and the U.S. Department of Justice (justice.gov). Although the fraud was related to a COVID-19 scheme, the commentary did not relate to the NFL's season or its policies. Thus, the

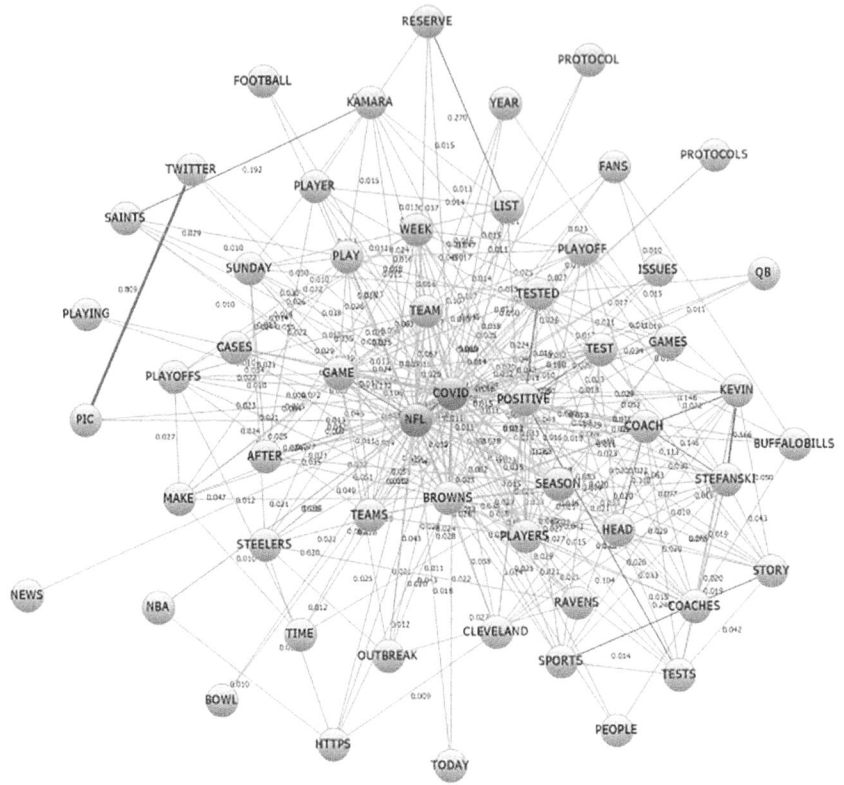

Figure 9.4. Semantic Network for Dec. 30 to Jan. 5 Timeframe

NFL's decision to launch the season was overshadowed by the player's misdeed (see Table 9.1).

Time 2 featured the first major COVID-19 outbreak of the season, and thus we focused on the keyword of "postponed." Key themes included critiques of the NFL's policies, criticism of President Donald Trump, and uncertainty about the NFL's plans to handle COVID-19 (see Table 9.1). At this point in the season, fans offered up ideas or solutions to prevent postponement or suggested what the NFL "should have done" instead, for example, scheduling in more bye weeks, to handle the inevitable postponements coming from a bubble-free environment. Additionally, this analysis came on the heels of President Trump taking credit for "bringing back football," which led to both sarcasm and earnest appeals to Trump to solve the situation. Others expressed skepticism that the NFL would be able to handle the inevitable postponements, bringing up

Table 9.1. Exemplary Quotes from Thematic Analysis of Twitter Conversation

Timeframe	Themes	Exemplary Quotes
Time 1: First game Sept. 10, 2020	News headlines	"NFL Player Charged for Role in $24 Million COVID-Relief Fraud Scheme"
	Political connections to COVID	"24M fraud scheme. That's fraud to defraud people who are already frauded by a hoax. Things get complicated . . ."
Time 2: First outbreak Week 4, Sept. 28-Oct. 1, 2020	Critique of NFL's policies	"Just schedule a buffer at the end of the season to make up ALL postponed games and skip all the stupid mid-season shuffling."
	Criticism of then-President Trump	"The NFL postponed their 1st game due to COVID. Imagine that! Yesterday BLOTUS was bragging about how he brought back football! . . . #BLOTUSHASTOGO"
	Uncertainty about the NFL's plans to handle COVID	"NFL games being postponed because of COVID already. Wow who could've seen this coming? A league with no bubble having an outbreak this early in the season? Oh right, everyone." " . . . They need a contingency plan so no more games lost. #coronavirus"
Time 3: Largest outbreak Week 12, Nov. 19-Dec. 2, 2020	Seriousness of COVID	". . . the NFL commissioner should never had the season because this covid-19 ain't no joke and I blame the NFL commissioner for this"
	Poor protocols, policies	"NFL is a joke. They never had a plan for this COVID stuff and it's showing." "NFL covid protocol is about as bad as you would think it would be . . . . Goddell is a joke"
	Unfair advantages	". . . And one team has received special treatment from the NFL with regards to COVID. What a joke"
	League comparisons	"Can't believe the NFL got lapped by MLB on handling covid"

Continued

Table 9.1. Continued

Timeframe	Themes	Exemplary Quotes
Time 4: Playoffs outbreak Wild Card Round, Dec. 30, 2020-Jan. 5, 2021	Unfair advantages & motives	"What would the NFL do if it lost one of his superstars to COVID during the playoffs?" "@nflcommish: "Ehhh, but the playoffs are close..." #NFL doesn't care anymore."
	Playoff-specific policies	"NFL playoffs are going to suck. 14 teams and at least 1 team will have a major roster shake up with covid. These teams should be bubbled"
	Integrity of playoffs	"Personally they should probably postpone the playoffs until this COVID spike between players calms down so ALL teams have a fair shot in the playoffs but the NFL doesn't care and won't do that"

past criticisms about player safety and surprise that the league admitted they had positive cases. However, most of the tweets under this keyword were factual in nature and expressed concern over the postponement—but belief the season would continue.

Time 3 included the largest outbreak of the season, leading to the postponement of a Thanksgiving game. Within keyworks "joke" and "handling," this is the first timeframe where we see actual fan outrage about the NFL's postponement policies. Fans believed the NFL's policies provided advantages to certain teams and players, in this case by postponing the Ravens' game until their team was healthy enough to face the then-undefeated Steelers. Fans considered the NFL's policies to be inconsistent and unfair, while others considered the entire season to be poorly orchestrated (see Table 9.1). Others blamed NFL commissioner Roger Goodell for holding a season in the first place, noting the seriousness of COVID-19, and contrasted the NFL's protocols to other leagues' (NFL was often considered worse). Notably, we didn't see any NFL response to the criticism on Twitter (X).

Time 4 continued some of the same themes as Time 3, but the NFL's decision was different: The playoff game continued as scheduled despite players on the Browns being inactive and coaches unable to be with the team due to COVID-19. Thus, fans continued to believe the NFL was implementing policies unfairly to favor certain teams and players. They continued to criticize the NFL's overall policies, many calling for a bubble environment like other leagues had successfully implemented for their playoffs (see Table 9.1). Other fans commented on the integrity of the playoffs given the possibility a team could lose key players due to COVID-19 and then fail to advance. Overall, the NFL's handling of the season continued to be critiqued until the end.

Discussion

This chapter attempted to understand the COVID-19 crisis in sports by examining fan and league interactions on social media. Given the unprecedented situation sports leagues were under during the COVID-19 pandemic—especially when it became clear the crisis would be long-term—leagues and fans had to determine what would constitute a successful, safe season. Leagues like the NFL moved forward with protocols in place to hold sporting events, likely due to financial pressures and a need to engage fans (Skinner & Smith, 2021). Our analysis demonstrated that fans were quite critical of NFL policies—yet the 2020 season was completed on-time and without any major setbacks.

Interestingly, our analysis found that the NFL made little use of image repair strategies on social media to engage fans. Instead, the league was either ignoring the need for image repair or did not see Twitter (X) as the location for these strategies. In fact, the league's perspective was notably absent from the data we examined, and fans seemed to anticipate that the NFL would do a terrible job handling COVID-19 even before the season got underway. Perhaps this lack of trust in the NFL is a result of previously unresolved crises, such as player misconduct (e.g., Brown, 2016) or concussion safety (e.g., Harker, 2021). Previous research has shown that fans continue to discuss the NFL's previous crises when the league comes under scrutiny for new situations (Harrison & Erlichman, 2022). Perhaps we are seeing more evidence for unresolved crises and their impact on fan relationships.

Additionally, fans made little use of image repair strategies to defend the NFL themselves (e.g., Brown & Billings, 2013). Again, this could be the result of Twitter (X) and the keywords used to conduct the search, but this may also be a result of how fans identify with the league. Fans discuss sports crises within their social networks because they seek to find others who identify with them and help them process the situation (Harker, 2021). Social media specifically is one way for fans to connect and reinforce their identity as a fan by finding others in these virtual communities (Guo et al., 2020; Lim & Brown-Devlin, 2021). However, in our study, fans used Twitter (X) to critique the NFL's policies and vent frustration with perceived rule inequities affecting their favorite teams. Thus, fans expressed identities of their favorite teams over that of the NFL and were quick to criticize the NFL when the team's well-being was at stake. It seemed like social media was a way to complain to the NFL rather than build relationships through crisis repair strategies (e.g., Brown & Billings, 2013).

Particularly of note, the fans' criticism for the league seemed to grow as the season went on. The week 1 conversation focused on the arrest of a player who committed fraud related to COVID-19, both overshadowing the opening game and the NFL's policies. The NFL didn't seem to be a part of this conversation (even though a player was implicated), perhaps unintentionally practicing diversion (e.g., Bruce & Tini, 2008) by allowing the player's transgression to supersede questions about the NFL's opening during the pandemic. However, as policies were implemented and the season continued, the NFL could not hide behind other headlines. Instead, fans on social media scrutinized the NFL's decisions. While this practice may seem counterproductive for building meaningful fan relationships, the NFL has a history of practicing diversion for other controversies (e.g., protests during the national anthem, concussions), which has resulted in minimal negative effects to reputation or fan perceptions (Harrison & Erlichman, 2022). We see that the NFL is maintaining such a strategy during the COVID-19 crisis.

Limitations and Future Research

We want to acknowledge certain limitations with this study. First of all, we analyzed specific timeframes during the NFL season, so our findings reflect only the conversation occurring during those specific dates. Thus, it is likely that we have not captured the entirety of the NFL and fan conversation about COVID-19 and the season. Secondly, the fact that we may not have found NFL crisis responses to fan criticisms may be due to our research method and focus on the Twitter (X) platform. We looked at the entire Twitter (X) conversation during these timeframes, focusing on keywords, and we did not examine specific responses from the NFL or specific spokespeople. The NFL may not have chosen to engage fans on Twitter, instead using traditional media or their own website to communicate strategies. However, our findings show that if the NFL did respond to comments or use crisis strategies on Twitter, they did not feature prominently in the fan conversation. Future research can determine how fans felt about the NFL's lack of response and if this strategy impacted fan perceptions of the NFL's reputation or image and if it impacted the quality of fan relationships. Additional studies may also be able to connect how the NFL's lack of communication during the season impacts financial outcomes such as advertising revenues and ratings.

Conclusion

At the time of writing this chapter, nearly every other major sports league based in the United States (e.g., NHL, NBA, Women's National Basketball Association, MLB, MLS) and internationally (e.g., English Premier League, Formula One) have returned to full, regularly scheduled seasons with normal travel. While testing and masking protocols largely remain in place, the NFL was the first league to play its full regular schedule and playoffs outside of a bubble. By completing the 2020 season with minimal interruptions, the NFL set the stage for other sports to attempt a similar feat. In some ways, the NFL showed them the blueprint—but not without uncertainty and criticism on the part of its fans. From concerns about player safety to beliefs that the season would be unfair based on the NFL's decisions, fans voiced their opinions about the 2020 season on social media, and most of those found in our analysis were negative. Yet, the NFL emerged from the crisis seemingly unscathed without directly addressing the fans' concerns on social media. As the 2021 NFL season gets underway, the sports world has learned to handle the ongoing crisis—mostly by operating business as usual. Yet to be seen are the long-term impacts of COVID-19, league policies, and their impacts on fan relationships.

Discussion Questions

1. How should the NFL have addressed fans' comments on Twitter (X) or other social media platforms? What could the league have done differently to respond, if anything?
2. Which of Coombs' (2007) crisis communication repair strategies may have been useful to address fans' comments during the 2020 season?
3. What could be some potential long-term consequences of the NFL's lack of response to fan comments on social media? How could this affect fan relationships?

4. When you post a critical comment on social media about your favorite team or league, do you expect the team or league to respond? What would you expect them to say? How would that impact your fandom?

Resources

1. Students and teachers can get a 30-day free trial version of Sprinklr by visiting: https://www.sprinklr.com/modern-research-lite/
2. Students and teachers can get a 14-day free trial of WordStat by visiting: https://provalisresearch.com/downloads/trial-versions/

References

Apstein, S. (2020, August 3). Rob Manfred blames players, but MLB's troubles are his fault. *Sports Illustrated.* https://www.si.com/mlb/2020/08/03/rob-manfred-Baseball-coronavirus-response

Austin, L., Liu, B.F., & Jin, Y. (2012). How audiences seek out crisis information: Exploring the social-mediated crisis communication model. *Journal of Applied Communication Research,* 40(2), 188–207. https://doi.org/10.1080/00909882.2012.654498

Battista, J. (2021, February 1). *How the NFL navigated through a pandemic and made it to the finish line of a historic season.* NFL. https://www.nfl.com/news/sidelines/2020-in-review-inside-the-most-unique-season-in-nfl-history

Beaton, A. (2021, January 5). Cleveland Browns head coach, 4 others test positive before playoff game. *The Wall Street Journal.* https://www.wsj.com/articles/cleveland-browns-covid-19-outbreak-kevin-stefanski-11609867536

Braun, V., & Clarke, V. (2006). Using thematic analysis in psychology. *Qualitative Research in Psychology,* 3, 77–101. https://doi.org/10.1191/1478088706qp063oa

Brown, K.A. (2016). Is apology the best policy? An experimental examination of the effectiveness of image repair strategies during criminal and noncriminal athlete transgressions. *Communication & Sport,* 4(1), 23–42. https://doi.org/10.1177/2167479514544950

Brown, N.A., & Billings, A.C. (2013). Sports fans as crisis communicators on social media websites. *Public Relations Review,* 39(1), 74–81. https://doi.org/10.1016/j.pubrev.2012.09.012

Bruce, T., & Tini, T. (2008). Unique crisis response strategies in sports public relations: Rugby league and the case for diversion. *Public Relations Review,* 34, 108–115. https://doi.org/10.1016/j.pubrev.2008.03.015

Coombs, W.T. (2006). Crisis management: A communicative approach. In C. Botan & V. Hazelton (Eds.), *Public relations theory II* (pp. 171–197). Routledge.

Coombs, W.T. (2007). Protecting organization reputations during a crisis: The development and application of situational crisis communication theory. *Corporate Reputation Review, 10*(3), 163–176. https://doi.org/10.1057/palgrave.crr.1550049

Curtis, C. (2020, March 11). *A minute-by-minute look at March 11, the night Rudy Gobert tested positive for COVID-19 and changed sports.* USA Today Sports. https://ftw.usatoday.com/lists/2020-covid-19-nba-rudy-gobert-march-11

Doerfel, M.L. (1998). What constitutes semantic network analysis? A comparison of research and methodologies. *Connections, 21*(2), 16–26. https://qualquant.org/wp-content/uploads/cda/Doerfel%20What%20constitutes%20semantic%20network%20analysis.pdf

Du Plessis, C. (2018). Social media crisis communication: Enhancing a discourse of renewal through dialogic content. *Public Relations Review, 44*(5), 829–838. https://doi.org/10.1016/j.pubrev.2018.10.003

Guo, S., Billings, A.C., Brown, K.A., & Vincent, J. (2020). The tweet heard round the world: Daryl Morey, the NBA, China, and attribution of responsibility. *Communication & Sport,* 1–18. Advanced publication. https://doi.org/10.1177/2167479520983254

Haigh, M.M., & Brubaker, P. (2010). Examining how image restoration strategy impacts perceptions of corporate social responsibility, organization-public relationships, and source credibility. *Corporate Communications: An International Journal, 15*(4), 453–468. https://doi.org/10.1108/13563281011085538

Harker, J.L. (2021). Let's talk sports: An egocentric discussion network analysis regarding NFL crisis perceptions. *Communication & Sport, 9*(4), 576–602. https://doi.org/10.1177/2167479519875970

Harrison, V., & Erlichman, S. (2022). NFL player protests, corporate social responsibility, and diversion in sports crisis. *Journal of Sports Media, 17*(1), 119–142. https://doi.org/10.1353/jsm.2022.0005

Hensley, J. (2020, December 1). *Inside the outbreak: The latest in the Raven's Covid-19 saga.* ESPN. https://www.espn.com/blog/baltimore-ravens/post/_/id/53840/inside-the-outbreak-how-covid-19-hit-lamar-jackson-and-the-ravens

Kim, Y., & Park, H. (2017). Is there still a PR problem online? Exploring the effects of different sources and crisis response strategies in online crisis communication via social media. *Corporate Reputation Review, 20*(1), 76–104. https://doi.org/10.1057/s41299-017-0016-5

Lim, H.S., & Brown-Devlin, N. (2021). The value of brand fans during a crisis: Exploring the roles of response strategy, source, and brand identification. *International Journal of Business Communication,* 1–29. Advanced publication https://doi.org/10.1177/2329488421999699

Liu, W., & Ni, L. (2021). Relationship matters: How government organization-public relationship impacts disaster recovery outcomes among multiethnic communities. *Public Relations Review, 47,* Article 102047. https://doi.org/10.1016/j.pubrev.2021.102047

Pyle, A.S., Morgoch, M.L., & Boatwright, B.C. (2019). SnowedOut Atlanta: Examining digital emergence on Facebook during a crisis. *Journal of Contingencies and Crisis Management, 27*(4), 414–422. https://doi.org/10.1111/1468-5973.12274

Rapoport, I., & Pelissero, T. (2020, November 29). *NFL playoff bubbles a subject of active discussion as COVID cases rise.* NFL.com. https://www.nfl.com/news/nfl-playoff-Bubbles-a-subject-of-active-discussion-as-covid-cases-rise

Schultz, F., Kleinnijenhuis, J., Oegema, D., Utz, S., & Van Atteveldt, W. (2012). Strategic framing in the BP crisis: A semantic network analysis of associative frames. *Public Relations Review*, 38(1), 97–107. https://doi.org/10.1016/j.pubrev.2011.08.003

Skinner, J., & Smith, A.C.T. (2021). Introduction: Sport and COVID-19—impacts and challenges for the future (volume 1). *European Sport Management Quarterly*, 21(3), 323–332. https://doi.org/10.1080/16184742.2021.1925725

Ulmer, R.R., Seeger, M.W., & Sellnow, T.L. (2007). Post-crisis communication and renewal: Expanding the parameters of post-crisis discourse. *Public Relations Review*, 33(2), 130–134. https://doi.org/10.1016/j.pubrev.2006.11.015

Vafeiadis, M., Bortree, D. S., Buckley, C., Diddi, P., & Xiao, A. (2020). Refuting fake news on social media: nonprofits, crisis response strategies and issue involvement. *Journal of Product & Brand Management*, 29(2), 209–222.Vafeiadis, M., Bortree, D. S., Buckley, C., Diddi, P., & Xiao, A. (2020). Refuting fake news on social media: nonprofits, crisis response strategies and issue involvement. Journal of Product & Brand Management, 29(2), 209–222.

Vaudreuil, N.J., Kennedy, A.J., Lombardo, S.J., & Kharrazi, F.D. (2021). Impact of COVID-19 on recovered athletes returning to competitive play in the NBA "bubble." *Orthopaedic Journal of Sports Medicine*, 9(3). https://doi.org/10.1177/23259671211004531

Young, R. (2021). Forced play: Was the MLB commissioner's decision to force a 2020 MLB season amid coronavirus unenforceable, or just a bad idea? *Jeffrey S. Moorad Sports Law Journal*, 28(2), 499–553. https://heinonline.org/HOL/P?h=hein.journals/vse28&i=527

· 1 0 ·

CORONAVIRUS AND JOURNALISM: A META-ANALYSIS OF EARLY RESEARCH ON JOURNALISM IN THE COVID-19 PANDEMIC

Gregory Perreault, Ella Hackett, & Alexis Handler

Growing up in Rio Grande Valley gave Edgar Sandoval, criminal justice reporter for *The New York Times*, the unique ability to report on the arrival of the coronavirus to that small Texas town. As he prepared himself to enter a tight-knit community where parties and gatherings were second nature, he realized the spread of the coronavirus might be more rapid than he anticipated. It wasn't until he was boarding the plane when he received a text that would change the course of his trip. "'It looks like all of the Sandovales have COVID,'" he read. Just like that, Sandoval would no longer be reporting from the sidelines.

Instead of having to get the feel of an unfamiliar town like he usually would do when reporting, Sandoval recalled the traditions and routines he grew up with. Instead of interviewing new faces for information, he sat on the phone with his mother as she lay in a hospital bed. Instead of researching sources, he consoled his close family and friends as they mourned loved ones. It could be said that many journalists alike would find themselves in similar positions. Positions that made them realize that for the first time in their careers, they were not separated from their story. They were not simply an observer anymore, but rather in the middle of the playing field.

Reader comments provided Sandoval with thanks. "Thanks for giving this tragedy a human face," one read. The reality of this pandemic is that it affected everyone, and everyone wanted to know they weren't alone (Sandoval, 2020). Journalists and their audiences alike have had to adapt their practices and come up with strategies as to how to cope with life-altering circumstances during the pandemic.

This is one of many stories exemplifying the reality of journalists dealing not only with their own lives being shifted, but how they would analyze the changes happening in the entire world, how they would tell their audience about it, and how their audience would receive it. This chapter conducts a meta-analysis of research done in journalism studies during the early stages of the coronavirus. Hence, this chapter reflects the topics central during this time; namely the impact COVID-19 had on journalists financially, emotionally, and practically; how their audiences dealt with information and whether they maintained healthy news habits; and the ways in which social media sources played a role in distributing misinformation.

Field Theory

In essence, Bourdieu's (1977, 2005) field theory operates as a sort of sport metaphor—imagining professional fields as operating on a field. Actors on the field are pulled in multiple directions as a result of the expectations of their profession's *game*. The essence of the theory emphasizes an interest in understanding the "reproduction of fields of intellectual or economic striving" (Lizardo, 2004, p. 377), a knowledge that is reproduced through journalism. Fields tend to fight for the preservation of their space, even as athletes push against the renegotiation of the field of play while in play. Journalism is no different. Research has demonstrated that the traditional values of journalism prove very resilient to calls for change or even to pressure from external forces (Vos et al., 2012; Perreault & Ferrucci, 2020; Perreault & Stanfield, 2019). Journalists operate with a *doxa*, a well of knowledge and experience that helps journalists understand their place within the field (Bourdieu, 2005). This *doxa* is operated through the *habitus*, the habits of the field or the "strategy generating principle enabling agents to cope with unforeseen and ever-changing situations" (Bourdieu, 1977, p. 77). This sort of principle has proven valuable in other sorts of unexpected challenges, allowing journalists to innately and almost unconsciously respond to a hate group rally with an understanding of their journalistic role (Perreault et al., 2020) or to the coronavirus pandemic with an understanding of how their practices need adapt (Perreault et al., 2021).

With the habitus, actors may mistake activities as natural when they actually have been culturally shaped. For example, Bourdieu (1977) uses an analogy of a baseball player who needs little conscious thought to know when to swing at a fastball. In a similar manner, journalists anticipate certain forms of journalistic coverage in such a manner so that they know how to report on them with little conscious thought.

The goal for actors on the field are forms of *capital*—economic, cultural, and social. Cultural capital is often referred to in terms of prestige, often reflected in terms of valued journalistic work such as investigative reporting, in-depth reporting and thoughtful commentary (Vos, 2012). Social capital is often connected to a journalist's social circle—or their social network. And economic capital refers to the whole of a news organization's financial resources.

Journalism During COVID-19

The COVID-19 pandemic placed journalists in an unprecedented situation similar to but never quite exact to that of other crises or disasters. Typically, journalists respond to chaotic situations by interpreting factual, official information and spreading it to the public in the interest of mitigating risk and helping people adapt to the crisis in question. An example of this is seen in tornado warning messages, which are broadcasted to the public during said tornadoes and are considered a trusted form of communication with journalists standing in as the remediaries of public information (Perreault et al., 2014). In the same regard as with natural disasters, the way that journalists relate to and share information with the public during a pandemic can differ given the specific challenges of the situation, but can offer the public a sense of comfort as they emanate the familiarity of normal practices used in everyday reporting (Perreault & Perreault, 2021). For example, journalists navigating COVID-19 conditions for their own personal well-being may opt to socially distance or use video conferencing software to support pandemic restrictions and keep all parties safe, but remain putting out relevant content for audiences.

When it comes to crisis and disaster communication, news reporting plays a vital role by connecting journalists and citizens through credible information. The cyclical nature of social media platforms further encourage this pattern by allowing for symmetric communication to occur among journalists, citizens and public information liaisons (Houston et al., 2015). Journalism itself serves the public as both a daily resource and a means to archive catastrophic moments in time. With regard to topics such as health and science (and applied subtopics including natural disasters and climate change), journalists without sufficient training or experience may run into challenges in trying to cover them (Hiles & Hinnant, 2014). The development of how journalists have covered climate change is just one example of this, as the progression of science over the last few decades heavily influenced the way in which the same narratives are translated through the press. Giving the public accurate, accessible information about scientific developments has been a difficult task for journalists to learn to keep up with (Brüggemann, 2017). While the purpose of journalism is to provide objective facts in a consistent manner, the profession often lacks the ability to wait on the process in which uncertainties surrounding a public health crisis are further evaluated and confirmed; the foundational knowledge around COVID-19 being a prime example.

Journalists are typically used to cover crises and disasters, and often focus on conflict as the main contributor to the news value of a story (Zelizer, 2015). During the pandemic, however, journalists took a specific communicative approach in the way they performed their work (Perreault & Perreault, 2021). Journalists had to adapt to reporting in a pandemic by utilizing skills from other crises, and within the first nine months of COVID-19's official outbreak experienced the back and forth of expectations, audiences' needs and general risks. These adaptations are not inherently new to the profession, but rather aided in demonstrating how the pandemic impacted the world that journalists are responsible to report on. Over time, four journalistic practices have been established: (1) research, (2) freedom of speech, (3) a pursuit of truth and accuracy, and (4) integration of ethical principles (Pavlik, 2013). Journalistic practice emphasizes the use of "history as a strategic resource, reminding their readers of the long and storied histories of their respective newspapers and giving them the impression that hundreds of years of history were on the line" (Finneman & Thomas, 2021, p. 14). These key practices establish the means by which journalism functions in a professional environment, as well as provide understanding of how journalists impact the coverage of news.

Living in a crisis while simultaneously covering it brings many challenges that are difficult to navigate. Although many journalists never experience trauma in their daily lives, those working locally may be more attuned to covering crises and disasters that directly affect both themselves and their target audiences (Perreault, 2020). These challenges have only been emphasized as

COVID-19 increased debates over safety, legitimacy of information, risk, and the personal and professional effects of such decisions.

Journalists use formal, pre-established networks to source information and develop stories to share with the public. However, the early days of a crisis can create doubt over whether or not available information is truly verified or trustworthy—even if said information comes from the same credible sources as used in past disasters. Therefore, journalists use specific frameworks to help them navigate the reporting. An example of this is seen when journalists cover dangerous actors, as research shows they operate as *storytellers* in order to mitigate coverage and avoid a balancing of truth and falsehood (Perreault et al., 2020). They operate as *enrichers* when catering to particular audiences and groups and enhance the experience of learning new information (Perreault & Bell, 2020), and operate as *disseminators* when seeking to remain objective within a volatile cultural space (Perreault et al., 2020). In crises, journalists frequently operate as *facilitators* to monitor the environment for "relevant information about events, conditions, trends, and threats" (Christians et al., 2010, p. 139) due to a perceived need for intervention; in other words, pulling from the understanding that journalists are responsive to society and have a significant impact on the public's decision-making during a crisis.

The countries highlighted in this sample all endured subjective circumstances that shaped concern relative to reporting the pandemic back to the public. The United States dealt with particular challenges in covering COVID-19 due to the fact that 2020 saw it operate under conservative political leadership that sought to undermine and dispute scientists and national health leaders. If journalism were to be considered as a "cultural act" that promotes the views of the already powerful (Gutsche, 2018, p. 7), it's evident that such circumstances make reporting in a pandemic harder than ever. Both the United States and the United Kingdom saw a surge in media interactions during the early stages, but fell back to pre-pandemic levels within months; triggering concerns about misinformation and magnifying the trustworthiness of messaging (Nielsen et al., 2020). This is to showcase that the different countries in this sample operate in various political and media environments, but that this discredits the commonality between the countries: that the trade press gave journalists a location to air grievances about the pandemic and negotiate the best ways to report in light of said pandemic.

This leads us to pose the following research questions:

> RQ1: How did research in journalism reflect on the role of the coronavirus on the work of journalists?

RQ2: How did research in journalism reflect on the role of the coronavirus on news audiences?

Method

The present study conducts a systematic review of research on journalism and the coronavirus pandemic ($n = 21$) published in academic peer-reviewed journals of high quality and wide international research. This research reflects the time frame of March 2020–August 2021. From the introduction of the coronavirus, lockdowns, and testing, to the introduction of the vaccination and the rise of the delta variant of the coronavirus amid concerns of vaccine hesitancy. The journals selected reflect an emphasis on work related to journalism, published in the Social Sciences Citation Index, and having work published on the coronavirus during the initial stages of pandemic reflection (March 2020–August 2021). The following journals were selected: *American Behavioral Scientist; Communication & Sport; Digital Journalism; European Journal of Communication; International Communication Gazette; International Journal of Communication; International Journal of Press & Politics; Journal of Communication; Journalism and Mass Communication Quarterly; Journalism: Theory, Criticism & Practice; Journalism Practice; Journalism Studies; Media & Communication; New Media & Society.*

To collect articles relevant to journalism and the coronavirus pandemic, we searched through Google Scholar, using the search terms "coronavirus AND journalism" and "COVID-19 AND journalism." After this, we screened all abstracts of research articles for coronavirus and journalism. If abstracts did not directly relate to journalism or if coronavirus was ancillary to the study (e.g., an anecdote to start off the study) it was excluded from analysis. Otherwise, research studies, theoretical/conceptual works and editorials were all included.

For the coding process, each article was coded for title, journal, author names, countries reflected by the author's institutions, methodologies, theoretical frameworks, keywords, subjects, and key findings. Analysis was conducted in the model of meta-analysis following the examples set by Hanusch and Vos (2020). Through this analysis, and approached through the lens of field theory, we sought to identify patterns in findings, trends in actors, nationalities, and methodological practices involved in this research. The goal of such research is to illuminate research gaps both theoretically and conceptually as well as to build a foundation of support based on the findings made on COVID and journalism in the early stages of this research.

Coronavirus Impact on Journalists

A dominant theme in the research published in the first year of the coronavirus pandemic reflected on the role the coronavirus played on the work of journalists. In regards to RQ 1, the strain on journalists was felt financially (Perreault & Perreault, 2021), but also in terms of workflow (Perreault et al., 2021).

While local journalism has long suffered under a weakened financial state (Perreault & Perreault, 2021), the coronavirus pandemic demonstrated in explicit form the results of a weakened local journalism initiative. Local journalism during the pandemic contributed directly to citizens' "potential for self-protection and safety" (Olsen et al., 2020, p. 674). However, during the same time period local advertisers drastically cut funds, forcing many news organizations to close (Perreault & Perreault, 2021). The United States, for example, estimated in 2020 to lose more than $30 billion in advertising during the pandemic (Alpert & Hagey, 2020). Similarly, news publishers in Scandinavia reported cancellation of advertising ranging between one-fifth and half of their expected revenue—and this was only in March and April of 2020 (Olsen et al., 2020). These are just two examples that are nevertheless representative of a significant loss of revenue for news worldwide, exacerbating the trends toward news deserts that have already been noted in journalism research (Abernathy, 2018). But it is worth noting that this is most dramatically felt in media systems dependent on advertising income. In other cases, where journalism is funded as a public good, news organizations at times even saw their financing increase—as in Europe where subscriptions rose drastically following the first months of the pandemic (Olsen et al., 2020).

Some journalistic niches were also financially as well as practically infeasible during the early stages of the pandemic—such as sports reporting—and hence, journalists were assigned to cover other topics (Sadri et al., 2021). In sports reporting, journalists were assigned to health, safety, and quality of life stories instead.

A perhaps obvious effect of the coronavirus pandemic is that journalists not only needed to work remotely, but indeed found there was much less they could cover in person. As a result, journalists were forced to work from their homes. As Ioan (2021) put it, "[T]he house, which up to COVID-19 was only a place to relax and recharge the batteries, usually during the night, suddenly turned into the place where the entire existence was concentrated 24/7" (p. 35). The result of this meant that journalists were at once never fully at work and never fully home—a reality that made the work of journalism all the more difficult (Ioan, 2021). While teleworking is a reality that has existed in journalism for years, it wasn't until the pandemic that it became a *mandated* way of life (García-Avilés, 2021). Most newsrooms, García-Avilés (2021) argues, "followed a conservative approach of 'doing journalism as usual.' ... maintaining standard practices from the physical newsroom and overseeing power relationships" (p. 18). Hence, the goal was to try to recreate the physical experience digitally; an approach that by nature required journalists to build employee cooperation and required editors to exert their power (García-Avilés, 2021).

This difficulty was amplified by the needs placed upon journalists during this time, namely to verify a wide range of information related to the pandemic that could fundamentally shape the response of their audience, but they were asked to do so with few resources. In general, the demands for innovation in journalism tend to put a heavy burden on journalists (Ferrucci & Perreault, 2021), but in this case in particular, journalists were being asked to innovate in relation to their practices; to respond to a pandemic with practices for gathering and verifying information (Ioan, 2021). These are long-held routines within journalism that nevertheless were stretched by the realities posed by the pandemic (Hoak, 2021). Hoak (2021) did not find any significant stress stemming from employer-employee relationships, although those commonly emerge in crisis situations. Logistical support, seemingly, was sufficient for the pandemic, but there were other areas which received less support. As in Ferrucci and Perreault (2021), they were being asked to do so with little training or resources; "journalists have neither the training nor the time necessary to verify the accuracy of the data obtained. Even more so since the situation is not clear even to specialists" (Ioan, 2021, p. 38). Hoak (2021) notes that the exceptional nature of the pandemic made journalists' normative commitment to obtaining and verifying information almost impossible to conduct.

> As the United States began to shut down in March, those long-held routines collapsed. Journalists were forced to embrace an unusual and constantly fluctuating norm that included using new technology with little to no training, disseminating news with no newsroom, online interviews, and remote television from their living rooms, and for those with families, figuring out how to "do journalism" while children homeschooled in the next room. (Hoak, 2021, p. 855)

Hoak (2021) further noted that in general, the introduction of new routines into journalism tends to result in increased stress on the part of journalists. Indeed as Hoak (2021) demonstrated, journalists in general reported higher than usual levels of stress particularly if they worked in the television medium—perhaps a result of having to balance the needs of clean visuals and audio in a home environment that could be chaotic with homeschooling and work-from-home. Furthermore, many journalists noted a sense of loneliness in their work according to Hoak (2021).

Research seemed to place the coronavirus within the broader trend of the growing dangers posed by climate change. Hence, the practices developed during the pandemic gain additional import given that they represent an initial run at operating amid extreme weather circumstances and reflect the challenges of reporting when free flow of information is impeded by its availability (Perreault et al., 2021). Furthermore, the challenges journalists faced in responding to pandemic conditions would seem to only have the ability to grow more acute in the future (Perreault & Perreault, 2021). However, it is encouraging to note how quickly and effectively journalists made changes in order to adapt to the needs of their audiences; reflecting that while circumstances may change, journalists' normative commitment did not.

Coronavirus Impact on Audiences

In regards to RQ 2, research conducted in the early stages of lockdown suggests that respective emotional, social, and contextual circumstances both promote and hinder the news habits shaped by audiences during the coronavirus. Broersma and Swart (2021) identified five groups of news users whose news habits provided examples of different responses to the pandemic. Those groups are: news avoiders, followers turned avoiders, stable news users, frequent news users and news junkies. Studies show that differing social context, lifestyles, levels of stress and anxiety, and emotional drives may explain these different behaviors.

Based on previous research, it was expected that the need for information at the beginning of the pandemic would surge (Broersma & Swart, 2021). Therefore, news consumption substantially increased (Ytre-Arne & Moe, 2021). All groups showed considerable interest in news early on in the pandemic; however, varying factors drove some individuals in the direction of news consumption, while others practiced avoiding it.

"Frequent news users" and "news junkies" formed and upheld good news habits, because the information they were receiving proved to be of importance or of good use to them. They recognized that forming habits that kept them up to date on the happenings of the pandemic would play a substantial role in their lives (Broersma & Swart, 2021). Social cues played a role in sustaining their news use habits (Broersma & Swart, 2021), as well as motivations to maintain political-social identities (Young & Bleakley, 2020).

The dependency theory of the media system "predicts that the dependence that people feel on the media tends to increase in crisis situations" (Ferreira & Borges, 2020, p. 110). When the social environment lost important components and became unpredictable, the dependence on the media increased. However, because information usually provided by the media was incomplete due to journalists' limited access to resources, feelings of ambiguity were evoked in the audience. Citizens knew that a crisis had occurred, but they did not know what it meant, how to interpret it or how to go forward. As a result, more information was sought out by the individual in an attempt to resolve this ambiguity—which increases the existing dependency on media (Ferreira & Borges, 2020).

While there was a pattern in "news avoiders" and "followers turned avoiders" participating in media consumption at first, the pursuit of information was not repeated, and habit of news use was not formed (Broersma & Swart, 2021). These groups tended to avoid news later on due to a number of factors. News avoidance has often been used as a strategy to escape emotionally unsettling news (Ytre-Arne & Moe, 2021). Broersma and Swart's study provided that many avoided news due to the belief that the circumstances did not affect them (2021).

Stress and anxiety played a role in both the consumption and avoidance of news. In the face of a public health crisis, individuals are more likely to engage in information-seeking behaviors in order to receive answers. This is due to increases in stress and anxiety (Young & Bleakley, 2020). For others, however, the constant reminder of positive COVID-19 cases, death tolls, government policies, etc., are constant reminders of ongoing feelings of stress, fear, and uncertainty, in which case avoiding the news would be this person's initial response (Broersma & Swart, 2021).

Audiences also had a politically polarized response to the coronavirus, which played a role in their media consumption as well. Individuals often sought social and political identity reinforcing media content (Young & Bleakley, 2020), which in turn kept them relevant in news facilitated conversations and social relations, as well as allowed them to relate to civic issues and public debate (Broersma & Swart, 2021).

In opposition to the extremes of diving into the media and avoiding it all together is finding a balance between the need for information and the need to cope with anxiety and stress (Ytre-Arne & Moe, 2021). With a constant opportunity to follow the news due to social media, television, and online news sites, citizens were buried in news daily. News became even more accessible when the lockdown eliminated the flow of daily life, and all anyone could do was sit in their house with the news running. While news consumption is not a bad thing, the information overload needed to be countered in order to minimize the amount of emotional distress and anxiety (Ytre-Arne & Moe, 2021).

The Moderating Role of Social Media in the Pandemic

In another theme responsive to RQ 2, social media during the pandemic instilled itself as a reliable, optimum resource for publics to intercommunicate with one another, and the COVID-19 pandemic did little to jeopardize that. It did, however, play a role in both undermining and enhancing public trust during the pandemic, as well as influencing the information and updates taken away (van Dijck & Alinejad, 2020). While impressions throughout different platforms varied across countries, citizens' ability to use the internet and access real-time updates transformed social media platforms into entire support systems. But for journalists, social media quickly turned the pandemic into a misinformation nightmare.

The beginning of the pandemic saw citizens of the world scrambling to get their hands on as much information as possible; even within those who didn't typically engage with news media. In a Dutch study on social psychology and habit formation during COVID-19, researchers found that "considerable life changes and disruptions in daily routines can give rise to the adaptation or formation of habits" (Broersma & Swart, 2021, p. 1) and that people began associating pandemic updates with positive rewards as the information pertained to relevant topics within their personal lives. Social media offers people the opportunity to talk back where traditional media does not, allowing them to feel heard around the world even when in the comfort of their homes. In a situation where entire countries were shutting down and keeping citizens isolated, this type of connection became more vital than ever before. When studying initial reactions to the pandemic from where it originated in Italy, it was concluded that the presence of social media allowed for "a sort of collective intelligence through which the unexpected was domesticated and the mounting feeling of astonishment recognized" (Vicari & Murru, 2020, p. 3).

These patterns stopped, however, upon the information turning into overstimulation and triggering a widespread pattern of news avoidance. Because the pandemic brought up so many different emotions, many people ceased to check the news as a coping skill to quite emotional and attentive drainage. Alternatively, some stopped engaging with news upon getting accustomed to the lockdown, at which point they felt confident and comfortable enough with the reality of the pandemic to step away from the calamity of it all. Others found themselves caught in a routine of "doomscrolling," in which they constantly kept up with media platforms in order to match the urgency of the pandemic and stay as updated as possible (Ytre-Arne & Moe, 2021). Further still, there were groups that sought to use irony as a means to cope with the influx of information; in other words, they never stopped engaging with the news, but didn't take it completely seriously, either. And although humor is a vital attribute to mitigate times of crisis, journalists soon found themselves scrambling among platforms to confirm, deny, and address the rumors and misinformation that arose in the aftermath.

Thanks to high levels of emotional content and vividness, it's known that false messages are shared online more frequently than accurate ones (Dunwoody, 2020), and to suggest that the pandemic led to increased emotional turmoil would be an understatement. At the beginning of the pandemic, news outlets prioritized health and safety as publics simultaneously took to social media to express their own thoughts; all while hurrying to digest as much information across platforms as possible. Despite consuming and questioning stories from all available sources at this time, studies showed that people still attributed greater credibility to traditional media due to the factual sources privileged by journalists (Ferreira & Borges, 2020). In this regard, many sectors within the journalism industry found themselves having to reframe the way that they communicated with their publics in order to maintain relevance and interest. Once the lockdown was established and sports were clearly put to the side, sports journalists shifted in emphasis to both highlight health and safety and defend journalism as being the public's first line of defense. This not only represents the malleability of journalism, but "highlights the integral role of journalism during a pandemic ... [representing] an aggressive attempt to reshape the media ecosystem and combat the spread of misinformation" (Sadri et al., 2021, p. 19). It's indisputable that citizens look to news media to be informed, especially with regards to a health crisis, and keeping various aspects of the industry centralized around the pandemic allowed for people to stay connected to credible and factual information.

Despite the general consensus that traditional media is more factual than social media, misinformation still impacted a good amount of the public's ability to understand the pandemic. The issue that many officials came across was found in determining the extent that they could limit misinformation without infringing on individual rights to express oneself. Since the start of the pandemic, 18 different governments implemented counter-measures through decrees and emergency legislation with the intention of discouraging the creation and spread of misinformation (Radu, 2020). Unfortunately, this also served to facilitate the flourishing of such misinformation by "undermining legitimate journalism and eroding trust in institutions of authority" (Radu, 2020, p. 3). In these situations, it's imperative that official sources aren't villainized to maintain public trust and keep people confident in returning to journalistic sources. A study conducted in Switzerland based on the dissemination of COVID-19 news revealed that "there is a gap between perception (trust) and reality (usage) of information sources ... [citizens] do not trust politicians, but they have a remarkably high degree of trust in their national government" (Liu et al., 2020, p. 155). Essentially, journalists and other public officials cannot connect with the public and combat misinformation if the strategy is to be on the offensive, as doing so only prompts further suspicion for audiences.

In conclusion, the pandemic has seen social media act as a coping mechanism, news outlet, social gathering and everything in between. It gives people the ability to validate themselves, engage directly with public officials and share individual experiences to help others. However, it also allowed for widespread misinformation, deceit, and panic to thrive where it otherwise would be written off by traditional media as irrelevant. At its best, social media effectively moderated between the factual information coming out of journalists and the emotional responses needed to be processed as citizens grew accustomed to isolation, safety procedures and an overall halt in daily life. Journalism as an industry found itself focusing all eyes on the pandemic in order to put out as much accurate information as possible, even within sectors where health and wellness are less of a priority. Even through the months of combating misinformation with reassurance, the pandemic clearly proved the relevance and necessity of journalism when it comes to public crises as being both a reliable and trusted source of information.

Conclusion

Taken together, this chapter synthesizes the research done of both timely and recurrent significance: the coronavirus. It is possible that the topic of the coronavirus is contextually situated. Perhaps it is one that will never be repeated.

The research perspective is that the coronavirus represents merely an initial foray into a host of climate and viral challenges that humanity will face in the years to come (Perreault et al., 2021). If this is the case, journalism could scarcely be more essential and more adaptable to change. From a field theory perspective, many professions tend to reflect strong boundaries. Journalism is often perceived as holding a strong boundary and professional identity (Vos et al., 2012), however, based on the research conducted during coronavirus it would seem that actually the opposite was represented during coronavirus. In order to innovate, journalism needed to be heteronomous—that is open to change and new actors—the ability to welcome in new ideas in order to be adaptable to change (Perreault & Ferrucci, 2020). However, this heteronomy causes some instability as we see here.

This study reflects a shift in journalistic *habitus* as journalists scrambled to reinvent their habits in order to better respond to the challenges before them (Bourdieu, 1977). However, their ability to respond and adapt with such grace is also reflective of their habitus in some ways. Journalists are in the habit of needing to respond to changes in the field and doing so in ways that do not jeopardize the field's normative commitments as reflected in journalistic doxa. Worth noting is that while journalists struggled in regard to their economic capital and worked to gain greater social capital during the pandemic, this, in many ways, simply reflected an extension of existing trends.

It is essential for journalists to pay close attention to their own habits in order to better prepare themselves for future crises. This way, scrambling to remain consistent during wavering circumstances—and future crises are inevitable—will be minimal. Instead, journalists will be better suited to adapt in an ever-changing industry.

Every study has limitations, and this one is no exception. Pandemic journalism is a rapidly evolving field that has evolved along with the coronavirus. For the purpose of clear analysis, this study had to pinpoint a particular time frame and this time frame while comprehensive at the time of writing—in late 2021—may in the long view not be representative of the lasting impact of the coronavirus overall.

Perhaps the pernicious effect of the pandemic may be the resulting shift in focus when analyzing journalistic research (Lewis, 2020). Shortly after the pandemic began, research in journalism studies began to show an increased focus on a range of topics from local journalism (Wenzel & Crittenden, 2021) to journalistic well-being (Wahl-Jorgensen, 2020)—topics that had received less attention in relation to scholarship on technology. Crises have a way of laying things bare and revealing areas that need further attention, and that has been as true for journalism as it is for journalism research.

Discussion Questions

1. Due to the international presence of the coronavirus, the pandemic became a political issue almost instantaneously. Seeing as journalists are responsible to present unbiased stories to the public, how did the pandemic force them to find new ways to report?
2. To what degree would you suggest that the isolation and social distancing contributed to a lack of full transparency within real-world events?
3. Do you believe that the journalism industry will ever return to a fully in-person state? Or will there always be an element of technology contributing to the "new normal?"
4. Long gone are the days where one's only source of information is from a newspaper. Do you think that the convenience of social media and high internet speed will ever replace the validity of receiving news from an official reporter?
5. How can we differentiate between reliable and unreliable news sources now that everything has become digitized and tones within stories aren't always specified?

References

Abernathy, P.M. (2018). *The expanding news desert*. Center for Innovation and Sustainability in Local Media, School of Media and Journalism, University of North Carolina at Chapel Hill. https://www.cislm.org/wp-content/uploads/2018/10/The-Expanding-News-Desert-10_14-Web.pdf

Alpert, L.I., & Hagey, K. (2020). Coronavirus is giving readers plenty of news. But local outlets are still teetering. *Wall Street Journal*. https://www.wsj.com/articles/news-outlets-win-audiences-yet-lose-revenue-during-coronavirus-crisis-11584708390

Bourdieu, P. (1977). Structures and the habitus. In V. Buckli (Ed.), *Material culture: Critical concepts in the social sciences* (Vol. 1, Part 1, pp. 72–95). Routledge.

Bourdieu, P. (2005). *The social structures of the economy*. Polity Press.

Broersma, M., & Swart, J. (2021). Do novel routines stick after the pandemic? The formation of news habits during COVID-19. *Journalism Studies*, 1–18. https://doi.org/10.1080/1461670X.2021.1932561

Brüggemann, M. (2017). Shifting roles of science journalists covering climate change. In *Oxford research encyclopedia of climate science*. https://doi.org/10.1093/acrefore/9780190228620.013.354

Christians, C.G., Glasser, T., McQuail, D., Nordenstreng, K., & White, R.A. (2010). *Normative theories of the media: Journalism in democratic societies*. University of Illinois Press.

van Dijck, J., & Alinejad, D. (2020). Social media and trust in scientific expertise: Debating the Covid-19 pandemic in the Netherlands. *Social Media+ Society*, 6(4), https://doi.org/10.1177/2056305120981057

Dunwoody, S. (2020). Science journalism and pandemic uncertainty. *Media and Communication*, 8(2), 471–474. https://doi.org/10.17645/mac.v8i2.3224

Ferreira, G.B., & Borges, S. (2020). Media and misinformation in times of COVID-19: How people informed themselves in the days following the Portuguese Declaration of the State of Emergency. *Journalism and Media*, 1(1), 108–121. https://doi.org/10.3390/journalmedia1010008

Ferrucci, P., & Perreault, G. (2021). The liability of newness: Journalism, innovation and the issue of core competencies. *Journalism Studies*, 22(11), 1436–1449. https://doi.org/10.1080/1461670X.2021.1916777

Finneman, T., & Thomas, R.J. (2021). "Our company is in survival mode": Metajournalistic discourse on COVID-19's impact on US community newspapers. *Journalism Practice*, 1–19. https://doi.org/10.1080/17512786.2021.1888149

García-Avilés, J.A. (2021). Journalism as usual? Managing disruption in virtual newsrooms during the COVID-19 crisis. *Digital Journalism*, 1–22. https://doi.org/10.1080/21670811.2021.1942112

Gutsche, R.E., Jr. (Ed.). (2018). *The Trump presidency, journalism, and democracy*. Routledge.

Hanusch, F., & Vos, T.P. (2020). Charting the development of a field: A systematic review of comparative studies of journalism. *International Communication Gazette*, 82(4), 319–341. https://doi.org/10.1177/1748048518822606

Hiles, S.S., & Hinnant, A. (2014). Climate change in the newsroom: Journalists' evolving standards of objectivity when covering global warming. *Science Communication*, 36(4), 428–453. https://doi.org/10.1177/1075547014534077

Hoak, G. (2021). Covering COVID: Journalists' stress and perceived organizational support while reporting on the pandemic. *Journalism & Mass Communication Quarterly*, 98(3), 854–874. https://doi.org/10.1177/10776990211015105

Houston, J.B., Hawthorne, J., Perreault, M.F., Park, E.H., Goldstein Hode, M., Halliwell, M.R., Turner McGowen, S.E., Davis, R., Vaid, S., McElderry, J.A. & Griffith, S.A. (2015). Social media and disasters: A functional framework for social media use in disaster planning, response, and research. *Disasters*, 39(1), 1–22. https://doi.org/10.1111/disa.12092

Ioan, A. (2021). Journalism-Between utopia and pandemic dystopia. *International Journal of Communication Research*, 11(1). https://www.ijcr.eu/articole/534_005%20Alexandru%20Ioan.pdf

Lewis, S.C. (2020). The objects and objectives of journalism research during the coronavirus pandemic and beyond. *Digital Journalism*, 8(5), 681–689. https://doi.org/10.1080/21670811.2020.1773292

Liu, Z., Shan, J., Delaloye, M., Piguet, J.G., & Glassey Balet, N. (2020). The role of public trust and media in managing the dissemination of COVID-19-related news in Switzerland. *Journalism and Media*, 1(1), 145–158. https://doi.org/10.3390/journalmedia1010010

Lizardo, O. (2004). The cognitive origins of Bourdieu's habitus. *Journal for the Theory of Social Behaviour*, 34(4), 375–401. https://doi.org/10.1111/j.1468-5914.2004.00255.x

Nielsen, R.K., Fletcher, R., Newman, N., Brennen, J.S., & Howard, P.N. (2020, April 15). *Navigating the "Infodemic": How people in six countries access and rate news and information about Coronavirus*. Reuters Institute for the Study of Journalism. https://reutersinstitute.politics.ox.ac.uk/infodemic-how-people-six-countries-access-and-rate-news-and-information-about-coronavirus

Olsen, R.K., Pickard, V., & Westlund, O. (2020). Communal news work: COVID-19 calls for collective funding of journalism. *Digital Journalism*, 8(5), 673–680. https://doi.org/10.1080/21670811.2020.1763186

Pavlik, J.V. (2013). Innovation and the future of journalism. *Digital Journalism*, 1(2), 181–193. https://doi.org/10.1080/21670811.2012.756666

Perreault, G., & Bell, T.R. (2020). Towards a "digital" sports journalism: Field theory, changing boundaries and evolving technologies. *Communication & Sport*, 10(3), 398–416. https://doi.org/10.1177/2167479520979958

Perreault, G.P., & Ferrucci, P. (2020). What is digital journalism? Defining the practice and role of the digital journalist. *Digital Journalism*, 8(10), 1298–1316. https://doi.org/10.1080/21670811.2020.1848442

Perreault, M.F., Houston, J.B., & Wilkins, L. (2014). Does scary matter?: Testing the effectiveness of new National Weather Service tornado warning messages. *Communication Studies*, 65(5), 484–499. https://doi.org/10.1080/10510974.2014.956942

Perreault, G., Johnson, B., & Klein, L. (2020). Covering hate: Field theory and journalistic role conception in reporting on White nationalist rallies. *Journalism Practice*, 16(6), 1117–1133. https://doi.org/10.1080/17512786.2020.1835525

Perreault, M.F., & Perreault, G.P. (2021). Journalists on COVID-19 journalism: Communication ecology of pandemic reporting. *American Behavioral Scientist*, 65(7), 976–991. https://journals.sagepub.com/doi/pdf/10.1177/00027642211992813

Perreault, G., Perreault, M.F., & Maares, P. (2021). Metajournalistic discourse as a stabilizer within the journalistic field: Journalistic practice in the Covid-19 pandemic. *Journalism Practice*, 1–19. https://doi.org/10.1080/17512786.2021.1949630

Perreault, G., & Stanfield, K. (2019). Mobile journalism as lifestyle journalism? Field Theory in the integration of mobile in the newsroom and mobile journalist role conception. *Journalism Practice*, 13(3), 331–348. https://doi.org/10.1080/17512786.2018.1424021

Radu, R. (2020). Covid-19. Fighting the "Infodemic": Legal Responses to COVID-19 Disinformation. *Social Media+ Society*, 6(3). https://doi.org/10.1177/2056305120948190

Sadri, S.R., Buzzelli, N.R., Gentile, P., & Billings, A.C. (2021). Sports journalism content when no sports occur: Framing athletics amidst the COVID-19 international pandemic. *Communication & Sport*, 10(3), 493–516. https://doi.org/10.1177%2F21674795211001937

Sandoval, E. (2020, July 14). I went home to Texas to cover the virus. Then my family got it. *The New York Times*. https://www.nytimes.com/2020/07/14/us/coronavirus-texas-rio-grande-valley-border.html

Vicari, S., & Murru, M.F. (2020). Covid-19. One platform, a thousand worlds: On Twitter irony in the early response to the COVID-19 pandemic in Italy. *Social Media+ Society*, 6(3), https://doi.org/10.1177/2056305120948254

Vos, T.P., Craft, S., & Ashley, S. (2012). New media, old criticism: Bloggers' press criticism and the journalistic field. *Journalism*, 13(7), 850–868. https://doi.org/10.1177/1464884911421705

Wahl-Jorgensen, K. (2020). An emotional turn in journalism studies?. *Digital Journalism*, 8(2), 175–194. https://doi.org/10.1080/21670811.2019.1697626

Wenzel, A.D., & Crittenden, L. (2021). Collaborating in a pandemic: Adapting local news infrastructure to meet information needs. *Journalism Practice*, 1–19. https://doi.org/10.1080/17512786.2021.1910986

Young, D.G., & Bleakley, A. (2020). Ideological health spirals: An integrated political and health communication approach to COVID interventions. *International Journal of Communication*, 14, 3509–3524. https://ijoc.org/index.php/ijoc/article/viewFile/15309/3139

Ytre-Arne, B., & Moe, H. (2021). Doomscrolling, monitoring and avoiding: News use in COVID-19 pandemic lockdown. *Journalism Studies*, 22(13), 1739–1755. https://doi.org/10.1080/1461670X.2021.1952475

Zelizer, B. (2015). Terms of choice: Uncertainty, journalism, and crisis. *Journal of Communication*, 65(5), 888–908. https://doi.org/10.1111/jcom.12157

· 11 ·

SIX FEET APART: A CASE STUDY OF URBAN AND RURAL MEDICAL PROFESSIONALS' AND HEALTH SYSTEMS' RESPONSES TO COVID-19

Melanie B. Richards & Ashleigh D. Bunn

> *When you know something is going to happen, have a plan in place on what you are going to do when it does happen, because we've known that there was going to be an outbreak of something—we're way past due for it . . . it should have been, "let's open up the playbook and see where we go."*
>
> —Rural Medical Provider Study Participant

COVID-19 Pandemic Timeline in Tennessee

In early 2020, COVID-19, the disease caused by the SARS-COV-2 virus, spread across the United States. Tennessee, as a state, was not an area initially impacted heavily by the virus. New COVID-19 case counts did not begin rising substantially in Tennessee until July 2020. Peak cases were then observed in December 2020 (coinciding with the timing of Thanksgiving and other winter gatherings) and September 2021 (coinciding with a return to school in person and a rise in the Delta variant). This trend was true for both urban and rural areas of the state.

Concurrent with disease spread, disease prevention and management were topics addressed in both health system and medical provider communications.

However, initial communications regarding how to best prevent the disease were often unclear, with vague and occasionally inconsistent information cascading down through major and regional health agencies, health systems, and medical practices. Seeming inconsistencies regarding preventative measures including social distancing, mask-wearing, and later, vaccination, frustrated individuals and families searching for information regarding how to best protect their loved ones and their communities. Many individuals went online at this time to do their own research. However, they were met face-to-face with an infodemic of even more vague, confusing, and, in many cases, contradictory information (Zarocostas, 2020).

Though Google searches regarding COVID-19 generally followed the new case counts for the state and in the regions (Google Trends, 2021), the highest number of "coronavirus"[1] related searches in Tennessee, by far, occurred at the beginning of the pandemic timeline in March 2020. This happened before state case counts started climbing. Searches then increased again in summer 2020, when case counts began to rise substantially in Tennessee (Tennessee Department of Health, 2021). This was true in both rural and urban areas. Early pandemic searches for disease-preventative information regarding "masks" were displaced by searches related to "COVID-19 vaccines" as the pandemic timeline wore on, while searches regarding "social distancing" remained relatively low in prevalence to other COVID-19–related topics throughout the course of the pandemic.

Social distancing was the initial disease-preventative behavior recommended by both health agencies and government entities on a larger scale. Though larger metro areas, like Los Angeles and New York City, enacted shelter-in-place orders in March 2020 as case counts quickly escalated, most smaller cities and rural areas issued social distancing recommendations in an attempt to slow the rapidly increasing epidemiological curve. Six feet of distance between individuals was the prevailing recommendation when social distancing measures were first enacted, based on expectations of how far larger virus droplets could move through the air unimpeded (Sheikh et al., 2020). However, other studies supported distances as low as 3 feet or as high as 15 feet, depending on the context of the interaction (Rabin, 2021; Reynolds, 2020).

Mask usage has been another disease-preventative behavior historically used to control disease spread, and in the past has most frequently been utilized by those in higher-risk health categories and by those living in geographical areas where there is a higher risk of virus exposure. Throughout the COVID-19 pandemic, both the United States Centers for Disease Control and Prevention

(CDC) and the World Health Organization (WHO) changed direction on mask guidelines over time. Early in the pandemic, both agencies recommended that only those who were ill or caregiving for the ill needed to wear masks (CDC, 2021; WHO, 2020). These initial recommendations occurred in the midst of panic buying of personal protective equipment (PPE) by individuals, which saw hospitals begin to lose access to various supplies, but most critically, N95 masks (Lee, 2020).

However, in April, both the CDC and the WHO changed their recommendations to suggest that all people wear masks to stop potential disease spread, especially when social distancing was not an option (CDC, 2021; WHO, 2020). The White House echoed these evolved recommendations in April (McDonald, 2020), though the President at that time, Donald Trump, added that he would not personally be following all recommended mask protocols. Being pro-mask, while portrayed as "anti-American" by some, was still a practice adopted (at least on occasion) by 86% of Americans in late June 2020 (Brenan, 2020).

Vaccination was another preventative health measure that, due to the relatively rapid development of medical solutions to combat the disease, increased in public conversations as the pandemic wore on. Upon pandemic onset, the vaccine development timeline was unknown. However, almost a year after the first verified COVID-19 case in the United States, the Pfizer-BioNTech vaccine was the first COVID-19 vaccine made available for broad distribution to individuals aged 16 and over under emergency use authorization by the Food and Drug Administration on December 11, 2020 (U.S. FDA, 2020). Other COVID-19 vaccines from Moderna and Johnson & Johnson/Janssen quickly followed as additional options for individuals aged 18 and over.

COVID in Tennessee: Population Health, Political, and Timeline Considerations

Even prior to the COVID-19 pandemic, many Tennessee residents faced overlapping health challenges concerning access to healthcare, healthcare quality, and public health conditions, with Tennessee ranking 40th in a recent U.S. News and World Reports list of all states for overall healthcare (Ziegler, 2021). These health-related issues exist in both rural and urban areas of Tennessee, though they affect slightly different demographic populations across the state, especially when examining regional population makeup by race and ethnicity.

Recent research has also shown that beliefs about the pandemic and preventative health behaviors are driven more by political affiliation than individual age and local infection incidence (Makridis & Rothwell, 2020). Tennessee is predominantly a conservative-leaning state, having voted solely for Republican gubernatorial and presidential candidates since 2011 and 2000, respectively (NGA, 2021; O'Neill, 2020). These political undercurrents impacted adoption of many disease-preventative behaviors in the state, including vaccination rates. According to the latest data available from the Mayo Clinic, Tennessee continues to maintain one of the lowest vaccination rates in the country compared to other states, with less than half (48.7%) of residents fully vaccinated (Mayo Clinic, 2021).

As another factor in the COVID-19 pandemic, the virus impacted Tennessee later in the spread timeline, which allowed time for regional systems and local providers to observe the changing climate both domestically and internationally and better prepare for community impact. However, the longer runway to virus impact yielded little change in virus effects. In March 2021, a year after the COVID-19 pandemic began in the United States, the state was ranked fifth for the highest number of COVID cases per 100,000 residents (Parker et al., 2021).

Guiding Literature and Theory

Crisis and Emergency Risk Communication Model

The Crisis and Emergency Risk Communication Model (CERC), developed by the Centers for Disease Control and Prevention (CDC), provides an "application of evidence-based principles to effectively communicate during emergencies," and assumes a typical pattern of crisis development: (1) pre-crisis, (2) initial crisis onset, (3) maintenance and mitigation, (4) resolution, and (5) evaluation (CDC, 2014; Reynolds & Seeger, 2005). Though originating and still applied as a practice-driven program by the CDC, the CERC model has since developed into a theoretical framework concerning expectations and best practices for crisis response (Veil et al., 2008).

In the CERC model, the first phase occurs pre-crisis, and includes monitoring of emerging risks, increasing the general public understanding of these risks, and preparing the public for the possibility of a crisis event. The second phase of the model includes the initial crisis event. Following this event, the public is encouraged to lean into self-efficacy behaviors and complete actions to help either mitigate or manage the crisis in both the second and third phases of the model (Lwin et al., 2018; Reynolds & Seeger,

2005). The CDC recommends that effective public health messaging in these phases should:

- Acknowledge fears.
- Express wishes.
- Give people things to do.
- Acknowledge shared misery.
- Give anticipatory guidance (foreshadow).
- Address the "what if" questions, when appropriate.
- Be a role model and ask more of people.
(CDC, 2014, p. 43)

During this study, which examined data from January 2020 through October 2021, the state of Tennessee was in phases one, two, and three of CERC regarding the COVID-19 pandemic, which included pre-crisis, the initial crisis event (defined as March 2020, concurrent with the definition of COVID-19 as a pandemic by the World Health Organization, President Trump's declaration of a national emergency due to the virus, and the first confirmed case of COVID-19 in Tennessee) and resolution (which has yet to occur at the time of this writing) (Tennessee Department of Health, 2020). Ideally, improved public understanding of ongoing disease factors, including risks and context should occur during these phases (Reynolds & Seeger, 2005).

Preventative Health Behaviors/Communications

Studies have shown that communications focused on "(a) disease symptoms, (b) personal efficacy actions, and (c) societal efficacy actions" are most impactful in risk communication (Evensen & Clarke, 2011). Messages that focus on efficacy have also been shown to have a stronger desired effect in terms of driving desired population behavior compared to those that enhance threat perceptions (Barnett et al., 2013).

In times of public health crisis, a consistent and coordinated response from trustworthy public health agencies can also make a positive impact in mitigating crisis effects (Cairns et al., 2013; Dickmann et al., 2014; Frieden, 2014; Ruiu, 2020; Tay et al., 2010). However, in the COVID-19 pandemic, five crisis communication failures have been identified: "i) mixed messages from multiple messengers; ii) delay in releasing information; iii) paternalistic attitudes; iv) lack of immediate reaction to rumors; and v) political confusion" (Ruiu, 2020). Widespread and instantaneous digital communication (e.g., via social media) further amplified these failures, as Walker (2016) predicted several years ago:

> Repeated tidal waves of messages and images will quickly overwhelm traditional information sources, including national governments, global news media outlets, and even on-the-ground first responders. As a result, hundreds of millions of people will receive unvetted and incorrect assertions, uncensored images, and unqualified guidance, all of which, if acted on, could endanger their own health, seriously damage their economies, and undermine the stability of their societies.

With so many inconsistent messages coming through to the public, people questioned and discussed which preventative measures were really necessary and their relative degree of efficacy (if any). Communities looked to their regional health systems and primary medical providers for direction, searched for information online, and discussed the topics with others. These COVID-19 preventative behavior conversations generally focused on three topic areas across the pandemic timeline: social distancing, mask usage, and, later, vaccines/vaccination. Media coverage of the virus spread added fuel to these public conversations and ensuing decisiveness continued even as major health agencies became more clear and concise about their recommendations for these three specific preventative health behaviors. This communication pattern aligns with recent findings regarding public health crisis media messages (Ophir & Jamieson, 2020).

Research Questions

In this study, the authors wished to examine these interrelated issues regarding preventative health behavior communication by examining three research questions:

> **RQ1:** How often did both urban and rural health systems in Tennessee communicate with the public via social media regarding COVID-19 disease-preventative health behaviors throughout the pandemic?
>
> **RQ2:** How did individual medical providers in both urban and rural areas of Tennessee communicate with the public and their patients regarding COVID-19 disease-preventative health behaviors throughout the pandemic?

RQ3: Were there observable communication patterns that differed regarding urban and rural healthcare systems' and providers' responses to COVID-19?

Methods

Health System Social Media Analytics

To address RQ1 and RQ3, the authors leveraged the Brandwatch Consumer Research platform (https://www.brandwatch.com/) for a quantitative content analysis of health system social media posts. Brandwatch is a social media listening and analysis tool which allows users to identify specific posts, topics, hashtags, or authors across social media platforms to better understand consumer trends, audience insights, and viral topics. For the purposes of this research, the authors defined a specific boolean query that would pull in social media post data related to four specific Covid-19 topics: "COVID," "masks," "social distancing," and "vaccination." In defining these topics, the authors specified topics for Brandwatch to "listen for" or scrape when analyzing public social media posts. The tool would then aggregate these post types enabling the authors to further cull the data.

As defined by Brandwatch, "A Mention is a single article of content with a message by an author with corresponding metadata returned as a result to a Query or Channel search, such as a Tweet, Comment, Blog Post, Forum Message, News Article, Image or Video" (Brandwatch, 2021). For the purposes of this study, the authors isolated mentions to look only at the original post content on Facebook, Twitter (X), or Instagram, excluding any comments. Retweets or shares are not considered in "mention" count, as this investigation focused on actual post volume and not virality of each post.

Additionally, the authors verified specific hospital systems for further segmentation. In creating these rule parameters, the authors were able to isolate social media posts by both key topic areas and the hospital system publishing them. To better control for content volume, authors limited data for the hospital systems by identifying and isolating for "original posted content" on Facebook, Instagram, and Twitter (X), only.

To further refine the data, authors then created "tags" for the aforementioned topics enabling them to segment the data in a trendline format based on topic. Quantitative data analytics (via examining the frequency of posts mentioning these topics and the trends in their frequency over time) were then applied. Social media data was included for analysis if posted by one of the three systems included in the study between January 1, 2020 and October 31, 2021.

Medical Provider In-depth Interviews

To address RQ2 and RQ3, following Institutional Review Board approval, in-depth interview respondents were recruited through the authors' personal networks and included regional health organization representatives working on the frontlines of the pandemic throughout the same time period of January 1, 2020 through October 31, 2021. The interviews allowed for increased understanding and interpretation of the effects of trends observed in the health system social media analytics, especially regarding how these trends affected individual provider response.

Interviews lasted 30–45 minutes and took place between September 1 and October 31, 2021, via Zoom web conferencing. Practitioner roles included adult primary care and dermatology nursing in the Nashville metro area and family practice and pediatrics in the Appalachian Highlands. Zoom effectively mitigated any risk of in-person contact regarding virus transmission and allowed for both audio and video recording of the interview during the session. The researchers accessed Zoom through their university and could provide this software free to participants with a link over email or extension via phone.

After interview completion and transcription (using Zoom's natural language processing capabilities), the authors edited the transcripts for accuracy and completed a thematic analysis of the four transcripts, particularly focusing on the topics related to the study's research questions. A first pass of the transcribed materials yielded field notes, which were then coded line by line using open and axial coding methods to identify themes and relationships (Glaser & Strauss, 1967; Krippendorff, 2004). The authors then discussed their independent findings, which were highly aligned from an intercoder reliability perspective, and determined final themes related to the topic of study and research questions.

Analysis and Findings

System Social Media Response to COVID-19

In aggregate, there was an initial spike in COVID-related mentions in March of 2020, followed by a more gradual increase in both COVID case counts and corresponding "COVID" mentions across social media platforms throughout the rest of 2020. Rural and urban system social posts roughly aligned with case count trends throughout the remainder of 2020 and the first half of 2021. However, from late July through October of 2021, urban system mentions of COVID-related topics typically remained well below the frequency of rural system posts.

Examined individually, the strongest case count alignment lies with the Rural Hospital System, which was also the first of the three systems to mention "COVID" on social media, with five mentions of "COVID" the week of February 24, 2020. From this point on, the Rural System posted fairly consistently about COVID, with mention peaks the week of April 6, 2020 (as the Pandemic took grip in the United States) and again the week of January 4, 2021 (reflecting a spike in case counts in the region). Following the January 2021 spike in COVID mentions (which hit a volume of 49, rivaling the early April 2020 peak of 52), mention volume began to consistently decrease as case counts waned into the summer of 2021. After weeks of minimal mentions (and in some cases none or only 1), mentions began to rise again at the end of July 2021, as the rural system began to battle its second massive COVID wave. Unfortunately, the Rural System quickly grew overwhelmed during this wave. From this point through the end of the research period (October 31, 2021), COVID mentions never dip below 20 mentions per week for the system.

In contrast, Urban System 1 didn't begin posting about "COVID" until the week following the Rural System's first post (week of March 2, 2020). Between that week and the following week (March 9), Urban System 1 only had four mentions of "COVID." In fact, Urban System 1 shared the lightest volume of COVID-related content during the early days of COVID, never reaching a COVID weekly mention volume of 25 or higher until the end of July 2020. Urban System 1's mentions of "COVID" seem to be less aligned with general case counts than the other systems. The highest mentioned volume of COVID among their posts occurs in the week of January 25, 2021, with 45 mentions of "COVID" as the overall case count volume of the first wave was reaching its low point. Mentions spiked again in the first two weeks of May 2021, but again, overall case counts are quite low during this timeframe.

Meanwhile, Urban System 2 also began highlighting "COVID" the week of March 2 with 3 mentions, but quickly grew to a peak the week of April 6, 2020, with 50 mentions of COVID in the system's social post content. Mention volume spiked again in mid-December 2020, with 43 mentions the week of December 13. From this peak, volume ebbed and flowed until dipping below 20 mentions per week in early May of 2021, mirroring a decrease in case counts. While there was a small increase in mention volume in Fall 2021 (during the Urban area's second wave), COVID-related mentions remained below 16 mentions weekly.

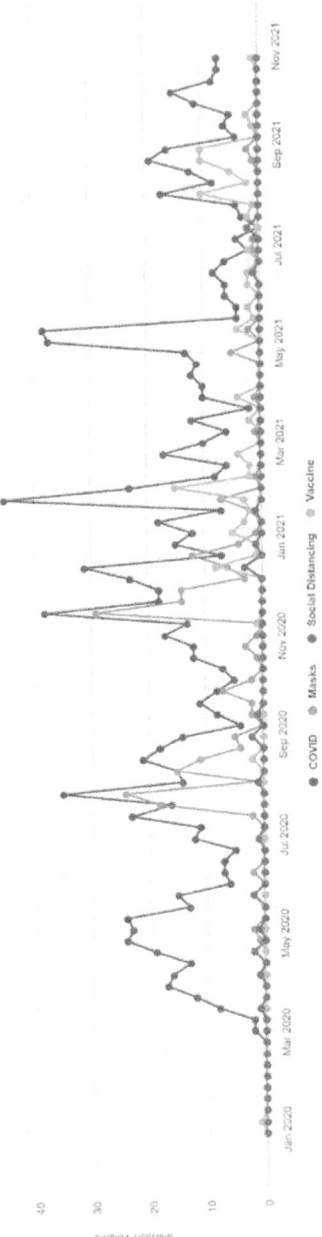

Figure 11.1: Tennessee Urban Health System 1 COVID-19 Social Media Response
Source: Brandwatch

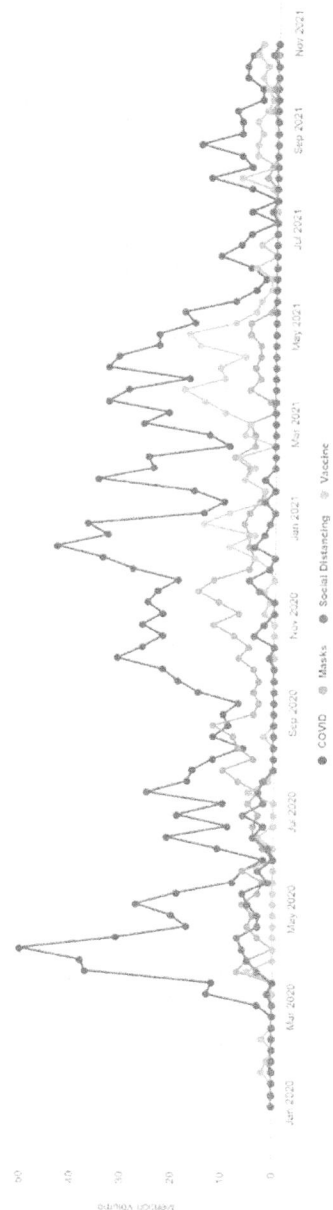

Figure 11.2: Tennessee Urban Health System 2 COVID-19 Social Media Response
Source: Brandwatch

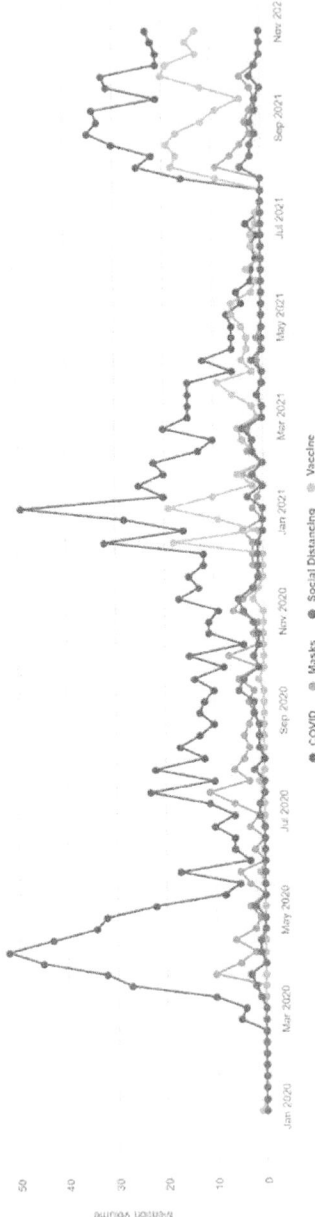

Figure 11.3: Tennessee Rural Health System COVID-19 Social Media Response
Source: Brandwatch

System Social Media Response: Disease Preventative Measures

While "social distancing" as a disease-preventative measure was frequently discussed in public conversation at the onset of the pandemic, very few healthcare system posts touched on this topic. "Social distancing" as a topic was first mentioned in early March at the onset of the Pandemic. Yet, at its height, "social distancing" was only mentioned eight times in a week. That said, it did achieve this peak five times in our study timeline (twice in April of 2020, once in May of 2020, once at the end of July, and again in mid-December of 2020).

When exploring "social distancing" as a topic across systems, it's worth noting that the Rural System and Urban System 2 carried the majority of mentions. Driving home the importance of "social distancing," Urban System 2 maintains consistent topic mentions from mid-March to July 2020 and again from October 2020 to January 2021. While Urban System 2 slows social distancing mentions to a near halt in February of 2021, the Rural System maintains its position, posting about social distancing throughout the rest of February. And while post mentions disappear during the summer months, the Rural System revisits the topic the week of August 2, 2021, and on through September. Urban System 1 mentions "Social Distancing" more lightly, with peak mention volume occurring the week of December 14, 2020, with three mentions.

Regarding mentions related to "masks," the Rural System doesn't produce nearly the same volume as the Urban Systems. Urban System 2 spreads the mask message, with consistent mentions beginning in March 2020 through May 2021. Urban System 1's mask messaging is more concentrated with the highest single-week mentions in the weeks of July 27 and November 16, 2020, with 24 and 29 mentions, respectively. However, Urban System 1 makes few mentions prior to July 2020 and mentions trail off beginning in February 2021. Our Rural systems mask mentions never exceed 11 mentions in a single week (with that peak occurring the week of July 13, 2020). Other spikes occurred early on, during the week of March 23, 2020, and then again as the Rural System began to hit its second wave, the week of August 2, 2021.

Generally speaking, "vaccines" were not discussed frequently by healthcare systems until December of 2020, when vaccinations in the United States began (at which point there were 35 collective mentions of "vaccine" across all three healthcare systems, representing the first of two "vaccine" related peaks). "Vaccine" mention volume dipped during the week of the Christmas holiday, but picked back up during the weeks of December 28, 2020, and January 4, 2021 (with mention volumes of 24 and 33, respectively). The second vaccine mention peak occurred the week of August 2, 2021, coinciding with the expected return to in-person K-12 schools and colleges/universities later that same month.

Urban System 1 only sparsely mentioned "vaccines" with a peak of 15 mentions the week of February 1, 2021. Excluding that peak, Urban System 1 had 10 or fewer vaccine mentions per week. Urban System 2 posted more frequently about "vaccines" with mention peaks of 9, 18, and 17 in the weeks of December 28, 2020, March 22, 2021, and April 26, 2021, respectively. However, it's the Rural System that appears to have really pushed out information related to "vaccines." The Rural System had five peaks with mention volumes at or over 18 during the time frame examined.

Medical Provider Communication Response to COVID-19

In addition to examining system communications, researchers also examined individual medical providers' experiences and their personal health communication responses. Upon analysis, urban and rural providers mentioned several consistent themes:

- Their initial awareness of the pandemic was personal and happened outside of health system communications
- They initially felt un/underprepared (and that their regional health system/s was also un/underprepared)
- They were disappointed with "official" sources of communication, such as major health agencies (e.g., CDC, NIH, WHO)
- Some providers (both urban and rural) spoke to patients about COVID-19 in advance of/outside of regional system communications
- They felt like both the virus and preventative measures that could help reduce virus transmission were unnecessarily politicized
- Social media use during the pandemic generally created more issues than benefits
- Though all providers faced some patient resistance in adopting preventative health measures (e.g., mask usage, vaccination), rural providers discussed encountering greater levels of patient opposition, which coincided with their perception of the general cultural climate in rural areas

Medical Provider COVID-19 Preventative Measure Communication

To support investigation of RQ2, a more thorough analysis was completed for comments regarding how individual providers communicated with both patients and the public regarding COVID-19 preventative measures. Four of our initial thematic findings were most pertinent in response to this research question.

First, individual providers were disappointed with "official" sources of communication, such as major health agencies (e.g., CDC, NIH, WHO). They found the information coming from these agencies was inconsistent and at times, blatantly contradictory to other disease preventative recommendations. This created additional challenges for providers when communicating to their patients regarding the "right" way to think about disease prevention. Many were especially frustrated by the seeming "flip-flopping" of agencies regarding guidance on mask usage for the general public. One provider also mentioned the same concern of inconsistencies regarding social distancing recommendations:

> Rural Provider 1: I think the CDC has not been a terribly reliable source of information . . . you can't say "stay out of crowds" and then say "except for these crowds" . . . people basically know that's bogus information. And then, they say, "well, if that's bogus information why will I believe something else?" I think as the information came in, you started getting different stories and that really (diminished) public confidence in any information coming out about COVID. Some of it was data that was honestly legitimate arguments within the academic community that most people did not understand. And they could draw conclusions from it, but the studies were not set up to show the conclusions people drew from it. I think there were a lot of mask studies, where they looked at particle size and aerosolized versus droplets, and I don't think most people understand a single thing about what the difference between aerosolized and droplets is. I think everyone had a consensus that masks help. If we stopped right there, we would have been good . . .

> Urban Provider 2: The CDC made some recommendations about wearing a mask, but many people lost trust in their recommendations because of the flip-flopping . . . I also feel like the WHO lost a little bit of their reputation for the average American because of some of the things they said that were a little discordant with other big institutions and then by really dragging their feet to call this an epidemic. With all these communication issues, "mask/don't mask," (it was) setting people up to not know who to trust. And so the CDC says something, "I'm not sure I can trust them, they didn't get their story straight on the math, you

know." So what I did was I looked at data from the ACIP (Advisory Committee on Immunization Practices).

Second, some providers (both urban and rural) spoke to patients about COVID-19 in advance of and/or in addition to regional system communications. The most direct example of this was a provider we interviewed in the urban Tennessee region. However, all providers mentioned critically looking at the information that was available themselves, drawing their own conclusions, and then communicating those conclusions to patients and others in the community.

> Urban Provider 2: Moving towards the end of March of 2020, when we started having a bit more (cases) in the United States and people first started recommending "work from home, try to stay home," I made the decision to use my electronic health platform system for the very first time to send a message out to all of my patients. It was just, "hey, we don't know what this is, but we do know that people are getting very sick from it and it's a real thing." Because I remember at that point in time, there was already a discussion of, "this is silly, we shouldn't be staying home, this isn't a real threat," on some platforms. So I said, "let's treat this with a little bit of respect, because we don't know what we're dealing with, and then I'll keep you updated as we know more." So that was one of the things that I've utilized during the pandemic is my ability to message my patients informational updates to try to keep information accurate. That was the first of what has become (approximately) 12 messages over the last year and a half, with updates. It was later than that when our CEO of our health system sent out a video directly to the patients … (but) once Tennessee started experiencing some of it, there was more communication from our institution directly, rather than just me.

Third, all providers felt like both the virus and preventative measures that could help reduce virus transmission were unnecessarily politicized. Providers saw this occur along "red and blue" county lines, with associated differences in rural and urban areas. However, as one provider stated, a virus doesn't care "who or what your political stances are," and this politicization of disease-preventative measures made aspects of their work regarding disease prevention much more difficult.

> Rural Provider 1: Nobody's interested in facts anymore, so that's kind of pointless. Initially, people were actually trying to find out about the disease, but at this point, everyone has an opinion about the disease and you're not likely to change it.
>
> Rural Provider 2: I think (not following recommended disease preventative behaviors) has a lot to do with COVID fatigue and I feel like it has become very political. Maybe it's just this area, but I have a hard time understanding the "removal of rights" theory when it comes to safety and protecting others.

> Urban Provider 1: Politics clearly have a part in it. People think that people are being microchipped, that it's going to cause infertility, just complete nonsense. People are more willing to take a monoclonal antibody, which is an experimental treatment, then take the antibody vaccine. If there's just no common sense in people, there's really not anything you can do about that.
>
> Urban Provider 2: It's very frustrating to me how this has fallen along political lines, because it's a public health thing, it's not a political thing. (A virus) doesn't really care who or what your political stances are. We notice areas that are more likely to vote liberal or neutral have better vaccine uptake compared to red counties or states.

Finally, providers felt that the public's social media use during the pandemic generally created more issues than benefits. However, some acknowledged that either side of most issues can be supported via social media and that people will typically view the information that naturally supports their own opinions. In the pandemic, this social media "echo chamber" effect was more readily apparent to providers when it came to patients' disease-preventative behavior adoption. This finding stood out somewhat in contrast to how medical systems were thinking about and utilizing social media.

> Urban Provider 2: The most interesting thing on social media is the algorithms. You click on one thing and it's going to send you a bunch more things like that. In general, the way that it affects people is pretty similar for anyone who uses it, it just depends on what you initially click on and what the algorithm starts feeding you. So, if you were someone who tends to be a little bit more science-minded or open-minded to the regular news updates and you click on that, you may get more information that says vaccines are safe. If you are the opposite and you click on one thing that says vaccines are unsafe or you need to be careful about this, it may feed you more information about that.
>
> Rural Provider 1: Social media gives (everyone an) equal voice. You know, a PhD is probably 10 steps below a singer. And I think that is a problem. Number one, politicians need to stay out of medicine . . . but also celebrities. I think people that don't have any knowledge need to not be spreading their influence as if they are knowledgeable. That's the biggest thing that has caused a lot of headaches.

Urban and Rural Differences in Provider Experiences During COVID-19

To better address RQ3, we also examined differences in medical provider experiences along urban and rural geographic lines. Though many similarities in experiences and perceptions existed across geographic locations, providers also observed some differences in rural and urban response to the virus.

For example, city mask mandates and other cultural norms around masking applied by businesses occurred more frequently in urban locations. In addition, some rural providers noted more cultural resistance to masking as a disease-preventative behavior.

> Urban Provider 1: The attitude in the city is much different than when you go to a suburb. I work in a suburb and so pretty much everyone I worked with didn't really know anyone that had it. They weren't that worried about it, and some of them already had it and they had no symptoms, so they were like "this is really not that big of a deal." So I would catch people, probably not even on purpose, but dropping their masks to talk. I work in a pretty small office so I'd have to constantly tell them to put it back up again. That was a challenge and it still is. In urban areas, if you walked into a coffee shop without a mask, they would tell you to leave.
>
> Rural Provider 1: I think we naturally have a bigger distrust of government than most places. I think that people feel like they're going to get taken advantage of. And I'm not exactly sure why that's so strong in this area. I think the churches have also made it more difficult by some of them taking a religious opinion on the disease and the vaccine, and I have no idea how that happened. That confuses me, but it's there, I mean there's pastors preaching about, "no one will come into this church with a mask", and I do not understand that.

Discussion

> **RQ1:** How often did both urban and rural health systems in Tennessee communicate with the public via social media regarding COVID-19 disease-preventative health behaviors throughout the pandemic?

All health systems maintained a social media presence within the COVID-19 pandemic. However, how strongly they enforced different preventative behaviors and both proactivity and consistency of messaging varied. All systems started messaging about the COVID-19 pandemic within, roughly, the same time frame. However, the rural system posted first, before either of the urban systems, and appeared to message with a bit more consistency throughout the pandemic compared to the urban systems. Rural system posts were also the most consistently aligned with new case counts for the region.

> **RQ2:** How did individual medical providers in both urban and rural areas of Tennessee communicate with the public and their patients regarding COVID-19 disease-preventative health behaviors throughout the pandemic?

Providers spoke to patients and broader community members directly, via both face-to-face conversations and email, and to a less prevalent extent, via social media. They took it upon themselves to do their own research in the face of changing agency recommendations, especially in regard to mask usage. Many communicated before or in addition to communications coming out of the regional health systems to provide greater clarity to their communities.

RQ3: Were there observable communication patterns that differed regarding urban and rural healthcare systems and provider response to COVID-19?

There were some differences in urban and rural systems and provider response observed in this study, though provider findings should be interpreted with some caution given the number of providers we spoke with (four in total, two per region). At a system level, researchers observed greater alignment in the amount of social media communication and case counts within the rural system. Topically, the urban systems pushed out considerably more information regarding mask usage, while the rural system pushed out more information on vaccines across social media channels, especially in the second wave of virus impact in that region (Fall of 2021). Related, at the provider level, those living and/or practicing in urban areas mentioned very little resistance to masks, while those living and/or practicing in rural areas faced a more oppositional cultural climate regarding mask usage.

In this study, researchers found that evolving COVID-19 preventative health behavior guidelines encouraged providers to follow pandemic news from official health agencies, major news outlets, and medical system sources closely. Many initially looked to the CDC, NIH, and WHO for information and updates, however, little information was shared by these organizations during the earliest stages of COVID-19 spread. Little information was shared by regional health systems at the pandemic onset as well. In the interviews, providers expressed frustration about inconsistencies (or absence of) communication and then changing guidelines. Several providers also mentioned that evolving communication around preventative measures (especially around mask usage and vaccines) created a frustrating foothold for divisiveness and politicization regarding individuals' personal pandemic responses.

When compared to the CERC model, COVID-19–related communication issues occurred in the first, second, and third model phases. However, perhaps the most damning deviation from the model occurred in the first phase. Again, in the CERC model, the first phase occurs pre-crisis, and includes monitoring of emerging risks, increasing the general public understanding of these risks, and preparing the public for the possibility of a crisis event (Lwin et al., 2018; Reynolds & Seeger, 2005). One medical provider directly spoke to the problems in this first phase (i.e., the absence of a "playbook" providers and medical agencies could use for this scenario) that then set the next phases of the CERC model up for challenges.

In summary, research findings from this study showed that the health systems' social media responses to the COVID-19 pandemic spiked at pandemic onset, and then varied slightly in their alignment with regional new case counts in each location throughout the remainder of 2020, with rural systems more closely aligned regarding post volume and case counts. Individual providers were typically more proactive than systems in their pandemic-related health communication response. Additionally, urban systems were more focused on mask-related communications, while the rural system focused more on vaccine-related communications.

When examining these findings in relation to the CERC model, opportunities exist for improved crisis communication in the case of future crises, particularly in phase one (pre-crisis). Both Urban and Rural systems missed the opportunity to shape public discourse regarding the pandemic in the CERC pre-crisis phase. While much research was still being conducted regarding the SARS-COV-2 virus, health systems could have shared general information regarding virus transmission, pandemic timelines, and general best practices for maintaining a healthy lifestyle in preparations for mass viral spread. While health systems made operational preparations in anticipation of the potential impact of high community positivity rates, addressing this potential eventuality from a social media perspective could have helped raise awareness to the importance of implementing greater preventative care to minimize community transmission.

Regular and consistent health messaging could establish health systems as a source of "truth" regarding pandemic information. In turn, this approach could empower providers with the opportunity to amplify this messaging, creating a strong information network that is consistent, accurate, and increases community understanding of pandemic ramifications and impact. The researchers hope that this study and studies of this nature will highlight the value and impact of both the voice of the health system and the individual provider in shaping pandemic perspectives.

Limitations

Within this study, researchers encountered several limitations. Limited health systems and a small number of providers across rural and urban areas were included in the study. Both samples (system and provider) could be expanded for future efforts. Additionally, some facilities included within a system might post more through subsidiary brands (e.g., individual hospitals, physician practices). However, only official system social media channels for Facebook, Twitter (X), and Instagram were analyzed for this study. Differences in rural and urban provider experiences noted in our findings should especially be interpreted with caution considering the small number of rural (two) and urban (two) providers interviewed. However, this directional finding is of interest and recommended as a topic for future in-depth study to better address regional differences in health communication challenges.

As another limitation and associated recommendation for future study, the authors did not examine virality of system posts in this research effort. This would be an interesting exploration to determine which posts did and did not achieve broader public engagement and possible determinants of virality. Finally, all trends in cases and mentions were examined directionally, but more detailed statistical analysis (e.g., to determine strength of correlation coefficients and statistical differences in regional systems) could be conducted in the future in order to determine strength of the observed relationships.

With the pandemic, there have been several additional challenges to discussing health, based on the responses of government leaders and political groups. The authors did not ask study participants to share their political views, so the information gathered around these topics was purely offered by the respondents on their own accord. Though we know political affiliation may affect provider response, this makes drawing specific conclusions about political affiliation difficult. From what respondents disclosed and we were able to observe, even medical provider respondents who shared certain views about preventative health behaviors did not all align in supporting a particular politician or party within this study.

Conclusion

The COVID-19 pandemic brought both health systems and providers many challenges, including mixed messages from major health agencies, politically and culturally driven responses to recommended preventative health behaviors, and social media amplification of divisive and inaccurate information. Some systems focused more on mask messages (urban) and some focused more on vaccine messages (rural). However, all utilized digital communication via social media to share recommended actions within their respective communities. Meanwhile, individual providers worked within the same chaotic communications environment, completing their own research and analysis of the available data, to affirm recommended preventative health behaviors to their patients.

Applications

1. Health-focused agencies and systems can better incorporate and follow the CERC model as best practice in the case of public health crises, particularly during phase 1 (pre-crisis).
2. Systems can better monitor grassroots provider communication (which may happen prior to system communication, as in this instance) and respond accordingly.
3. Health systems and providers can collaborate on regional health communication efforts to improve community adoption of disease-preventative measures.

    (a) Providers can also help to amplify system recommendations (and vice versa).

4. Findings can help continue to inform standards for best practices in public health crisis communication.

Discussion Questions

1. Thinking about all the phases of the CERC model and applying this as best practice, what could have been improved regarding health system/provider communication with the public during this time period?
2. From a grassroots perspective, could providers have influenced Health Systems communication during this time period? What power do providers wield as the owners of community relationships?

3. How would social media post virality impact such a study? Does it lend a greater voice to some health systems over others? Does this make a difference in the case of urban versus rural systems?

Resources

1. CERC Model: https://emergency.cdc.gov/cerc/
2. Reynolds, B., & Seeger, M. (2005). Crisis and Emergency Risk Communication as An Integrative Model. *Journal of Health Communication, 10,* 43–55. https://doi.org/10.1080/10810730590904571
3. Hewitt, A.M., Spencer, S.S., Ramloll, R., & Trotta, H. (2008). Expanding CERC beyond public health: sharing best practices with healthcare managers via virtual learning. *Health Promotion Practice, 9*(4 Suppl), 83S–87S. https://doi.org/10.1177/1524839908319090

Note

1 "Coronavirus" was examined as a term in this analysis due to much higher search volume at pandemic onset compared to "COVID" or "COVID-19." In early June 2020, this trend changed, with "COVID" achieving higher search volume throughout the remainder of the timeline examined.

References

Barnett, D., Thompson, C., Semon, N., Errett, N., Harrison, K., Anderson, M., Ferrell, J., Freiheit, J., Hudson, R., McKee, M., Mejia-Echeverry, A., Spitzer, J., Balicer, R., Links, J., & Storey, J. (2013). EPPM and willingness to respond: The role of risk and efficacy communication in strengthening public health emergency response systems. *Health Communication, 29*(6), 598–609. https://doi.org/10.1080/10410236.2013.785474

Brandwatch. (2021). *Mentions.* https://developers.brandwatch.com/docs/mentions

Brenan, M. (2020). *More mask use, worry about lack of social distancing in U.S.* Gallup. https://news.gallup.com/poll/313463/mask-worry-lack-social-distancing.aspx

Cairns, G., Andrade, M., & MacDonald, L. (2013). Reputation, relationships, risk communication, and the role of trust in the prevention and control of communicable disease: A review. *Journal of Health Communication, 18*(12), 1550–1565. https://doi.org/10.1080/10810730.2013.840696

CDC. (2021). *Guidance for wearing masks: Help slow the spread of COVID-19.* https://www.cdc.gov/coronavirus/2019-ncov/prevent-getting-sick/cloth-face-cover-guidance.html

Centers for Disease Control and Prevention. (2014). *Crisis and emergency risk communication: 2014 edition.* U.S. Department of Health and Human Services, Centers for Disease Control and Prevention.

Dickmann, P., Biedenkopf, N., Keeping, S., Eickmann, M., & Becker, S. (2014). Risk communication and crisis communication in infectious disease outbreaks in Germany: What is being done, and what needs to be done. *Disaster Medicine and Public Health Preparedness,* 8(3), 206–211. https://doi.org/10.1017/dmp.2014.36

Evensen, D., & Clarke, C. (2011). Efficacy Information in media coverage of infectious disease risks: An ill predicament? *Science Communication,* 34(3), 392–418. https://doi.org/10.1177/1075547011421020

Frieden, T.R. (2014). Six components necessary for effective public health program implementation. *American Journal of Public Health,* 104(1), 17–22. https://doi.org/10.2105/AJPH.2013.301608

Glaser, B., & Strauss, A. (1967). *The discovery of grounded theory: Strategies for qualitative research.* Aldine Publishing.

Google Trends. (2021). https://trends.google.com/trends/yis/2021/GLOBAL/

Krippendorff, K. (2004). *Content analysis: An introduction to its methodology.* Sage.

Lee, B. (2020). Despite COVID-19 coronavirus, here is why you should stop buying face masks. *Forbes.* https://www.forbes.com/sites/brucelee/2020/02/29/despite-covid-19-coronavirus-here-is-why-you-should-stop-buying-face-masks/#134189ed2ab8

Lwin, M., Lu, J., Sheldenkar, A., & Schulz, P. (2018). Strategic uses of Facebook in Zika outbreak communication: Implications for the crisis and emergency risk communication model. *International Journal of Environmental Research and Public Health,* 15(9), 1974. https://doi.org/10.3390/ijerph15091974

Makridis, C., & Rothwell, J.T. (2020). *The real cost of political polarization: Evidence from the COVID-19 pandemic.* SSRN. http://dx.doi.org/10.2139/ssrn.3638373

Mayo Clinic. (2021). *U.S. COVID-19 vaccine tracker: See your state's progress.* https://www.mayoclinic.org/coronavirus-covid-19/vaccine-tracker

McDonald, J. (2020). *COVID-19 face mask advice, explained.* FactCheck.org. https://www.factcheck.org/2020/04/covid-19-face-mask-advice-explained

National Governors Association. (2021). https://www.nga.org/former-governors/tennesse

O'Neill, A. (2020). *Number of electoral votes from Tennessee designated to each party's candidate in U.S. presidential elections from 1796 to 2020.* Statista. https://www.statista.com/statistics/1130787/tennessee-electoral-votes-since-1796/

Ophir, Y., & Jamieson, K.H. (2020). The effects of Zika virus risk coverage on familiarity, knowledge and behavior in the US—A time series analysis combining content analysis and a nationally representative survey. *Health Communication,* 35(1), 35–45. https://doi.org/10.1080/10410236.2018.1536958

Parker, J.J., Octaria, R., Smith, M.D., Chao, S.J., Davis, M.B., Goodson, C., Warkentin, J., Werner, D., & Fill, M.A. (2021). Characteristics, comorbidities, and data gaps for coronavirus disease deaths, Tennessee, USA. *Emerging Infectious Diseases, 27*(10), 2521–2528. https://doi.org/10.3201/eid2710.211070

Rabin, R.C. (2021). A new study suggests 3 feet, not 6 feet, is sufficient distance for school students, with mask-wearing and other safety measures kept in place. *New York Times.* https://www.nytimes.com/2021/03/14/health/Covid-schools-social-distancing-3-feet.html

Reynolds, G. (2020). For runners, is 15 feet the new 6 feet for social distancing? *New York Times.* https://www.nytimes.com/2020/04/15/well/move/running-social-distancing.html

Reynolds, B., & Seeger, M. (2005). Crisis and emergency risk communication as an integrative model. *Journal of Health Communication, 10*(1), 43–55, https://doi.org/10.1080/10810730590904571

Ruiu, M.L. (2020). Mismanagement of Covid-19: Lessons learned from Italy. *Journal of Risk Research, 23*(7–8), 1007–1020. https://doi.org/10.1080/13669877.2020.1758755

Sheikh, K., Gorman, J., & Chang, K. (2020). Stay 6 feet apart, we're told. But how far can air carry coronavirus? *New York Times.* https://www.nytimes.com/2020/04/14/health/coronavirus-six-feet.html

Tay, J., Ng, Y.F., Cutter, J.L., and James, L. (2010). Influenza A (H1N1-2009) pandemic in Singapore—Public health control measures implemented and lessons learnt. *Annals Academy of Medicine, Singapore, 39*(4), 313–324. https://annals.edu.sg/pdf/39VolNo4Apr2010/V39N4p313.pdf

Tennessee Department of Health. (2020). *TDH announces first case of covid-19 in Tennessee.* https://www.tn.gov/health/news/2020/3/5/tdh-announces-first-case-of-covid-19-in-tennessee.html

Tennessee Department of Health. (2021). *New cases by public health report date, region.*

U.S. Food & Drug Administration. (2020). *FDA takes key action in fight against COVID-19 by issuing emergency use authorization for first COVID-19 vaccine.* https://www.fda.gov/news-events/press-announcements/fda-takes-key-action-fight-against-covid-19-issuing-emergency-use-authorization-first-covid-19

Veil, S., Reynolds, B., Sellnow, T.L., & Seeger, M.W. (2008). CERC as a theoretical framework for research and practice. *Health Promotion Practice, 9*(4-Suppl), 26S–34S. https://journals.sagepub.com/doi/pdf/10.1177/1524839908322113

Walker, J. (2016). Civil society's role in a public health crisis. *Issues in Science and Technology, 32*(4), 43–48. https://login.iris.etsu.edu:3443/login?url=https://search.proquest.com/docview/1812403611?accountid=10771

World Health Organization. (2020, April 2). *Advice on the use of masks in the context of COVID-19: Interim guidance.* https://www.who.int/publications-detail/advice-on-the-use-of-masks-in-the-community-during-home-care-and-in-healthcare-settings-in-the-context-of-the-novel-coronavirus-(2019-ncov)-outbreak

Zarocostas, J. (2020). How to fight an infodemic. *The Lancet Journal: World Report, 395*(10225), 676. https://doi.org/10.1016/S0140-6736(20)30461-X

Ziegler, B. (2021). *Health care rankings.* U.S. News & World Reports. https://www.usnews.com/news/best-states/rankings/health-care

· 1 2 ·

IS THERE A DIFFERENCE? GENERATIONAL RESPONSE TO COVID AND MEDIA USAGE

Carrie Reif-Stice, Steven Venette, Sarah Smith-Frigerio, Nazanin Bani Amerian, & Joel Iverson

With the outbreak of the COVID-19 pandemic in March 2020, stay-at-home orders shut down all non-essential businesses, travel, and closed schools across the United States. However, by May, states, such as Arizona, Texas, and Florida, started lifting restrictions on businesses and in-person gatherings (Hawkins et al., 2020). For example, on May 18, 2020, Florida Governor Ron DeSantis relaxed COVID-19 safety protocols, reopened businesses, and encouraged tourism by declaring Florida an "open state" destination (Rohrer & Santana, 2020). By July, all major theme parks, including Disney World, resumed operation and beaches and parks reopened. Although touted as a success by government officials, the state's plan for recovery was marred by a spike in COVID-19 infection rates, hospitalizations, and deaths (Waymer & Sasson, 2020). Governor DeSantis blamed the COVID-19 surge on young adults (i.e., 25- to 34-year-olds) who were breaking rules by socializing at large events and not observing social distancing guidelines (Brown, 2020). Images and videos of large groups of young adults flocking to Florida's bars and beaches, violating COVID-19 guidelines, circulated new outlets, the internet, and social media. In other words, young adults were framed as reckless "spreaders of the virus" and responsible for the second wave of the COVID-19 virus.

The framing of young people as irresponsible, careless, and dismissive of COVID-19 risks is flawed and misleading. Several studies have indicated that young adults have a sense of responsibility to prevent the transmission of COVID-19 to others and engage in protective behaviors (DeJonckheere et al., 2021; Wilson et al., 2020). Inaccurate media portrayals of young people as being "spreaders" may negatively impact perceptions of risk, alter preventative behaviors, and undermine public health response. Additionally, older adults continued to spread, contract, and die from the virus at a similar rate as people under 30 (Moore, 2020). Although some research finds older generations to be risk-averse (Albert & Duffy, 2012), other studies find a more complex and nuanced relationship between risk perception and generational differences (Bonem et al., 2015). Given the novelty of COVID-19, individuals have turned to different channels, such as news channels, social media platforms, and healthcare professionals, to get information. Thus, difference in media usage could result in differences in risk and efficacy perceptions among generations. This study investigates the relationships between generational differences, risk perception, and media consumption related to COVID-19. Alongside discussion of implications of our findings, we discuss the limitations of the current study and offer directions for future research.

What Is Risk?

Risk, and how humans perceive it, is a complex phenomenon because scholars and laypersons alike disagree about the definition and assessment of risk. That said, scholars have several commonalities when seeking to explicate risk. Risk is recognized as a threat to individuals, and the complex interrelationship between natural and social worlds influences the classification of risks. Proutheau and Heath (2009) mention uncertainty as a central part of risk in their definition, stating "risks are defined as probabilistic occurrences that can have positive or negative outcomes of various magnitudes" (p. 576). All forms of risk comprise basic common elements: (1) context, (2) action, (3) conditions, and (4) consequences (Alberts, 2006).

Social dimensions are crucial in risk assessment and management (Latour, 2003). Since risk is a social construct, it can appear and disappear, requiring constant consideration. Stah et al. (2003) purported that "risks should be studied in context, their relation to specific projects, to characteristics of projects, to participating groups and so on should be emphasized" (p. 20). Factors such as framing of the problem, the comprehensibility of risks, and the communication to individuals who may be impacted by the hazard, affect uncertainty in the society (Jackson & Cornell, 2013). In other words, risks shift with geographical, cultural, economic, and political contexts. Uncertainty, too, is a product of the societies and cultures through which make it modulated and meaningful (Jackson & Cornell, 2013).

Risk perception is also contextual. Risk perception studies often focus on people's judgment when characterizing and evaluating hazardous activities. Put another way, risk perception deals with intuitive risk judgments. Most society experiences hazards as both firsthand, and secondhand through the news media. What people mean when they refer to something "risky" helps illuminate the factors underlying their perception of risk (Slovic, 1987).

Threat Susceptibility, Severity, and Efficacy

According to the Extended Parallel Processing Model (EPPM), perceptions of risk and behavioral intention to mitigate risks directly relate to an individual's perceptions of threat susceptibility, threat severity, and efficacy (Witte, 1992). Threat susceptibility is an individual's perception that a risk—such as contracting COVID-19—could reasonably happen to them. Threat severity explains the amount of harm or danger resulting from a potential risk encounter (e.g., severe illness, hospitalization, or death from COVID-19). Perceived efficacy articulates individual beliefs regarding the likelihood that recommended behaviors will keep them safe or mitigate harm (e.g., social distancing, wearing masks, and washing hands prevent the spread of COVID-19). Efficacy can be further broken down into self-efficacy (i.e., I can do the things needed to keep me safe), response efficacy (i.e., these behaviors do, in fact, keep people safe), and system efficacy (i.e., systems in place within our society will help keep us safe; Bani Amerian & Venette, 2020). When evaluating fear/danger appeals in health messaging, audiences are willing to accept and act upon the recommendations if they perceive the threat as being real, likely to cause negative outcomes, and the behavior recommendations as reasonable and likely to work. If the risk is seen as unlikely to happen, not severe, or if the behaviors seem untenable or unlikely to mitigate the risk, then audiences will reject the messaging.

Extensive scholarship evaluates the effectiveness of health-related risk messaging using the EPPM model. Studies in recent years include exploring the role of EPPM in anti-smoking cessation (Wong & Cappella, 2009), in HPV vaccines (Carcioppolo et al., 2013), climate change (Feldman et al., 2017), and the potential effects of repeated messaging (Shi & Smith, 2016). Recent studies of risk perceptions and behavioral intentions related to COVID-19 also provide interesting insights. Roberto et al. (2021) found threat severity, threat susceptibility and perceived efficacy help explain a significant amount of the variance in behavioral intentions among college students exposed to social distancing messaging. Additionally, Chung and Jones-Jhang (2021) found partisan media usage was associated with (un)willingness to perceive COVID-19 as a threat and associated with (un)willingness to engage in recommended behavioral changes to mitigate the risk of contracting COVID-19. Given these insights, we explore generational risk perception as well as differences in media use as it relates to risk messaging.

Generational Risk Perception

Communicating risk is integral to motivating change in risk-taking behaviors and promoting self-protective behaviors. For health professionals, creating effective interventions can reduce risk, prevent the outbreak of disease, and improve well-being (Rimal & Real, 2003). The complex process of crafting risk messages involves accounting for people receiving and processing the information. For example, perceived level of risk depends on demographic variables, such as gender, education, and socioeconomic status (Savage, 1993; Sund et al., 2015). Age-related differences must also be considered when determining individuals' perceptions of risk.

When examining the age-related risk, older generations are often stereotyped as more cautious compared to younger adults (Mather et al., 2012). Although some research finds older generations to be risk-averse (Albert & Duffy, 2012), other studies find a more complex and nuanced relationship between risk perception and generational differences (Bonem et al., 2015). In the face of a pandemic, understanding generational risk behavior and decision-making is important in decreasing the likelihood of infection, transmission, and disease severity (Bish & Michi, 2010; Henrich & Holmes, 2009). Research exploring the outbreak of H1N1 found older adults more likely to engage in protective behaviors, such as handwashing (Jones & Salthe, 2009). However, Rubin et al. (2009) found younger adults, especially females, more likely to follow recommended behaviors. Other studies indicate no significant relationship between age and the perceived likelihood of engaging in protective behaviors during the H1N1 outbreak (Ibuka et al., 2010).

With the outbreak of COVID-19, scholars should examine risk perception and age-related differences throughout the course of the global pandemic. Studies on risk perception and COVID-19 show conflicting results regarding generational differences. For example, in a study of Italian citizens and risk perception, Carlucci et al. (2020) demonstrate older adults (60 and over) and younger adults (18–29) are likely to engage in risk-taking behaviors and defy quarantine guidelines. Yet, Marschalk and colleagues (2021) found no generational differences between Generation X, Generation Y, and Baby Boomers in COVID-19 risk perception (Calucci et al., 2020). Despite the conflicting evidence, several studies show perceived vulnerability to COVID-19 decreases as age increases (Bruine de Bruin, 2020; Nueburger & Egger, 2021; Rosi et al., 2021). However, older adults have greater perception of risk severity, including higher risk of mortality and hospitalizations, compared to younger adults (Bruine de Bruin, 2020; Rosi et al., 2021). Put simply, despite an increased risk of contracting the virus with fatal consequences, older adults may underestimate the threat and fail to take protective actions. Based on the literature, the following prediction is made:

H1: Perceptions of risk of COVID-19 will vary by generation.

News Media Usage

When faced with a health crisis, individuals often seek out information to manage uncertainty and improve well-being (Brashers, 2007). Although medical providers are the most trusted source of health information, individuals use other information avenues. For example, family members, friends, and loved ones serve as a primary source of medical information (Baiocchi-Wagner, 2015). However, given the novelty of the COVID-19 pandemic, individuals increasingly turned to different media channels to access health-related information. Throughout the crisis, television networks, such as *CNN, ABC, CBS,* and *Foxnews,* have record numbers of viewers looking for COVID-19 updates and information on preventative actions (Deaven, 2020). Most importantly, at least 48% of all Americans reported getting some COVID-19 news from social media (Walker & Matsa, 2021). Older adults indicated using *Facebook* as a trusted and accurate news source for COVID-19 information (Sakya et al., 2021). Because information-seeking increases during times of uncertainty, and differences in media usage could result in differences in risk and efficacy perceptions, we propose the following research question:

> RQ1: Which information sources will influence perceptions of susceptibility, severity, and efficacy?

Method

Following IRB approval, a web-based questionnaire was administered using Amazon's Mechanical Turk (MTurk). MTurk has been found to be a reliable and valid method of data collection (Hauser & Schwarz, 2016; Sheehan, 2017). Furthermore, in the context of communication research, MTurk has demonstrated the ability to capture a diverse sample and high level of data quality (Sheehan, 2017). The questionnaire collected information on perceptions of system efficacy, response efficacy, self-efficacy, severity, susceptibility, and source information.

Adults 18 years or older were eligible to participate through the MTurk worker pool. Participation was voluntary and workers could quit the survey at any point. Participants who entered a valid code into the MTurk system were paid $0.05. After providing consent, respondents were connected to Qualtrics to complete the survey.

Between September 28, 2021, and September 29, 2021, the researchers received a total of 1,283 responses. However, after cleaning the data, only 263 responses were kept in the final data set. To ensure valid responses, three validity checks were included in the survey. Questions asked participants the extent to which they agreed they were taking a survey. If participants could not consistently agree they were taking a survey, their response was dismissed. Additionally, respondents who did not answer more than half of the questions were eliminated. Anyone whose age did not correspond with the generation selected by a latitude of two generations was removed. In other words, if an individual identified as being 25 but selected being a member of the Greatest Generation, the survey was removed from the data set. Finally, respondents were allowed to indicate they received a low level of information from all news sources. However, if they demonstrated heavy reliance on watching *Fox News*, participants could not also overly rely on *CNN* and *MSNBC* as a new source. Responses were also removed for putting the same answer for all sources of information.

Participants

Seventy-eight percent of the sample were White, 4% Black or African American, 1% American Indian or Alaska Native, 13% Asian, 1% Native Hawaiian or Pacific Islander, and 3% identified as other or did not report. Within the sample, 46% identified as male, 52% as female, 2% as non-binary or third gender or not reported. Thirteen percent of the sample identified as Hispanic or Latinx, and 87% who did not identify as a member of that group. In terms of age distribution, 22% reported being between 19 and 29, 34% between 30 and 39, 21% between 40 and 49, 10% between 50 and 59, 12% between 60 and 69, and 1% as 70 and over. Finally, under 1% of the sample indicated belonging to the Silent Generation (i.e., 76–92 years old), 17% to the Baby Boomer Generation (i.e., 57–75 years old), 26% to Generation X (i.e., 41–56 years old), 49% to Generation Y (i.e., 25–40 years old), 7% to Generation Z (i.e., 24 years old and under), and 1% did not identify.

Scales

Scales measuring perceptions of threat susceptibility, threat severity, self-efficacy, and response efficacy were developed using Witte's (1996) Risk Behaviour Diagnostic Scale as a model. The score for each variable was generated using the mean value of the appropriate items. Using the mean provided an acceptable way to adjust for missing responses.

Perceptions of Threat Susceptibility

A four-item scale was constructed. The items were "My loved ones are at risk for catching COVID-19," "It is possible that one of my loved ones will catch COVID-19," "I believe that I could be a victim of COVID-19," and "Anyone could be a victim of COVID-19." Items were rated on a 5-point Likert-type scale, with higher scores indicating greater perception of susceptibility (1 = strongly disagree) to 5 (strongly agree). All items loaded on a single dimension using factor analysis, indicating good validity. Internal reliability for the scale was high ($\alpha = 0.83$).

Perceptions of Threat Severity

Perceptions of threat severity were assessed using six items ($\alpha = 0.82$). The scale items were "COVID-19 poses a serious risk to my loved ones," "COVID-19 is a severe threat to my loved ones," "My friends or family members could die from COVID-19," "COVID-19 is a legitimate threat to me," "I could die if I contracted COVID-19," and "My health could be permanently damaged if I contracted Covid." Items were rated on a 5-point Likert-type scale, with higher scores indicating greater perception of severity (1 = strongly disagree) to 5 (strongly agree). All items loaded on a single factor. Internal reliability for the scale was extremely high ($\alpha = 0.92$).

Perceptions of Self-efficacy

Perceptions of self-efficacy were measured using four items. These items were "I have the ability to receive the COVID-19 vaccine," "I can use social distancing," "If I am exposed to Covid, I can quarantine myself," and "I can take action to protect myself from COVID-19." Items were rated using a 5-point Likert-type scale, with higher scores indicating greater perceptions of self-efficacy (1 = strongly disagree) to 5 (strongly agree). All items loaded on a single factor. Internal reliability for the scale was acceptable ($\alpha = 0.79$).

Perceptions of Response Efficacy

Perceptions of response efficacy were assessed using four items. Response-efficacy prompts were "Personal protection, such as masks, are effective in reducing the threat of COVID-19," "Social distancing is effective in reducing the threat of COVID-19," "Actions that I take are effective in reducing the threat of COVID-19," and "Actions that I take are effective at protecting others from COVID-19." Items were rated on a 5-point Likert scale, with higher scores indicating greater perceptions of response efficacy (1 = strongly disagree) to 5 (strongly agree). Again, all items loaded on a single dimension. Internal reliability for the scale was high ($\alpha = 0.85$).

Perceptions of System Efficacy

To measure perceptions of system efficacy, a 7-item scale was created using Bani Amerian and Venette (2020) as a guide. The scale reflected participants' perceptions of how well other individuals and organizations protect them from COVID-19. The items read, "Government agencies provide resources that help me respond to the outbreak," "Organizations or agencies exist that will save people who catch the disease," "The medical system can respond effectively to the disease," "Hospitals and emergency rooms can provide effective care," "I believe there are organizations or agencies that want to protect me from COVID-19," "Government services are available to help me respond to COVID-19," and "Pharmaceutical researchers and scientists want to protect me from COVID-19." Items were rated on a 5-point Likert-type scale, with higher scores indicating greater perceived system efficacy (1 = strongly disagree) to 5 (strongly agree). All items loaded on a single dimension. Internal reliability for the scale was high (α = 0.89).

Discriminating Value

Witte (1996) suggested the score for the perception of the hazard can be subtracted from the perceived efficacy value. A positive score predicts that the respondent has a *danger control* orientation. In other words, the person should be motivated to respond to the threat. A negative score suggests that the individual is in *fear control*. This orientation exists when the person is concerned about controlling their emotional state (e.g., fear or anger), rather than reducing the threat. In this study, the mean of the susceptibility and severity items were subtracted from the mean of the three efficacy subscales to produce the discriminating value.

News Source Information

To measure news source information, the researchers created a list of information sources related to COVID-19. Information sources included, for example, *Facebook*, *MSNBC*, *Fox News*, and *TikTok*. Participants were asked to rate the extent to which they rely on each source for Covid-related information using a scale from 0 (not at all) to 10 (all the time).

Data Analysis

ANOVA was used to test for differences in means for discriminating values for the generations. Additionally, a regression-based causal model was constructed using *SPSS AMOS*. Paths were drawn from generation to each of the 25 information sources. Paths were also included from each information source to susceptibility, severity, self-efficacy, response efficacy, and system efficacy, respectively. Finally, paths were included from generation to susceptibility, severity, and the three efficacy variables.

Errors were allowed to covary for information sources. Additionally, susceptibility and severity were allowed to covary, as were self-efficacy, response efficacy, and system efficacy. Nonsignificant paths were trimmed. Final model fit was acceptable (GFI = .94, CFI = .96, IFI = .97, RMSEA = .06, PCLOSE = .04).

Results

For discriminating values, no significant differences existed between generations (F[4, 258] = .45, p = .77). Table 12.1 lists the means and dispersion for each group. Notably, the means for every generation are positive. This result suggests that each generation, on average, has a danger control orientation toward COVID-19.

Some generational differences existed regarding information sources relied upon for COVID-19. Perhaps not surprisingly, younger generations reported relying more on the social media platforms Facebook (b = .34, p = .026), Instagram (b = .41, p = .001), YouTube (b = .56, p < .001), and Reddit (b = 54, p < .001). More recent generations were also more likely to depend on friends and family for COVID-19 information (b = .35, p = .016). Older respondents depended on news websites more frequently (b = -.36, p = .03).

The perception of the COVID-19 hazard is determined by two subdimensions: susceptibility/probability and consequences/severity. Perception of the likelihood of being affected by COVID-19 was moderately high (M = 4.02, SD = .89). No statistically significant differences existed between generations (F[4] = .36, p = .84). Information source was found to significantly influence this perception in two instances. The more people rely on Fox News as a source of COVID-19 information, the less likely they thought they would be affected by the virus (b = -.09, SE = .02, p < .001). The more the respondent relied on their healthcare providers, their perception of probability was higher (b = .06, SE = .02, p < .001).

Perceptions of the consequences of COVID-19 were moderate overall (M = 3.89, SD = 1.08). Again, no significant differences were found based on generations (F[4] = 1.23, p = .30). Four information sources were identified as

Table 12.1. Average Discriminating Value for Generations

Generation	Mean	SD
Baby Boomers	.228	.827
X	.274	.836
Y	.319	.689
Z	.135	.525
Overall	.285	.746

influencing perceptions of impact. People who relied on CBS News were more likely to believe that the consequences of COVID-19 would be higher ($b = .05$, $SE = .02$, $p = .002$). Similarly, as the respondents increased their use of health care providers as an information source, their perception of potential impact also increased ($b = .08$, $SE = .02$, $p < .001$). Conversely, reliance on Fox News was associated with lower perceptions of severity ($b = -.08$, $SE = .02$, $p < .001$).

Efficacy was measured using three subdimensions (self-efficacy, response efficacy, and system efficacy). Self-efficacy was high among respondents ($M = 4.64$, $SD = .54$), meaning people believe they have actions they could take to protect themselves or others. The more that people relied on their healthcare providers for information, the higher their perception of self-efficacy ($b = .04$, $SE = .01$, $p < .001$). Increased use of TikTok as an information source was related with lower perceptions that people have actions they can take ($b = -.068$, $SE = .02$, $p < .001$).

Response efficacy is the belief that actions taken in response to COVID-19 would be effective in decreasing the hazard. Respondents generally perceived response efficacy was high ($M = 4.34$, $SD = .84$). Five information sources were found to influence participants' perceptions. Increased use of national or international newspapers was associated with greater belief that actions would be effective ($b = .03$, $SE = .01$, $p = .007$). Similarly, increased use of news websites was linked to higher response efficacy ($b = .03$, $SE = .01$, $p = .021$). Again, healthcare providers positively influenced higher perceptions of this type of efficacy ($b = .05$, $SE = .02$, $p = .001$). Conversely, two social media sources were associated with lower perceptions of response efficacy: TikTok ($b = -.08$, $SE = .03$, $p < .016$) and YouTube ($b = -.04$, $SE = .01$, $p = .002$).

System efficacy, or the perception that some entity will act on one's behalf to mitigate or avoid the hazard, was relatively low overall ($M = 3.74$, $SD = 1.08$). Increased use of talk radio was associated with lower system efficacy ($b = -.05$, $SE = .02$, $p = .02$). Three sources were linked with higher beliefs that others would act to protect them: Facebook ($b = .04$, $SE = .02$, $p = .043$), Fox News ($b = .06$, $SE = .02$, $p = .002$), and health care providers ($b = .07$, $SE = .02$, $p < .001$).

Discussion

The hypothesis predicted that perceptions of the risk of COVID-19 will vary by generation. The data do not support the hypothesis. In fact, the generations perceptions of the overall risk, measured using the calculated discriminating score, were highly similar. Although adults 65 and over are more vulnerable and at greater risk for COVID-19, several studies indicate that older generations have a lower risk perception of contracting the virus compared to younger adults (Pasion et al., 2020; Rosi et al., 2021). Younger adults are also more likely to engage in protective behaviors, such as social distancing and wearing a mask, to avoid illness (Pasion et al., 2020; Rosi et al., 2021). Contrary to these previous findings, this study did not find an overarching generational divide regarding perceptions of risk and COVID-19. Instead, our findings showed perceptions of risk were moderately high regardless of generation.

To explain the differing results, we must consider the changing and long-lasting nature of the global pandemic. Prior research examined risk perception and generational divide during the initial stages of the COVID-19 outbreak in 2020 (Bruine de Bruine, 2020; Paison et al., 2020; Nueburger & Egger, 2021). At the time of this study (October 2021), the pandemic was ongoing for almost two years and in its fourth wave (WHO, 2021). We think that, in our study, the possibility of perceived risk being evenly distributed across generations is linked to the outbreak of the highly contagious Delta variant. Unlike initial strands of COVID-19, the Delta variant poses a significant threat to both younger and older generations. Although individuals between the ages of 65 and 74 have a high vaccination rate (Whiteman et al., 2021), the number of COVID-19 deaths increased in 2021. However, individuals between the ages of 35–65 saw the largest increase of Covid deaths and hospitalizations from 2020, particularly among healthy individuals with no preexisting conditions (CDC, 2021). Certainly, no generation was exempt from the risk of COVID-19. This may help explain why perceptions of the hazard were overall invariant.

The research question sought to explore which information sources might influence perceptions of risk and perceptions of efficacy. Several interesting results were found in our study. For susceptibility, use of Fox News was associated with lower perceptions while information from one's healthcare provider was associated with higher perceptions of susceptibility. For severity, perceptions were lower among regular viewers of *Fox News* while higher among those viewing *CBS News* and seeking information from their healthcare providers. Perceptions of self-efficacy increased with information from healthcare providers while it decreased with use of *TikTok*. Perceptions of response efficacy were higher for individuals who used national and international news sources, as well as news websites, and information from healthcare professionals. Perceptions of response efficacy were lower for individuals who relied on

TikTok and *YouTube* for information. Finally, perceptions of system efficacy were higher for those who sought information from *Fox News*, *Facebook*, and healthcare providers, while talk radio was associated with lower perceptions of system efficacy.

Interestingly, social media use—often seen as more frequently used by younger generations, except for *Facebook*—resulted in lower perceptions of efficacy (Auxier & Anderson, 2021). Additionally, information-seeking from traditional news sources (Matsa & Naseer, 2021) and healthcare professionals is typically seen as more frequent in older generations, and is associated with higher levels of perceived susceptibility, severity, and efficacy, except for *Fox News*. Given no observed differences in perceptions of risk and efficacy among generations in this study, but differences based on media use emerged, and evidence points to generational differences in media use, we postulate that potential differences may be driven more by where individuals seek their information and less by the generation to which they belong. In other words, public officials and healthcare practitioners, by understanding the influence of media usage on risk perceptions, can create effective strategies to mitigate and contain future outbreaks. Based on these findings, less emphasis can be placed on crafting messages that specifically target risk perception and efficacy beliefs across generational divides. Instead, practitioners should encourage media outlets to avoid sharing misinformation, such as conspiracy theories, altered images, and fabricated news, that create confusion and undermine public health response.

Hopefully, the findings in this study may help to clarify the mixed results existing in the literature, to date.

Limitations and Future Research

Several limitations were identified in our study. First, the cross-sectional, one-time measurement design cannot fully assess the complex relationships between the variables. Longitudinal studies are needed to confirm the relationships highlighted in this study. Second, data was assessed by self-reported measures, which could potentially introduce bias in the interpretation of the results. Additionally, because of the political nature of COVID-19, participants could have also intentionally withheld information or provided incorrect responses (Kerlinger & Lee, 2008). Future studies could use more naturalistic approaches, such as interviews, to develop a nuanced understanding of how media messages employing targeted demographics may (or may not) contribute to a generational divide in risk perception.

Finally, MTurk is associated with capturing a diverse sample (Sheehan, 2017); however, this study demonstrated some issues with generalizability. For example, while the sampled population was diverse in terms of gender, most respondents were Caucasian (80%), between the ages of 30–39 (34%), identifying as Generation Y (25–40 years old). Furthermore, despite being the second largest racial and ethnic group (Flores, 2017), 87% of respondents did not identify as Hispanic or Latinx. Because of the lack of diversity, the research findings are not wholly representative and do not capture a racially and ethnically diverse sample. In addition, although Baby Boomers are the second largest generation in terms of population (Fry, 2020), most respondents identified as Generation X (i.e., 41–56 years old) and Generation Y (i.e., 25–40 years old). Future studies should use participant recruitment strategies to ensure adequate representation of the population within the sample.

Other avenues of future research should consider exploring different diseases, as well as COVID-19 within different contexts (e.g., other nations). Additionally, future studies should seek to take a longitudinal approach, and measure potential differences over several points in time, particularly since the COVID-19 pandemic continues, and is likely to remain endemically. Finally, a more detailed analysis of information-seeking behaviors, especially the differences in news and social media use, is certainly warranted. While some effort was taken in this study to break down information sources and news/social media use, even more attention is needed in this area. Nevertheless, this study provides important insights into the varying results on generational differences currently existing in the literature, and points to the need for further elaboration on information-seeking behaviors as they relate to perceptions of susceptibility, severity, and efficacy related to the COVID-19 pandemic.

Discussion Questions

1. What are potential reasons why individuals did not perceive threat severity and susceptibility to COVID-19?
2. What roles does the media play in disseminating health information?
3. What other factors may contribute to the mixed results regarding generational perception of risk and COVID-19?
4. What type of social media messaging would improve risk perception and efficacy among older and younger adults?
5. Where do you access health-related information? How do those sources influence your own threat and efficacy perceptions?

References

Albert, S.M., & Duffy, J. (2012). Differences in risk aversion between young and old adults. *Neurosci Neuroecon, 2012*(1), 1–12. https://doi.org/10.2147/NAN.S27184

Alberts, C.J. (2006). *Common elements of risk*. Carnegie-Mellon University.

Auxier, B., & Anderson, M. (2021, April 7). *Social media use in 2021*. Pew Research Center. https://www.pewresearch.org/internet/2021/04/07/social-media-use-in-2021/

Bani-Amerina, N., & Venette, S. (2020). *Self-efficacy and EPPM* [Poster]. International Crisis Risk Communication Conference, Orlando, FL.

Baiocchi-Wagner, E. (2015). Future directions in communication research: Individual health behaviors and the influence of family communication. *Health Communication, 30*(8), 810–819. https://doi.org/10.1080/10410236.2013.845492

Bish, A., & Michie, S. (2010). Demographic and attitudinal determinant of protective behaviours during a pandemic: A review. *British Journal of Health Psychology, 15*(4), 797–824. https://doi.org/10.1348/135910710X485826

Bonem, E.M., Ellsworth, P.C., & Gonzalez, R. (2015). Age differences in risk: Perceptions, intentions and domains. *Journal of Behavioral Decision Making, 28*(4), 317–330. https://doi.org/10.1002/bdm.1848

Brashers, D.E. (2007). A theory of communication and uncertainty management. In B.B. Whaley & W. Samter (Eds.), *Explaining communication: Contemporary theory and exemplars* (pp. 201–218). Lawrence Erlbaum Associates Publishers.

Brown, L. (2020, June 29). Gov. DeSantis blames young people partying for coronavirus surge. *New York Post.* https://nypost.com/2020/06/29/gov-desantis-blames-young-people-partying-for-coronavirus-surge/

Bruine de Bruin, W. (2020). Age differences in COVID-19 risk perceptions and mental health: Evidence from a national US survey conducted in March 2020. *The Journal of Gerontology, 76*, e24–e29. https://doi.org/10.1093/geronb/gbaa074

Carcioppolo, N., Jensen, J.D., Wilson, S.R., Collins, W.B., Carrion, M., & Linnemeier, G. (2013). Examining HPV threat-to-efficacy ratios in the Extended Parallel Process Model. *Health Communication, 28*(1), 20–28. http://dx.doi.org/10.1080/10410236.2012.719478

Carlucci, L., D'ambrosio, I., & Balsamo, M. (2020). Demographic and attitudinal factors of adherence to quarantine guidelines during COVID-19: The Italian model. *Frontiers in Psychology, 11*. https://doi.org/10.3389/fpsyg.2020.559288

Chung, M., & Jones-Jang, S.M. (2021). Red media, blue media, Trump briefings, and COVID-19: Examining how information sources predict risk preventive behaviors via threat and efficacy. *Health Communication*, 1–8. https://doi.org/10.1080/10410236.2021.1914386

Deaven, K. (2020). *Cable news is politicizing Coronavirus coverage*. The University of Texas at Austin. https://mediaengagement.org/blogs/politicized-coronavirus-coverage/

DeJonckheere, M., Waselewski, M., Amaro, X. Frank, A., & Chua, K. (2021). Views on COVID-19 and use of face coverings among U.S. Youth. *Elsevier Public Health Emergency Collection, 68*(5), 873–881. https://doi.org/10.1016/j.jadohealth.2021.02.05

Feldman, L., Hart, P.S., & Milosevic, T. (2017). Polarizing news? Representations of threat and efficacy in leading US newspapers' coverage of climate change. *Public Understanding of Science, 26*(4), 481–497. https://doi.org/10.1177/0963662515595348

Flores, A. (2017). *How the U.S. Hispanic population is changing.* Pew Research Center. https://www.pewresearch.org/fact-tank/2017/09/18/how-the-u-s-hispanic-population-is-changing

Fry, R. (2020). *Millennials overtake Baby Boomers as America's largest generation.* Pew Research Center. https://www.pewresearch.org/fact-tank/2020/04/28/millennials-overtake-baby-boomers-as-americas-largest-generation/

Hauser, D.J., & Schwarz, N. (2016). Attentive Turkers: MTurk participants perform better on online attention checks than do subject pool participants. *Behavior Research Methods, 48*(1), 400–407. https://doi.org/10.3758/s13428-015-0578-z

Hawkins, D., Birnbaum, M., Kornfield, M., O'Grady, K.C., Lati, M., & Sonmez, F. (2020, June 29). Arizona, Florida, Texas are latest coronavirus epicenters. *The Washington Post.* https://www.washingtonpost.com/nation/2020/06/28/coronavirus-live-updates-us/

Henrich, N., & Holmes, B. (2009). The public's acceptance of novel vaccines during a pandemic: A focus group study and its application to influenza H1N1. *Emerging Health Threats Journal, 21*(4), 1–7. https://doi.org/10.3402/ehtj.v2i0.7088

Ibuka, Y., Chapman, G.B., Meyers, L.A., Li, M., & Galvani, A.P. (2010). The dynamics of risk perceptions and precautionary behavior in response to 2009 (H1N1) pandemic influenza. *BMC Infectious Diseases, 10*, 269–271. https://doi.org/10.1186/1471-2334-10-296

Jackson, M., & Cornell, S.E. (2013). Social science perspectives on the knowledge construction of natural hazards risk and uncertainty. In L.H. Rougier & R.S.J. Sparks (Eds.), *Assessment of risk and uncertainty for natural hazards* (pp. 502–547). Cambridge University Press.

Jones, J.H., & Salathé, M. (2009). Early assessment of anxiety and behavioral response to novel swine-origin influenza A (H1N1). *PLoS One, 4*(12), Article e8032. https://doi.org/10.1371/journal.pone.0008032

Kerlinger, F.N., & Lee, H.B. (2008). *Foundations of behavioral research.* Harcourt College Publishers.

Latour, B. (2003). Is re-modernization occurring-and if so, how to prove it? A commentary on Ulrich Beck. *Theory, Culture & Society, 20*(2), 35–48. https://doi.org/10.1177/0263276403020002002

Marschalk, E.E., Kotta, I., Kalcz-Janosi, K., Szabo, K., & Jancso-Farcas, S. (2021). Psychological predictors of COVID-19 prevention behavior in Hungarian women across different generations. *Frontiers in Psychology, 12*, 1–7. https://doi.org/10.3389/fpsyg.2021.596543

Mather, M., Mazar, M., Gorlick, Lighthall, N.R., Buregeno, J., Schoeke, A., & Ariely, D. (2012). Risk preferences and aging: The "Certainty Effect" in older adults' decision making. *Psychological Aging, 27*(4), 801–816. https://doi.org/10.1037/a003017

Matsa, K.E., & Naseer, S. (2021, November 8). *News platform fact sheet.* Pew Research Center. https://www.pewresearch.org/journalism/fact-sheet/news-platform-fact-sheet/

Moore, D. (2020, November 16). *An increasing share of the state's COVID cases are in people under 30, but other age groups have been infected at similar rates.* Boston Globe. https://www.bostonglobe.com/2020/11/16/nation/are-young-people-blame-recent-COVID-19-surges-experts-say-numbers-are-not-conclusive/

Neuburger, L., & Egger, R. (2021). Travel risk perception and travel behavior during the COVID-19 pandemic 2020: A case study of the DACH region. *Current Issues in Tourism*, *24*(7), 1003–1016. https://doi.org/10.1080/13683500.2020.1803807

Paison, R., Paiva, T.O., Fernandes, C., & Barbosa, F. (2020). The AGE effect on protective behaviors during the COVID-19 outbreak: Sociodemographic, perceptions, and psychological accounts. *Frontiers in Psychology*, *11*, 1–14. https://doi.org/10.3389/fpsyg.2020.561785

Proutheau, S., & Heath, R.L. (2009). Precautionary principle and biotechnology: Regulators are from Mars and activists are from Venus. In R.L. Heath & H.D. O'Hair (Eds.), *Handbook of risk and crisis communication* (pp. 576–589). Routledge.

Rimal, R., & Real, K. (2003). Understanding of perceived norms on behaviors. *Communication Theory*, *13*(2), 184–203. https://doi.org/10.1111/j.1468-2885.2003.tb00288.x

Roberto, A.J., Zhou, X., & Lu, A.H. (2021). The effects of perceived threat and efficacy on college students' social distancing behavior during the COVID-19 pandemic. *Journal of Health Communication*, 1–8. https://doi.org/10.1080/10810730.2021.1903628

Rohrer, G., & Santana, M. (2020, May 15). *Florida reopens gyms and fitness centers, expands restaurant seating*. Orlando Sentinel. https://www.orlandosentinel.com/coronavirus/jobs-economy/os-ne-coronavirus-desantis-friday-20200515-ofphjhbiknazborp73jgc6p3im-story.html

Rosi, A., Tijmen van Vugt, F., Lecce, S., Ceccato, I., Vallarino, M., Rapisarda, F., Vecchi, T., & Cavallni, E. (2021). Risk perception in a real-world situation (COVID-19): How it changes from 18 to 87 years old. *Frontiers in Psychology*, *12*, 1–8. https://doi.org/10.3389/fpsyg.2021.646558

Rubin, J., Amlôt, R., Page, L., & Wessely, S. (2009). Public perceptions, anxiety, and behavior change in relation to the Swine Flu outbreak: Cross sectional telephone survey. *British Medical Journal*, *339*, 1–8, https://doi.org/10.1136/bmj.b2651

Sakya, S.M., Van Scoy, L.J., Garman, J.C., Miller, E.L., Synder, B., Wasserman, E., Chinchilli, V.M., & Lennon, R.P. (2021). The impact of COVID-19-related changes in media consumption on public knowledge: Results of a cross-sectional survey of Pennsylvania adults. *Current Medical Research and Opinion*, *37*(6), 911–915. https://doi.org/10.1080/03007995.2021.1901679

Savage, I. (1993). Demographic influences on risk perceptions. *Risk Analysis*, *13*(4), 413–420. https://doi.org/10.1111/j.1539-6924.1993.tb00741.x

Sheehan, K. (2017). Crowdsourcing research: Data collection with Amazon's Mechanical Turk. *Communication Monographs*, *85*(1), 140–156. https://doi.org/10.1080/03637751.2017.1342043

Shi, J., & Smith, S.W. (2016). The effects of fear appeal message repetition on perceived threat, perceived efficacy, and behavioral intention in the extended parallel process model. *Health Communication*, *31*(3), 275–286. https://doi.org/10.1080/10410236.2014.948145

Slovic, P. (1987). Perception of risk. *Science*, *236*, 280–285. https://doi.org/10.1126/science.3563507

Stahl, B.C., Lichtenstein, Y., & Mangan, A. (2003). The limits of risk management: A social construction approach. *Communications of the International Information Management*

Association, 3(3), 15–22. https://www.researchgate.net/profile/Bernd-Stahl-2/publication/228895562_The_Limits_of_Risk_Management-A_social_construction_approach/links/09e4150c24ee851f2e000000/The-Limits-of-Risk-Management-A-social-construction-approach.pdf

Sund, B., Svensson, M., & Anderson, H. (2015). Demographic determinants of incident experience and risk perception: Do high-risk groups accurately perceive themselves as high-risk? *Journal of Risk Research*, 20(1), 99–117. https://doi.org/10.1080/13669877.2015.1042499

Walker, M., & Masta, K.E. (2021, September 20). *News consumption across social media in 2021*. Pew Research Center. https://www.pewresearch.org/journalism/2021/09/20/news-consumption-across-social-media-in-2021/

Waymer, J., & Sasson, A.M. (2020, July 7). *Florida sees worrying spike in coronavirus cases, potential to "overwhelm our hospitals" after reopening*. The Florida Times-Union. https://www.jacksonville.com/story/news/coronavirus/2020/07/07/florida-sees-worrying-spike-in-coronavirus-cases-potential-to-overwhelm-our-hospitals-after-reopening/112287034/

Whiteman A, Wang A, McCain K, et al. Demographic and Social Factors Associated with COVID-19 Vaccination Initiation Among Adults Aged ≥65 Years — United States, December 14, 2020–April 10, 2021. MMWR Morb Mortal Wkly Rep 2021; 70:725–730. DOI: http://dx.doi.org/10.15585/mmwr.mm7019e4external icon

Wilson, R.F., Sharma, A.J., Schluechtermann, S., Currie, D.W., Mangan, J., Kaplan, B., Goffard, K., Salomon, J., Casteel, S. Mukasa, A., Euhardy, N., Ruiz, A., Bautista, G., Bailey, E., Westergaard, R., & Gieryn, D. (2020, October 16). Factors influencing risk for COVID-19 exposure among young adults aged 18–23 years—Winnebago County, Wisconsin, March–July 2020. *Morbidity and Mortality Weekly Report*. https://www.cdc.gov/mmwr/volumes/69/wr/mm6941e2.htm

Witte, K. (1992). Putting the fear back into fear appeals: The extended parallel processing model. *Communication Monographs*, 59(4), 329–349. https://doi.org/10.1080/03637759209376276

Witte, K. (1996). Predicting risk behaviors: Development and validation of a diagnostic scale. *Journal of Health Communication*, 1(4), 317–342. https://doi.org/10.1080/108107396127988

Wong, N.C., & Cappella, J.N. (2009). Antismoking threat and efficacy appeals: Effects on smoking cessation intentions for smokers with low and high readiness to quit. *Journal of Applied Communication Research*, 37(1), 1–20. https://doi.org/10.1080/00909880802593928

World Health Organization. (2021, September 23). *Managing the COVID-19 infodemic: Promoting healthy behaviours and mitigating the harm from misinformation and disinformation*. https://www.who.int/news/item/23-09-2020-managing-the-COVID-19-infodemic-promoting-healthy-behaviours-and-mitigating-the-harm-from-misinformation-and-disinformation

· 1 3 ·

SPEAKING DIRECTLY TO INDIGENOUS COMMUNITIES VIA SOCIAL MEDIA: NATIVE FEMALE POLITICIANS MANAGE COMMUNITY INFORMATION BY ADDRESSING CRISES WITHIN A PANDEMIC

Victoria L. LaPoe, Benjamin R. LaPoe II, Candi S. Carter Olson, Cristina L. Azocar, & Jayne Yerrick

Indigenous Women in the Political Spotlight

The 2020 elections brought many new Native American women into national leadership positions, which allowed them to speak to and for Native American nations throughout the United States. In addition to Deb Haaland, the first Native person to work as a Cabinet secretary, and Sharice Davids, one of the first two Native women to serve in Congress, there were many other Indigenous politicians who had historic election victories in 2020. Yvette Herrell's (Cherokee) election, paired with Rep. Haaland's, made New Mexico the first state to have two Indigenous women congressional delegates (Aratani, 2020). Kansas state Rep. Stephanie Byers (Chickasaw) also became Kanas' first transgender lawmaker (Aratani, 2020). Christina Haswood (Diné) joined the group of trailblazing Indigenous women as the youngest person in the Kansas Legislature at age 26, and Doreen Garlid (Diné) became Tempe, Arizona's first

Native person to serve on city council (Aratani, 2020). Gabriella Cázares-Kelly (Tohono O'odham) was elected to hold a countywide seat in Pima county (AZ), the first Native person to do so (Silversmith, 2020). Each of these politicians ensured Indigenous women had unprecedented political representation in the United States (Center for American Women and Politics, 2020).

These women were joined by record-breaking numbers of Indigenous women who ran for office in 2020 (Center for American Women and Politics, 2020). Out of the 114 Indigenous candidates who ran for public office in 2020, 67 were women (Chavez, 2020). In addition, the highest number of Indigenous women in history ran for the U.S. House of Representatives, 15, and Senate, three (Center for American Women and Politics, 2020), giving the House of Representatives an historic number of Native women (Chavez, 2020).

Issues Faced by Indigenous Female Politicians

The increase in Indigenous female politicians provided Indigenous communities with an empathetic resource to help address ongoing crises, including historical erasure and Missing and Murdered Indigenous Women and Girls (MMIWG). Today, Indigenous communities and politicians regularly deal with erasure, the practice of eliminating Native people and cultures to access their land and resources (Orr et al., 2019). Secretary Haaland faced a serious instance of erasure during her Senate confirmation hearing, largely from Republican senators. Sen. Mike Lee, R-Utah, was especially aggressive when he questioned Haaland about the Antiquities Act, a law providing protection for cultural and natural resources. Lee said 28 of the national monuments created in the past 40 years are in Utah, "impoverishing" its residents (Amehae, 2021). In her answer, Haaland explained the area, Bear Ears National Monument, was "the Pueblo Indians' Ancestral homeland" (Amehae, 2021, para. 11). Lee interrupted Haaland by saying he was concerned with the "people who have some sort of connection to the land," meaning, ranchers and oil and gas workers (Amehae, 2021). A. Gay Kingman, Executive Director of the Great Plains Tribal Chairmen's Association and a former head of the National Congress of American Indians, explained the problematic nature of Lee's remarks:

> Dismissing a Pueblo woman's deep connection to her ancestral homeland demonstrated immense disrespect. The tone of this hearing was in stark contrast to what we witnessed with Ryan Zinke and David Bernhardt, the last two Interior Secretaries,

about both of whom we had serious questions on ethics and conflicts of interests that were never answered. I hope this is not systemic in U.S. Senate hearings now, that white men are treated with a measure of respect not accorded to women, and most especially to women of color? (Amehae, 2021, para. 12)

Haaland was confirmed as Secretary of the Interior, but Lee's interjection was still harmful to Haaland and Indigenous communities. He dismissed Haaland's connection to her ancestral homeland, and consequently contributed to the erasure of Indigenous women.

Lee's comments are not surprising considering mainstream media repeatedly fail to properly cover Indigenous peoples, which contributes to the erasure of Indigenous identity. A prime example of the erasure of Indigenous peoples by mainstream media involved CNN political commentator Rick Santorum. In April 2021, Santorum made racist remarks about Native peoples at a Young America's Foundation event:

> We came here and created a blank slate. We birthed a nation from nothing. I mean, there was nothing here. I mean, yes, we have Native Americans, but candidly there isn't much Native American culture in American culture. (Romero, 2021, para. 8)

Native advocacy groups worked together to have Santorum fired. IllumiNative, the National Congress of American Indians, NDN Collective, and the Native American Rights Fund held a "day of action" in response to the comments by promoting the hashtag #RemoveRick and hosting a Twitter (X) chat featuring Native journalists (Bendery, 2021). CNN fired Santorum in May 2021 (Romero, 2021), but the network continued to contribute to the erasure of Indigenous identity.

CNN Anchor Poppy Harlow also participated in the erasure of Indigenous peoples in April 2021 when she referred to Gov. Peggy Flanagan as a white woman (Bendery, 2021). Harlow was incorrect, as Flanagan is a citizen of the White Earth Band of Ojibwe, which has been widely stated. Not only is Flanagan a Native woman, but she is also the highest-ranking Native woman elected to U.S. executive office in history (Bendery, 2021). Prior to these two incidents CNN was under fire for releasing a poll that included a "something else" category. The catch-all category was intended to include Native peoples (Bendery, 2021). Native advocacy groups have called out CNN for "ignoring, silencing, and evading accountability to Native peoples" because of multiple erasure incidents (Bendery, 2021, para. 8). However, many Indigenous officials have used their platforms to give a voice to Native issues to counter politicians and the media ignoring and silencing them.

Indigenous women in politics are speaking out about one of the most severe crises facing Indigenous communities: MMIWG. In 2016, the National Crime Information Center reported 5,712 American Indian and Alaska Native women and girls were missing (Native Womens Wilderness, n.d.). The U.S. Department of Justice missing persons database reported just 116 cases of missing Native women in 2016 (Native Womens Wilderness, n.d.). Not only do great disparities exist in the number of reported cases, but law enforcement typically struggles to substantively investigate the cases. Jurisdictional issues between state, local, and tribal law enforcement make solving the cases exceptionally difficult (Native Womens Wilderness, n.d.). The high number of MMIWG cases reflects the heightened risk of violence Indigenous women face. According to the National Institute of Justice Report, more than four out of every five Indigenous women have experienced some form of violence (Native Womens Wilderness, n.d.). Indigenous women are ten times more likely to be murdered than all other ethnicities, and the third leading cause of death for Indigenous women is murder (Native Womens Wilderness, n.d.).

To combat the pervasive issue of MMIWG, politicians like Haaland have taken steps to raise awareness and help solve cases. Haaland created the Missing and Murdered Unit to serve as a task force focused on analyzing and solving cases of missing and murdered Indigenous peoples (Native Womens Wilderness, n.d.). Operation Lady Justice, a task force established in 2019, focuses on solving MMIWG cases by making improvements to data collection, investigative responses, and policies (Native Womens Wilderness, n.d.). The Not Invisible Act was created in 2019 to reduce violence within Native lands and against Native peoples. Notably, it is the first bill introduced and passed by four Native members of federally recognized tribes, including Sharice Davids, Deb Haaland, Tom Cole (Chickasaw Nation), and Markwayne Mullin (Cherokee Nation) (U.S. Representative Sharice Davids, 2020). Additionally, Savanna's Act became law in 2020 requiring the U.S. Department of Justice to properly address the cases of MMIWG by reviewing and developing policies and protocols (Native Womens Wilderness, n.d.). To raise awareness for MMIWG, the White House declared May 5, 2019, as the National Day of Awareness for Missing and Murdered Native Women and Girls (Native Womens Wilderness, n.d.). These initiatives, led by Indigenous officials, all have made a difference in raising awareness and solving cases of MMIWG.

Analyzing the crisis communication of Indigenous female politicians is critical because Indigenous communities faced a triple threat in 2020: the ongoing COVID-19 pandemic, continued erasure of Indigenous heritage, and high cases of MMIWG. Social media provided Indigenous women leaders a way to bypass mainstream media's episodic framing and its tendency to "index" opinions reported in the media to only those represented by non-Indigenous elites. Episodic framing and indexing erase Indigenous voices, but during the tumult of 2020, social media allowed Indigenous women to sidestep mainstream media's dominant narratives, directly contradict those narratives, and speak directly to Indigenous people seeking leadership and insight into issues impacting Native American nations.

Literature Review

One of the most common ways Indigenous officials raise awareness for MMIWG is through social media. Social media platforms provide Indigenous politicians the opportunity to connect directly with their audiences about the crises Native communities face (Wharton Business Daily, 2020). During the pandemic, Indigenous culture was spread on social media through hashtags like #ChangeTheName, #NativeTikTok, #MMIW, and #SomethingElse (Nielsen, 2020). Social media was also an especially effective form of crisis communication for Indigenous officials during the COVID-19 pandemic, a time when in-person interaction was severely limited. Social media amplified Indigenous officials' voices to wider audiences, as 96% of Native Americans own smartphones with access to social media (Nielsen, 2020).

COVID-19, Framing, and Indexing

The ongoing COVID-19 pandemic profoundly affected Indigenous communities throughout the world. In the United States, Indigenous politicians used their platforms to respond to the pandemic and support Indigenous peoples. Due to various social, economic, and health inequities, Native communities experienced greater difficulties because of the pandemic (Hill & Artiga, 2021). As of June 2, 2021, the Centers for Disease Control and Prevention (CDC) reported 6,585 Native people died from COVID-19, which is the highest COVID-19 death rate of any ethnic group in the United States (Bennett-Begaye et al., 2021). The death rate of Native peoples from COVID-19 is likely even higher than the CDC reports. Native peoples experienced what Abigail Echo-Hawk, director of the Urban Indian Health Institute, refers to as "data genocide" (Bennett-Begaye et al., 2021). The real number of Indigenous deaths from COVID-19 might never be known, mostly because of limited communication between local, state, federal, and tribal data-reporting systems (Bennett-Begaye et al., 2021). Although an accurate death toll remains uncertain, it is clear which factors had the most negative impact on Native peoples. Individuals belonging to Indigenous households earning less than $45,000 a year, those living on reservations, and Indigenous peoples who identify as transgender or gender nonconforming experienced some of the most serious hardships during the pandemic. These individuals were more likely to have inadequate access to personal protective equipment (PPE) and experience more adverse effects on employment, finances, and overall well-being (IllumiNative, 2020a). The high death toll, inaccurate data, and lack of access to PPE demonstrate the serious disadvantages Native communities encountered during the pandemic.

Past research on media coverage of Indigenous communities during the COVID-19 pandemic demonstrated many mainstream media outlets relied on episodic framing, meaning news media focused on specific incidents rather than broader context (Iyengar, 1996; LaPoe et al., 2021). Conversely, many Indigenous media outlets covered COVID-19 with a combination of both episodic and thematic framing, meaning they looked both at specific incidents and put those incidents within either historical or geographical context (Iyengar, 1996; LaPoe et al., 2021). When mainstream media rely on episodic framing to cover COVID-19, the blame for the issues related to COVID-19 within Indigenous communities is placed on Indigenous peoples. For example, Indigenous peoples were blamed for the lack of resources and significant health disparities their communities experienced during the pandemic (LaPoe et al., 2021). In addition to concentrating on episodic reporting, non-Indigenous news sources tend to "index" mainstream debates to privilege the viewpoints of prominent, often non-Native government officials (Bennett, 1990). This is demonstrated in the lack of Indigenous sources used by mainstream media when reporting on Indigenous communities (Azocar et al., 2021). When covering COVID-19 in Indigenous communities, mainstream media frequently quote federal or state officials in news stories before including tribal members (Azocar et al., 2021). In addition, many mainstream media outlets fail to interview tribal officials, and instead rely on information from press releases or websites (Azocar et al., 2021).

Indigenous officials may be able to break this pattern by speaking directly to Indigenous communities through social media. By framing themselves on social media, Indigenous politicians may not need to rely on mainstream media to discuss Indigenous issues. Instead, they may have the power to directly draw attention to the crises facing Indigenous communities that may not have been covered by mainstream news media.

Indigenous leaders particularly used social media to sidestep mainstream narratives throughout the COVID-19 pandemic. Although Native peoples were disproportionately affected by the pandemic, Native communities handled the COVID-19 pandemic and the vaccination process much better than other communities in terms of vaccination rates (Hill & Artiga, 2021). With the assistance of leading Indigenous politicians, Native communities responded to COVID-19 with a collective effort to get as many individuals vaccinated as possible. Due to this effort in Indian Country, Native peoples achieved the highest vaccination rate of all racial/ethnic groups in the United States early on, once vaccines became available (Hill & Artiga, 2021).

Social media allowed Indigenous communities to respond to the pandemic in a highly effective manner. Tribal leaders distributed COVID-19 vaccines strategically so the needs and preferences of Native communities were met, which resulted in a high vaccination rate among Native peoples (Hill & Artiga, 2021). In addition to tribal leadership, prominent Indigenous female politicians also played a major role in achieving a high vaccination rate. During the pandemic, leading Indigenous female politicians used social media to connect with Indigenous communities. Deb Haaland (Laguna and Jemez Pueblos), who was selected by President Joe Biden to be Secretary of the Interior, and Rep. Sharice Davids (Ho-Chunk Nation) of Kansas frequently used social media to communicate about the pandemic (Chavez, 2020). They both often hosted Instagram lives to discuss the importance of getting the COVID-19 vaccine and address any concerns viewers had. By talking directly to their audience through social media, Haaland and Davids made themselves accessible to Native peoples who were concerned about the pandemic and the vaccination process (Wharton Business Daily, 2020).

Sovereignty, Power, and Policy

While tribes are sovereign, voting in non-tribal elections may mean hurdles for some Indigenous peoples. According to the Indigenous Futures Survey, which surveyed over 6,400 Native peoples from 401 tribes, the main four barriers to voting included delayed absentee ballots, work schedules, the long distance of polling places, and long voting lines (IllumiNative, 2020b). Indigenous peoples living in North Dakota also have faced an additional barrier to voting. In 2013, the state began requiring individuals to have a valid ID to vote, with their name, birth date, and current residential address. The requirement served as an obstacle for many Indigenous voters, as those living on reservations disproportionately lacked street addresses (Lyon, 2020). Therefore, many of the Indigenous votes were ineligible. It was not until 2020 that North Dakota, after facing a lawsuit, agreed that tribal addresses would be considered valid and Indigenous members of the Spirit Lake Nation and Standing Rock Sioux Tribe could vote with tribal IDs (Lyon, 2020).

Despite imposed outside barriers, Indigenous peoples remain politically active, and have high voting rates (IllumiNative, 2020b). The Indigenous Futures Survey found 77% of participants voted in the last local, state, or national election. According to the survey, 82% of Indigenous voters were motivated by a candidate's platform and political affiliation, 80% of voters cared about a candidate's track record on Native issues, 40% were motivated by opposition to other candidates, and 31% were motivated if the candidate is Native (IllumiNative, 2020b).

The majority of Indigenous people (95%) who were surveyed said they engaged in some form of civic engagement in the past year (IllumiNative, 2020b). Many of the participants reported they were involved with the protests following the murder of George Floyd, in political rallies, and were in contact with political officials (IllumiNative, 2020b). Indigenous officials assisted this process by sharing information about avenues for civic engagement on their social media sites.

Distrust of the Federal Government

One of the key reasons Indigenous peoples have high levels of political engagement appears to be distrust of the federal government to effectively handle Indigenous concerns (IllumiNative, 2020b). Just 4% of participants said they trusted the federal government, while 95% of participants reported they do not trust the U.S. government to make good decisions about Native issues. Additionally, 91% of participants do not trust their local and state governments (IllumiNative, 2020b). However, more than 10 times as many participants trusted their tribal government over the federal government (IllumiNative, 2020b). With little-to-no faith in the federal government, many Native peoples are hopeful future generations will gain more political representation in the U.S. government. In 2020, there was more Indigenous representation in the U.S. government, and one respondent in the survey was hopeful for continued success in the future:

I want future generations to get educated and excited about voting, census and running for Tribal government and then onto Congress. We have to be the change we want to see for our next 7 generations. (IllumiNative, 2020b, p. 55)

Politicians' Use of Social Media

Through social media, many of the current Indigenous officials helped Indigenous communities navigate the hardships of the pandemic, while also discussing erasure of identity and MMIWG. Much of the crisis communication Indigenous politicians had with the public was on social media. Indigenous politicians like Interior Secretary Haaland, Rep. Davids, and Rep. Haswood regularly use social media to connect with supporters, enabling them to connect with communities through one-on-one discussions.

TikTok and Instagram

Social media platforms TikTok and Instagram were important Indigenous communication tools throughout the COVID-19 pandemic. Pew Research Center found 71% of 18 to 29-year-olds use Instagram (Auxier & Anderson, 2021). New Mexico Representative and now Interior Secretary Haaland and Rep. Davids actively used Instagram, including its live-streaming video platform, to connect with followers during the pandemic. TikTok is even more popular with young people. TikTok, a video-sharing app, has about 100 million monthly active users in the United States (Sherman, 2020). TikTok has drastically gained popularity over the past few years, as monthly TikTok users have increased by 800% since January 2018 (Sherman, 2020) and has given Indigenous creators the unique opportunity to share more about Indigenous cultures and issues. Erin Tapahe (Diné) is a young Indigenous woman who started to use TikTok in mid-July 2020 to share her father's art project, "Art Heals: The Jingle Dress Project" after the pandemic caused many of his shows and exhibitions to be canceled (Pember, 2020). Since then, she has gained over 75,000 followers on the app. Tapahe says she uses TikTok to "share the strength and successes of Native people" (Pember, 2020, para. 7). In September 2020, Tapahe was hired by TikTok through the Creative Learning Fund to continue sharing videos about Native history and cultures (Pember, 2020). Rep. Haswood is also popular on TikTok, with over 143,700 followers as of February 2024. She regularly posts about her culture and her experience as a Kansas State legislator. Through social media, Rep. Haswood can talk candidly with audience members and engage with them through the comment section.

Social Media Transformed Politics

As Rep. Haswood's TikTok account shows, social media sites give Indigenous politicians an opportunity to talk directly with their supporters ("How Social Media," 2020). With social media, leaders can discuss policy and form personal connections with audience members by sharing intimate details of their lives, making politicians more accessible to the public than ever before (Wharton Business Daily, 2020). The humanization made possible by social media is a key advantage for politicians. For example, Secretary Haaland and Rep. Davids used Instagram Live to discuss COVID-19 and to address important issues related to navigating the COVID-19 pandemic, like mental health concerns, the vaccination process, and relief bills.

Social media include powerful tools for Indigenous politicians to use for crisis communication, such as live events that allow for community questions and answers in real time. This chapter seeks to answer the following research questions:

> **RQ1:** How did Indigenous female politicians use social media to connect with Native communities through crises, such as the COVID-19 pandemic, MMIWG, and erasures?
>
> **RQ2:** How did Indigenous officials frame themselves on their social media sites to respond to crises such as the COVID-19 pandemic, addressing MMIWG, and continued erasure?
>
> **RQ3:** What does it mean when officials from marginalized communities can directly speak to citizens of their communities?

Method

Data Collection Design and Procedure

We conducted a qualitative thematic analysis of Instagram and TikTok posts from March 12, 2020, when the COVID-19 pandemic became a widespread concern in the United States, until May 5, 2021, marking two weeks after the National Day of Awareness for MMIW. We collected posts noting the date, theme, account, content, and hashtags of each post. Instagram and TikTok posts were found via the search engines within the apps by a professor and research assistant. To select posts, we searched the hashtags #MaskUp, #MasksSaveLives, #MMIWG, #MMIW, #nativetiktok, and #NoMoreStolenSisters, along with each Indigenous politician's name. Posts were also found by visiting Indigenous politicians' Instagram pages to find any posts related to COVID-19, MMIWG, and erasure. We examined the Instagram accounts of Sec. Haaland, Rep. Davids, Rep. Yvette Herrell (Cherokee), and Rep. Haswood (Diné). Additionally, we looked at Haswood's TikTok account because she is very popular on the app. We looked at social media accounts of these women because they are leading Indigenous female politicians actively using social media to communicate with their audiences. The posts were selected if they had any mention of COVID-19, erasure, Indigenous politicians, or MMIWG. For purposes of analysis the posts were organized into three categories: COVID-19, Indigenous politicians, and MMIWG. We collected 33 posts related to COVID-19, 56 posts related to Indigenous politicians, and 25 posts related to MMIWG, for a total of 114 posts.

Qualitative Thematic Analysis

Conducting a qualitative thematic analysis involves analyzing "multiple forms of data from diverse media to understand the mediated construction of an illuminating case" (Phillips & Chagnon, 2018, p. 52). A thematic analysis assists in revealing patterns or themes within the crisis communication of Indigenous officials on Instagram and TikTok. We first thoroughly examined the posts to become familiar with the content, and then coded the groups based on the emergent themes (Miller, 2020). After coding the posts, we established broader themes for the data (Miller, 2020). By further analyzing the posts, we refined the themes in order to understand the relationships between theme (Miller, 2020). The thematic analysis allowed us to assign meaning to each theme and make critical connections between the data (Miller, 2020). This process can provide critical insight into what the themes might ask the audience to "believe, understand, feel, or think about" (LaPoe & LaPoe, 2018).

Case Study

We chose to use a case study to investigate our research questions. A case study is defined as "an in-depth, multifaceted investigation, using qualitative research methods, of a single social phenomenon" (Morland et al., 1992, p. 2).

Case studies seek to apply the findings to a larger group or phenomenon (Gerring, 2004). For a case study to be successful, it must investigate a phenomenon with clear content and established boundaries (Morland et al., 1992). Utilizing a case study helps us understand more about the development of crisis communication among Indigenous politicians throughout the COVID-19 pandemic (Morland et al., 1992). This type of research provided a more in-depth look at the social media use of Indigenous officials. Although case studies can "explain, describe, or explore events or phenomena in the everyday contexts in which they occur" (Crowe et al., 2011, para. 8), this method of analysis has been criticized for not having enough scientific rigor and not allowing for generalization (Crowe et al., 2011). We addressed these concerns by being transparent about our case selection and the methods we chose to use in the study (Crowe et al., 2011).

Findings and Discussion

RQ1: How Did Indigenous Female Politicians Use Social Media to Connect with Native Communities Through Crises Such As the COVID-19 Pandemic, Addressing MMIWG, and Continued Erasure?

Indigenous officials used social media to communicate with the public throughout the COVID-19 pandemic, a time when in-person communication was rare. They used social media to address COVID-19, while also providing support for issues like MMIWG and erasure. Three key themes emerged in their communication on social media: establishing unity, spreading information, and encouraging safety.

Establishing Unity

Throughout the COVID-19 pandemic, Indigenous officials urged audience members to work together to overcome the pandemic and battle MMIWG. Themes of unity were evident among Indigenous politicians' Instagram posts and were indicated by the hashtags they used. Representative examples of these hashtags include:

- New Mexico Rep. Haaland regularly added "#AllTogetherNM" to her Instagram posts at the beginning of the pandemic when she urged audience members to social distance and wear masks (Haaland, 2020f).

- New Mexico Rep. Yvette Herrell frequently used "#WeAreNewMexico" on her Instagram posts regarding COVID-19 (Herrell, 2020).
- Once vaccines were made available to the public, Sec. Haaland continued to use unifying language when she advised her supporters to get vaccinated. Sec. Haaland tagged her vaccine-related posts with "#WeCanDoThis" (Haaland, 2021d).

In addition to hashtags, the language Indigenous politicians used in the captions of Instagram posts also attempted to establish unity throughout the pandemic. Politicians commonly used the words "we" and "our" when discussing the difficulties of the COVID-19 pandemic and MMIWG on social media, as the following examples illustrate:

- In her Instagram post for Kansas Day, Rep. Christina Haswood captioned it by saying, "Seeing our community rise to current challenges and take care of one another inspires me to work harder and be a strong advocate each day. We are resilient" (Haswood, 2021a).
- On Missing and Murdered Indigenous Persons Awareness Day in 2021, Rep. Haswood wrote the caption: "The MMIP epidemic impacts us all, no matter our geographical location. It's going to take all hands on deck to come together to prevent and save the lives of our relatives" (Haswood, 2021f).

Indigenous officials also attempted to establish unity throughout the pandemic by encouraging community-based efforts. Officials took to social media to urge followers to help their communities by volunteering and supporting local businesses. Both Rep. Davids and Rep. Haaland posted on Instagram about their efforts volunteering with local food banks (Davids, 2020c). Rep. Haaland's post directly asked followers to join her in volunteering: "If you are able, please donate or volunteer" (Haaland, 2020f). Many politicians also advocated for supporting local businesses throughout the pandemic. For instance, both Rep. Haaland and Rep. Haswood requested their Instagram followers consider shopping from local coffee shops (Haaland, 2020d; Haswood, 2020b). In the caption on Rep. Haaland's small business post, she engaged with her followers by writing: "Did you support a small business today? If so, share in the comments!" (Haaland, 2020d). These types of social media posts indicate Indigenous politicians promoted community-based efforts and unity during the pandemic.

Spreading Critical Information

Social media was a valuable tool that Indigenous politicians used to spread crucial information to the public throughout the COVID-19 pandemic. Many leaders used Instagram to inform the public about the U.S. government's COVID-19 relief efforts and resources. For example, Rep. Haaland posted about the Cares Act and the Families First Coronavirus Response Bill on Instagram (Haaland, 2020b, 2020c). In these posts, she detailed the benefits the efforts entailed. Furthermore, Indigenous officials also provided support to the public by sharing information on social media about the video calls they hosted. A key example is Rep. Davids' post about the virtual roundtable she hosted to educate the public on voting rights under COVID-19 (Davids, 2020b). In addition, Rep. Haswood posted on Instagram about the "Virtual Townhalls" she held to support the public during the pandemic (Haswood, 2021h).

Social media was used to inform the public about the pandemic, but it also was used by politicians to discuss MMIWG. Indigenous officials regularly shared information about the policy changes they have made to combat MMIWG. Rep. Haswood frequently made posts to update her Instagram followers about the MMIP bill she worked on (Haswood, 2021b, 2021j). She also was active on TikTok and frequently shared videos about the MMIP bill (Haswood, 2021c). In addition, it is important to note the prevalence of statistics in MMIWG posts. Other creators often included statistics about MMIWG when addressing the issue on social media (Louie, 2020; MMIWG, 2021). These statistics provided the public with essential information about MMIWG.

Encouraging Safety

When posting about COVID-19 on social media, Indigenous politicians encouraged practicing safety measures by promoting social distancing, wearing masks, staying home, and getting vaccinated. Social distancing and staying home was a key focus of the Instagram posts of Indigenous officials, especially at the beginning of the pandemic. Rep. Haaland and Rep. Davids both shared posts about staying home during the pandemic (Davids, 2020a; Haaland, 2020g). It was commonplace for Indigenous representatives to advise their followers to wear masks to protect themselves from the virus (Haswood, 2020e). Once vaccines were made available to the public, Indigenous officials also regularly shared information about the vaccines, including information about where to get vaccinated and the benefits of being vaccinated (Haaland, 2021d; Haswood, 2021k).

RQ2: How Did Indigenous Officials Frame Themselves on Their Social Media Sites to Respond to Crises Such As the COVID-19 Pandemic, Addressing MMIWG, and Continued Erasure?

Leading by Example

Indigenous officials framed themselves as individuals who lead by example through social media posts. When Indigenous politicians shared posts urging their followers to participate in COVID alleviation efforts, like wearing a mask or volunteering, they were often pictured doing the action they encouraged. For instance, Indigenous officials were regularly pictured wearing masks on social media, even if the caption was unrelated to mask-wearing. In many of their posts, Rep. Davids, Rep. Haaland, and Rep. Haswood wore masks, while often encouraging their supporters to follow their lead (Davids, 2020d, 2020e; Haswood, 2020e).

Indigenous leaders also led by example by posting pictures of themselves volunteering. We noticed a similar trend with posts regarding supporting small businesses. When urging followers to support local businesses, Indigenous officials shared photographs of themselves visiting and buying an item from the business (Haaland, 2020d; Haswood, 2020b). Indigenous politicians also shared photographs of themselves after getting their COVID-19 vaccine. Many politicians would also share their personal reasons for getting vaccinated and tell supporters to follow their lead in their posts (Haaland, 2021d; Haswood, 2021k).

Highlighting Native Culture and Traditions

Indigenous officials often framed themselves as leaders who are proud of their Indigenous culture on social media. One of the main ways Indigenous politicians framed themselves in this way was through wearing traditional clothing in the photos they shared on social media. Representative examples include:

- Rep. Haswood shared a photograph of being sworn into office while wearing regalia. She wore traditional Diné regalia, including a velveteen skirt, moccasins, and a red blouse. She then shared the Vogue article about it on her Instagram page (Haswood, 2021e).
- Sec. Haaland posted the photos InStyle magazine took of her wearing regalia (Haaland, 2021a).

- Sec. Haaland shared a photograph of her wearing a traditional ribbon skirt while being sworn in as Secretary of the Interior (Haaland, 2021b).

They also expressed pride in their Native culture by spreading information about Indigenous history and issues on social media. For example, Rep. Haswood used her Instagram page to publicly recognize Native American Legislative Day and Indigenous Peoples Day to educate the public about the significance of each day (Haswood, 2020c, 2021d). In addition, Sec. Haaland used her social media platform to advocate for the protection of Indigenous lands (Haaland, 2020a). Each of the Indigenous politicians we examined in our case study posted about MMIWG at some point on social media.

Collaborative Team that Supports One Another

Indigenous officials framed themselves as a united force on social media by creating multiple posts in support of one another. This support is illustrated by the following Instagram posts:

- Rep. Davids and Rep. Haswood posed for an Instagram picture after sharing dinner together (Haswood, 2020d).
- Rep. Haswood thanked Indigenous politician Rep. Dr. Ponka-We Victors (Tohono O'odham Nation of Arizona & Southern Ponca Nation of Oklahoma) on Instagram for her help on the MMIP bill (Haswood, 2021g).
- Rep. Davids and Rep. Haswood hosted an online series together and promoted it on Instagram (Haswood, 2020a).
- Rep. Haaland and Rep. Haswood hosted a joint virtual fundraiser and promoted it on Instagram (Haswood, 2020d).
- Rep. Haaland and Rep. Davids hosted an Instagram Live to discuss the COVID-19 vaccine and to address any concerns from the public about the vaccine (Davids & Haaland, 2021).

Haaland and Haswood Regularly Framed Themselves with the Color Turquoise

A common visual theme found among Sec. Haaland's and Rep. Haswood's posts was the color turquoise, a nod to their Nations. The two politicians frequently wore the color found in their homelands' regions, often in the form of jewelry. Also, many of the posts about the two officials included the color turquoise. Representative examples include:

- In the Instagram post Rep. Haswood made after her first COVID-19 vaccine dose, she is wearing a turquoise ring, bracelet, and necklace (Haswood, 2021k).
- In a video of Sec. Haaland posted on TikTok, she is seen wearing turquoise earrings (Now This Politics, 2020).
- A drawing of Haaland found on Instagram depicts her wearing turquoise earrings and standing against a turquoise background (Agency, 2021).

Wearing Red for MMIWG

Indigenous officials framed themselves by wearing red, the color associated with the movement against MMIWG when addressing MMIWG in the following posts:

- In an Instagram post, Sec. Haaland lays a red shawl over an empty chair in her office to honor Missing and Murdered Indigenous Persons Awareness Day (Haaland, 2021c).
- Rep. Haswood shared an image of her testifying for her MMIP bill. In the image, she is seen wearing a red sweater (Haswood, 2021j).
- Rep. Haswood wore a red scarf and wrote on a sign in red marker when she posted on Instagram for Missing and Murdered Indigenous Persons Awareness Day (Haswood, 2020f).

RQ3: What Does It Mean When Officials from Marginalized Communities Can Directly Speak to Citizens of Their Communities?

Forming Connections by Sharing Personal Stories and Anecdotes

Since social media allows leaders to directly speak to citizens of their communities, Indigenous leaders can form close connections by sharing personal stories and anecdotes. Many Indigenous politicians used social media to reveal more about their personal lives, which may lead to deeper connections between officials and supporters. Representative examples of these personal connections included the following:

- Rep. Haswood shared her experience getting her first vaccine dose on Instagram, including details about how long she waited and the side effects she felt after the vaccine (Haswood, 2021k).
- Sec. Haaland shared she got vaccinated because she wants to be able to visit her mother in the senior facility where she lives (Haaland, 2021d).
- Rep. Davids opened up about feeling anxious during the pandemic in an Instagram post (Davids, 2020a).
- Rep. Haaland mentioned on her Instagram page she was worried about her elderly mother's safety due to the virus (Haaland, 2020e).

Sharing Critical Information with Affected Marginalized Communities

Indigenous politicians used social media to share critical information about Indigenous issues. On social media, Indigenous officials often communicated about the efforts they were taking in the fight against MMIWG. Rep. Haswood shared many details about her MMIP bill on social media (Haswood, 2021i). This kept the public informed about how she was supporting Indigenous communities.

Indigenous officials also posted on social media as advocates for Indigenous peoples and solving Indigenous issues. For example, Rep. Haswood posted on Instagram in honor of Native American Legislative Day and acknowledged Tribal Nations have been disproportionately affected by COVID-19 (Haswood, 2021d). In addition, Sec. Haaland captioned one Instagram post with her promise to protect all the stolen land (Haaland, 2020a).

Differences Between Instagram and TikTok Posts

It is important to note the differences in the content we examined on Instagram and TikTok. One of the most evident differences between the two social media apps is the format of the posts. TikTok exclusively has video posts, while most of the Instagram posts were photographs. However, Indigenous politicians at times did share some videos on Instagram to share more detailed information. Another notable difference between the two apps is most of the TikTok posts we examined addressed MMIWG, rather than issues like COVID-19 and erasure. With Instagram, there were fewer posts related to MMIWG and more COVID-19 posts. In addition, Instagram was the most-used app by Indigenous politicians. Each official we included in our research had an official Instagram account, but that was not the case with TikTok. In fact, Rep. Haswood was the only Indigenous politician we included in our study who actively ran a TikTok page.

Conclusion

In 2020, social media allowed female Native politicians to fight past gatekeepers and traditional informational news norms and routines to strengthen Indigenous communities during COVID-19, spread information about MMIWG beyond Native American communities, and confront and combat mediated erasures of Indigenous identities and issues. Through social media, they distributed information directly to communities during crises. This was essential as the federal government continued erecting bureaucratic and unnecessary hurdles, such as the CARES Act, for Indigenous communities attempting to rebuild during the pandemic (Spears et al., 2021). Female politicians specifically used Instagram and TikTok to establish unity, spread community safety health measures, and to flex their support of each other. This support included sharing personal stories, nods to their tribal traditions, and visually working with one another to collaborate on producing social media messages, such as live events, to answer community questions in real time.

Indigenous communities have had their own media and language for hundreds of years, and Indigenous politicians speaking directly to their communities supports this historical sovereign tradition, but within the new platform of social media (LaPoe & LaPoe, 2017). While trust of, and barriers within, the federal government continue to be an issue for tribal relations, social media provided an empowering moment where Indigenous politicians chose how they were represented and chose the most appropriate crisis communication to address COVID-19 in their communities. Dine' reporter Marley Shebala discussed, in a Fall 2021 talk to Ohio University journalism Honors students, what reporting meant to her as an Indigenous person: "We are art. If you are art, you are sacred and take care of yourself." She furthered this statement by saying that everything is connected: trees are alive, coal is Mother Earth's liver and so, environmental racism, injustice, climate damage (which she emphatically noted was more accurate), the Indian Child Welfare Act, boarding school history and trauma, and so on, is all connected. She said, "[I]t can't be separated." And, while Indigenous communities are not monolithic, Shebala's discussion highlights the mission of this chapter: addressing issues within issues, as a pandemic raged. Future research should continue analyzing the evolution of social media and evaluate further how both Indigenous and non-Indigenous media represent sources and stories in comparison to officials.

Resources

1. Illuminative: https://illuminative.org
2. Global Investigative Journalism Network. Guide for Indigenous Investigative Journalists: https://gijn.org/gijn-naja-guide-for-indigenous-investigative-journalists/
3. National Indigenous Women's Resource Center: https://www.niwrc.org
4. Native American Journalists Association. Reporting Guides: https://najanewsroom.com/reporting-guides/

References

Agency, M. [@marlenaagency]. (2021, March 17). *Congratulations to Deb Haaland, our new Secretary of Interiors AND the first Native American to hold a cabinet position* [Photograph]. Instagram. https://www.instagram.com/p/CMiE6TLBI23/?utm_medium=copy_link

Amehae, A. (2021, February 23). *Haaland retains her composure in the face of "immense disrespect" in confirmation hearing*. Native News Online. https://nativenewsonline.net/currents/haaland-retains-her-composure-in-the-face-of-immense-disrespect-in-confirmation-hearing

Aratani, L. (2020, November 4). Record number of Native American women elected to Congress. *The Guardian*. https://www.theguardian.com/us-news/2020/nov/04/native-american-women-elected-congress-record-number

Auxier, B., & Anderson, M. (2021, April 7). *Social media use in 2021*. Pew Research Center. https://www.pewresearch.org/internet/2021/04/07/social-media-use-in-2021/

Azocar, C.L., LaPoe, V., Olson, C.S., LaPoe, B., & Hazarika, B. (2021). Indigenous communities and COVID 19: Reporting on resources and resilience. *Howard Journal of Communications*, 1–17. https://doi.org/10.1080/10646175.2021.1892552

Bendery, J. (2021, May 20). *Native groups launch "day of action" amid CNN's silence on Rick Santorum's racism*. HuffPost. https://www.huffpost.com/entry/cnn-rick-santorum-racism-native-americans-letter_n_60a68815e4b0d45b752686cc

Bennett, W.L. (1990). Toward a theory of press-state relations in the United States. *Journal of Communication*, 40(2), 103–127. https://doi.org/10.1111/j.1460-2466.1990.tb02265.x

Bennett-Begaye, J., Clahchischiligi, S., & Trudeau, C. (2021, June 8). *A broken system: The number of Indigenous people who died from coronavirus may never be known*. High Country News.

https://www.hcn.org/articles/indigenous-affairs-covid19-a-broken-system-the-number-of-indigenous-people-who-died-from-coronavirus-may-never-be-known

Center for American Women and Politics. (2020). *Native American women candidates in 2020*. https://cawp.rutgers.edu/election-analysis/native-american-women-candidates-2020

Chavez, A. (2020, December 28). *Indigenous candidates made history in 2020*. Indian Country Today. https://indiancountrytoday.com/news/indigenous-candidates-made history-in-2020

Crowe, S., Cresswell, K., Robertson, A., Huby, G., Avery, A., & Sheikh, A. (2011). The case study approach. *BMC Medical Research Methodology*, 11(1). https://doi.org/10.1186/1471-2288-11-100

Davids, S. [@shariceforcongress]. (2020a, March 17). *Checking in on everyone while I'm working from home today & practicing social distancing like I hope everyone is too* [Video]. Instagram. https://www.instagram.com/tv/B92AdTIp8Fw/?utm_source=ig_web_copy_link

Davids, S. [@shariceforcongress]. (2020b, May 19). *Join Let America Vote Founder @JasonKander, End Citizens United and Let America Vote President Tiffany Miller* [Photograph]. Instagram. https://www.instagram.com/p/CAYANNHpb4T/?utm_source=ig_web_copy_link

Davids, S. [@shariceforcongress]. (2020c, October 12). *Last week I had the chance to help deliver groceries to folks in #KS03 during a community food bank* [Photograph]. Instagram. https://www.instagram.com/p/CGQUXUlJmJX/?utm_source=ig_web_copy_link

Davids, S. [@shariceforcongress]. (2020d, July 29). *Let's all do our part to keep those around us safe and healthy. #MaskUpKC* [Video]. Instagram. https://www.instagram.com/p/CDOtL7ZJLU3/?utm_medium=copy_link

Davids, S. [@shariceforcongress]. (2020e, June 30). *Masks help keep yourself & those around you safe* [Photograph]. Instagram. https://www.instagram.com/p/CCEFjhSJDgU/?utm_source=ig_web_copy_link

Davids, S., & Haaland, D. [@repdebhaaland & repdavids]. (2021, February 5). *Rep. Haaland and Rep. Davids host an Instagram Live to discuss the COVID-19 vaccine* [Live Video]. Instagram.

Gerring, J. (2004). What is a case study and what is it good for? *American Political Science Review*, 98(2), 341–354. https://doi.org/10.4135/9781473915480.n7

Haaland, D. [@debhaalandnm]. (2020a, December 28). *#DebForInterior* [Video]. Instagram. https://www.instagram.com/tv/CJXGBJYHqPV/?utm_source=ig_web_copy_link

Haaland, D. [@debhaalandnm]. (2020b, April 10). *In Congress we passed the #CaresAct, the most significant stimulus package ever passed* [Photograph]. Instagram. https://www.instagram.com/p/B-0WmJehuWd/?utm_source=ig_web_copy_link

Haaland, D. [@secdebhaaland]. (2021a, June 24). *I never really understood what representation meant until I became one of the first Indigenous women in Congress* [Photograph]. Instagram. https://www.instagram.com/p/CQgUZpzpMXD/?utm_source=ig_web_copy_link

Haaland, D. [@secdebhaaland]. (2021b, March 18). *Thank you @POTUS Biden and @VP Harris. I am honored and ready to work* [Photograph]. Instagram. https://www.instagram.com/p/CMkSEMfpf0p/?utm_source=ig_web_copy_link

Haaland, D. [@debhaalandnm]. (2020c, March 12). *The House of Representatives introduced the Families First Coronavirus Response Bill* [Photograph]. Instagram. https://www.instagram.com/p/B9paMgyFumS/?utm_source=ig_web_copy_link

Haaland, D. [@debhaalandnm]. (2020d, November 19). *This pandemic has taken its toll on small businesses all around our state* [Photograph]. Instagram. https://www.instagram.com/p/CHycNeOls88/?utm_source=ig_web_copy_link

Haaland, D. [@debhaalandnm]. (2020e, March 17). *Today I am thinking of my elderly mother* [Photograph]. Instagram. https://www.instagram.com/p/B92ozmjlVG6/?utm_source=ig_web_copy_link

Haaland, D. [@debhaalandnm]. (2021c, May 5). *Today is Missing and Murdered Indigenous Persons Awareness Day* [Video]. Instagram. https://www.instagram.com/reel/COgl9mcJQDF/?utm_source=ig_web_copy_link

Haaland, D. [@debhaalandnm]. (2020f, April 17). *We all have to pitch in and do what we can to help during this time* [Photograph]. Instagram. https://www.instagram.com/p/B_Gs9PNlwwt/?utm_source=ig_web_copy_link

Haaland, D. [@secdebhaaland]. (2021d, June 10). *We are a community* [Video]. Instagram. https://www.instagram.com/reel/CP8rpDkJWJt/?utm_source=ig_web_copy_link

Haaland, D. [@debhaalandnm]. (2020g, April 17). *We are #AllTogetherNM, and today I am thinking of all of you* [Photograph]. Instagram. https://www.instagram.com/p/B_GfBfKoMtd/?utm_source=ig_web_copy_link

Haswood, C. [@haswoodforks]. (2020a, August 19). *A great conversation with Congresswoman Sharice Davids* [Photograph]. Instagram. https://www.instagram.com/p/CEF5ve5p3iH/?utm_source=ig_web_copy_link

Haswood, C. [@haswoodforks]. (2020b, May 29). *Glad to support a small local and award winning bakery @1900barker and Cafe* [Photograph]. Instagram. https://www.instagram.com/p/CAywfkHJ86W/?utm_source=ig_web_copy_link

Haswood, C. [@haswoodforks]. (2020c, October 12). *Happy Indigenous Peoples Day!!!* [Photograph]. Instagram. https://www.instagram.com/p/CGQaYdXJzr_/?utm_source=ig_web_copy_link

Haswood, C. [@haswoodforks]. (2021a, January 29). *Happy Kansas Day!!* [Photograph]. Instagram. https://www.instagram.com/p/CKosMQ3J5gt/?utm_source=ig_web_copy_link

Haswood, C. [@haswoodforks]. (2021b, March 18). *HB 2008—the MMIP bill, passed out of the Senate Federal and State Committee unanimously!* [Photograph]. Instagram. https://www.instagram.com/p/CMk0QoFJYsv/?utm_source=ig_web_copy_link

Haswood, C. [@haswoodforks]. (2021c, January 30). *HB 2008—MMIP, my Well speech* [Video]. TikTok. https://vm.tiktok.com/ZMdgV3PNS/

Haswood, C. [@haswoodforks]. (2021d, February 3). *In honor of Native American legislative day, I lead the pledge of allegiance on the House floor* [Photograph]. Instagram. https://www.instagram.com/p/CK2ekwrpk7e/?utm_source=ig_web_copy_link

Haswood, C. [@haswoodforks]. (2021e, January 11). *It is an honor to take this oath today to represent the community I was born and raised in* [Video]. Instagram. https://www.instagram.com/p/CJ7MYFlpdyj/?utm_source=ig_web_copy_link

Haswood, C. [@haswoodforks]. (2020d, July 18). *Join Rep. Haaland and Christina for a virtual discussion on the role of Native American women in politics* [Photograph]. Instagram. https://www.instagram.com/p/CCykUfCpHOt/?utm_source=ig_web_copy_link

Haswood, C. [@haswoodforks]. (2020e, July 23). *MASK UP—our community needs us* [Photograph]. Instagram. https://www.instagram.com/p/CC_IzmGpNEG/?utm_source=ig_web_copy_link

Haswood, C. [@haswoodforks]. (2021f, May 5). *May 5, National Awareness on Missing and Murdered Indigenous Peoples* [Photograph]. Instagram. https://www.instagram.com/p/COgPPrspSB3/?utm_source=ig_web_copy_link

Haswood, C. [@christinahaswood]. (2021g, April 10). *MY FIRST BILL got signed by the Governor this week* [Photograph]. Instagram. https://www.instagram.com/p/CNfEnUwL0vS/?utm_source=ig_web_copy_link

Haswood, C. [@christinahaswood]. (2020f, May 5). *Native and Indigenous women, men, boys, girls, trans, and non binary gender are stolen, murdered, and experience violence at higher rates than any other race* [Photograph]. Instagram. https://www.instagram.com/p/B_0s16XlNj5/?utm_source=ig_web_copy_link

Haswood, C. [@haswoodforks]. (2021h, April 24). *Our April town hall for HD 10 residents is tomorrow at 3pm via zoom!* [Photograph]. Instagram. https://www.instagram.com/p/COEPMb9JnvG/?utm_source=ig_web_copy_link

Haswood, C. [@haswoodforks]. (2021i, April 7). *Our Missing and Murdered Indigenous Peoples bill was signed into law today by Governor Kelly* [Photograph]. Instagram. https://www.instagram.com/p/CNYGD0Wp6lx/?utm_source=ig_web_copy_link

Haswood, C. [@christinahaswood]. (2021j, March 19). *Testified for Rep. Dr. Victors and I bill, HB 2008—MMIP Bill* [Photograph]. Instagram. https://www.instagram.com/p/CMngCfUrTBy/?utm_source=ig_web_copy_link

Haswood, C. [@haswoodforks]. (2021k, January 30). *This week, I received my first COVID vaccine from Haskell Health Center which is an Indian Health Services (IHS) clinic here in District 10* [Photograph]. Instagram. https://www.instagram.com/p/CKrQ3PPpmUU/?utm_source=ig_web_copy_link

Herrell, Y. [@yvetteherrell2020]. (2020, April 11). *Take today to cherish your family & the many blessings we have* [Photograph]. Instagram. https://www.instagram.com/p/B-2KnnEJtei/?utm_source=ig_web_copy_link

Hill, L., & Artiga, S. (2021, April 9). *COVID-19 Vaccination among American Indian and Alaska Native People*. Kaiser Family Foundation. https://www.kff.org/racial-equity-and-health-policy/issue-brief/covid-19-vaccination-american-indian-alaska-native-people/

IllumiNative. (2020a). The impact of COVID-19 on Indigenous people. *IllumiNative*. http://indigenousfutures.illuminatives.org/wp-content/uploads/2018/04/Illuminative_COVID_report_FINAL_1.pdf

IllumiNative. (2020b). From protests, to the ballot box, and beyond: Building Indigenous POWER. *Indigenous Futures Survey*. http://indigenousfutures.illuminatives.org/wp-content/uploads/Indigenous_Futures_Survey_Report.pdf

Iyengar, S. (1996). Framing responsibility for political issues. *The Annals of the American Academy of Political and Social Science, 546*, 59–70. https://www-jstororg.proxy.library.ohio.edu/stable/1048170?seq=1#metadata_info_tab_contents

LaPoe, B.R., & LaPoe, V. (2018). *Resistance advocacy as news digital black press covers the tea party*. Lexington Books.

LaPoe, V., & LaPoe, B. (2017). *Indian Country: Telling a story in a digital age*. Michigan State Press.

LaPoe, V., Azocar, C., LaPoe, B., Hazarika, B., & Jain, P. (2021). A comparative analysis of health news in Indigenous and mainstream media. *Health Communication, 37*(9), 1192–1203. https://doi.org/10.1080/10410236.2021.1945179

Lyon, G. (2020, April 24). Victory for Native American voting rights in North Dakota! *Campaign Legal Center*.https://campaignlegal.org/update/victory-native-american-voting-rights-north-dakota

Louie, G. [@geronimo.warrior]. (2020, May 5). *More than 5,000 cases of missing/murdered Indigenous women and girls have been documented* [Video]. TikTok. https://vm.tiktok.com/ZMdgq21bH/

Miller, S.P.M. (2020). Thematic analysis. In *Salem Press encyclopedia*.

MMIWG. [@mmiwg2s]. (2021, May 28). *TikTok: Delloliod* [Video]. Instagram. https://www.instagram.com/p/CPcIXKDjUAN/?utm_source=ig_web_copy_link

Morland, J., Feagin, J., Orum, A., & Sjoberg, G. (1992). A case for the case study. *Social Forces, 71*, 240–242. https://doi.org/10.2307/2579984

Native Womens Wilderness. (n.d.). *Murdered and missing indigenous women*. https://www.nativewomenswilderness.org/mmiw

Nielsen. (2020, November 20). *Invisible no more: The rise of native American power in media*. https://www.nielsen.com/us/en/insights/infographic/2020/invisible-no-more-the-rise-of-native-american-power-in-media/

Now This Politics. [@nowthispolitics]. (2020, December 19). *If confirmed, Deb Haaland would become the first Native American Cabinet secretary in American history* [Video]. TikTok. https://vm.tiktok.com/ZMdggnKLF/

Orr, R., Sharratt, K., & Iqbal, M. (2019). American Indian erasure and the logic of elimination: An experimental study of depiction and support for resources and rights for tribes. *Journal of Ethnic and Migration Studies, 45*(11), 2078–2099, https://doi.org/10.1080/1369183X.2017.1421061S

Pember, M.A. (2020, September 16). *TikTok posts can help us heal*. Indian Country Today. https://indiancountrytoday.com/news/tiktok-posts-can-help-us-heal

Phillips, N.D., & Chagnon, N. (n.d.). "Six months is a joke": Carceral feminism and penal populism in the wake of the Stanford sexual assault case. *Feminist Criminology, 15*(1), 47–69. https://doi-org.proxy.library.ohio.edu/10.1177/1557085118789782

Romero, D. (2021, May 22). *CNN drops Rick Santorum following remarks about Native Americans*. NBC News. https://www.nbcnews.com/politics/politics-news/cnn-drops-rick-santorum-following-remarks-about-native-americans-n1268250

Sherman, A. (2020, August 24). *TikTok reveals detailed user numbers for the first time*. CNBC. https://www.cnbc.com/2020/08/24/tiktok-reveals-us-global-user-growth-numbers-for-first-time.html

Silversmith, S. (2020, December 3). *Gabriella Cázares-Kelly is the first Native American elected to a Pima Countywide seat*. The Arizona Republic. https://www.azcentral.com/story/news/politics/elections/2020/12/03/gabriella-cazares-kelly-makes-history-pima-county-election/6353273002/

Spears, N.M., Wallis, B., & Wilkes, M. (2021, August 26). *COVID relief funds highlight complexity of issues*. Indian Country Today. https://indiancountrytoday.com/news/covidrelief-funds-highlight-complexity-ofissues?fbclid=IwAR3wIYEaeWlYkH2I2w8I-A29iMuBNUOjS1wcrPd5ynoE5d5_5qDkA wmjviZc

U.S. Representative Sharice Davids. (2020a, September 22). *Rep. Davids applauds passage of bill to increase focus on missing and murdered indigenous women*. https://davids.house.gov/media/press-releases/rep-davids-applauds-passage-bill-increasefocus-missing-and-murdered-indigenous

U.S. Representative Sharice Davids. (2021, January 26). *Davids re-introduces bill to increase supply of equipment needed to fight COVID*. https://davids.house.gov/media/press-releases/davids-re-introduces-bill-increase-supply-equipment-needed-fight-covid

Utah State University Digital Exhibits. (n.d.). *Erasing Native American religious traditions: Cultural erasure continues*. http://exhibits.usu.edu/exhibits/show/religiouserasureofnativeameric/culturalerasurecontinues

Wharton Business Daily. (2020, August 17). *How social media is shaping political campaigns*. https://knowledge.wharton.upenn.edu/article/how-social-media-is-shaping-political-campaigns/

· 1 4 ·

COPING WITH A PANDEMIC USING SOCIAL MEDIA: NURSES' EXPRESSIONS OF INDIVIDUAL AND COMMUNITY RESILIENCE ON TIKTOK

Sarah Smith-Frigerio & J. Brian Houston

> *How many people did I kill? How many people did I condemn to death because I recommended somebody else [to the ICU] who had a better chance ... How many people died because of my suggestions? How do you live with yourself, after that? How do you just ... I'm sorry. I really am sorry.*
>
> —Nurse's TikTok post

Stories of the difficulties nurses and other healthcare workers have faced with each wave of COVID-19 hospitalizations and deaths have pervaded social media (e.g., Frier, 2020; IUPUI, 2021) and news media (e.g., Garcia, 2021). Many of these stories describe the psychological distress nurses and other healthcare workers have faced throughout the pandemic. At times these stories have focused on the heroic work of nurses and healthcare as they responded to a global pandemic, and at other times the stories have described the resistance that COVID-19 deniers and anti-vaxxers displayed as nurses and healthcare workers tried to provide lifesaving care. Some stories describe how nurses exhibit resilience while trying to manage their mental health reactions (e.g., by seeking social support and utilizing mental health treatment), yet also describe how difficult it has been to remain resilient given the challenges. This challenge is of substantial concern, because of the role resilience plays in nurses both remaining on the job and being able to perform their jobs effectively. Nearly one in five healthcare workers have quit their jobs during the pandemic (Galvin, 2021), and two-thirds of critical care nurses have considered quitting because of COVID-19 (Kalter, 2021).

Resilience is generally understood to be the ability "to adapt positively in the face of stress, risk, and adversity" (First et al., 2021, p. 942). For example, when an individual experiences a major stressor such as the COVID-19 pandemic, that experience is likely to have some sort of negative effect on the person. This negative effect might involve the individual experiencing increased anxiety, or having some sleep problems, or not functioning as well at work as they might normally. Major stressors and their negative effects can lead to job burnout and compassion fatigue, especially in the helping professions (Adams et al., 2008). However, if despite these challenges the individual can utilize resources to cope with the stressor and ultimately function in a manner similar to the way they functioned before the event, that person could be considered to be resilient. Thus, resilience does not mean that an individual is not affected by adversity, but instead, it means that they can utilize internal and external resources to cope with those challenges.

Resilience is a construct that can be conceptualized at many different levels (Buzzanell & Houston, 2018). Examples include individual resilience, family resilience, organizational resilience, community resilience, national resilience, and more. When considering the resilience of nurses, relevant levels include the resilience of individual nurses, the resilience of health care organizations that nurses work in, and the community resilience of those in the nursing profession. In the current study, we focus on individual, and especially, community nursing resilience.

Individual nursing resilience is the ability of any single nurse to be resilient when experiencing professional stress, risk, or adversity. Research indicates that a variety of factors can contribute to the resilience of individual nurses. These protective factors include having perceptions of self-efficacy (the belief that nurses can succeed in their work), ensuring work-life balance (including practicing self-care or taking care of oneself), using humor in the workplace to deal with stress, maintaining an optimistic outlook during work, being realistic about what they can do in the workplace, and utilizing social support (Cooper et al., 2020; Yu et al., 2019). A variety of workplace experiences serve as risk factors that can work against individual nursing resilience. These include workplace stress, burnout, bullying, and traumatic experiences (Yu et al., 2019).

In addition to individual nursing resilience, it can be useful to consider the collective or community resilience of nurses. A community can be based in a single place (a geographic community) or can involve members who are not necessarily located in the same area (non-geographic community; Skupin & Fabrikant, 2003). The nursing community is a collection of individuals who are members of a community due to their professional role but are not necessarily located in the same place. At the same time, one could consider a community of nurses who all work at the same healthcare organization and thus have a geographic component to their collective.

Community resilience is more than just simply a collection of individual people who are resilient (Houston, 2015; 2018). Community resilience "emerges from collective activity in which individuals join together in efforts that foster response and recovery for the whole" (Pfefferbaum & Klomp, 2013, p. 279). In other words, community resilience requires community members to interact in some way with the well-being of the overall community in mind.

Given the importance of a community needing to work together to foster resilience, Houston et al. (2015) posited that communication is particularly important to community resilience. They presented a model of community resilience that included four components: communication systems and resources, community relationships, strategic communication processes, and community attributes.

Communication systems and resources include the variety of communication modalities that a community utilizes to interact in ways that help facilitate resilience. This can include traditional media (television, radio, newspapers), social media (Facebook, Twitter (X), TikTok), in-person interactions, and more. Generally, having more accessible "places" for community members to interact can contribute to more opportunities for resilience building. Community relationships include the many different types of social connections and capital that exist within a community. This can involve community members supporting each other (social support), connections between citizens and government, and other partnerships.

Strategic communication processes involve a variety of deliberations, planning processes, and storytelling that can help foster resilience. This can include formal and informal processes, and strategic communication can occur via a variety of communication systems and resources and may involve many different community relationships. Finally, community resilience includes a community attribute component. This component addresses the different aspects of a community that can influence what sort of relationships and strategic processes can occur in the community. Examples of community attributes include how diverse or flexible a community is and what type of economic resources are available.

When applying this community resilience model to social media platforms, strategic communication and relationship building becomes prominent (Houston, 2019). In other words, if we consider how communities use social media to foster community resilience, strategic communication and relationship-building processes appear most important. For example, in terms of strategic communication, community members may use social media to share information, raise awareness, promote action, and tell and hear stories. These efforts may often be intended to affect change within the community. Regarding relationship building, community members may use social media to provide and receive support, develop connections, build community, and organize groups. This relationship forming can help sustain community members as they cope with a crisis or stressor and may also build the networks that can accomplish the strategic communication described previously.

Developing integrated perspectives on resilience levels is needed to develop robust multi-level conceptualizations of human resilience (Houston & Buzzanell, 2018). In this chapter, we examine individual and community nursing resilience as depicted in the social media platform TikTok. TikTok has over 689 million users, with over 100 million monthly users in the United States, making it one of the fastest-growing social media platforms (Sehl, 2021). Though TikTok is a newer social media platform, it is not solely for young people as only 25% of TikTok users are 19 or younger (Statista, 2021). In fact, in the United States, 48% of individuals aged 18–29 and 20% of individuals aged 30–49 use the social media platform (Sehl, 2021). While not the most frequently used social media platform in the United States—due, in part, to its newness—TikTok provides a unique perspective into social media content creation and interactions, and provides a substantial amount of content from health care professionals and public health experts. These professionals are using the platform to share health messaging about COVID-19 to increase health and well-being, and corrective communication to combat COVID-19 misinformation and disinformation (Smith-Frigerio & Reif-Stice, 2021).

In the current study, we consider individual resilience practices such as using humor and practicing self-care and include community resilience dimensions such as strategic communication and relationship building. Some aspects of these dimensions apply to both individual and community levels (e.g., social support). The research questions that guided us during our inquiry are:

RQ1: Which elements of individual and community resilience are present in nurses' TikTok posts, and how do they describe these elements?

RQ2: Which elements of individual and community resilience do nurses describe as lacking in their TikTok posts, and what suggestions do they have for addressing these needs?

Method

To answer our research questions, we analyzed TikTok videos about COVID-19 posted by self-identified nurses. Using a variety of hashtag search terms (i.e., #nurse, #nursesoftiktok, #covid, #covid19, #icunurse, #resilience, #resiliency, #mentalhealth), we collected 50 TikTok posts from self-identified nurses. The most common hashtags identified in collected posts were #nursesoftiktok and #covid. Before analyzing a post, we confirmed that the post's creator identified as a nurse, that the post included content about COVID-19, that the post was from 2020 or 2021, and that the post did not include misinformation about COVID-19. Only four posts were found to contain misinformation and were thus excluded from the analysis. The 50 analyzed posts were approximately 15 seconds to 3 minutes in length. Posts had anywhere from 500 to 2.5 million views, although most had between 100,000 and 700,000 views. All posts collected were public, with publicly available comments, and there was no evidence that creators were under the age of 18 (i.e., many creators share their age in their bios). Nevertheless, we have elected not to share names, screen names, or other identifying information about creators or commenters in our findings to protect identities. All posts were from nurses working in the United States.

We conducted our analysis using the iterative approach described by Tracy (2019), to develop a nuanced understanding of how nurses were communicating about COVID-19, COVID-19 treatments, and their personal experiences in providing care to COVID-19 patients. We reviewed and coded the data three times, looking carefully at the visual and audio elements of the posts, as well as the words on screen and captions. Additionally, we reviewed the first five comments in each post (when available), looking for sentiment and important statements. On TikTok, comments are typically ordered by likes and replies, with more replies or likes moving a comment to the top of the list. While it is difficult to manually capture post comments for analysis, reviewing the top five comments did provide context for sentiment, support, agreement, or disagreement. Throughout the process of coding and theme analysis, we employed analytic memoing during coding and theme generation, as recommended by Charmaz (2014). This also allowed us to engage in the level of rigorous analysis Rankl et al. (2021) say results from open and transparent communication among multiple researchers as to the nature of codes and themes present in the data. From this analysis, we identified the following five themes that we describe in the findings: Storytelling to show the nursing experience, creating peer support when social support is lacking, sharing information to educate the public, calls to bolster community attributes, and the role of dark humor. Given the number of themes identified, and the various pieces within the communication framework of community resilience, we provide some discussion specific to each theme after describing the theme in the findings. The chapter's discussion section will then focus on answering the research questions and addressing larger practical and theoretical implications.

Findings

Storytelling to Show the Nursing Experience

The most common theme that arose from our data—present in 20 posts—involved storytelling. Nurses creating content on TikTok realized many individuals outside of healthcare had no concept of patients' or healthcare professionals' experience on the COVID floor or in the intensive care unit (ICU). Nurse creators were cognizant of hospital policy and the Health Insurance Portability and Accountability Act (HIPPA) with regard to patient privacy, but within these confines shared some of their experiences in caring for COVID patients. For instance, one post includes the word "Exhausted," with no other words or sounds, while a montage of clips plays during the post showing the nurse creator taking off PPE gear, sitting in the driver's seat of their car, brushing their teeth, and then beginning to cry while sitting at a dining table. A second nurse creator's post includes red words on a black screen, with the sounds of multiple medical alarms and beeps audible in the background. The words on the screen describe what the alarms mean and how they know the patient is dying. The caption reads, "The sound of COVID." Another video shows a gloved hand holding the hand of a patient, while words on the screen say, "Holding the hand of a patient as she is actively dying of COVID. Hardest part of my job." Lastly, an additional post describes the anguish and second-guessing one pediatric nurse experiences after their pediatric patient dies by displaying an overwhelming number of questions on the screen over a video of her crying. The TikTok audio "Turn it Off" plays in the background, and when the audio reaches the point where it states, "turn it off," she stops crying, takes on an impassive look, and the words on the screen tell the viewer that the next coding pediatric patient was placed in her care five minutes after the previous patient died.

Storytelling and relating one's lived experience in treating COVID patients is important to these nurse creators. As will be discussed later in this chapter, nurses appear to be creating community narratives through strategic communication processes to bolster other areas—such as community attributes and community relationships—where they did not perceive themselves as having as much community resilience (Houston et al., 2015). Comments were generally supportive of the nurse creators' sharing, even going so far as to commiserate with creators. Although, in a few instances, commenters also accused the nurse creators of lying. This ties into the second-most prevalent theme that emerged from our data—creating peer support when social support is lacking.

Creating Peer Support when Social Support Is Lacking

We found that nurses creating content on TikTok did not always feel supported by their healthcare employers, and with the rise of the U.S. fourth wave in cases due to the delta variant, they no longer felt supported by their local communities or the public they served.

Thirteen of the posts included calls for social support or attempted to provide support to fellow nurses working directly with COVID-19. For instance, one nurse creator, sitting in a car during what appears to be a break, explains that they are struggling with being treated poorly by family members, and "going from being a hero to a sheep" as COVID-19 has continued. The nurse creator then asks for advice about how to remain caring and empathetic now that the same family members who have disparaged them have tested positive for COVID-19 and are scared and seeking comfort from them. Commenters generally agreed that it was not the nurse creator's responsibility to do this emotional labor, and confirmed they had similar experiences in their social networks. In another highly emotional post, a nurse creator reflects on the fact that throughout the pandemic she has been involved in the decision-making process about who has the best chance for survival, and therefore, who should receive an ICU bed. She laments that the blood of those who've died because they weren't able to access ICU care is on her hands. Commenters on this post—many of whom identify as also being in healthcare—remind her that she has not killed anyone as she and others on her team are doing the best they can in the most difficult circumstances, and suggest that she is experiencing trauma and that it would be okay for her to seek help.

In other posts, nurse creators attempted to provide peer support to fellow nurses. In one post, the nurse creator advocates for nurses to take travel positions (which typically pay more than permanent positions and include significant perks) and not feel guilty about doing so. Commenters agreed and stated it was perfectly fine to make this money. A few commenters who identified as current nursing students stated they were going to work harder in their studies and try to finish their programs earlier—both to help nurses currently working in the field and to take travel positions that would help them financially. Another creator dueted (dueting involves a creator making a post that includes the video from a previous post, with both posts typically shown side-by-side) a fellow nurse, where they both agreed that it was time for nurses to know their worth and stated: "[B]urnout is real. It's okay to take a break sometimes." Comments on this post agreed with the sentiment.

The lack of social support from employers and the public, as well as the desire to provide peer support to one another online, mirrors previous studies that describe how public health officials supported one another during COVID online via Reddit (Valiavska & Smith-Frigerio, 2022) and how those with stigmatized mental health concerns may gravitate to online spaces to receive and provide peer support (Smith-Frigerio, 2021). When considering Houston and colleagues' (2015) framework, we understand these posts as an attempt to augment or bolster community resilience in the community relationships element. Our next theme, which involves sharing COVID-19 and vaccine information to a broader public, also falls within the area of community relationships.

Sharing Information to Educate Publics

Nurses also took the opportunity to create content to share COVID-19 and vaccine information, as well as to correct misinformation. These posts appear to be directed toward a public audience and are not necessarily meant for fellow healthcare providers. Eleven of the analyzed posts were included in this theme, and topics included correcting vaccine misinformation, discussing why hospitals were full, exploring the reasons behind the nursing staff shortage, recognizing the number of healthcare professionals that have died from COVID-19, and discussing the fourth wave of COVID-19 cases and hospitalizations. It is important to note that these posts also demonstrated a level of compassion and disaster fatigue (Worley et al., 2023). For instance, one post combating vaccine misinformation warned, "Don't even think about asking me if it has a microchip." A post on hospitals being overwhelmed with the fourth wave of cases stated, "What happens when we run out of beds? If you aren't familiar with disaster triage, look it up." Another post warned that nurses were about to get more annoying, "because we have to let you know what's coming down the pipe." Finally, one creator, focused on how COVID-19 deaths are reported, stated: "Do not ask what comorbidities they had. It does not matter," because they were alive before contracting COVID-19. Comments on these posts were mixed, with some commenters supporting the messaging of the posts, and others criticizing the posts by creators. This resistance to posts sharing information and correcting misinformation could further contribute to disaster fatigue. We will discuss the implications of potential disaster fatigue in the discussion.

In our analysis, we came to understand efforts to share information and educate the public as related to citizen engagement (within community relationships) and citizens and organizations reinforcing official information (within communication systems and resources) in Houston and colleagues' (2015) model. Communication systems and resources may be formal (e.g., traditional news media and social media content from official sources), but also allow for more informal interactions, such as those witnessed in TikTok posts created by nurses. As Houston et al. (2015) point out, these systems and resources are important in information sharing, meaning-making, and fostering connections to support community resilience, and reinforcing messaging from official sources in informal interactions can be beneficial. Additionally, citizen engagement is important to fostering connections, information sharing, as well as advocacy and activism work. This approach likely worked to support, or bolster, other areas within the framework that nurses perceived as lacking. In the next theme, we demonstrate the community attributes creators perceived as lacking and their impact on community resilience.

Calls to Bolster Community Attributes

Nurses noted several concepts within the communication framework for community resilience that they perceived as inadequate or missing altogether. These items included five posts concerning lack of economic resources, an additional five posts discussing a lack of efficacy, and two posts focused on a lack of flexibility. Lack of economic resources focused on the lack of nursing staff, typically due to lack of adequate pay (especially when compared to the much higher pay of travel nursing staff), and lack of hospital equipment and beds. Lack of efficacy involved posts addressing feelings of helplessness, especially in the face of the fourth wave of COVID-19 hospitalizations, and perceptions of not being able to do anything about administrative decisions made by hospital systems. One important illustrative example of both a lack of economic resources and a lack of efficacy could be found in a nurse creator's post describing that for Nurse's Week, hospital administrators brought in speakers for self-care and resilience workshops, while not offering retention bonuses, adequate staffing, or the medical equipment needed by nurses to do their jobs effectively. Lack of flexibility was described by nurse creators as not being able to handle or manage the situations they faced within the profession any longer, with one commenter agreeing on a post—where the creator stated they could not do this anymore—by stating, "many of you haven't been putting people in body bags the last year and half and it shows."

Nurses were, in effect, calling out the constructs within community resilience that were inadequate or missing in what appears to be an effort to draw the attention of a broader audience. While not explicitly stated, we can reasonably assume that they were looking to remedy these perceived deficiencies. This is an interesting theme to note, particularly considering the communication framework for community resilience. There is no set formula for how many constructs within the model must be present for community resilience to be achieved. This is due to the authors' (Houston et al., 2015) conceptualization of community resilience not as a trait or an outcome, but as a process. Further exploration of how missing or inadequate functions of community resilience are negotiated is warranted.

The Role of Dark Humor

In our final—and unanticipated—theme, we note the dark humor witnessed in seven of the TikTok posts. Dark humor typically represents disastrous or terrifying issues or events in a humorous light and is often seen as a coping mechanism. Included in this theme were posts addressing "what covid-deniers think I do," showing different departments of nurses trying to unload their anti-vaccination colleagues onto other departments, explaining how nurses try not to bring home COVID-19 to their families, and stating "if the covid doesn't kill me, the Lysol fumes will." Another post in this theme used the sound, "I'm not saying she deserved it, but I am saying that God's timing is always right" when describing an anti-vaccination supervisor who lost their job.

While few, the posts involving dark humor helped nurse creators express their frustrations and fears surrounding their work during COVID-19. The role of dark humor is not discussed at length in community resilience literature, but the use of humor has been described as a part of social support (Henman, 2001), which can bolster individual resilience (Fluri, 2019). Social support is within the communication framework for community resilience. Also, the use of humor may impact community narratives and community storytelling. Future research should explore the use of humor, including dark humor, and its potential relationships with community resilience.

Discussion

The first research question asked what elements of individual and community resilience were present in nurse creators' content, and how they described these elements. In the current study, we identified some elements of individual resilience and several elements of community resilience, including storytelling to create community narratives, development of peer support where social support was lacking, use of dark humor, and sharing information to educate the public. Additionally, the themes demonstrated that messaging from nurse creators was occurring within several areas of Houston and colleagues' (2015) communication model of community resilience. These areas include bolstering strategic communication processes, such as critical reflection and community storytelling; community relationships, particularly support; and communication systems and resources, with a focus on citizen engagement and reinforcing official information. It is interesting to note that three of the four areas described by Houston et al. (2015) were employed here, but the area of community attributes was not. This becomes relevant when considering the second research question.

The second research question focused on elements of individual and community resilience that nurse creators described as lacking during the pandemic, and how they thought these inadequacies might best be addressed. Our analysis showed that nurse creators actively identified areas of community resilience that they found lacking, including the economic resources of their health systems, a perceived lack of efficacy to do their jobs effectively, and a lack of flexibility in both the profession and in their daily work. It is interesting to note the areas that nurse creators perceive as lacking all fall within the community attributes area of the communication model for community resilience.

While posts from nurse creators that we analyzed focus substantially on community resilience, it is also prudent to discuss posts focused on individual resilience. For instance, the use of dark humor—which can also be seen as indicative of fostering peer support in the communication model for community resilience—was an interesting individual resilience trait present in our findings. Social support, along with factors such as work-life balance and perceived efficacy, is important to individual resilience as well (Cooper et al., 2020; Yu et al., 2019). While there is overlap in protective communicative factors in both individual and community resilience, it is important to remember that a group of resilient individuals does not equate to a resilient community (Houston, 2015; 2018). Overall, our findings identified a range of potential risk factors and resilience adaptive capacities—both at the individual and community levels—present within the COVID-19 posts of nurse creators.

Practical and Theoretical Implications

Several practical implications result from the findings of our study. First, nurse creators in our collected data openly spoke on topics related to psychological distress and experienced secondary trauma. As mentioned before, workplace stressors (Yu et al., 2019) and secondary trauma can result in compassion fatigue among those who work in the helping professions (Adams et al., 2008). It would be prudent for health administrators—and the community at large—to prioritize and even augment, trauma-informed mental health care services for those working in the health professions during the pandemic to address the substantially higher needs for this type of care. Compassion fatigue and job burnout can result in many healthcare professionals—especially nurses—leaving the profession (Galvin, 2021; Kalter, 2021). Our findings demonstrate that both the healthcare industry and society at large must find ways to develop and augment community resilience capacities—particularly those identified by nurses and other healthcare professionals as lacking. If not addressed, healthcare systems run the risk of not being able to provide the appropriate standard of care to their respective communities.

Theoretical implications result from our analysis as well. This study provides additional nuance to our understanding of how the constructs identified within the communication model of community resilience can present within messaging on a social media platform. Additionally, nurse creators' posts provided insights into what was needed (and what was missing) from their perspectives of community resilience. Given that community resilience is communicative and a process (rather than a trait or an outcome), theorizing about the communication framework for community resilience has not focused on a checklist of "must-haves" or optional elements, but further investigation into the needs of community members—possibly delineated by crisis/disaster events—may prove beneficial.

Limitations and Future Directions

There are limitations to our research. This study focused on one subset of healthcare professionals during a specific period (i.e., the pandemic) posting content on one social media platform, with a limited number of posts and comments. Yet, these limitations can help guide future research. Future research should investigate other healthcare professions (e.g., respiratory therapists, physicians, etc.) and other professions/industries significantly impacted by the pandemic. Comparative studies could investigate if the messages from nurse creators change based on the social media platform used. Finally, future studies should explore burnout, compassion fatigue and disaster fatigue during crises or disasters on a broader, societal scale (Worley et al., 2023). Nursing is a complex, high-stress helping profession even when there is not a pandemic. How might traumatic events or disasters, over a prolonged period, further negatively impact the helping professions? Nevertheless, our study provides a meaningful look into what characteristics of individual and community resilience were present in nurses' TikTok posts as well as which ones were missing and provides many avenues for future inquiry.

Discussion Questions

1. What do you think motivated nurses to post about COVID-19 and their work on TikTok?
2. How might nurses' posts on TikTok about COVID-19 differ from their posts on Facebook, Twitter (X), or Instagram? How might they be similar?
3. How could we determine if nurses' posts on TikTok about COVID-19 made a difference in the working lives of those nurses?

4. This chapter described a model of communication and community resilience. Did you notice anything that was missing from that model, and if so, what?
5. How do you think the TikTok posts from nurses described in this chapter affected people who saw those posts?

References

Adams, R.E., Figley, C.R., & Boscarino, J.A. (2008). The compassion fatigue scale: Its use with social workers following urban disaster. *Research on Social Work Practice, 18*(3), 238–250. https://doi.org/10.1177/1049731507310190

Buzzanell, P.M., & Houston, J.B. (2018). Communication and resilience: Multilevel applications and insights—A Journal of Applied Communication Research forum. *Journal of Applied Communication Research, 46*(1), 1–4. https://doi.org/10.1080/00909882.2017.1412086

Charmaz, K. (2014). *Constructing grounded theory.* Sage.

Cooper, A.L., Brown, J.A., Rees, C.S., & Leslie, G.D. (2020). Nurse resilience: A concept analysis. *International Journal of Mental Health Nursing, 29*(4), 553–575. https://doi.org/10.1111/inm.12721

First, J.M., Yu, M., & Houston, J.B. (2021). The Disaster Adaptation and Resilience Scale: Development and validation of an individual-level protection measure. *Disasters, 45*(4), 939–967. https://doi.org/10.1111/disa.12452

Fluri, J.L. (2019). What's so funny in Afghanistan?: Jocular geopolitics and the everyday use of humor in spaces of protracted precarity. *Political Geography, 68,* 125–130. https://doi.org/10.1016/j.polgeo.2018.08.011

Frier, S. (2020, December 24). *Nurses celebrating Covid-19 vaccines battle social media scorn.* Bloomberg. https://www.bloomberg.com/news/articles/2020-12-24/nurses-celebrating-covid-19-vaccines-battle-social-media-scorn

Galvin, G. (2021, October 4). *Nearly 1 in 5 Health care workers have quit their jobs during the pandemic.* Morning Consult. https://morningconsult.com/2021/10/04/health-care-workers-series-part-2-workforce/

Garcia, K. (2021, October 1). Nurses have had a tough year (and then some). You can learn from their resilience. *Los Angeles Times.* https://www.latimes.com/california/story/2021-10-01/nurses-have-had-a-tough-year-and-then-some-how-theyve-stayed-resilient

Henman, L.D. (2001). Humor as a coping mechanism: Lessons from POWs. *Humor, 14*(1), 83–94. https://doi.org/10.1515/humr.14.1.83

Houston, J.B. (2015). Bouncing forward: Assessing advances in community resilience assessment, intervention, and theory to guide future work. *American Behavioral Scientist, 59*(2), 175–180. https://doi.org/10.1177/0002764214550294

Houston, J.B. (2018). Community resilience and communication: Dynamic interconnections between and among individuals, families, and organizations. *Journal of Applied Communication Research, 46*(1), 19–22. https://doi.org/10.1080/00909882.2018.1426704

Houston, J.B. (2019). Community resilience and social media: A primer on opportunities to foster collective adaptation using new technologies. In K.K. Stephens (Ed.), *New media in times of crisis* (pp. 177–192). Routledge.

Houston, J.B., & Buzzanell, P.M. (2018). Communication and resilience: Concluding thoughts and key issues for future research. *Journal of Applied Communication Research*, 46(1), 26–27. https://doi.org/10.1080/00909882.2018.1426691

Houston, J.B., Spialek, M.L., Cox, J., Greenwood, M.M., & First, J. (2015). The centrality of communication and media in fostering community resilience: A framework for assessment and intervention. *American Behavioral Scientist*, 59(2), 270–283. https://www.doi.org/10.1177/0002764214548563

IUPUI. (2021). Twitter offers crucial insight into thoughts, needs of nurses during pandemic. *Indiana University Research Impact—Coronavirus*. https://research.impact.iu.edu/our-strengths/coronavirus/nurses-and-twitter.html

Kalter, L. (2021, September 20). *Survey: 2/3 of critical care nurses consider quitting due to COVID-19*. WebMD Health News. https://www.webmd.com/lung/news/20210920/survey-critical-care-nurses-consider-quitting-due-covid

Pfefferbaum, R.L., & Klomp, R.W. (2013). Community resilience, disasters, and the public's health. In F.G. Murphy (Ed.), *Community engagement, organization, and development for public health practice* (pp. 275–298). Springer Publishing Company.

Rankl, F., Johnson, G.A., & Vindrola-Padros, C. (2021). Examining what we know in relation to how we know it: A team-based reflexivity model for rapid qualitative health research. *Qualitative Health Research*. https://doi.org/10.1177/1049732321998062

Sehl, K. (2021, May 5). *23 important TikTok stats marketers need to know in 2021*. Hootsuite. https://blog.hootsuite.com/tiktok-stats/

Skupin, A., & Fabrikant, S.I. (2003). Spatialization methods: A cartographic research agenda for non-geographic information visualization. *Cartography and Geographic Information Science*, 30(2), 99–119. https://doi.org/10.1559/152304003100011081

Smith-Frigerio, S. (2021). "You are not alone": The importance of online peer support in grassroots advocacy groups' social media messaging. *Health Communication*, 1–10. https://doi.org/10.1080/10410236.2020.1808415

Smith-Frigerio, S., & Reif-Stice, C. (2021). *"Hey! Dr. Kat, epidemiologist.": Corrective health messaging on TikTok to reduce COVID-19 misinformation* [Conference presentation]. 2021 ICRC Conference, Orlando, FL, United States.

Statista Research Department. (2021). *Distribution of TikTok users in the United States as of March 2021, by age group*. Statista. https://www.statista.com/statistics/1095186/tiktok-us-users-age/

Tracy, S.J. (2019). *Qualitative research methods: Collecting evidence, crafting analysis, communicating impact*. John Wiley & Sons.

Valiavska, A., & Smith-Frigerio, S. (2022). Politics and public health: Analysis of Twitter and Reddit posts concerning the role of politics in the public health response to COVID-19. *Health Communication*, 1–10. https://doi.org/10.1080/10410236.2022.2063497

Worley, M., Smith-Frigerio, S., & Houston, J.B. (2023). "Disaster fatigue, communication, and resilience: Insights from natural hazards, human-caused disasters, and public health crises." in Sellnow, Timothy L., and Deanna D. Sellnow, eds. Communicating Risk and Safety. Vol. 24. Walter de Gruyter GmbH & Co KG.

Yu, F., Raphael, D., Mackay, L., Smith, M., & King, A. (2019). Personal and work-related factors associated with nurse resilience: A systematic review. *International Journal of Nursing Studies*, 93, 129–140. https://doi.org/10.1016/j.ijnurstu.2019.02.014

· 1 5 ·

POLITICAL RHETORIC AND CRISES COMMUNICATION DURING A GLOBAL PANDEMIC

Joel Lansing Reed & Monique Luisi

Throughout the COVID-19 pandemic, massive shortages of personal protective equipment (PPE), ventilators, and other medical devices threatened the safety of frontline healthcare workers, prevented access to lifesaving treatment, and slowed pandemic response. At all levels of government, leaders turned their attention and their rhetoric to securing that very equipment needed to address the emerging crisis. This was not always the circumstance. In the years leading up to the first U.S. confirmed case of COVID-19, a different public health crisis directly connected to the sterilization of medical equipment, including PPE, rocked communities across the country.

In 2016, the Environmental Protection Agency (EPA) announced findings that the nation's most common sterilizing agent for medical equipment, ethylene oxide (EtO), was 30 times more carcinogenic than previously believed (Rimer, 2019). Many of the facilities using EtO to sterilize ventilators, PPE, and other important medical equipment operated in populous areas. Suburban neighborhoods in Illinois and Georgia housed these facilities with minimal protections to prevent citizens' exposure to potentially cancer-causing EtO emissions. Two years after the initial Environmental Protection Agency (EPA) report, studies indicated increased rates of cancer among residents in neighborhoods surrounding EtO sterilization facilities (Illinois Department of Public

Health, 2019). Residents erupted in protest, resulting in the closure of several sterilization sites despite health industry objections that closing facilities could result in PPE and ventilator shortages.

In March 2020, industry concerns were realized when the COVID-19 pandemic supercharged the need for mass equipment sterilization. With the increased need for sterilized ventilator tubes, masks, gowns, face shields, and other forms of PPE, leaders at local, state, and national levels faced competing pressures: to reopen the facilities capable of sterilizing lifesaving equipment, or keep facilities shuttered and protect neighboring communities from further exposure to the toxic EtO emissions linked to the deaths of their friends, family, and neighbors.

In the pages that follow, we outline the challenges faced by political communicators when two public health crises collided. Rather than focusing exclusively on COVID-19 crisis communication, we argue for a dynamic *crises communication* view of pandemic response, in which rhetors are forced to balance competing claims for the allocation of material resources, attention, and values in the midst of multiple crises. We describe the crises at the intersection of PPE and EtO forged by the COVID-19 pandemic, offer a discussion of the extant literature on political rhetoric in the COVID-19 pandemic, and analyze the rhetorical construction of these conflicting crises. Our analysis, a *rhetorical criticism*, examines responses from rhetors in communities that house major EtO facilities. We also examine the rhetoric of leaders of affected states, members of U.S. Congress, federal officials, and sterilization companies to reveal the intricacies of the conflict between the EtO and COVID-19 health crises. Our analysis is followed by a discussion of how COVID-19 came to dominate crisis response, and the role of silence in rendering fenceline communities expendable in the face of a global pandemic.

Personal Protection and Medical Equipment Shortages

By late January 2020, when the first lab-confirmed U.S. COVID-19 case was documented, a predictable pattern had emerged for countries already in the throes of the pandemic. Early cases overwhelmed hospital capacity, strained health workers, and rapidly depleted supplies vital for treatment. The World Health Organization (WHO) (2020) noted that declining availability of personal protective equipment (PPE), such as masks, gloves, gowns, and face shields, was putting health workers at risk worldwide. By the end of March, U.S. hospitals reported lack of access to PPE (Miroff, 2020). Facing severe shortages, nurses and other health workers began reusing masks for several consecutive working shifts, or turning to untested, makeshift alternatives (Wells & Winowiecki, 2020). The shortages created deep concern for healthcare workers, prompting some U.S. health officials to initially discourage the public from purchasing masks out of fear that these purchases would further strain the already limited supplies.

The lack of ventilators and other medical devices needed to treat serious cases of COVID-19 was equally concerning. By mid-March 2020, emergency stockpiles of ventilators were dramatically insufficient to meet the demands of a respiratory pandemic (Ranney et al., 2020). The U.S. Federal Government turned its efforts to mass-producing ventilators and securing additional stockpiles from overseas. Within weeks, U.S. automotive manufacturers and other industrial facilities transformed production lines and shifted resources toward the creation of lifesaving artificial ventilation systems (Albergotti & Siddiqui, 2020).

Concerns over lack of access to these supplies dominated politics at local, state, and national levels. In late March 2020, a survey of members of The United States Conference of Mayors (2020) revealed that 85% feared their community did not have sufficient access to ventilators, and 88% believed that their communities did not have the necessary supplies of PPE. With the federal government largely deferring to states for short-term COVID response, governors of nearly every state joined the fight over limited supplies of existing resources nationally and internationally. In addition to their efforts to secure new supplies, governors began implementing measures to preserve available PPE supplies and incentivize new manufacturing of vital equipment (National Governors Association, 2020). At the federal level, it was Senate Minority Leader Chuck Schumer who first highlighted the need for ventilators in a March 16th address on the Senate floor (166, Cong. Rec. S1748, 2020). Across all levels of government, there was a concerted effort to address the emerging global health crisis and remedy supply shortages.

Some causes of the supply shortages were obvious. These included insufficient national stockpiles and increasing global demand. Shortages were further exacerbated by massive supply chain disruptions brought on by the pandemic. While these were often the most frequently cited culprits for supply shortages, another major factor lurked not far behind in discussions of PPE and medical equipment access: the lack of effective equipment sterilization. The CDC

(2008) defines sterilization as a process that "destroys all microorganisms on the surface of an article or in a fluid to prevent disease transmission associated with the use of that item" (para. 2). In health settings, sterilization of equipment is essential to protect healthcare workers from exposure to viral or bacterial diseases and prevent secondary infection among patients. To understand the role of sterilization in supply shortages requires discussion of a different public health crisis, one affecting several U.S. neighborhoods and other communities around the world that border medical device sterilization facilities.

Ethylene Oxide Air Pollution Crisis

Ethylene Oxide (EtO) is a gaseous chemical compound first discovered by chemist Charles-Adolphe Wurtz in 1859 (American Chemical Society, 2019). Since the mid-nineteenth century, science has revealed a wide range of uses for EtO. For example, EtO is used to make the glycols in antifreeze and in the manufacturing of synthetic materials. It is also sometimes used as insecticide fumigant for grain and tobacco. In 1937, Chicago-based chemists Carroll Griffith and Lloyd Hall (1940), who had pioneered the use of EtO in food fumigation, sought a patent for the use of EtO for medical device sterilization, which the federal government granted in 1940. Over the next 80 years, EtO became the industry standard for sterilizing medical devices, including ventilator components, catheters, syringes, surgical telescopes, anesthesia masks, and certain forms of PPE.

Thirty-seven years later, in 1978, Sterigenics opened its first sterilization facility in California (Sterigenics, 2020). As of 2021, Sterigenics reported operating 48 facilities in 13 countries sterilizing medical equipment and PPE with EtO and a range of other chemical and radiation sterilization techniques. In the Fall 2019, Sterigenics and other companies, including Medline Industries, Viant, and Becton, Dickinson, and Company, all relied heavily on EtO for sterilization of vital medical supplies (Advanced Medical Technology Association, 2019). By some estimates, EtO is now used to sterilize more than half of all reusable medical equipment in the United States.

The sterilization industry eased the significant burden of purchasing new devices for health care providers and helped maintain steady supplies of ventilators, gowns, syringes, and surgical kits for the nation's hospitals. But in 2016, new findings from the Environmental Protection Agency (EPA) regarding the toxicity of EtO sparked widespread concern in communities housing sterilization facilities (EPA, 2016). The EPA discovered that EtO was between 30 and 60 times more carcinogenic than suggested by previous estimates (Rimer, 2019). A follow-up report from the EPA warned of increased cancer risk for residents living around a Sterigenics facility in Willowbrook, Illinois, estimating that residents' risk of cancer was nine times higher than the general population (Hawthorne, 2018). Fears seemed to be confirmed in 2019 when the Illinois Department of Public Health released findings that showed increased incidences of Hodgkin's lymphoma and breast cancer among women living in areas close to the Willowbrook Sterigenics facility. Stories from those with cancer or those who had died from the disease in surrounding neighborhoods dominated headlines in the months that followed (e.g., Sterman et al., 2020).

The 2019 report was followed by months of public outrage and a pressure campaign targeting elected officials and industry leaders, demanding they close EtO facilities in populated areas. Scholars have labeled the neighborhoods surrounding air-polluting businesses as *fenceline communities* (Burke, 1999). Some of the fenceline communities living with exposure to toxic EtO emissions organized through formal and informal networks to lobby lawmakers to end sterilization in their communities. Others without access to information or resources remained unaware of their elevated risk of disease. Finally, between September and October 2019, Sterigenics announced plans to permanently close its Willowbrook facility and temporarily halt operations at another facility in Cobb County, GA, at least until necessary changes could be made to reduce the risks of EtO exposure for surrounding neighborhoods.

While many communities were still living with the threat of EtO, progress seemed on the horizon for fenceline communities around the United States, but just weeks after the first facility closures, a then unidentified respiratory infection began circulating in Hubei Province in Central China, nearly 7,000 miles away from the Sterigenics facility in Willowbrook. Later known as the novel coronavirus, or COVID-19, the infections resulted in a global pandemic, killing over 6 million people as of March 2022, increasing demand for sterile medical equipment, and bringing these two public health crises into direct conflict.

The Political Rhetoric Around COVID-19

Much of the early literature on political responses to COVID-19 has treated the pandemic as a singular crisis (e.g., Callahan, 2021; Montiel et al., 2021;

Neville-Shepard, 2021). Others have analyzed the confluence of racism and COVID-19 as *intersecting* crises (e.g., Croucher et al., 2020). As COVID-19 scholarship continues to develop, researchers should devote increased attention to parallel, intersecting, and conflicting crises. We understand parallel crises to refer to independent difficulties or disasters that grow alongside one another without an obvious causal relationship but still competing for the attention and resources required for restoration (e.g., wildfires in California and chemical spills in the Gulf of Mexico). By intersecting crises, we refer to two or more difficulties or disasters that are directly exacerbated by or compounded by one another (e.g., COVID-19 and systemic racism). In contrast to parallel or intersecting crises, we present COVID-19 and the EtO emissions as *conflicting* crises. Conflicting crises arise when the proposed or enacted solutions to one crisis exacerbate or compound a different crisis. In the pages that follow, we outline our method of analysis before turning our attention to national, state, and local rhetoric on the conflicting crises of equipment shortages and EtO exposure.

Applying Rhetorical Criticism

Sonja Foss (1989) defines rhetorical criticism as "the investigation and evaluation of rhetorical acts and artifacts for the purpose of understanding rhetorical processes" (p. 5). Criticism moves beyond simple description of a text by emphasizing elements of context, identity, and social structures to understand how texts relate to one another and come to construct our realities through language. Here, we rely on Hoffman and Ford's (2009) process for rhetorical analysis. In their formulation, criticism begins with a description of the strategies and context surrounding a piece, or pieces, of rhetoric before considering how those contexts and strategies relate to other texts of a similar type. Critics then conduct a series of systematic readings, emphasizing the evaluative and investigative components highlighted Foss's definition of criticism. Critics use the insights gleaned from their readings to advance an argument about the relationship between texts and the realities they construct.

Lloyd Bitzer's generative 1968 essay offers a lens for understanding the relationship between rhetoric and its context. Rhetoric, according to Bitzer, responds to an *exigence*, which can be at least partially resolved through rhetoric. Rhetors then address exigencies as a call for audiences to become party to the solution. Later critics have challenged or expanded Bitzer's notion of a rhetorical situation (e.g., Edbauer, 2005; Smith & Lybarger, 1996; Vatz, 1973), but the view of rhetors as either addressing or constituting a singular crisis or challenge through rhetoric remains a dominant theme of rhetorical scholarship. In our case, we address the collision of two public health exigencies, in which the potential solutions of one exigence amplify the other.

To understand the complexities of political communication before and during the COVID-19 pandemic, we analyzed rhetorical artifacts from national, state, and local levels as well as corporate responses to government rhetoric. The use of multiple texts from multiple rhetors allowed us to engage in close-textual-intertextual analysis (Ceccarelli, 2010), reading not only an initial piece of rhetoric but also the rhetoric that emerged in response. Close-textual-intertextual analysis allowed us to see the rhetorical context of the pandemic and revealed elements missing from public discourse. At the national level, we used the *Congressional Record* to identify discussions of EtO, sterilization, and equipment shortages as well as publicly available correspondence from federal officials. We then turned to speeches, press releases, and official statements of governors in Illinois and Georgia, two of the states with the greatest vulnerability from ethylene oxide emissions. We looked at county-level statements to see how the most proximate levels of government differed in their discussion of these conflicting crises. Finally, we analyzed industry statements to understand the role organizations played in constructing this crisis collision and demanding the reopening or continued operation of sterilization facilities.

The Rhetoric of Collision

Industry leaders had long expressed fears about equipment shortages should the government or public force the closure of sterilization facilities or curtail the use of EtO in the sterilization process. For example, in response to community concerns about the Cobb County, Georgia facility in 2019, Sterigenics (2021) released a statement pledging to reduce emissions but also reminding critics of the importance of sterilization: "E[t]O is a vital resource in the sterilization of medical products and devices. Our Atlanta facility sterilizes many products including surgical kits, radiological syringes, catheters, hospital gowns, and IV administration sets which are essential in today's hospitals." Similarly, in much of their external communication, Sterigenics labeled their organization "a leading provider of mission-critical sterilization services." Sterigenics and other sterilizing organizations worked to communicate and remind stakeholders how important they are to the everyday operation of hospitals and doctors' offices.

While Sterigenics' framing of their importance in the early stages of the EtO crisis centered on the need for a range of sterile medical equipment, with the start of the COVID-19 pandemic, their narrative shifted to focus almost exclusively on pandemic response. The Sterigenics website soon prominently featured regular updates about the pandemic, and the company reframed their role directly around COVID-19. In a letter to suppliers in March 2020, Sterigenics' parent company Sotera Health wrote:

> At Sterigenics, we sterilize products that are being used specifically for COVID-19 response. For example, we process facemasks and other Personal Protective Equipment (or PPE's) for COVID-19 response. We also process the sterilizing swabs being used in the COVID-19 tests that help to diagnose patients with the virus.

This new framing put a specific crisis context on the work of sterilizers. While they had long argued for the value of EtO from a health access perspective, the pandemic sharpened this approach, giving a clear human face to the work of sterilization and tapping into global fears about the disease. Companies shifted their public identities from chemical companies to disaster response companies.

Internal and external stakeholders seized on this new framing of the importance of medical device sterilization and began reexamining the decision to close Sterigenics facilities in Illinois and Georgia. Journalists started seeking out comments from industry leaders and free-market think tanks published op-eds about the conflict. As the President of a Pennsylvania-based healthcare company told journalists:

> Everyone approves of eliminating the emissions to keep people safe. Taking EtO factories offline until enhanced safety goals could be achieved may have seemed smart at the time, but in hindsight with this pandemic, it may have inadvertently contributed to equipment shortages. (Clinical Oncology News, 2020, para. 4)

Utilitarian framing was common among rhetors questioning the plant closures and working to protect the continued operation of others. While nothing had changed about the risks of EtO exposure or EtO protections, the public health calculus had changed. Comments like these implied that attention and resources should be devoted to addressing the new crisis even at the expense of the health and safety of those living in fenceline communities around EtO sterilization plants.

Calls from medical providers and sterilization industry representatives grew louder as shortages continued to prevent safe and effective treatment of COVID-19. Angela Logomasini (2020), a fellow with the libertarian think tank the Competitive Enterprise Institute, penned an op-ed blasting the EPA's assessment of acceptable levels of EtO and faulting what she labeled "junk science" for medical device shortages. From Logomasini's perspective, EtO never posed a significant risk to the public, but Logomasini's op-ed did not provide any alternative explanations for the elevated incidences of cancer surrounding EtO facilities.

A similar op-ed by Ross Marchand (2020) of the conservative think tank Foundation for Economic Education blamed the EPA for COVID-19 deaths and blasted the agency's cautious approach to regulating carcinogenic chemicals. Marchand positioned this caution as emblematic of the problems with government bureaucracy, saying: "Regulatory foot-dragging will cost millions of lives and untold billions of dollars in lost economic activity" (para. 8). He went on to argue, "It's time for regulators to rely on real-world evidence and empower health care providers to lead the charge against the coronavirus. Millions of lives depend on the right regulatory approach and philosophy" (para. 9). Both Marchand and Logomasini blamed government efforts to protect fenceline communities for the risks now being faced by the public at large. Marchand's rhetoric engaged the national discourse around COVID-19 while eschewing local discussions of cancer risk and long-term health effects from exposure to toxic chemicals.

With the stage set, we investigate these very questions of proximity and scale in EtO and COVID-19 conflict framing.

A Local Crisis in a Global Pandemic

On March 20 and April 3, respectively, the governors of Illinois and Georgia issued "stay-at-home" orders for all non-essential workers in their states. Early in the COVID-19 pandemic, the home became a symbol of safety. This safety was of particular privilege for those with the access and agency to retreat into their places of residence and avoid potential exposure to the virus (Yalçın & Düzen, 2021). Many U.S. Americans stayed home with the promise that social distancing could reduce or even eliminate the risk of infection. While home was a symbol of safety for millions, for the nearly 300,000 Americans living near EtO facilities, home was imbued with the fear of toxic chemical exposure and associated long-term health risks. The pandemic further amplified these risks, as recently closed facilities reopened and others accelerated operations to meet the growing demand for sterile equipment.

Fenceline communities affected by EtO are disproportionately low-income communities of color (Kaswan, 2020). Crisis rhetoric surrounding COVID-19 framed the health and safety of low-income, fenceline communities as a necessary sacrifice to slow the spread of a *larger* public health crisis gripping the nation. This rhetoric of expendability was most palpable in Cobb County, GA, where officials reopened an EtO facility just weeks after closing it to protect neighbors from cancer-causing emissions.

In February 2020, before large-scale equipment shortages, Georgia county officials released a statement plainly dismissing the possibility the facility could reopen. In their statement, officials said, "The safety of our residents is our utmost concern" (Cobb County—State of Georgia, 2020a, para. 6), but just one month later, the same officials allowed the facility to reopen for the narrow purpose of sterilizing PPE. Concerned that the limited reopening was insufficient to meet growing needs for sterile medical equipment, federal employees attempted to bypass Cobb County health officials and appeal directly to the State of Georgia. Laura Trueman, then Director of the Office of Intergovernmental and External Affairs for HHS, penned a fiery email to the state criticizing Cobb County's narrow reopening, asking for the facility to be brought back to full operating capacity (Ryan, 2020). Trueman wrote:

> Finally, we don't think that one county should be allowed to jeopardize the nation's response to an unprecedented national pandemic. My understanding is that this particular plant represented 4% of the total U.S. capacity for Ethylene Oxide Sterilization. If it remains shuttered, there are national implications. (para. 19)

Trueman framed Cobb County's closure of the facility as a selfish attempt to protect one small group of U.S. Americans at the expense of thousands, or possibly millions, of others. Inherent in this positioning is the notion that the health of fenceline communities is expendable when national interests are better served by polluting the air of local residents.

The emergency order allowing the Cobb County facility to reopen contained 12 *whereas clauses* justifying the authorization. Like Trueman's email, these clauses positioned the interests of fenceline residents against the backdrop of a global crisis. Community concerns were juxtaposed with the sheer scale of COVID-19 and the massive supply chain disruptions that stretched worldwide. The order cited Governor Kemp's State Public Health Emergency designation, President Trump's National Public Health Emergency designation, and the World Health Organization's designation of COVID-19 as "a world health emergency and global pandemic." When situated within the context of a global crisis, the concerns of those most immediately affected by the sterilization process begin to fade in comparison.

Sterigenics, the company that operates the Cobb County facility, filed a 54-page lawsuit against the county in district court (Cobb County—State of Georgia, 2020b). The suit argued that the community was obstructing access to PPE and other lifesaving equipment, placing the nation at risk. The suit dismissed the risks posed by EtO exposure in Cobb County and accused local officials of placing politics over the safety of the nation. The suit begins:

> Defendants Dawe and Gobble are unlawfully precluding Sterigenics' longstanding operation of its medical products sterilization facility in Cobb County, Georgia. [. . .] They are thereby preventing millions of essential and lifesaving medical products Sterigenics' facility is responsible for sterilizing from reaching healthcare providers who need them for patient care.

In total, the lawsuit made 17 references to the emerging COVID-19 pandemic with only vague references to the toxicity or carcinogenic effects of EtO. The suit cited state and national COVID-19 infection numbers, PPE shortages, and the growing need for ventilators, IV sets, medical tubing, and catheters for the nation.

In the previously mentioned email, Laura Trueman attempted to remind state and county officials that their authority paled in comparison to that of the federal government and that those at the top levels of executive leadership could force the county's hand and bring them into line with national crisis response. She told state leaders:

> We hope you will use whatever communication channels you have to encourage the county to expand the decree to full production of all medical items and extend it until the nation's threat and need is over. Conversations on next steps from the Federal Government are occurring at the highest levels, should the situation not change.

The thinly veiled threat of federal intervention was a call for state and local officials to conform to "the nation's threat and need," even if that meant sacrificing the safety of local residents. Importantly, these narratives of sacrifice were never directed to individuals who would be exposed to EtO. Instead, county, state, and federal officials preferred private correspondence and appeals to government actors that could reopen facilities against the interests of fenceline communities. The following section further details the rhetoric of silence that marginalized those at risk from EtO during the height of equipment shortages.

Rhetoric of Silence

In many cases, the emerging conflict between the COVID-19 and EtO crises was met with overwhelming silence from elected officials, agencies, and corporations. Even those who had boasted about their role in closing EtO facilities just months earlier fell silent when it became clear that a conflict was emerging between protecting citizens at risk for EtO exposure and protecting those who might die without access to sterile medical equipment like PPE and ventilators. For almost a year after the pandemic reached the United States, elected officials at state and national levels seemed to avoid public discussion of the conflict altogether.

In the months leading up to the COVID-19 pandemic, elected officials at all levels were outspoken in support of communities living with the risks from EtO exposure. For example, in January 2019, six members of the federal congressional delegation from Illinois penned a letter to the EPA calling on the agency to take action against the Medline and Sterigenics facilities in their state (Casten, 2019). The same members issued a public statement a month later once again demanding action. On February 12, 2019, Senator Dick Durbin spoke on the Senate floor detailing the narratives of whistleblowers who accused the Willowbrook facility of negligently releasing large quantities of EtO into the surrounding community and highlighting findings that Willowbrook showed increased rates of cancer in areas around the Sterigenics plant (U.S. Congress—Senate, 2019). In August 2019, Georgia Governor Brian Kemp took credit for Sterigenics' decision to dramatically curtail EtO emissions in the state (King, 2020). Local activist groups like Stop Sterigenics organized protests outside government buildings, amassed a significant social media following, and developed media relations operations to engage with journalists.

By the time COVID-19 began to spread across the United States, some progress had already been made in reducing EtO emissions, including new restrictions implemented by the State of Illinois, which forced the Sterigenics facility in Willowbrook to cease operations and the Medline facility in Lake County to undergo renovation. Facilities in other states underwent voluntary transformations to reduce EtO emissions. But, just as progress was being made, other facilities came back online and existing facilities ramped up sterilization efforts to meet the demands resulting from the COVID-19 pandemic. It was also clear that closure of some facilities was contributing to PPE and other medical equipment shortages. Despite the clear conflict, once vocal politicians and agencies fell silent rather than risk being assessed blame for either local emissions or global supply shortages.

Rhetorics of silence often work to marginalize and exclude non-dominant groups in a society (Brown, 2009; Glenn, 2004). Silence on a particular public health crisis signals the value rhetors place on its victims and the effects of the crisis. At the end of March 2020, the Inspector General (IG) of the EPA detailed failures of the agency to alert those in fenceline communities of the risks of EtO. The EPA IG proposed coordinating with the Food and Drug Administration (FDA) to alert communities about their risk. Despite this warning, FDA messaging focused largely on equipment shortages resulting from facility closures while remaining mostly silent on the risks of EtO to fenceline communities.

In a letter dated March 19, FDA commissioner Stephen Hahn (2020) requested that Georgia Governor Brian Kemp help reopen the Cobb County facility to prevent supply shortages. In the letter, Hahn spoke only in general terms about the facility closures, saying, "Due to the recent challenges with the closure of some commercial sterilizers, such as the Sterigenics facility located in Cobb County, the supply of critical PPE during the COVID-19 outbreak has been further limited." Some FDA documents named the cause of the closures, but only as a secondary concern to supply shortages and typically by sharing a single link from the National Institutes of Health describing the connection between EtO and cancer. An FDA (2021) web page titled "Ethylene Oxide Sterilization Facility Updates" provided the statuses of facility closures and discussed potential ramifications on device shortages with each closure but did not provide any information about the causes that prompted the closures or about the risks that EtO posed to surrounding communities.

Between March 2020 and November 2021, the Congressional Record contained just nine mentions of ethylene oxide, most in the text of legislation or amendments unrelated to device sterilization. During the same time period, PPE was mentioned almost 400 times and COVID-19 almost 4,300 times. While multiple members discussed the EtO crisis in House and Senate floor speeches in the months before March 2020, the crisis was not addressed in either chamber in the months that followed. In July 2020, Rep. Bill Foster mentioned the dangers of EtO in a committee hearing on environmental justice and COVID-19 marking the only committee reference to EtO risks in the year following the first case of COVID-19 in the United States.

A separate report from the EPA Inspector General in April 2021 exposed efforts of Trump Administration political appointees to obstruct testing of emissions in Illinois and prevent EPA employees from alerting residents to the risks posed by EtO. The report identified specific attempts to silence career EPA officials from discussing the risks of EtO in fenceline communities. The Inspector General accused EPA officials of violating the mission of the agency by withholding information from publics about the dangers of EtO:

> The EPA's mission statement asserts that the Agency works to ensure that "[a]ll parts of society—communities, individuals, businesses, and state, local and tribal governments—have access to accurate information sufficient to effectively participate in managing human health and environmental risks." The EPA's risk communication guidance also states that communities have the right to participate in decision-making processes that affect their lives and livelihoods. The EPA's actions have not been consistent with its mission or guidance on risk communication. (para. 4)

As the IG report indicates, the rhetoric of silence moved beyond a redirecting of attention toward the global pandemic. In some cases, government silence was an orchestrated attempt to avoid further supply chain disruptions that were already hindering COVID-19 response. Rhetors may have hoped that keeping fenceline communities unaware of their risks would strengthen the capacity of healthcare organizations to save lives of healthcare workers and those infected with COVID-19.

Through silence, rhetors further marginalized those at greatest risk of cancer and other long-term health implications from EtO exposure. The COVID-19 pandemic drew attention away from a variety of public health crises, but the EtO crisis stands out as an example of political willingness to exacerbate a different public health crisis in the name of remedying the effects of COVID-19. Questions of conflict and allocation are central to understanding political communication. Our concluding paragraphs stress the importance of a *crises* (rather than crisis) approach to the study of political communication in a public health emergency.

The Politics of Public Health in Conflicting Crises

Political scientist David Easton (1965) famously defined politics as "the authoritative allocation of values" (p. 80). Easton viewed politics fundamentally as a question of allocation. He further elaborated: "The fundamental fact confronting all societies is that scarcity of some valued things prevail. It inevitably leads to disputes over their allocation" (p. 53). Political communication frequently, perhaps even centrally, addresses the allocation of things of value within a society. Crises and disasters bring these questions of allocation into stark relief. At the beginning of the COVID-19 pandemic, things of value—such as time, attention, media coverage, compassion, medical equipment, and other material resources—were either organically or artificially limited in supply. These limitations impacted a wide variety of public health crises. Depression (Wang et al., 2020), domestic violence (Kofman & Garfin, 2020), opioid use disorder (Khatri & Perrone, 2020), hunger (Paslakis et al., 2021), and dozens of other crises were exacerbated by the COVID-19 pandemic. In the case of EtO emissions and COVID-19, the question of values was associated with human lives and how to value the lives of those suffering from COVID-19 in comparison to other vulnerable populations in fenceline communities facing increased risk of cancer from toxic chemical emissions.

Limited resources to address COVID-19 rendered some bodies expendable. Rhetorics of expendability abounded during the pandemic. Importantly, shortages of medical equipment, further exacerbated by EtO facility closures, forced difficult conversations about rationing care and prioritizing treatment of the deadly disease (Andrews et al., 2021). In some of the hardest-hit areas of the planet, health officials made decisions to prioritize care for younger patients and patients without comorbid conditions because those patients had the best chance for survival (Doebrich et al., 2020). These conversations and decisions intensified calls for social justice in health care and demanded solutions to supply chain disruptions. In these same conversations, the dominant focus on COVID-19 as a singular global crisis, however, obscured those bodies made expendable by the very solutions to these shortages. The scope of the COVID-19 pandemic, the silence of elected officials, and the reframing of the sterilization industry denied a voice to fenceline communities and even offered their health and well-being as a sacrifice to preserve those infected with COVID-19.

Analysis of political communication in times of crisis should be concerned with questions of allocation across crises and strive to understand the interrelation of these crises. Focusing on interrelations makes visible those who were rendered expendable by the combined or conflicting effects of multiple crisis situations. These conflicts do not lend themselves to easy answers. The difficult work of political communication in a crisis or disaster requires reconciling conflict and creating opportunities for change. Future political leaders will continue to confront questions that put lives in conflict. The EtO example illustrates how local concerns and smaller public health crises were dismissed or silenced during a global pandemic and how vulnerable communities became expendable in the context of crisis response.

Practical Applications

Future political communicators, health communicators, and affiliates can glean valuable insight from the conflicting EtO emissions and COVID-19 crises. Conflicting crises, like the ones presented here, force discussions of relative risk and require actors to weigh decisions based on probability, proximity, immediacy, and magnitude. While weighing these factors, we advise that rhetors should be cautious to avoid false dichotomies, prevent politicization, clearly communicate risks to all affected publics, and articulate pathways forward.

1. *Avoid false dichotomies*—Even when conflicts between crises ultimately prove inexorable, starting from the perspective of a fixed choice between two or more negative health outcomes closes off potential solutions and immediately renders some stakeholders expendable. Actors in this case study presented addressing the EtO crisis and reducing supply shortages as either/or propositions. Even when crises come into conflict, political leaders should resist the impulse to frame conflicts as either/or decisions. Instead, efforts should center attention on solutions that minimize risks to all communities.
2. *Prevent politicization*—In times of crisis, publics need reliable and apolitical sources of information to effectively assess risk and respond appropriately to those risks (Houston, 2012). Politicization of the COVID-19 pandemic created serious barriers to effective crisis response (Halpern, 2020). In this case, corporations and think tanks attempted to sow doubt about the effects of EtO and many political leaders avoided the discussion altogether out of fear of political ramifications. Politicization is especially troubling in times of conflicting crises. Politicization risks pitting affected publics against one another in competition for scarce resources, including government attention and concern.
3. *Clearly communicate risks to all affected publics*—Political leaders, public officials, and businesses should reveal important information affecting fenceline communities and allow opportunities for public input. As observed in the case study, once the conflict between the two crises becomes evident, leaders often fall publicly silent, even as some now

public correspondence suggests that conversations were continuing out of public view. For example, Trueman's email to Georgia officials directly acknowledged the potential effects on Cobb County residents but dismissed concerns relative to the national interest. The email was in the form of direct correspondence and was only revealed to residents after decisions were made. Similarly, political appointees in the federal government attempted to stop the disclosure of health risks to those surrounding EtO facilities.

4. *Articulate pathways forward*—From this pandemic, we have learned that the need for sterilization will remain. As citizens in fenceline communities may feel that efforts to close the facilities utilizing carcinogenic chemicals have been abandoned, efforts to protect their safety now, and in the future should be clearly communicated. This communication not only serves to keep these residents informed, but also functions to build relationships and trust with the residents of fenceline communities.

Definitions

Fenceline communities—those areas bordering or adjacent to a company and directly impacted by that company's operations, including chemical, biological, or physical hazards, emissions, odors, traffic, parking, and noise (Burke, 1999).
Conflicting crises—Situations of difficulty, danger, risk, or threat that are exacerbated or compounded by proposed or implemented solutions to a different situation of difficulty.

Recommendations for Research

Future research should investigate the rhetoric surrounding parallel, intersecting, and conflicting crises. Within the context of COVID-19, scholars should consider the implications of U.S. American crisis response on other parts of the globe and investigate how COVID-19 affected health and income inequalities globally. The relationship between COVID-19 and other crises requires urgent attention, including COVID's effects on hunger, social isolation, substance use disorders, and global climate change. Analyzing the relationship between these crises can reveal new facets of inequity and further foreground marginalized voices.

Discussion Questions

1. How could federal officials have worked better to communicate with fenceline communities about the conflict between EtO and COVID-19? Should these officials have been more receptive to the concerns of these communities?
2. Was silence an appropriate or ethical response for political officials facing conflicting crises? When may silence be the best approach, or the worst?
3. What responsibilities do local officials have in a national crisis? What responsibilities do they have to themselves, their constituents, and what responsibilities do they have to the nation?

Resources

1. The United States Conference of Mayors offers guidance on best practices, essential resources, and relevant press releases in their COVID-19 issue guide at USMayors.org/COVID-19
2. Individuals and organizations in the United States can assess risk of exposure to carcinogenic air pollutants in their communities using the EPA's AirToxScreen Mapping Tool located at epa.gov/AirToxScreen

References

165 Cong. Rec. S1565-S1568 (2019). (statement of Sen. Durbin)

166 Cong. Rec. S1748–S1753 (2020). (statement of Sen. Schumer)

Advanced Medical Technology Association. (2019, February 21). *Ethylene oxide (EO): Overview of EO use with medical devices*. AdvaMed. https://www.reginfo.gov/public/do/eoDownloadDocument?pubId=&eodoc=true&documentID=4815

Albergotti, R., & Siddiqui, F. (2020, April 4). Ford and GM are undertaking a warlike effort to produce ventilators. It may fall short and come too late. *Washington Post*. https://www.washingtonpost.com/business/2020/04/04/ventilators-coronavirus-ford-gm/

American Chemical Society. (2019, November 8). *Ethylene oxide*. Molecule of the Week Archive. https://www.acs.org/content/acs/en/molecule-of-the-week/archive/e/ ethylene-oxide.html

Andrews, E.E., Ayers, K.B., Brown, K.S., Dunn, D.S., & Pilarski, C.R. (2021). No body is expendable: Medical rationing and disability justice during the COVID-19 pandemic. *American Psychologist, 76*(3), 451–461. http://dx.doi.org/10.1037/amp0000709

Bitzer, L.F. (1968). The rhetorical situation. *Philosophy & Rhetoric*, 1–14. http://www.jstor.org/stable/40236733

Brown, M.T. (2009). LGBT aging and rhetorical silence. *Sexuality Research and Social Policy Journal of NSRC*, 6(4), 65–78. https://doi.org/10.1525/srsp.2009.6.4.65

Burke, E.M. (1999). *Corporate community relations: The principle of the neighbor of choice*. Greenwood Publishing Group.

Callahan, J.M. (2021). The United States: Politics versus science? In D. Lilleker, I.A. Coman, M. Gregor & E. Novelli (Eds.), *Political communication and COVID-19* (pp. 67–78). Routledge. https://doi.org/10.4324/9781003120254

Casten, S. (2019, July 23). *Casten, Durbin, Duckworth, Lipinski, Foster, and Schneider press EPA for strict ethylene oxide standards*. Office of Sean Casten. https://casten.house.gov/media/press-releases/casten-durbin-duckworth-lipinski-foster-and-schneider-press-epa-strict-ethylene

Ceccarelli, L. (2010). *Shaping science with rhetoric*. University of Chicago Press.

Centers for Disease Control and Prevention. (2008). *Sterilization: Guideline for disinfection and sterilization in healthcare facilities*. https://www.cdc.gov/infectioncontrol/guidelines/disinfection/sterilization/index.html

Clinical Oncology News. (2020). *Sterilization has been a problem for months—Then COVID-19 hit*. https://www.clinicaloncology.com/COVID-19/Article/05-20/--Sterilization-Has-Been-a-Problem-for-Months%E2%80%94Then-COVID-19-Hit/58055

Cobb County—State of Georgia. (2020a, February 27). *Cobb County issues a statement regarding the ongoing investigation into Sterigenics' Certificate of Occupancy*. Cobb County: Communications. https://www.cobbcounty.org/communications/news/latest-sterigenics-plant-situation

Cobb County—State of Georgia. (2020b, March 25). *Order pursuant to declaration of emergency in Cobb County permitting temporary resumption of operations by Sterigenics for the sterilization of personal protective equipment (PPE) necessary to combat the COVID-19 pandemic*. Cobb County: Communications. https://www.cobbcounty.org/communications/news/latest-sterigenics-plant-situation

Croucher, S.M., Nguyen, T., & Rahmani, D. (2020). Prejudice toward Asian Americans in the COVID-19 pandemic: The effects of social media use in the United States. *Frontiers in Communication*, 5(39), 1–12. https://doi.org/10.3389/fcomm.2020.00039

Doebrich, A., Quirici, M., & Lunsford, C. (2020). COVID-19 and the need for disability conscious medical education, training, and practice. *Journal of Pediatric Rehabilitation Medicine*, 13(3), 393–404. https://doi.org/10.3233/prm-200763

Easton, D. (1965). *A framework for political analysis*. Prentice-Hall.

Edbauer, J. (2005). Unframing models of public distribution: From rhetorical situation to rhetorical ecologies. *Rhetoric Society Quarterly*, 35(4), 5–24. https://www.jstor.org/stable/40232607

Environmental Protection Agency. (2016). *Ethylene oxide*. EPA.gov. https://www.epa.gov/sites/default/files/2016-09/documents/ethylene-oxide.pdf

Foss, S.K. (1989). Rhetorical criticism as the asking of questions. *Communication Education*, 38(3), 191–196. https://doi.org/10.1080/03634528909378755

Foster, W. (2020, July 14). *Hearing before Committee on Science, Space, and Technology: Sweltering in place: COVID-19, extreme heat, and environmental justice.* Congress.gov. https://www.congress.gov/event/116th-congress/house-event/LC65628/text?s=1&r=9

Glenn, C. (2004). *Unspoken: A rhetoric of silence.* Southern Illinois University Press.

Griffith, C.L., & Hall, L.A. (1940). *Sterilizing colloid materials* (U.S. Patent No. 2,189,949). U.S. Patent and Trademark Office. https://patentimages.storage.googleapis.com/0f/db/bb/b58c3ebbc70a87/US2189949.pdf

Hahn, S.M. (2020, March 19). *Letter to the Hon. Brian Kemp.* U.S. Food and Drug Administration. https://s3.amazonaws.com/jnswire/jns-media/d7/73/11408978/fda_letter_re_sterigenics.pdf

Halpern, L.W. (2020). The politicization of COVID-19. *American Journal of Nursing [AJN], 120*(11), 19–20. https://doi.org/10.1097/01.naj.0000721912.74581.d7

Hawthorne, M. (2018, August 28). High cancer risk in southeast DuPage County linked to company co-owned by Rauner's former firm. *Chicago Tribune.* https://www.chicagotribune.com/news/breaking/ct-met-dupage-cancer-pollution-rauner-20180827-story.html

Hoffman, M.F., & Ford, D.J. (2009). *Organizational rhetoric: Situations and strategies.* Sage Publications. https://us.sagepub.com/en-us/nam/organizational-rhetoric/book231664

Houston, J.B. (2012). Public disaster mental/behavioral health communication: Intervention across disaster phases. *Journal of Emergency Management, 10*(3), 283–292. https://doi.org/oi:10.5055/jem.2012.0106

Illinois Department of Public Health. (2019, March 29). *Cancer incidence assessment near Sterigenics in Willowbrook, IL 1995–2015.* State of Illinois. https://www.documentcloud.org/documents/5784030-2019-3-29-Sterigenics-Willowbrook-Cancer.html

Kaswan, A. (10 June 2020) Blog: "Black Lives Matter and the Environment." ComingClean. https://comingcleaninc.org/latest-news/in-the-news/blog-black-lives-matter-and-environment

Khatri, U.G., & Perrone, J. (2020). Opioid use disorder and COVID-19: Crashing of the crises. *Journal of Addiction Medicine, 14*(4), 6–7. https://doi.org/10.1097/adm.0000000000000684

King, M. (2020, August 5). *New ethylene oxide regulation signed into law by Gov. Kemp.* Alive. https://www.11alive.com/article/news/health/new-ethylene-oxide-regulation-signed-into-law-by-gov-kemp/85-f7fc4f81-f7a6-430e-841d-6af4f8457b3f

Kofman, Y.B., & Garfin, D.R. (2020). Home is not always a haven: The domestic violence crisis amid the COVID-19 pandemic. *Psychological Trauma: Theory, Research, Practice, and Policy, 12*(S1), 199–201. https://psycnet.apa.org/doi/10.1037/tra0000866

Logomasini, A. (2020, December 14). Opinion: The seriously dangerous consequences of junk science. *The Detroit News.* https://www.detroitnews.com/story/opinion/2020/12/15/opinion-seriously-dangerous-consequences-junk-science/6540662002/

Marchand, R. (2020, July 9). Op-Ed: Precautionary principle punishes pandemic patients. *The Center Square.* https://www.thecentersquare.com/national/op-ed-precautionary-principle-punishes-pandemic-patients/article_e128b6bc-c1f2-11ea-a1c0-5b3c337cfd05.html

Miroff, N. (2020, March 27). U.S. cities have acute shortages of masks, test kits, ventilators as they face coronavirus threat. *Washington Post.* https://www.washingtonpost.com/national/coronavirus-mayors-mask-equipment-shortage/2020/03/27/fc2a45a4-701f-11ea-96a0-df4c5d9284af_story.html

Montiel, C.J., Uyheng, J., & Dela Paz, E. (2021). The language of pandemic leaderships: Mapping political rhetoric during the COVID-19 outbreak. *Political Psychology, 42*(5), 747–766. https://doi.org/10.1111/pops.12753

National Governors Association. (2020, April 13). *Governor actions to address PPE and ventilator shortages.* Nga.org. https://www.nga.org/wp-content/uploads/2020/04/NGA-Medical-Equipment-Memo.pdf

Neville-Shepard, M. (2021). Masks and emasculation: Populist crisis rhetoric and the 2020 presidential election. *American Behavioral Scientist (Advance online publication),* 1–15. https://doi.org/10.1177/00027642211011223

Paslakis, G., Dimitropoulos, G., & Katzman, D.K. (2021). A call to action to address COVID-19–induced global food insecurity to prevent hunger, malnutrition, and eating pathology. *Nutrition Reviews, 79*(1), 114–116. https://doi.org/10.1093/nutrit/nuaa069

Ranney, M.L., Griffeth, V., & Jha, A.K. (2020). Critical supply shortages—the need for ventilators and personal protective equipment during the Covid-19 pandemic. *New England Journal of Medicine, 382*(18), 41. https://doi.org/10.1056/nejmp2006141

Rimer, K. (2019). *U.S. EPA's National Air Toxics Assessment (NATA) and ethylene oxide.* EPA. https://www.epa.gov/sites/default/files/2019-08/documents/nata_overview_-_kelly_rimer.pdf

Ryan, C. (2020, March 27). *Feds threaten action against Cobb County if it doesn't expand sterilization order.* CBS 46. cbs46.com/news/feds-threaten-action-against-cobb-county-if-it-doesnt-expand-sterilization-order/article_edb514a4-7092-11ea-acf9-a7546c2c92e0.html

Smith, C.R., & Lybarger, S. (1996). Bitzer's model reconstructed. *Communication Quarterly, 44*(2), 197–213. https://doi.org/10.1080/01463379609370010

Sotera Health. (2020, March 23). *Supplier letter—Business continuity.* Sotera Health. https://sterigenics.com/wp-content/uploads/2020/03/Sotera-Health-Supplier-COVID-19-Letter-3_23_2020-signed.pdf

Sterigenics. (2020). *Company overview.* https://sterigenics.com/about-us/

Sterigenics. (2021). *Sterigenics comments on ruling in New Mexico litigation as of June 29, 2021.* https://investors.soterahealth.com/static-files/569c1219-a071-463b-bdd7-aa24782bb0bb

Sterman, J., Brauer, A., & Nejman, A. (2020, September 14). *Invisible gas may pose a cancer risk in towns, but experts say the EPA is failing to warn.* Sinclair Broadcast Group. https://wjla.com/news/spotlight-on-america/invisible-gas-may-pose-a-cancer-risk-in-towns-but-experts-say-the-epa-is-failing-to-warn

United States Conference of Mayors, The. (2020, March 27). *Shortages of COVID-19 emergency equipment in U.S. cities: A survey of the nation's mayors.* USMayors. https://www.usmayors.org/issues/covid-19/equipment-survey/

U.S. Food and Drug Administration. (2021). *Ethylene oxide sterilization facility updates*. FDA. https://www.fda.gov/medical-devices/general-hospital-devices-and-supplies/ethylene-oxide-sterilization-facility-updates

Vatz, R.E. (1973). The myth of the rhetorical situation. *Philosophy & Rhetoric*, 6(3), 154–161. https://www.jstor.org/stable/40236848

Wang, X., Hegde, S., Son, C., Keller, B., Smith, A., & Sasangohar, F. (2020). Investigating mental health of US college students during the COVID-19 pandemic: Cross-sectional survey study. *Journal of medical Internet research*, 22(9), Article e22817. https://www.jmir.org/2020/9/e22817/

Wells, K., & Winowiecki, E. (2020, March 20). *Some healthcare workers turn to homemade masks amidst "controlled chaos" of dwindling supplies*. Michigan Radio. https://www.michiganradio.org/news/2020-03-20/some-healthcare-workers-turn-to-homemade-masks-amidst-controlled-chaos-of-dwindling-supplies

World Health Organization. (2020, March 3). *Shortage of personal protective equipment endangering health workers worldwide*. https://www.who.int/news/item/03-03-2020-shortage-of-personal-protective-equipment-endangering-health-workers-worldwide

Yalçın, M.G., & Düzen, N.E. (2021). Altered meanings of home before and during COVID-19 pandemic. *Human Arenas*, 1–13. https://doi.org/10.1007/s42087-021-00185-3

· 1 6 ·

"IT SPREAD LIKE WILDFIRE" AND "FLOODED HOSPITALS" COMPOUNDING CRISIS: CLIMATE, WILDFIRES, AND HURRICANES DURING THE PANDEMIC

Mildred Perreault & Bipulendra Adhikari

During the COVID-19 Pandemic, the COP26 Climate Change Summit in the United Kingdom made it clear that climate change concerns had not halted the risks and impacts of climate change, but rather made it more visible. Concerns about climate change have grown in the last 20 years, and the frequency and severity of natural disasters have accompanied that growth. COVID-19 surfaced at a time when climate change coverage was becoming more prominent, and therefore, the ways in which they have both been covered and the challenges for coverage have been similar (Franklin et al., 2021; Perreault et al., 2021).

Reporters likened the pandemic to a natural disaster in their reporting, for example, a "disease that spread like wildfire" (Beasely, 2021) and "hospitals flooded with patients" (Gilligan, 2021). Covering conflict is central to journalism practice (McGregor, 2002). Journalistic organizations have made recommendations for best practices when reporting crises and disasters (Franklin et al., 2021; Seeger & Sellnow, 2016), but for many reasons, journalists do not always apply them.

After an investigation of four different natural disasters, this chapter will address two questions: (1) What can crisis communications experts consider when working with these journalists? and (2) What might the implications be for covering elongated crises like climate change?

News organizations struggle to cover disasters because of the demands of the 24/7 news cycle (Boenker, 2012) and to understand and simplify scientific information that often connects climate change (Appelgren & Jönsson, 2021) and natural disasters (Mackie, 2014). The focus on conflict during crises and lack of support for long-term coverage of disasters prioritizes the most immediate threat. Journalists point to climate-related problems in their own areas but lack the time and knowledge to elaborate on the "how and why" issues tying disasters directly to climate change.

This study aimed:

- To examine how journalists dealt with the two narratives of climate change and natural disasters in the midst of the global COVID-19 crisis.
- To gain a broader understanding of how systems of response might be weakened or strengthened while occurring alongside COVID-19 responses.

Researchers selected four disasters based on impact in loss of life and economic strain from several different countries (Hubbard, 2020; Woodall, 2021). These included Oregon/California wildfires in the United States, bushfires in Australia, typhoon Amphan in India, and an earthquake followed by a tropical storm in Haiti.

Each disaster would have been considered high impact even if it had occurred in a year unaffected by the COVID-19 pandemic. Two were chosen in North America and two were chosen in the India and Oceania region. News sources from three countries were part of the evaluation. These disasters were identified by researchers as unique and impactful based on the data supplied by Reliefweb.int, and made publicly available on their websites, through Statista.com and the U.S. News and World Report Websites (Reliefweb.int, 2022; Navarre, 2021; Statista.com, 2022).

The Disasters

Considering that disasters are an increasing indicator of climate change, examining natural disasters that occurred at the height of the COVID-19 pandemic might provide insights into how journalists covered multiple, overlapping crises.

Wildfires in California and Oregon

The 2021 summer wildfire season in California produced significant challenges for emergency responders in California and Oregon. Our analysis looked at two fires that occurred in July through September 2021.

The Bootleg fire started in late July and continued into August and affected states, including California, Idaho, Montana, Oregon and then later Nevada and into New Mexico (Incident Information System U.S. Forest Service, 2021a). More than 5,000 people were working to contain it as of August 1. In September 2021, more than 240,400 acres were affected and more than 4,000 homes were burnt down (Associated Press, 2021), and covered 665 square miles (Incident Information System U.S. Forest Service, 2021a). A second slightly smaller fire (about the size of the city of San Diego) killed many people and had a substantive economic impact (Incident Information System U.S. Forest Service, 2021b).

Australian Bushfires

Australia was hit by one of the worst wildfires (often called bushfires) starting in September 2019 and into February 2020. The wildfire season was dubbed as "Black Summer." The bushfires destroyed 18.6 million hectares of land including most populated Australian states—New South Wales and Victoria—and killed at least 33 people and about 1 billion animals. Australian states were prompted to declare a state of emergency urging residents and tourists to evacuate. The brush fires have had long-term physical, ecological, biodiversity, public health, economic, and climate change impacts within the country and across borders (New Zealand and South American countries).

Cyclone Amphan (India)

On May 20, 2020, Cyclone Amphan, with a wind speed of 185 kilometers per hour (115 miles/h), cut a swathe across the eastern Indian city of Kolkata (West Bengal state), killing 86 people, mostly due to electrocution or the collapse of homes.

The cyclone, which is considered as one of the worst in the last decade, posed damages of around $13.5 billion and affected 70% of the West Bengal population. The impacts of the cyclone were also felt in Bangladesh, Bhutan, and Sri Lanka. Bangladesh newspaper Dhaka Tribune reported that around

83,000 homes were either destroyed or damaged in the country, costing around $1.5 billion. The rescue and relief operations in the cyclone-hit areas were affected by COVID-19 pandemic restrictions.

India is among the most COVID-19-affected (including its variants) countries in the world with more than 455,000 deaths (as reported by Ministry of Health and Family Welfare, Government of India in October 2021). The first COVID-19 case was reported on January 30, 2020, and India's preparedness and response to mitigate COVID-19 have varied across its 29 states (Lancet, 2020). Gujarat state had high fatalities, while the low industrialized state Kerala suffered less (Israelsen & Malji, 2021).

2021 Haiti Earthquake

The earthquake that hit in 2021 was reminiscent of the earthquake that hit Port au Prince in 2010. As of late September 2021, more than 2,200 people had died, more than 12,000 were reported injured and hundreds were still missing. The earthquake was followed by tropical storm Grace, which made recovery conditions more challenging. Then tropical depression Grace hit on August 16, 2021 (Stevenson & Sanon, 2021).

The 7.2 magnitude earthquake took place on August 14 (Communications and Publishing USGS, 2021). It hit west of Port au Prince, and was a shallow earthquake in that it hit a broader area but resonated closer to the surface, according to the Center for Disaster Philosophy (2021). When hurricane Grace made landfall as a tropical depression on August 16, there were more than five inches of rain in some areas, causing flooding and landslides. In addition, earlier in the year Haiti's President Jean Dominique was assassinated, which provided a challenging situation for response as the government was investigating several key leaders for involvement in the plot. Haiti also had a very low vaccination rate (Our World in Data, 2021).

Literature Review

When considering how a crisis affects people, systems, and governments, it is valuable to consider the different levels of response—individual, organizational, and community. For this study, the researchers identified the different types of disaster responses included in news stories in the shadow of COVID-19 (March 2020 through September 2021).

Communication Ecology, Disaster and Crisis Communication, and COVID-19

Researchers have identified several different components that interact to create an environment where people feel empowered and able to respond to a crisis. This ecosystem, or ecology model, is specifically the crisis and disaster communication ecology (Spialek et al., 2016). COVID-19 continued to pose threats globally from November 2019 well into 2022, making it what has been termed an *elongated crisis*. Organizations and communities that experience elongated crises often face long-term challenges in recovery and resilience. What can change the way they respond is the information and resources they have to address the crisis head-on. Communication ecology considers interactions between different groups and information sources; so in considering a COVID-19 communication ecology, it is necessary to how information is produced by journalists and others.

Information sources can change the way that people overall conceptualize a crisis, respond to a crisis and even their long-term processing and coping with that crisis (Houston et al., 2015; Kiesler & Sproull, 1982). Researchers have considered the impacts of information such as news messages, crisis warnings and interpersonal communication (Jin et al., 2014; Perreault et al., 2014). How national journalists choose to cover crises can change the conversations about crises, as well as how those crises are remembered (Austin et al., 2012). Previous crisis experience can change the way that an organization responds to crises in the future, but also public perception (Hale et al., 2005).

Disasters are often described as a sudden disruption of routine events in society as they lead to collective stress. Though there is no uniformity in a definition of disaster, there is one useful definition, as it can be described in different terms. The United Nations Office for Disaster Risk Reduction (UNISDR) defines disaster as:

> A serious disruption of the functioning of a community or a society at any scale due to hazardous events interacting with conditions of exposure, vulnerability and capacity, leading to one or more of the following: human, material, economic and environmental losses and impacts. (UNISDR, 2009, p. 9)

Disasters are not only a socially constructed crisis but also economic, human, and environmental degradation (a process through which the natural environment is compromised). Disasters are a collective stress situation, which leads to social disruption and psychological dislocation in the society (Barton,

1969). This definition gives four dimensions to study disaster: impact, duration, speed of impact and society's response or preparedness. The case studies for this research are selected based on these four dimensions particularly focusing on their impacts on human lives and livelihoods.

News and Media Coverage of Natural Disasters

Disasters expose people to new realities. People need information to address demands, consequences, and to cope with new realities. Newspapers, television, radio, and social media sites form the basis of information sources in disaster situations.

A disaster event can be categorized into three stages: pre, present, and post, although it is sometimes difficult to identify these stages in events like earthquakes, wildfires, hurricanes etc. (Wukich, 2016). Apart from an immediate effect, these events are likely to cause long-term havoc. Though social media can be an immediate source of information in disasters, authenticity of information is always questionable (Jung & Park, 2014), yet news organizations often release content through social media channels (Houston et al., 2015). Trust of information and its sources are important aspects of disaster communication. In addition, news organizations have faced challenges because of limited resources, time, and the demands of technology (Barnes et al., 2008), or certain crises receive different types of coverage depending on the severity (Benson, 2018; Perreault & Perreault, 2021).

News coverage of natural disasters can provide a summary and insight into the disaster and crisis communication ecology around a disaster, and can frame how the disaster is thought about in crisis and disaster communication situations (Houston et al., 2012). Community responses to disasters have been found to have a positive link to individuals' disaster-coping outcomes (Liu, 2020). Best practices in crisis communication have been linked to sharing information about safety and facilitating relocation and recovery in a crisis (Seegar, 2006; Veil et al., 2020).

Similarly, journalists use their previous knowledge or their *collective memory* about crisis or crisis experience to mitigate how they interact with the crisis that follows that initial experience (Allan, 2013). In the case of COVID-19, journalists may interact with crises that follow differently—for better or worse— depending upon what their sources are, their communities, the information or their personal networks before the crisis or in previous crisis situations that they've had to mitigate (Perreault & Perreault, 2021; Perreault et al., 2021).

In addition, the news coverage of crises and disasters on the local level could provide strategies for covering more complex issues like climate change (Djalante & Thomalla, 2012). Overall research has shown local connections to issues make them more relevant, this issue of proximity often creates an opportunity for connection for readers and communities to the conflicts at hand (Bowden et al., 2021; Milfont et al., 2014; Stoddart & Smith, 2016). That said, isolating crises is often necessary in times of crisis and disaster response and journalists may struggle with balancing coverage of multiple issues in one story.

Compounding Crises

Public relations practitioners operating and compounding crises often use legitimate U.S. organizational responses and social capital established with their state stakeholder network to reduce risk perceptions for their public. Compounding crises are often difficult to respond to, because organizations and agencies might already be strapped for resources (Viel & Anthony, 2017). Similarly, the intersectionality of the global crisis of the COVID-19 pandemic and natural disasters (many heightened in intensity by climate change) have exposed many structural inequities, new injustices, vulnerabilities, and systemic challenges to crisis and disaster responses for public and private organizations (Sultana, 2021). In addition, organizations and stakeholders must meet the needs of the media and remain accessible in a crisis in order to provide valuable information to the public (Veil & Husted, 2012). But this is a reciprocal relationship in that organizations that partner with media can provide more credible and trustworthy information (Heath, 2006; Seegar, 2006; Veil & Ojeda, 2010).

Narratives with personalized content, or stories of personal experience are more persuasive when asking people to take action in a disaster or crisis (Clementson, 2020; Seeger & Sellnow, 2016).

Adapting to Crisis Within a Crisis

While for this study we examined compounding crises, it must also be acknowledged that all of these crises take place within the elongated response to COVID-19. Regardless of the crisis, all individuals must adapt to crises and disasters in order to move past them. Most people and organizations come to the crisis or disaster with some prior knowledge or some training that influences the way that they respond.

So what is a compounding crisis at its simplest? The idea of a compounding crisis is one that is second or third in a string of other crises simultaneously—a crisis with a response that depends on depleted resources. It exists within the first crisis, and often yields its response capacities to that crisis. The new crisis is introduced, even before the previous crisis is resolved, and therefore the impact of the first crisis may deplete the ability of stakeholders to respond to the second crisis as it is taking place.

The notion of a crisis arising with other vulnerabilities already existing as a result of because of first crisis is a reality given the pandemic because a lot of times, that means that disaster resources, financial capacities, aid, and even people's personal mental health capacities have already been exhausted, as a result.

International Perspectives

By examining four different crises, the chapter provides a comprehensive international perspective—as these countries have varied approaches to public health, funding for crisis response and even socioeconomic classifications (Reinhart & Rogonoff, 2009; World Bank, 2021; Scientific American, 2021). Some countries were impacted by COVID-19 more than others, and several of the countries we are examining in this chapter had a very small capacity to respond to crises, even if they aren't health crises. For example, as we mentioned in the examples, Haiti and India had gaps in access to healthcare and therefore do not have vaccines or other measures to guarantee treatment for COVID-19.

In addition to the above-mentioned criteria, issues surrounding COVID-19 and disaster events were seized as an opportunity to strengthen political domination, mostly in India, where the disaster response was often influenced by political meddling (Rahman, 2020).

There were sporadic events reported in the media on misappropriate distributions of relief supplies (supplies were directed to party cadres rather than the disaster-affected people), mobilize party cadres to gain support (as a public relations stunt) and embezzlement of government funds, among others (more details on individual analysis sections below). These events emphasize the differences on disaster responses, where sometimes referred as Western-style disaster responses are not suitable for under-developed and developing countries, based on locations or countries and how one may not be able to understand the disaster based on media reports. This international perspective also focuses on cultural influences to understand disaster responses and mitigation (Mercer et.al., 2012) in various countries.

This research considers the following questions:

RQ1: How do different countries respond to natural disasters that occurred during the COVID-19 crisis?

RQ2: How do responses to natural disasters and COVID-19 overlap in different countries?

Methodology

Researchers identified four internationally covered disasters and then pulled articles from the search engine Newsbank in the weeks following each disaster. Articles included in the data set were pulled with search terms for the name of and location of the natural disasters indicated above. Duplicates were excluded. There were more than 1,180 articles in the total dataset. Because the goal was to observe 1–5 months of coverage, a longer time period was sometimes needed to gather a data set of at least 20 articles.

In addition, articles that were news roundups (contain news briefs), editorials or duplicates were excluded from the sample. News sources included the top four United States-based newspapers during that time (*USA Today, The Wall Street Journal, the New York Times, The Washington Post*), the top 5 Australian papers (*The Sydney Morning Herald, The Age, The Australian, the Herald Sun,* and *The Daily Telegraph*), and the top English papers in India (*The Times of India, Hindustan Times, Indian Express* and *The Telegraph*) for three weeks to four months following the four disasters. Researchers selected the fifth article when possible, although some articles were not long enough to analyze, so they moved to the next article that fit the criteria. They examined at least 20 articles, so for some disasters this meant a longer time period. Stories were included if they were long enough (more than 300 words) and had three or more sources referenced. Because the disasters were all different and written about in different publications, this criteria to provide consistency across the data.

After an initial read, researchers developed a list of potential themes. Then researchers independently coded articles for the themes and discussed how these findings were represented with each disaster to better understand them. The researchers then returned to the data to clarify these themes and how they demonstrated cross-coverage of COVID-19 and that disaster. After analysis, the researchers returned to discuss how these disasters were similar and different and how they might contribute to the idea of compounding crises.

Then the researchers coded different themes in the articles and identified the different sources quoted for each. The researchers came up with six different themes (other mentions concerning COVID-19). These included (1) Financial and Life Impact Factors—the cost, how many homes were destroyed, how many people died, lack of electricity and food, human trafficking; (2) Humanitarian—relocation, relief aid, support from others; (3) Cultural impacts—religion, economic station, education level and access to health care or other relief, economic industry, volunteerism; (4) Political—party politics, president and other factors, relief; (5) Environmental/Climate Concerns—previous disasters, clean up from debris; (6) Communication—misinformation, risk reduction, lack, tech issue. These different themes were then summarized and unpacked concerning each disaster and then across cases, for within and between case analyses.

- For the wildfires in Oregon/California, a total of 1104 articles were present during the time period selected for all the disasters; only 241 were written in the month following the onset of the wildfire and dealt specifically with the wildfires we identified (there were 12 different named wildfires in the region from March 2020 to September 2021). Of those articles, 30 were analyzed based on our study exclusion criteria.
- For Cyclone Amphan, there were 803 total in an initial search. Of those, 45 news articles were selected from four widely published newspapers in the two months after the cyclone hit June to August 2020. There were 45 total articles. Of these, 12 news articles reported COVID-19 and cyclone Amphan together, while 33 articles reported cyclone Amphan only. We analyzed 23 articles in this data set that fit our exclusion criteria.
- For the Australian brush fires, there were 200 articles collected from five different Australian newspapers. In order to gather enough data the researchers had to examine a longer time period between January 2, 2020 and May 31, 2020. For the purpose of this study only 20 articles met the criteria.
- For the Haiti Earthquake, in the three months following the disaster, 172 news articles discussed geological disasters. For this study, a total of 105 articles in the three weeks after the earthquake were used, and 35 were analyzed based on the study criteria.

Because of the large dataset, the number of articles and analysis for each natural disaster differed slightly, these are also included under each natural disaster in the findings sections.

Findings

Wildfires in California and Oregon

The 2021 summer wildfire season in California produced a lot of challenges for emergency responders and California, Oregon, and other Western states. Researchers analyzed 30 articles based on our study criteria. There was very little mention of COVID-19 in relation to the 2021 summer wildfire season.

Communication Factors

Getting information out about wildfires that stretch over thousands of miles is something the journalists struggle to contextualize well. Since most of these reports are from national and international news organizations, there are some challenges to getting local and regional context or sources. Also, there are several mentions of the internet and electricity being out.

> The fires erupted as the West was in the grip of the second bout of dangerously high temperatures in just a few weeks. A climate-change-driven megadrought is contributing to conditions that make fires even more dangerous, scientists say. (Brian Stieglitz For Dailymail.Com, 2021)

Political Factors

Several articles discussed the parties involved in response. These included firefighters and political representatives. Almost all articles included at least two sources from these groups. Often articles included a discussion of funding or responses that were not well funded, the costs of relocating people, or understaffing to put out fires.

Environmental Factors

Several references are made to the warming climate internationally discussing how temperatures have been rising internationally. These are normally included early in the stories or in quotes from scientific sources. Geography and topography are often discussed in these articles—discussing how desert, mountainous, and heavily forested regions are difficult to access and respond to. Also, that communication is difficult in these areas. As a result, often regions or states rather than towns are discussed—for example, the articles about these fires mention Oregon, California, Utah, and other outlying states that might be impacted by the fires spreading.

Financial and Life Impact Factors

As mentioned in the political factors themes, the discussion of a lack of money to respond to the wildfires is key. Public officials respond with information about long-term costs or impacts on smaller communities. Death counts are indicated in most of the articles, and those often discuss the inability of rural hospitals to respond given injuries from the fires.

Australian Brush Fires

The dataset for the Australian bushfires had fewer mentions of COVID-19 than compared to other disasters. There were 200 articles collected from five different Australian newspapers between January 2 and May 31, 2020. Only 20 articles met the criteria. That said, the analysis generated four themes, consistent with the other four cases.

Communication Factors

Miscommunication and misinformation were two major factors that contributed to this theme. There were four topics in this theme—arsonists arrested who were responsible for bushfires, mental health issues, domestic violence and climate change. Newspapers covered the Australian bushfires mostly through a cultural and environmental lens, social aspects were overshadowed with the onset of the COVID-19 pandemic. There were news articles that reflected mental health and domestic violence following social distancing rules.

> Australia's bushfires were started by arsonists. False. The latest coronavirus has been found in energy drinks. False. The disease is a bioweapon that escaped a lab. False. (The Sydney Morning Herald, February 12, 2020)

Political Factors

The political theme was the second largest theme developed in the content analysis of the newspapers. The theme had three major sub-themes—Prime Minister Scott Morrison greeted badly by locals affected by bushfires, the country closing its borders except for its citizens and permanent residents and Australia on head-to-head with China demanding an international investigation on the origin of COVID-19.

Environmental Factors

The other theme in this disaster category is environmental factors with the majority of newspapers reporting issues like climate change and impacts of fire on flora and fauna. The majority of news articles under this category were reported following a report carried out by the World Weather Attribution consortium, which suggested that 30% of Australian bushfires were contributed by climate change (Ghosh, 2020).

Financial and Life Impact Factors

The final theme under this category is financial and life impact factors. This theme has three sub-themes—recovery from the bushfires and COVID-19, foreigners stuck in bushfires affected areas and border closure following COVID-19 and effects on the economy following the COVID-19 pandemic and Australia's head-to-head with China over the virus COVID-19 origin investigation.

> Backpackers will be granted special visa benefits to help rebuild homes, fences and farms in bushfire-ravaged communities. (The Australian, February 16, 2020)

Cyclone Amphan

Our study examined 45 news articles related to Cyclone Amphan and COVID-19 were reviewed between June to August 2020. The content analysis of these articles found that 12 news articles reported COVID-19 and cyclone Amphan together, while 33 articles reported cyclone Amphan only. The content analysis of these news articles generated four major themes—financial and life impact factors, humanitarian factors, cultural impact factors and political impact factors—and 21 sub-themes.

Financial and Life Impact Factors

The newspaper articles ($n = 12$) under this theme have eight sub-themes: human and animal/bird casualties, insurance claims, human trafficking, financial hardships, effects of disaster and pandemic in child education, low employment rate, relief for the victims and public movement across the states for employment. Most articles reported negative effects of disaster and pandemic in employment opportunities and financial hardships.

> We have a home neither here nor there, but the money is better there. So what's the harm in going back? (*Hindustan Times*, July 3, 2020)
>
> [A worker's response when he was asked if he fears contracting COVID-19 when he goes to places looking for employment]

Humanitarian Factors

The newspaper articles under this theme ($n = 10$) have four sub-themes: people struggle to return to their home villages after lockdowns and lack of employment in big cities, support and pledges from people outside the disaster and pandemic area (outside India or cyclone affected region), relief packages, assurances, and promise from the prime minister and chief minister to remain calm and positive.

> Long queues at bus stands across the city and traffic choke points at some busy interactions marked the first day of Unlock 1.0 on Monday morning. (*Times of India*, June 2, 2020)
>
> [Public had to struggle to commute due to lack of private buses, metro and autos operating in full swing]

Cultural Impact Factors

There were four sub-themes ($n = 8$): economic impacts on society (i.e., men leaving their homes in search of jobs and leaving behind economically dependent families), education of children (children had to drop school to support their parents and local schools were affected by disaster, and parents could not afford school), and lastly people ditch buses for bicycles fearing contracting COVID-19 during their commute and access to healthcare/relief packages remains uneven among the population.

> After 25 years, Anindya Sundar Dutta has decided to ride a bicycle. He repaired his daughter's cycle that was lying at a corner of the house for three years so that he could reach his Theatre Road office from his Baguiati residence. (*Times of India*, June 2, 2020)

Political Impact Factors

The majority of newspapers covered the news stories surrounding political issues and its impacts. The articles in this category ($n = 15$) generated five sub-themes: political intervention on relief distribution, political parties recruiting cadres in the name of relief distribution volunteers, financial embezzling under political protection, inter-party cadres conflicts and opposition parties criticizing government's response to cyclone and COVID-19.

> Trinamul Congress's youth wing chief Abhishek Banerjee on Saturday urged 5.5 lakh youths, who registered in the Bangla'r Jubo Shokti (Bengal's Youth Power) initiative launched on June 11, to each take up 10 families in distress in the wake of Covid-19 and Cyclone Amphan and "take care" of them. (*The Telegraph*, July 19, 2020)

2021 Haiti Earthquake

For the 2021 earthquake, 35 articles were analyzed based on the study criteria. Articles reported that Haiti's health system was already fragile. When the "U.S. government donated 500,000 shots of the Moderna coronavirus vaccine through the Covax aid initiative—Haiti was the only country in the Americas that hadn't received a single vaccine dose" (Arnesen et al., August 17, 2021, *Washington Post*).

Communication Factors

Discussion of the difficulty to reach rural communities was mentioned in ($n = 20$) many articles. There were several mentions of the challenges of getting an accurate count of those who had passed away from the earthquake or COVID-19. Compounding factors related to damage done to the island nation's infrastructure in 2010 as well as other hurricanes and tropical storms. At least one of these factors was mentioned in all of the articles. Concerns for communication and access to resources included technology failure, although access to news was limited because the earthquake took place in a more rural region of Haiti than in 2010.

Political Factors

With the assassination of the Haitian President Jovenel Moïse not long before the earthquake a variety of narratives contextualize this as an added challenge. Of the articles half discussed challenges related to the assassination by name and the other half referenced political unrest. After Moïse died, several people stepped down or were asked to resign from the Haitian government. There were also several incidents of gang violence in response to his death.

> Martinor Gerardin, mayor of L'Asile, a town of 52,000 northeast of Les Cayes, said most homes there, too, were destroyed or severely damaged. He estimated that 50

residents had been killed and 500 injured. Scores of cows and goats in the rural community had been buried under rubble, he said, threatening the inhabitants' livelihoods.No aid from the government or nonprofit groups had arrived by Monday, he said. "We need tents and water urgently," he said. (Arnesen et al., *Washington Post*, August 17, 2021)

Environmental Factors

The fact that it was warm and hurricane season was a complicating factor for disaster and humanitarian responses. There are three articles that indicated U.S. military response or aid being sent by the United Kingdom and the Royal Family. A few articles mentioned groups present to help with long-term environmental effects. Climate change is mentioned in several *USA Today* articles as a contributing factor to the challenges Haiti faces, but mainly because of hurricanes becoming more intense and more common in frequency.

Discussion

COVID-19 was not covered in relation to natural disasters despite its pervasiveness in the communities experiencing disaster. Perhaps this is because journalists are being forced to consider multiple issues at the same time with limited resources? National and regional newspapers tended to prioritize coverage based on getting coverage to the riskiest crises first. When covering multiple crises journalists prioritizes the issues that require immediate action to preserve life and resources. Although political and longer-term economic concerns were mentioned, they were rarely the focal point for coverage. This is similar to how natural disasters have been covered in the past.

Comparisons

When looking at the themes (1) Financial and Life Impact Factors, (2) Humanitarian, (3) Cultural impacts, (4) Political, (5) Environmental/Climate Concerns, and (6) Communication across the different cases, the researchers determined there were a variety of productive but also problematic approaches to coverage. Emphasizing catastrophe over actionable approaches has been found to be counterproductive in crisis communication messaging, so when journalists neglect to emphasize connections to issues of local relevance this could become overwhelming for individuals in the midst of the cris(es).

Often journalists are mitigating which issue to give preference to, or address first, lacking the capacities for a synergistic approach (or one that can spread out coverage). Similarly the COVID-19 pandemic, which is an elongated crisis, became a footnote in stories about these disasters, similar to how broader connections to climate change have become. While science is still examining the direct relationships between COVID-19 and climate change, the connections between disasters and climate change are clear.

Natural disasters stretch resources and are made worse as a result of the effects of climate change—specifically, the intensity of changing weather patterns. Professional structures may also have an impact. The journalists who fly in to report on disasters may not have the same expertise as those who report on public health. In addition, the journalistic focus on timeliness makes an immediate crisis more salient, attention-getting, and appealing to audiences.

People perceive natural disasters and longer-term crises like climate change differently (Dey & Lewis, 2021). Journalism research also shows that writing about climate change or disasters can be challenging for journalists, but also difficult for policymakers and nonprofits given the complexities of science and the demands of the news cycle.

While the cases were unique in their impact, strategies for response, and recovery; took place in different regions, countries, and political systems; they provide a breadth of the experiences and potential challenges for long-term understanding of the complexities of disaster responses, reporting and competing and personalized narratives in news coverage. COVID-19 complicates reporting and crisis response in similar ways to how natural disasters do.

Regardless of the country, disasters challenge the resources of journalists and news organizations to adequately address two competing issues of conflict. In each of the five natural disaster situations, journalists default to the most pressing disaster or the most current concern, even with the elongated challenges of COVID-19 looming in the background. Similar to the findings in studies of organizational resource management in crisis (Viel & Anthony, 2017), news organizations must decide what to cover because of three factors: time, space, and audience attention (Benson, 2018). In addition, a number of the stories include personal stories or accounts, which have been found to provide more impact (Clementson, 2020; Seeger & Sellnow, 2016).

What we found the most interesting was the prioritization of the disaster over the elongated crisis of COVID-19 in most stories, regardless of the country in which they were reported.

Practical Applications

The practical application of this study is that expecting journalists to have the resources and knowledge to cover two issues may be unrealistic given the constraints of the news, but journalists can still address what they can in ways that provide better context when possible.

Government officials have an obligation to consider making these connections when possible and providing compelling and relevant data as well as actions people can take in a disaster or crisis. Those learning the field of crisis communication should consider the challenges of reporting on deadlines, 24/7 news cycles, and social media publishing about crisis situations. Clear, concise, and transparent information are useful tips for communicating clearly at any stage of a crisis.

Journalists should stick to the most pertinent facts that will allow audiences to respond quickly, update that information as it becomes available (Janetsky, 2020) and focus as much on the local as they can (Franklin et al., 2021). Given the observations from this study, we offer these four recommendations:

1. Connect with experts who can provide context at the time of the crisis, but also as the crisis becomes less new.
2. Crisis communicators should be prepared with statements and content and for a long-term relationship with journalists.
3. While deadline reporting is valuable, long-term coverage and analysis is more likely to empower communities to respond to crises. Journalists and communicators can directly change the public crisis narrative.
4. When there are multiple complex disasters and crises going on, communicators should provide direct information and make connections to ongoing efforts to address both crises in a tangible way.

Connections between natural disasters and climate change effects were articulated by several reporters. These stories lacked a focus on individual experiences, which have been found to make the public more aware of climate change. That said, while reporters for national and international news sources are reporting on these connections, only a few narratives addressed climate change and disaster impacts at the local level.

Discussion Questions

1. How do the disasters differ in scope and impact as far as coverage? What are some similarities between the narratives used to cover

different disasters in different countries? What is different? Why do you think this is?
2. How have political influences created certain narratives concerning these natural disasters?
3. Which disasters were more challenging to communicate given the constraints or challenges of the COVID-19 Pandemic?
4. How might different media models (government versus independent) play into the way news coverage of these disasters was reported?
5. How might the news coverage of these crises be similar to the news coverage of other political crises? What might be the long-term implications for crisis communication in these situations?

Resources

1. The United Nations Framework Convention on Climate Change: https://unfccc.int/sites/default/files/resource/Communicating%20climate%20change_Insights%20from%20CDKNs%20experience.pdf
2. Incident Information System, United States Forest Service: https://inciweb.nwcg.gov
3. Climate Communication Science and Outreach Website: https://climatecommunication.org/resources/
4. National Geographic Resources Library: https://www.nationalgeographic.org/activity/natural-disasters-and-climate-change/
5. 54 Great Resources on Climate Change News: https://onlinepublichealth.gwu.edu/resources/sources-for-climate-news/

References

Allan, S. (2013). *Citizen witnessing: Revisioning journalism in times of crisis.* John Wiley & Sons.
Appelgren, E., & Jönsson, A. M. (2021). Engaging citizens for climate change—challenges for journalism. *Digital Journalism,* 9(6), 755-772.
Austin, L., Fisher Liu, B., & Jin, Y. (2012). How audiences seek out crisis information: Exploring the social-mediated crisis communication model. *Journal of Applied Communication Research,* 40(2), 188–207. https://doi.org/10.1080/00909882.2012.654498
Associated Press. (2021, August 5). *The Dixie Fire has destroyed most of a historic northern California town.* National Public Radio. https://www.npr.org/2021/08/05/1025087402/the-dixie-fire-has-destroyed-most-of-a-historic-northern-california-town

Barnes, M.D., Hanson, C.L., Novilla, L.M., Meacham, A.T., McIntyre, E., & Erickson, B.C. (2008). Analysis of media agenda setting during and after Hurricane Katrina: Implications for emergency preparedness, disaster response, and disaster policy. *American Journal of Public Health*, 98(4), 604–610. https://doi.org/10.2105/AJPH.2007.112235

Barton, A.H. (1969). *Communities in disaster: A sociological analysis of collective stress situations* (1st ed.). Doubleday.

Beasely, D. (2021, August 2). Delta spreads "like wildfire" as doctors study whether it makes patients sicker. *Reuters*. https://www.reuters.com/business/healthcare-pharmaceuticals/delta-spreads-like-wildfire-doctors-study-whether-it-makes-patients-sicker-2021-08-02/

Benson, R. (2018). Can foundations solve the journalism crisis?. *Journalism*, 19(8), 1059–1077. https://doi.org/10.1177/1464884917724612

Boenker, K. (2012). *Communicating Global Climate Change: Framing Patterns in the US 24-Hour News Cycle, 2007-2009*. University of Washington.

Bowden, V., Nyberg, D., & Wright, C. (2021). "We're going under": The role of local news media in dislocating climate change adaptation. *Environmental Communication*, 15(5), 625–640. https://doi.org/10.1080/17524032.2021.1877762

Communications and Publishing, United States Geological Survey. (2021, August 16). *Featured story: Magnitude 7.2 earthquake in Haiti*. https://www.usgs.gov/news/featured-story/magnitude-72-earthquake-haiti

Clementson, D.E. (2020). Narrative persuasion, identification, attitudes, and trustworthiness in crisis communication. *Public Relations Review*, 46(2), Article 101889. https://doi.org/10.1016/j.pubrev.2020.101889

Dey, R., & Lewis, S.C. (2021). Natural disasters linked to climate change. In T.M. Letcher (Ed.), *The impacts of climate change: A comprehensive study of physical, biophysical, social, and political issues* (pp. 177–193). Elsevier.

Djalante, R., & Thomalla, F. (2012). Disaster risk reduction and climate change adaptation in Indonesia: Institutional challenges and opportunities for integration. *International Journal of Disaster Resilience in the Built Environment*, 3(2), 166–180. https://doi.org/10.1108/17595901211245260

Franklin, T., Abernathy, P.M., & Jacob, M. (2021, December 17). *How the local news crisis affects coverage of COVID-19 and the climate . . . and vice versa*. Poynter. https://www.poynter.org/reporting-editing/2021/how-the-local-news-crisis-affects-coverage-of-covid-19-and-the-climate-and-vice-versa/

Gilligan, H.T. (2021, September 14). *Hospitals in California's Central Valley flooded with COVID-19 patients*. California Health Care Foundation. https://www.chcf.org/blog/hospitals-central-valley-flooded-covid-19-patients/

Ghosh, P. (2020, June 4). *Climate change boosted Australia bushfire risk by at least 30%*. BBC. https://www.bbc.com/news/science-environment-51742646

Hale, J.E., Dulek, R.E., & Hale, D.P. (2005). Crisis response communication challenges: Building theory from qualitative data. *The Journal of Business Communication (1973)*, 42(2), 112–134. https://doi.org/10.1177/0021943605274751

Heath, R.L. (2006). Best practices in crisis communication: Evolution of practice through research. *Journal of Applied Communication Research*, 34(3), 245–248. https://doi.org/10.1080/00909880600771577

Houston, J.B., Pfefferbaum, B., & Rosenholtz, C.E. (2012). Disaster news: Framing and frame changing in coverage of major US natural disasters, 2000–2010. *Journalism & Mass Communication Quarterly, 89*(4), 606–623. https://doi.org/10.1177/1077699012456022

Houston, J.B., Hawthorne, J., Perreault, M.F., Park, E.H., Goldstein Hode, M., Halliwell, M.R., Turner McGowen, S.E., Davis, R., Vaid, S., McEldery, J.A., & Griffith, S.A., 2015. Social media and disasters: A functional framework for social media use in disaster planning, response, and research. *Disasters, 39*(1), 1–22. https://doi.org/10.1111/disa.12092

Hubbard, K. (2020, December 22). Here are 10 of the deadliest natural disasters in 2020: Storms, fires, earthquakes and other disasters claimed hundreds of lives around the world this year. *U.S. News and World Report*. https://www.usnews.com/news/best-countries/slideshows/here-are-10-of-the-deadliest-natural-disasters-in-2020

Incident Information System, United States Forest Service (2021a). *Bootleg Fire*. https://inciweb.nwcg.gov/incident/7609/

Incident Information System, United States Forest Service (2021b). *Dixie Fire (CA)*. https://inciweb.nwcg.gov/incident/7690/

Israelsen, S., & Malji, A. (2021). COVID-19 in India: A comparative analysis of the Kerala and Gujarat development models' initial responses. *Progress in Development Studies, 21*(4), 397–418. https://doi.org/10.1177/14649934211030462

Janetsky, M. (2020, August 17) *How the pandemic is throwing international reporting into crisis*. Poynter Center for Crisis Reporting. https://www.poynter.org/reporting-editing/2020/how-the-pandemic-is-throwing-international-reporting-into-crisis/

Jin, Y., Liu, B.F., & Austin, L.L. (2014). Examining the role of social media in effective crisis management: The effects of crisis origin, information form, and source on publics' crisis responses. *Communication Research, 41*(1), 74–94. https://doi.org/10.1177/0093650211423918

Jung, K., & Park, H.W. (2014). Citizens' social media use and homeland security information policy: Some evidence from Twitter users during the 2013 North Korea nuclear test. *Government Information Quarterly, 31*(4), 563–573. https://doi.org/10.1016/j.ijdrr.2019.101232

Kiesler, S., & Sproull, L. (1982). Managerial response to changing environments: Perspectives on problem sensing from social cognition. *Administrative science quarterly*, 548–570. https://doi.org/10.2307/2392530

The Lancet (2020). India under COVID-19 lockdown. *Lancet (London, England), 395*(10233), 1315. https://doi.org/10.1016/S0140-6736(20)30938-7

Liu, W. (2020). Disaster communication ecology in multiethnic communities: Understanding disaster coping and community resilience from a communication resource approach. *Journal of International and Intercultural Communication, 15*(1), 1–24. https://doi.org/10.1080/17513057.2020.1854329

Mackie, B. (2014). *Warning fatigue: Insights from the Australian bushfire context*. University of Canterbury. http://dx.doi.org/10.26021/4033

McGregor, J. (2002, July). Restating news values: Contemporary criteria for selecting the news. In *Proceedings of the ANZCA 2002 Conference, Coolangatta. Communication: Reconstructed for the 21st Century*.

Mercer, J., Gaillard, J.C., Crowley, K., Shannon, R., Alexander, B., Day, S., & Becker, J. (2012). Culture and disaster risk reduction: Lessons and opportunities. *Environmental Hazards*, 11(2), 74–95. https://doi.org/10.1080/17477891.2011.609876

Milfont, T. L., Evans, L., Sibley, C. G., Ries, J., & Cunningham, A. (2014). Proximity to coast is linked to climate change belief. *PLoS One*, 9(7), e103180.

Navarre, B. (2021, December 23). *10 of the deadliest natural disasters in 2021*. U.S. News. https://www.usnews.com/news/best-countries/slideshows/here-are-10-of-the-deadliest-natural-disasters-in-2021

Perreault, M. F., Houston, J. B., & Wilkins, L. (2014). Does scary matter?: Testing the effectiveness of new National Weather Service tornado warning messages. *Communication Studies*, 65(5), 484-499.

Perreault, M.F., & Perreault, G.P. (2021). Journalists on COVID-19 journalism: Communication ecology of pandemic reporting. *American Behavioral Scientist*, 65(7), 976–991. https://doi.org/10.1177/0002764221992813

Perreault, G., Perreault, M.F., & Maares, P. (2021). Metajournalistic discourse as a stabilizer within the journalistic field: Journalistic practice in the COVID-19 pandemic. *Journalism Practice*, 1–19. https://doi.org/10.1080/17512786.2021.1949630

Rahman, S.Y. (2020). "Social distancing" during COVID-19: The metaphors and politics of pandemic response in India. *Health Sociology Review*, 29(2), 131–139. https://doi.org/10.1080/14461242.2020.1790404

Reliefweb.int (2022, April 22). *2021 Disasters in numbers*. https://reliefweb.int/report/world/2021-disasters-numbers

Reinhart, C.M., & Rogoff, K.S. (2009). The aftermath of financial crises. *American Economic Review*, 99(2), 466–472. https://doi.org/10.1257/aer.99.2.466

Seeger, M.W. (2006). Best practices in crisis communication: An expert panel process. *Journal of Applied Communication Research*, 34(3), 232–244. https://doi.org/10.1080/00909880600769944

Seeger, M., & Sellnow, T.L. (2016). *Narratives of crisis: Telling stories of ruin and renewal*. Stanford University Press.

Scientific American. (2021). *Natural disasters*. https://www.scientificamerican.com/natural-disasters/

Spialek, M.L., Czlapinski, H.M., & Houston, J.B. (2016). Disaster communication ecology and community resilience perceptions following the 2013 Central Illinois tornadoes. *International Journal of Disaster Risk Reduction*, 17, 154–160. https://doi.org/10.1016/j.ijdrr.2016.04.006

Statista.com. (2022). *Countries with the most natural disasters in 2021*. https://www.statista.com/statistics/269652/countries-with-the-most-natural-disasters/

Stevenson, M., & Sanon, E. (2021, August 17). *Death toll from Haiti's weekend earthquake rises to 1941*. Associated Press. https://apnews.com/article/health-caribbean-coronavirus-pandemic-haiti-earthquakes-93ff6b258c62b6a3246a1dd1d6307799

Stoddart, M. C., & Smith, J. (2016). The endangered arctic, the arctic as resource frontier: Canadian news media narratives of climate change and the north. *Canadian Review of Sociology/Revue canadienne de sociologie*, 53(3), 316-336.

Sultana, F. (2021). Climate change, COVID-19, and the co-production of injustices: A feminist reading of overlapping crises. *Social & Cultural Geography, 22*(4), 447–460. https://doi.org/10.1080/14649365.2021.1910994

UNISDR. (2009). *2009 UNISDR terminology on disaster risk reduction*. United Nations International. https://www.undrr.org/publication/2009-unisdr-terminology-disaster-risk-reduction#:~:text=The%20UNISDR%20Terminology%20aims%20to,authorities%2C%20practitioners%20and%20the%20public

Veil, S.R., & Anthony, K.E. (2017). Exploring public relations challenges in compounding crises: The pariah effect of toxic trailers. *Journal of Public Relations Research, 29*(4), 141–157. https://doi.org/10.1080/1062726X.2017.1355805

Veil, S.R., Anthony, K.E., Sellnow, T.L., Staricek, N., Young, L.E., & Cupp, P. (2020). Revisiting the best practices in risk and crisis communication: A multi-case analysis. In H.D. O'Hair & M.J. O'Hair (Eds.), *The handbook of applied communication research*, pp. 377–396. https://doi.org/10.1002/9781119399926.ch23

Veil, S.R., & Husted, R.A. (2012). Best practices as an assessment for crisis communication. *Journal of Communication Management, 16*(2), 1–32. https://www.emerald.com/insight/content/doi/10.1108/13632541211217560/full/html?casa_token=v39nJC2ssZUAAAAA:pFbxqixVRnEzKDPQD5gfdI29NUxERt335FYfHMqlW8AwZEDMCSEPL8SitMXBR-vNjiuMF3cEuuadzVT5l3RJOa1m5ndriLI4WxmAE4TJXXzCaK7gdrHe

Veil, S.R., & Ojeda, F. (2010). Establishing media partnerships in crisis response. *Communication Studies, 60*(4), 412–429. https://doi.org/10.1080/10510974.2010.491336

Woodall, M. (2021, October 4). *What we're watching: Weekly disaster update*. Center for Disaster Philanthropy. https://disasterphilanthropy.org/blog/other/what-were-watching-weekly-disaster-update/

World Bank. (2021). *Disaster risk management overview*. https://www.worldbank.org/en/topic/disasterriskmanagement/overview#1

Wukich, C. (2016). Government social media messages across disaster phases. *Journal of Contingencies and Crisis Management, 24*(4), 230–243. https://doi.org/10.1111/1468-5973.12119

· 17 ·

COMMUNICATING ABOUT COVID-19 AND BLACK LIVES MATTER: A CASE STUDY OF MEMES, TWITTER & REDDIT

Mia Moody-Ramirez

Protests are beautiful and incredibly important, but you can't just keep having protests forever, you actually have to have change.

—Tzipporah Goins, Black Lives Matter protest leader

During the early days of the COVID-19 pandemic, social media feeds were flooded with messages containing misinformation about where the virus originated, how it spread and who would die from it. For example, one common myth about the disease was Black people would be *less* susceptible because of their darker skin. One Facebook post in 2019 read, "People of Color May Be Immune to the Coronavirus Because of Melanin." Facebook would later flag it as false as part of the site's effort to combat fake news and misinformation (PolitiFact, 2021). Data from the CDC revealed evidence to the contrary, as the death rates of Black people would prove much higher than their White counterparts (Reeves et al., 2020). The cause of higher infection rates in the racial group would later be attributed to occupations, inability to social distance, and geographical locations.

In 2021, two years after the COVID-19 pandemic began, Americans still navigated the myths and misinformation communicated in messages associated with the virus. The idea that levels of immunity varied based on race was just one of the controversies associated with the virus (Yearby & Mohapatra, 2020). The Black Lives Matter (BLM) movement shifted from spotlighting police brutality to systemic racism, as headlines about health disparities and concerns about COVID-19 overtook those about police brutality (Mirzoeff, 2011). The COVID-19 pandemic, in fact, amplified the ordinary inequalities between Brown, Black, and White communities, such as unemployment, healthcare, and education. In most instances, Black and impoverished communities were often hit hardest. Social media users noticed. In 2020, Twitter (X) disclosed the most-used hashtag on the site was #COVID19, or variations of it, being retweeted some 400 million times. The second-most popular hashtag in the world was #BlackLivesMatter. The name of the third most tweeted person in the world was George Floyd ("Twitter trends 2020," 2020). Floyd's death was different because it was caught on camera, which produced a deeper connection with people. In addition, the pandemic offered a captive audience during which people were at home and more likely to pay attention to social injustices.

To explore the communication that arose after Floyd's death, this chapter explores how the pandemic helped America examine society's deeply rooted structural health inequities and systemic racism issues. First, it highlights the history and changing narratives of the BLM movement; then it examines the messages that emerged in memes, Twitter, and Reddit posts during the COVID-19 pandemic.

Black Lives Matter Movement

Social media platforms popularized the #BlackLivesMatter movement, which Patrisse Cullors, Opal Tometi, and Alicia Garza founded in July of 2013. According to the organization's website, its mission is to eradicate White supremacy and build local power to intervene in violence inflicted on Black communities by the state and vigilantes. Inclusive of other marginalized groups, such as members of the LGBT community, Black lives are at the forefront of its concerns because of the injustices inflicted on the group due to police brutality and racial profiling. The phrase "Black Lives Matter" debuted in a Facebook post shared by Alicia Garza in response to the acquittal of George Zimmerman (Edrington & Gallagher, 2019).

During 2019–2021, Americans lived in the middle of two crises—a racial reckoning and the COVID-19 pandemic. Black people were 3.5 times more likely than their White counterparts to be killed by a police officer in the

United States (Ray, 2020). Being killed by the police was a leading cause of death for Black men in America (Merelli, 2020).

Photos of police killings captured on cell-phone video clips or photographs and the protests that resulted became one defining feature of the BLM movement (Mirzeoff, 2011). The intensity of the Black Lives Matter movement continued to evolve in 2019 at the onset of the COVID-19 pandemic. In 2020, with the COVID-19 pandemic as a backdrop, the Black Lives Matter movement gained momentum. A tipping point occurred on May 25, 2020, when White police officers murdered George Floyd by placing his knee on his neck for almost nine minutes while Floyd, who allegedly used a counterfeit $20 bill, was in handcuffs. Panda et al. (2020) noted that although police brutality and COVID-19 are separate social-political issues, they intersect. As with police brutality deaths, the COVID-19 death rate was higher among Black people than in the United States population overall. From inadequate healthcare to a disproportionate share of frontline essential workers, the U.S. Black population was impacted.

In the modest research on the COVID-19 pandemic, Hart et al. (2020) concluded: "Americans have been divided in their perceptions of the government response, confidence in scientists, and support for protective actions" (p. 680). In another study, Panda et al. (2020) examined the polarization of U.S. politicians on Twitter. They found that Democrats frame the issue in terms of public health and police brutality, while Republicans are more likely to focus on small businesses and the economy, while criticizing perceived protest violence. The researchers also noted a few Democratic politicians connected George Floyd's murder to police brutality, and the killings of Breonna Taylor and Ahmaud Arbery, suggesting a recognition of larger social patterns at play. In contrast, while some Republicans addressed George Floyd's death, condemning it and calling for justice, there is little discussion of systemic problems with policing.

Yearby (2020) concluded racial and ethnic disparities are being replicated in COVID-19 infections and death rates. For example, African Americans make up just 12% of the population in Washtenaw County, Michigan, but suffered 46% of COVID-19 infections. In an article on the COVID-19 pandemic and how it impacted Black people, Yearby (2020) notes three distinct levels of racism: institutional, interpersonal, and structural. The article includes statistics indicating African Americans accounted for higher rates of COVID-19–related deaths in Milwaukee, Wisconsin, and Louisiana. Higher death rates are a result of historical and current practices of racism that cause disparities in exposure, susceptibility, and treatment.

A primary goal of Critical Race Theory (CRT) is to re-center inquiry and experience from a marginalized perspective. Legal scholars Derrick Bell (1992), Kimberlé Crenshaw (1995) and Richard Delgado and Jean Stefancic (2017) among other scholars, studied race, racism, and power and placed them in a broader context to include economics, history, and other factors.

In their recommendations for future research, Mills and Unsworth (2018) asserted that critical race approaches need to critique the production of digital texts and to evaluate the potential of techno-cultures for racial justice. They add that visual representations of race online have the potential to tell scholars how race is represented. The two ask scholars to inquire about who controls access to digital texts, and to examine how this control is either protected as White property—or extended to all races. Orbe and Allen (2008) encouraged communication scholars to consider the problem of dichotomization of race that is not resolved by simply including the research about neglected racialized groups.

Research Questions

Based on this review of the literature and suggestions from other scholars, this chapter addresses two research questions:

RQ1: What themes emerge in tweets, memes, and Reddit posts that emphasize BLM and COVID-19?

As with many ideas that are controversial, social media platforms were instrumental in fueling grassroots efforts regarding the COVID-19 pandemic and the Black Lives Matter movement.

RQ2: What are the implications for Critical Race Theory?

Critical Race Theory is relevant to the Black Lives Matter Movement and the COVID-19 pandemic, as Black people have been shown to be significantly more likely to be impacted by them both. An outgrowth of the civil rights movement, CRT advances an understanding of law as deeply connected to lived experiences and social power—particularly for marginalized groups.

Public opinion is influenced by mass media cultural narratives. There is a strong relationship between White people's perceptions of Black people and their judgments of crime and punishment (Hurwitz & Peffley, 2010). Mina found memes can amplify concerns about the "harmful encroachment of the state into aspects of daily life" (2019, p. 2) in their study of #Ferguson, #BlackLivesMatter, and Hong Kong's #UmbrellaRevolution protests.

Scholars must continue to examine representations on new media platforms to establish a baseline for stereotypes of marginalized groups.

Twitter, memes, and Reddit are important platforms for disseminating messages about race and social inequities. They will help extend the literature on this topic.

Methodology

A qualitative content analysis of the messages communicated in memes, on Twitter, and Reddit served as the means of analysis for this study. Individuals acted as gatekeepers, or interpreters of politically charged topics by selectively choosing to cover one or both sides of an issue—often putting forth their own interpretation, or by highlighting one issue over another.

I used the keywords "BLM" and "COVID-19" to gather three types of data: (1) tweets, (2) memes and (3) Reddit posts during the pandemic and after Floyd's death. The search returned 52 tweets, highlighted because of their popularity in the news and frequent retweets. Similarly, I used the same keywords to collect Reddit posts and memes. The search returned 18 Reddit posts and 24 memes.

The rationale for using memes and social media is that content creators/citizen journalists foster internal story patterns for readers that frame public debate and influence readers in decision-making. Memes and social media platforms, such as Twitter and Reddit, are updated regularly with content from everyday individuals.

The interactive nature of social media offers individuals the opportunity to receive information on a topic—in this case the COVID-19 pandemic—in real time. According to a 2021 Pew study, YouTube and Facebook continue to dominate the online landscape, with adults saying they use them at the rate of 81% and 69%. YouTube and Reddit were the only two platforms that experienced a statistically significant growth since 2019 (Auxier & Anderson, 2021). About 84% of adults aged 18–29 said they use any social media sites, which is like the share of those ages 30–49 who say they use them (81%). Reddit, a social news website and forum whose site's name is a play on the words "I read it," was the only other platform polled that experienced statistically significant growth during this period—increasing from 11% in

2019 to 18%. Reddit is free, but registration is required to use the website's basic features.

Individuals create memes using a digital photo, cartoon, or stock image, adding text and reposting it. Media scholars have analyzed memes from various perspectives, including defining and identifying the role memetic texts play in influencing politics, protests, and online conversations (i.e., Dawkins, 2006; Hristova, 2014).

COVID-19 and Twitter

An analysis of the tweets in my sample revealed five distinctive groups of underlying themes: politics, racism, medical, economics, and immigration (Table 17.1). The intensity and perception of the movement continued to evolve in 2020 at the onset of the COVID-19 pandemic. The pandemic was more than a health concern. It was a politically divisive issue that featured prominently in the 2020 presidential campaign and continues to separate the right and left wings of American politics, as citizens expressed their political identifications through pandemic-related behaviors like mask-wearing.

Table 17.1. Themes in Tweets Containing COVID-19 and Black Lives Matter

Politics: What were the conflicting themes in political messages, Germ warfare—bio war, Christmas gift from foreign leadership issues, president's briefings
Racism/Xenophobia: Were there elevated death rates of certain groups and populations, melanin resistant, Wuhan market, intolerance, hate crimes against Asians
Medical: Race, Asthma related, malaria medication, shortage of medical equipment, Hotspots: nursing homes, hospitals, cruises, beaches, conferences, New York, New Orleans, and California
Economics: Lagging economy, interest rate, Stock market crash
Immigration: Not allowing passengers to enter United States from certain countries and vice versa
Racism/Xenophobia: Were there elevated death rates of certain groups and populations, melanin resistant, Wuhan market, intolerance, hate crimes against Asians
Medical: Race, Asthma related, malaria medication, shortage of medical equipment, Hotspots: nursing homes, hospitals, cruises, beaches, conferences, New York, New Orleans, and California
Economics: Lagging economy, interest rate, Stock market crash
Immigration: Not allowing passengers to enter United States from certain countries and vice versa

While the BLM protests intensified over the summer of 2020, Pew researchers found that support for the movement among U.S. adults declined from 67% supporting the protests in June 2020 to about 55% in September 2020. The decline was based on how individuals depicted the movement and whether they focused on protests, conspiracy theories and the idea that BLM supports violence.

In general, the top tweets framed the Black Lives Matter movement and COVID-19 negatively. Posts included the idea BLM wants to abolish capitalism & vaccine passports and the COVID-19 pandemic ignited the spread of expressions of intolerance, exclusion, and hate. Politically themed posts emphasized Former President Donald Trump's statements about Floyd's death in tweets. He described New York City painting the BLM rallying cry on Fifth Avenue a "symbol of hate" (Cohen, 2020, para. 1). In another tweet, Trump said, "I feel very, very badly" about George Floyd's death while handcuffed and in the custody of Minneapolis police. "That's a very shocking sight."

The former president's language got more negative as violence ensued in Minneapolis BLM rallies. "These THUGS are dishonoring the memory of George Floyd, and I won't let that happen," he tweeted. "Just spoke to Governor Tim Walz and told him that the Military is with him all the way. Any difficulty and we will assume control but, when the looting starts, the shooting starts. Thank you."

The Guardian, on May 29, 2020, stated Twitter (X) hid the tweet behind a warning that it "glorifies violence." Two hours later, Twitter (X) added a notice to the tweet: "This tweet violated the Twitter Rules about glorifying violence. However, Twitter has determined that it may be in the public's interest for the tweet to remain accessible." The warning was accompanied by a link to its policies about public interest exceptions. A political-themed tweet focused on the idea that Republicans, Trump in particular, were responsible for the pandemic.

Tweets also depicted President Joe Biden as not doing enough. One tweet stated: "Remember Biden wanted to keep children segregated in schools, & in general. Sucked as a senator. Worst President ever. He wants to give illegal immigrants a half mil just cuz. What about BLM? They don't get it first. Wow, how rude. Also wants to open camps like Australia for COVID-19." Another stated, "God. No. You're a joke. You support BLM but cut housing subsidies. You executed bizarre COVID-19 policies like indoor masking for everyone unless in a bar or restaurant. Not to mention you're corrupt, how many of your admin including you have been investigated."

Tweets linked to articles that discussed how "the outbreak, the virus has exploited and worsened inequalities in the United States. CDC figures, when adjusted for age and population, show that Black, Latino and Native American people are two to three times more likely than whites to die of COVID-19."

Sample tweets that mentioned COVID-19 and race include: "What a missed opportunity—if COVID-19 had been named 'antifa' or 'BLM' it would have been immediately eradicated in the US." and "The deadliest disease is not COVID-19, it's racism." "'Science tells us that humanity started in Africa. We are all shades of black.' @CrystalREmery #racism #BlackLivesMatter #racisme," and also "I've said many times being in a constant state of fear and anger causes the body defenses to breakdown & how convenient was it that Covid-19 & all those racial brutal police injustices became known in the same year. [eyeroll emoji]."

COVID-19 and Protests

Many Twitter (X) users speculated that people would die after participating in BLM rallies. One article stated, "Black Lives Matter protests haven't led to COVID-19 spikes. It may be due to people staying home." However, it was also noted that protestors wore masks and were in an outdoor setting where the virus doesn't typically spread. A study published by the National Bureau of Economic Research found that as the protests grew, many people opted to stay home and avoid going out.

Themes in Memes

Previous studies provide an indication that memes are an effective means to communicate persuasive messages (Shifman, 2013). Researchers have studied them from various perspectives including the role they play in influencing political protests and other forms of online conversations (i.e., Dawkins, 1992; Hristova, 2014). Previous studies indicate memes have the power to change public opinion (Hristova, 2014; Harlow, 2013).

In this case study, individuals used memes to communicate messages about the pandemic and the Black Lives Matter movement in a humorous manner.

There was much less variation in memes that contained the terms BLM and COVID-19. The three main themes that surfaced were protest, racism/xenophobia, and blackface. Most of the memes in my sample focused on

Table 17.2. Themes in Memes Containing COVID-19 and Black Lives Matter

Protest: Individuals are going to get sick attending BLM rallies
Racism/Xenophobia: Were there elevated death rates of certain groups and populations, melanin resistant, Wuhan market, intolerance, hate crimes against Asians
Blackface: A connection to blackface and use of face masks for protection

protests and the idea that BLM protests might lead to a spike in COVID-19 infection rates, as seen in Table 17.2.

Some memes focused on a blackface theme that featured White people wearing black or brown medical masks with various captions regarding BLM and the pandemic. Other memes focused on racism and xenophobia and the idea people used the pandemic as an excuse to discriminate against marginalized groups.

Themes in Reddit Content

Reddit content is socially curated and promoted by site members through voting. Reddit is composed of subcommunities, known as subreddits, which have a specific topic—in this case, COVID-19 and BLM. Reddit posts were fewer in number and far less likely to focus on a diversity of topics. Posts focused on the likelihood that protests would cause a spike in COVID-19 infection rates (Table 17. 3). Another group of posts focused on the vaccination debate and if individuals should be forced to get vaccinated. Posts in this category highlighted the idea that marchers would be part of a group forced to get vaccinated.

Conclusion

After George Floyd's death, activists advocated for policies during the pandemic that would empower individuals who live in over-policed communities.

Table 17.3. Themes in Reddit Posts Containing COVID-19 and Black Lives Matter

Protest: Individuals are going to get sick attending BLM rallies
Just the facts: News reports
Vaccines: The vaccination debate

They examined defunding the institution of law enforcement, identifying how police abuse resources, and reallocating funds back into communities. Americans began weeding out racist symbols in American culture: Major companies began rebranding their products perceived as racist. Confederate statues were removed, and police departments reconsidered how they operate.

Social media content provided a space for groups to network, support one another and express concerns about current issues (Bock & Figueroa, 2018). As with many ideas that are controversial, COVID-19 sparked a multitude of discussions and debates among people on the opposite side of various political spectrums.

BLM protest efforts were likened to the Civil Rights movement of the 1950s and 1960s. In general, the top tweets depicted the Black Lives Matter Movement and the COVID-19 pandemic negatively. While memes and Reddit posts focused on news items, the virus in general and the safety of protestors, tweets were multifaceted and more likely to focus on the many themes faced by members of the Black community. Tweets mentioned class struggle and systemic racism in the context of BLM and COVID-19. Other tweets stated that the revival of the #BlackLivesMatter movement amid the pandemic has shown the need for new ways of addressing racism. Individuals focused on protests, conspiracy theories and the idea that BLM supporters advocate for violence. The tweets that emphasized COVID-19 and BLM often characterized the movement as violent, racist, and Black people as thugs. Study findings highlight the importance of using CRT to expand beyond race, racism, and power to also examine the economics, history, and cultural context of issues when examining social and political issues.

Much of the 2021 debate around CRT was inspired by social movements such as BLM. The idea that CRT may expose students to damaging or racist ideas that might damage their self-esteem fueled the debate when CRT grew more contentious in 2021. Legislatures across the country advocated limiting what public school teachers may teach regarding the nation's historical treatment of people of color.

This study is important because it offers a look at how individuals used three platform types with different messages regarding the COVID-19 pandemic. It continues the vein of research on how individuals used social media platforms to disseminate messages during the twenty-first century. As with newspaper headlines, memes, Twitter (X), and Reddit posts include words or phrases that frame information in a way that may influence readers to take action.

Social media content influences public opinion. Individuals who engage in sharing content on social media seek to criticize or support a viewpoint. Individuals used social media posts and memes during the pandemic to share persuasive messages about the BLM movement. In this case, memes, Twitter (X), and Reddit posts provided a snapshot of how Americans felt about the BLM movement during the pandemic.

Practical Application: COVID-19, BLM Meme Exercise

Read

1. Shifman, L. (2013). Memes in a digital world: Reconciling with a conceptual troublemaker. *Journal of Computer-Mediated Communication, 18*(3), 362–377. https://doi.org/10.1111/jcc4.12013
2. Twitter trends 2020: COVID and BlackLivesMatter dominate: https://www.dw.com/en/twitter-trends-2020-covid-and-blacklivesmatter-dominate/a-55859738

Find

1. Find an example of a meme online that illustrates a topic related to BLM and COVID-19 pandemic. Share this meme with peers in class and discuss why you chose it.

Create

1. Create your own meme illustrating an issue relating to COVID-19 and the Black Lives Matter movement. Use any online meme generator (i.e., https://meme-generator.com/). Be prepared to discuss why you chose a certain microaggression for discussion.

References

Auxier, B., & Anderson, M. (2021). *Social media use in 2021.* Pew Research Center, 1, 1–4.

Bell, D. (1992). *Faces at the bottom of the well: The permanence of racism.* Hachette UK.

Bock, E., & Figueroa, E. (2018). Faith and reason: An analysis of the homologies of Black and Blue Lives Facebook pages. *New Media and Society, 20*(9), 3097–3118. https://doi.org/10.1177/1461444817740822

Cohen, M. (2020, July 1). Trump: Black Lives Matter is a "symbol of hate." *Politico*. https://www.politico.com/news/2020/07/01/trump-black-lives-matter-347051

Dawkins, R. (2006). *The selfish gene* (30th anniversary ed.). Oxford; Oxford University Press. Print

Delgado, R., & Stefancic, J. (2017). *Critical race theory (third edition): An introduction*. New York University Press.

Edrington, C., & Gallagher, V. (2019). Race and visibility: How and why visual images of Black Lives Matter. *Visual Communication Quarterly, 26*(4), 195–207. https://doi.org/10.1080/15551393.2019.1679635

Harlow, S. (2013). Fue Una "Revolución de Facebook": Explorando La Narrativa de Los Meme Difundidos Durante Las Protestas Egipcias [It was a "Facebook revolution": Exploring the meme-like spread of narratives during the Egyptian protests]. *Revista De Comunicación, 12*(1), 59–82. https://revistadecomunicacion.com/article/view/2731

Harris, C. I. (1995). Whiteness as Property. In Crenshaw, K., Gotanda, N., & Peller, G. (Eds.). (1995). *Critical race theory: The key writings that formed the movement*. The New Press. https://www.google.com/books/edition/Critical_Race_Theory/lLXTyrlM59MC?hl=en&gbpv=1&dq=Crenshaw+Critical+race+theory.+The+key+writings+that+formed+the+movement+&pg=PR11&printsec=frontcover

Hart, P.S., Chinn, S., & Soroka, S. (2020). Politicization and polarization in COVID-19 news coverage. *Science Communication, 42*(5), 679–697. https://doi.org/10.1177/1075547020950735

Hristova, S. (2014). Visual memes as neutralizers of political dissent. *TripleC: Journal for a Global Sustainable Information Society, 12*(1), 265–276. https://doi.org/10.31269/triplec.v12i1.507

Hurwitz, J., & Peffley, M. (2010). And justice for some: Race, crime, and punishment in the U.S. criminal justice system. *Canadian Journal of Political Science, 43*(2), 457–479. https://doi.org/10.1017/S0008423910000120

Merelli, A. (2020). *Black people are at the center of two public health crises in the US: Covid-19 and police brutality*. Quartz. https://qz.com/1862403/black-people-are-at-thecenter-of-two-public-health-crises-in-the-us-covid-19-and-police-brutality/2

Mills, K., & Unsworth, L. (2018). The multimodal construction of race: A review of critical race theory research. *Language & Education: An International Journal, 32*(4), 313–332. https://doi-org.ezproxy.baylor.edu/10.1080/09500782.2018.1434787

Mina, A. (2019). *Memes to movements: How the world's most viral media is changing social protest and power*. Beacon Press.

Mirzoeff. (2011). *The right to look: A counterhistory of visuality*. Duke University Press.

Orbe, M., & Allen, B. (2008). "Race Matters" in the Journal of Applied Communication Research. *Howard Journal of Communications, 19*(3). 201–220. https://doi.org/10.1080/10646170802218115

Panda, A., Siddarth, D. & Pal, J. (2020) *COVID, BLM, and the polarization of US politicians on Twitter*. ArXiv. https://arxiv.org/pdf/2008.03263.pdf.

Pew Research Center. (2021). *More than half of national legislators in the UK tweeted about George Floyd or "Black Lives Matter" in the weeks after Floyd's Death in Minneapolis*. https://www.pewresearch.org/wp-content/uploads/2020/08/ft_2020.08.04_blmlegislators_01.png

Ray, R. (2020, May 30). *Bad apples come from rotten trees in policing.* Brookings. https://www.brookings.edu/blog/up-front/2020/05/30/bad-apples-come-from-rotten-trees-inpolicing/

Reeves, T., Ford, S., & Richard, V. (2020, June 16). *Race gaps in COVID-19 deaths are even bigger than they appear.* Brookings. https://www.brookings.edu/blog/up-front/2020/06/16/race-gaps-in-covid-19-deaths-are-even-bigger-than-they-appear/

Shifman, L. (2013). Memes in a digital world: Reconciling with a conceptual troublemaker. *Journal of Computer-Mediated Communication, 18*(3), 362–377. https://doi.org/10.1111/jcc4.12013

witter trends 2020: COVID and BlackLivesMatter dominate. https://www.dw.com/en/twitter-trends-2020-covid-and-blacklivesmatter-dominate/a-55859738

Yearby, R. (2020). Structural racism and health disparities: Reconfiguring the social determinants of health framework to include the root cause. *Journal of Law, Medicine & Ethics, 48*(3), 518–526.

Yearby, R., & Mohapatra, S. (2020). Law, structural racism, and the COVID-19 pandemic. *Journal of Law and the Biosciences, 7*(1), 1–20. https://doi.org/10.1093/jlb/lsaa036

· 18 ·

CALLING COVID-19 THE "CHINESE VIRUS": WHAT TYPES OF #CHINESEVIRUS MESSAGES GET ATTENTION ON FACEBOOK PAGES?

Juan Liu

> *Disease names really do matter to the people who are directly affected. We've seen certain disease names provoke a backlash against members of particular religious or ethnic communities . . .*
> —Dr. Keiji Fukuda, Assistant Director General for Health Security, the World Health Organization (WHO), 2015

At a news briefing on March 18 2020, when asked by a reporter about a White House official repeatedly using the term "Kung flu" and whether calling it a "Chinese virus" endangered Asian Americans, President Trump said, "[I]t's not racist at all. It comes from China, that's why." Since the coronavirus pandemic started appearing in the United States in January of 2020, Asian Americans have shared stories of minor aggression to blatant attacks from people blaming them for the pandemic. Here are some attacks reported by news media (BBC, 2021):

- An 84-year-old Thai immigrant in San Francisco, California, died in February of 2021 after being violently shoved to the ground during his morning walk.

- An 89-year-old Chinese woman was slapped and set on fire by two people in Brooklyn, New York.
- Two Asian American women were stabbed at a San Francisco bus stop.
- In Los Angeles, a 16-year-old boy of Asian descent said other students had bullied him and accused him of carrying the virus.

Throughout U.S. history, pandemics and epidemics have bred misinformation, fear, anxiety, and scapegoating, ultimately leading to a surge in racial and ethnic discrimination. The COVID-19 pandemic is no exception. As the coronavirus spreads, an accompanying pandemic of xenophobia, fear, and scapegoating have negatively affected individuals from marginalized backgrounds (Kantamneni, 2020; Shah, 2020). The Centers for Disease Control and Prevention (2020) warned linking COVID-19 with certain groups can lead to social stigma, which results in negative consequences including labeling, stereotyping, and discrimination. Upwards of 80,000 tweets containing "#ChineseVirus" reflect the ease with which racist slurs can be communicated online (Croucher et al., 2020).

Politicians' deliberate use of stigma-related terms encouraged racism against Asian communities. Despite guidance from the WHO and the rise of hate crimes, the Trump Administration has frequently referred to COVID-19 as "Chinese virus," "Wuhan virus," or "Kung Flu" (Riechmann & Tang, 2020). Anxiety and fear about the coronavirus have been widespread, and racist incidents, including hate crimes and Asian-focused racism, frequently occurred, particularly in the United States (Kandil, 2020). By June 2021, more than 9,000 anti-Asian attacks have been reported (Associated Press, 2021). The nonprofit organization, Stop AAPI Hate (2021) warned that even the large spike in anti-Asian hate crimes may represent a fraction of the incidents that have occurred. A recent survey from the Pew Research Center suggested that 45% of Asian adults have experienced at least one incident since the pandemic (Ruiz et al., 2021). The Asian population as the fastest-growing racial group in the United States (Yam & Venkatraman, 2021) becomes the target of blame, discrimination, harassment, racism, and hateful attacks. On March 16, 2021, a shooting spree happened at three spas in Atlanta, and the suspect, Robert Aaron Long, killed eight people. Six of the victims were women of Asian descent (Chappell & Jones, 2021). However, the suspect was not accused of a hate crime, though it occurred amid a spike in anti-Asian violence.

Phrases such as "Wuhan virus," "Chinese Virus" and "China Virus" have been prevalent among influential politicians, social media users, and mass media to refer to SARS-CoV-2 that caused the COVID-19 pandemic (Darling-Hammond et al., 2020; Rovetta & Bhagavathula, 2020). Referring to the novel coronavirus as "Chinese Virus" or "China Virus" has the potential to stigmatize and blame Asians for the spread of COVID-19 (Cho et al., 2021; Croucher et al., 2020; Ozturk, 2021). Against this backdrop and based upon attribution theory and fairness theory, this study examined how racist hashtags (e.g., #ChineseVirus, #ChinaVirus) have been used on Facebook pages and what types of #ChineseVirus messages get the most attention and engagement. In this research, content analysis was used to analyze the social media discourse with racist hashtags (e.g., #ChineseVirus). The present study provides policy suggestions for social media platforms to intervene and combat the rising racism and xenophobia.

Anti-Asian Hashtags and Racism Spiked Along With Coronavirus

Social media acting as a civic forum facilitated national conversations about key political and social issues. People often use hashtags to express agreement and solidarity. For instance, in the aftermath of the death of George Floyd, the #BlackLivesMatter has surged and went viral on Twitter (X) (Anderson et al., 2020). Researchers also examined hashtags on social media to identify the association between the use of racist hashtags and hate crimes targeting minority groups. Müller and Schwarz (2020) found that Trump's anti-Muslim tweets containing the hashtags "#StopIslam" and "#BanIslam" led to waves of anti-Muslim sentiment and predicted the frequency of hate crimes.

With the advent of social media, the rise of misinformation, conspiracy theory, and stereotyping has contributed to the spread of xenophobia. The "echo chambers" on social media, in which people tend to distribute inaccurate and racist messages with others who were subject to existing prejudice against various groups, likely perpetuated their racist attitudes (Criss et al., 2020). Social media has become a tool to either discriminate against Asian communities or to fight against prejudice (Croucher et al., 2020). Former President Donald Trump posting a tweet using the phrase "Chinese Virus" helped spark anti-Asian Twitter (X) content (Reja, 2021; Yam, 2020). For instance, Hswen and colleagues (2021) examined whether tweets with #covid19 and #chinesevirus will differ in terms of anti-Asian sentiment. Their analysis suggested the hashtag #chinesevirus was related to more than twice as many hate expressions compared with #covid19 and anti-Asian hashtags rose particularly after Trump calling coronavirus as "Chinese Virus" (Hswen et al., 2021). Similarly, comparing the prevalence of "Chinese virus" tweets before and after the presidential reference, Budhwani and Sun (2020) suggested there was a substantial increase of stigmatizing tweets referring to coronavirus as the "Chinese virus." Trump was identified as the most prominent influencer in the #Chinavirus and #Chinesevirus Twitter (X) network (Chong & Chen, 2021). By analyzing the tweets containing hashtags (e.g., #chinavirus) relevant to anti-Asian hate and COVID-19, Ziems et al. (2020) observed a spike of hate trend between March 16 and March 19, a time when former President Trump attempted to shift blame for the spread of coronavirus to China. When a user sends his or her first hate tweet against Asians, hateful users then become more vocal, engaged, and vicious by participating in the discourse (Ziems et al., 2020).

Social media platforms facilitate public expressions of racism and xenophobia (Depoux et al., 2020), and hate speech is contagious on social media (Velásquez et al., 2020; Ziems et al., 2020). The popularity of #ChineseVirus reinforces the proliferation of many other racist hashtags that express hostility against racial cultural identities (e.g., #Kungflu, #chopstickchins) and racial exclusion, such as #sinophobia (Hswen et al., 2021; Pei & Mehta, 2020). Specifically, negative sentiment containing two racist hashtags (i.e., #Chinesevirus and #Chinavirus) was prevalent on Twitter (X), and an increasing number of users expressed race-based discrimination and blame, especially when COVID-19 became the global pandemic (Pei & Mehta, 2020).

Malicious COVID-19 content, including hate speech, misinformation, and disinformation not only spread quickly but also are weaponized and stigmatized against Asian communities (Budhawani & Sun, 2020; Velásquez et al., 2020). The surge of online harassment of Asians and Asian Americans is accompanied using racist hashtags (Rubin & Wilson, 2021). When conservative social and news media started using stigmatizing terminology such as "Chinese virus," Darling-Hammond et al. (2020) found an increase in bias against Asian Americans. Similarly, a report analyzing hate speech and racist hashtags found the growth of 900% in hate speech on Twitter (X) targeted at China and the Chinese (LIGHT, 2020). Scholars also observed the dissemination of Sinophobic content and the emergence of new Sinophobic slurs on Twitter (X) (Tahmasbi et al., 2021).

Social media played a vital role in publicizing racialized attacks or hate crimes against Asian Americans (Gover et al., 2020). For instance, bystanders posted videos on Twitter (X) exposing incidents of anti-Asian hate crime, which was reported by the news media (Doubek, 2021). Twitter (X) hashtags such as #StopAsianHate, #StopAAPIHate, and #HateIsAVirus trended on social media calling on people to speak up and stand up for those who are affected by and vulnerable to racist violence (Fan et al., 2021; Robert, 2021). Hence, the racist hashtags and Trump's reference to the "Chinese virus" have fueled hatred and generated major repercussions for both Asians and Asian Americans in the United States (Hswen et al., 2021; Rubin & Wilson, 2021; Ziems et al., 2020). While prior studies have found the presence of anti-Asian sentiment on social media, the literature on this matter has mainly been situated on the Twitter (X) platform.

Prior literature did not examine how racist hashtags influenced online engagement, and it is necessary to examine how anti-Asian hashtags and discourse spread on other social media platforms. The study poses the following research question:

RQ#1: What kinds of #ChineseVirus messaging get the most attention and engagement on Facebook pages?

Attribution Theory

When encountering uncertainties and unpredicted negative situations, people have a propensity to involve themselves in an attribution process to find the causes of the event and determine who should be responsible (Weiner, 1985). As anti-Asian sentiment and hate crimes increase, media and government officials blame Asians for the spread of COVID-19 (Croucher et al., 2020). Attribution theory posits that individuals make sense of crises by identifying the causes of the crisis (Coombs, 2007; Weiner, 1985). The outbreak of the pandemic generated negative occurrences and triggered strong motivations among people to search for attributions. Polling conducted between March and April 2020 indicated that 78% of Republicans and 40% of Democrats attributed blame to China for the coronavirus entering the United States, while only 20% of Republicans and 60% of Democrats blamed the U.S. government (Lin & Pham, 2020).

Attribution theory posits that people either attribute responsibility for the negative event to the situation or the person in that situation (Coombs, 2007). Spontaneous evaluations of adverse situations involve the assessment of the belief blaming individuals or a group (Alicke, 2000). The recipients of this blame are often those who evoke unfavorable expectations (Alicke, 2000).

Trump's rhetoric on COVID-19 and blaming China elicited a resurgence of discrimination and stereotypes of Asian Americans (Rubin & Wilson, 2021). Specifically, Ipsos (2020) reports that about one-third of Americans blamed Asian people for the coronavirus and among those who believed a specific group or organization was responsible, 66% blamed Chinese people. In addition to Trump continuing to blame China and the Chinese for coronavirus, U.S. Senator Tom Cotton even spread a conspiracy theory that coronavirus is a Chinese biological weapon and leaked from a Chinese lab (Bostock, 2020).

Prior studies suggest that commenting can influence the attribution of responsibility in a crisis (von Sikorski & Hanelt, 2016). More opinionated comments generate a stronger influence on readers and may result in other users posting biased messages as well (Goncalves, 2018; Hsueh et al., 2015). Prejudice, racism, and violence against minority groups who were blamed for the spread of COVID-19 are linked to individuals' social media use and social media messages have introduced or strengthened the belief that China poses a realistic and symbolic threat to America (Croucher et al., 2020).

Fairness Theory

People's cognitive tendency to discover the causes of an unanticipated crisis is in line with attribution theory. However, when attempting to comprehend the uncertainties or negative events, individuals not only attribute responsibilities but also make judgments of fairness. Fairness refers to "the quality of conforming to a standard of moral conduct" (McComas et al., 2008, p. 1540). People consider the events detrimental and unfair if they perceive the events violate the core values, expectations, and moral standards (Roh, 2017). Individuals judging the fairness of an event are often influenced by their preexisting perceptions and expectations about the fairness of the parties involved (Jones & Skarlicki, 2013). The judgment of fairness guides people in how to react to unanticipated situations and affects their ensuing behavior (Cropanzano et al., 2001).

Fairness theory involves three key elements: (a) a presence of harmful situation, (b) an individual or target accountable for things that threaten a person's well-being, and (c) the event or the action violating moral tenet (Folger & Cropanzano, 2001). Fairness theory posits that individuals make judgments of fairness and reflect them in their cognitive and affective behavior (Folger & Cropanzano, 2001). When people face an instance of unfair treatment or unanticipated events, they are likely to hold someone accountable for an action that endangers a person's physical or psychological well-being. When people discover the fairness of one's actions, they decide whether to hold that person accountable for those actions. Fairness theory differs from attribution theory in that it explains why individuals sometimes act toward certain unjust or unexpected events in which they are not directly involved or that do not result in immediate harm to them (Roh, 2017).

Fairness theory is applicable to this study because it accounts for why people get outraged and act even though the situations that activated their judgment evaluation did not pose any immediate threat to them (Folger & Cropanzano, 2001). Existing research suggests that associating the pandemic to a social group leads to anti-Asian attitudes in the mass public and anti-Asian attitudes are linked with concern about the virus (Reny & Barreto, 2020). Political elites' referring to coronavirus as the "Chinese Virus" in the early stages of the pandemic reinforced anti-Asian attitudes (Reny & Barreto, 2020). The racist hashtags manifesting in racially charged, xenophobic sentiment and political elites' blame rhetoric trigger preexisting anti-Asian attitudes, influencing emotional and behavioral reactions to the pandemic (Hswen et al., 2021). Based on attribution and fairness theory, this study examined the relationship between affective responses and racist hashtags.

RQ#2: To what extent does the presence of #Chinesevirus or #Chinavirus vary depending on the type of emotional reactions?

Methodology

Data Collection

To collect the social media messages labeling COVID-19 as "Chinese Virus," the study conducted a content analysis using data from CrowdTangle, which is a public insights tool owned and managed by Facebook to analyze public accounts and understand how public content spreads on social media (Bleakley, 2021). Quantitative content analysis was helpful to identify typical patterns or characteristics of social media messages (Riffe et al., 2019). The Facebook posts in the study were from Facebook pages, which are places on Facebook where people (e.g., artists or bloggers), businesses, organizations, and nonprofits can connect with their fans or followers.

Analyzing hashtags can identify what topics and groups the users tend to be connected to, given hashtags can archive messages and distribute information to reach out to users outside of the direct networks (Feduskho et al., 2019).

Therefore, the study focused on Facebook pages whose administrators were based in the United States and contained racist hashtags. Facebook pages whose administrators were based outside the United States or their posts didn't have #ChineseVirus were excluded in the analysis. By applying the filter criteria mentioned above, the study retrieved a total of 624 posts containing #ChineseVirus as well as other relevant racist hashtags, including #ChinaVirus, #Kungflu, #Wuhanvirus, #CCPvirus from 256 Facebook pages between March 11, 2020, and August 17, 2021. The time frame was chosen from early March that President Trump started labeling the coronavirus as "Chinese Virus" to the time the book chapter was written. Types of Facebook pages range from the nonprofit, person, news sites, fan pages, entertainment, community, to political organizations, etc.

Content Analysis and Coding

The unit of analysis is a Facebook post, which could be a link, a text post, an image, or a video shared by a public page. Based upon prior studies of analyzing racist hashtags on Twitter (X) (Hswen et al., 2021; Pei & Mehta, 2020), the study identified five categories to code the content of Facebook posts, including 1 = informing and combating bias against Asian ethnic groups, 2 = criticizing Chinese Communist Party or the policies implemented by the Chinese government, 3 = spreading conspiracy stories, 4 = expressing anti-Asian opinions, and 0 = others.

Intercoder Reliability

Two independent coders with expertise in social media and crisis communication were trained to code the theme of each Facebook post. A random subsample (15%) of the data was calculated for intercoder reliability by using Cohen's Kappa and the agreement ranged from .83 to .97. Disagreements in coding between the two raters were adjudicated by the author.

Measures

Facebook Posts with #ChineseVirus

The content of each Facebook post was coded into five categories, with 1 = informing and combating bias against Asian ethnic groups, 2 = criticizing CCP or the policies implemented by the Chinese government, 3 = spreading conspiracy stories, 4 = expressing anti-Asian opinions, and 0 = others.

Total Interactions

Based on the dataset, total interactions are the aggregate of reactions, comments, shares, and likes received on each post (M = 128.1, SD = 415.1).

Media Type of Facebook Posts

In the sample, 120 (19.9%) posts contain only hyperlinks (coded as 1), 65 (10.4%) posts contain only texts (coded as 2), 278 (44.6%) posts have pictures (coded as 3), and 157 (25.2%%) have videos (coded as 4).

The Number of Emotional Reactions

Users can react to posts on Facebook to communicate a range of emotional responses ranging from like, wow, sad, angry, love, and haha. Each person can give only one of the reaction types and give it only once. In the sample, the average number of for each reaction form: Likes (M = 46.93, SD = 187.59), Love (M = 3.91, SD = 23.42), Wow (M = 2.61, SD = 10.1), Haha (M = 7.52, SD = 37.07), Sad (M = 2.72, SD = 12.8), Angry (M = 11.56, SD = 74.37), Care (M = 0.16, SD = 1.87).

Results

RQ1 asked what kinds of #ChineseVirus messages get the most interaction or attention on Facebook. An ANOVA was conducted and post hoc analysis featuring categories of messages as the independent variable, and the total interactions as the dependent variable. The results showed that there was a significant main effect of the categories of messages on the number of total interactions $F\ (4,\ 619) = 10.23$, $p < .001$, $\eta_p^2 = .062$. Specifically, messages using #ChineseVirus to spread conspiracy theories (M = 309.16, SD = 759) received more interactions than others (M = 58.35, SD = 257.4), $p < .001$. Posts using #ChineseVirus to inform and combat anti-Asian bias (M = 348.61, SD = 744.1) received more interactions than others (M = 58.35, SD = 257.4), $p < .001$. Furthermore, messages with #ChineseVirus spreading conspiracy stories received more interactions (M = 309.16, SD = 759) than other anti-Asian expressions (M = 90.77, SD = 180.3). Posts containing racist hashtags to inform and combat anti-Asian bias gained more interactions (M = 348.61.16, SD = 7444.1) than anti-Asian expressions (M = 90.77, SD = 180.3), as shown in Figure 18.1.

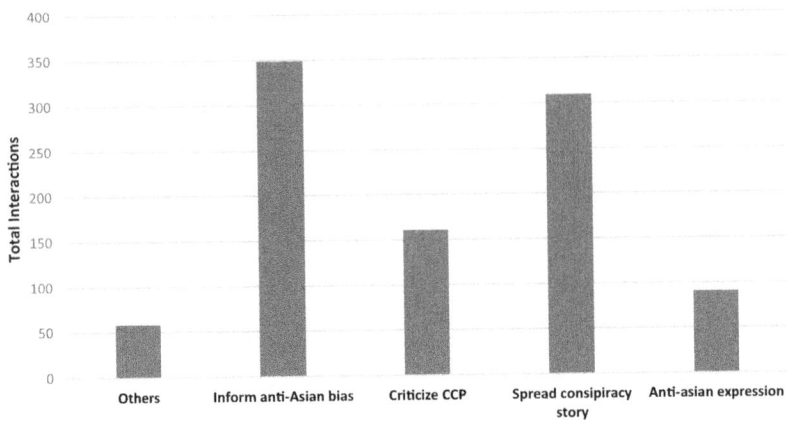

Figure 18.1. Total Interactions among Five Categories of Facebook Posts Containing #ChineseVirus or #ChinaVirus

RQ2 asked whether the use of #ChineseVirus among Facebook posts varies depending on the type of emotional reactions. Hierarchical multiple regression analyses were performed to examine RQ2. First, media types of Facebook posts were entered in the control block, followed by emotional reactions. Results showed a positive association between the "wow" reaction and #ChineseVirus messaging ($\beta = .104$, $p = .024$). The presented regression models accounted for

Table 18.1. Hierarchical Regression Predicting the #ChineseVirus Messaging on Facebook

	Model 1			Model 2		
Variable	B	SE (B)	β	B	SE (B)	β
Type	.131	.062	.085*	.124	.062	.080*
Like				.000	.001	.056
Love				-.001	.004	-.017
Wow				.017	.007	.104*
Haha				.003	.002	.061
Sad				.000	.008	-.001
Angry				-.001	.001	-.058
Care				.055	.035	.063
R^2	.007			.027		

Note: Coefficients are standardized regression coefficients (betas).
*$p < .05$.

a total variance of 2.7% for #ChineseVirus messaging. The media type of the post (β = .085, p = .034) was a positive predictor of #ChineseVirus messaging, as shown in Table 18.1. Results showed that media types and emotional reaction of shock (wow face) positively predict the presence of #ChineseVirus messaging.

Discussion

After Trump's frequent use of racist hashtags (i.e., #Chinesevirus), Asians have increasingly become the targets of hate crimes (Hswen et al., 2021; Wu et al., 2021). The growing use of racist hashtags and hateful words potentially contributed to the rise of anti-Asian sentiment (Gover et al., 2020). Through content analysis, the study investigates the presence of racist hashtags on Facebook pages and identified three unique characteristics of #ChineseVirus used by Facebook pages that were worth discussing.

First, #Chinesevirus appeared on Facebook pages not only to criticize Chinese Communist Party or the Chinese government, spread conspiracy beliefs, and express anti-Asian hate but also to inform and combat bias against Asian ethnic groups. The content analysis indicates #ChineseVirus appeared on many Facebook pages, such as CBS News, Truthout, VICE News, USA Today, The Daily Beast, WDTN-TV, Rasmussen Reports, Trump Resistance Movement, etc., to raise awareness of or combat anti-Asian bias. For instance, the Facebook page of CBS News (2021) posted, "[R]esearchers found that those who used the hashtag #chinesevirus were significantly more likely to use other overtly racist hashtags."

A closer examination of those pages indicated that many of them belonged to the news media. A hashtag often plays as a channel for users to seek information of similar interest and to reach out beyond their network community (Bruns & Burgess, 2011). During public health crises, news media are expected to act in a socially responsible way to reduce the spread of discriminatory language (Ittefaq et al., 2022). However, the findings indicated #ChineseVirus was also used by news media on their Facebook pages. The same term which was actively used by news media may reinforce audiences' preexisting attitudes and prejudice against Chinese and Asian Americans (Holt et al., 2022).

Second, the study revealed that #ChineseVirus appearing in posts of spreading conspiracy stories get more interactions compared with posts that express anti-Asian sentiment or other content. Consistent with the attribution and fairness theory which posits that an unanticipated crisis motivates people to make causal explanations and seek an individual or a group accountable for events that threaten a person's well-being (Coombs, 2007; Folger & Cropanzano, 2001; Weiner, 1985), the findings suggested #ChineseVirus appeared on Facebook pages to attribute blame to China for the spread and creation of the coronavirus. For instance, #ChineseVirus was accompanied with other hashtags like #BeijingJoe to disseminate conspiracy theories, as shown in one Facebook page, Colorado for Donald Trump 2020:

> #BeijingJoe ... we had the #ChineseVirus that was sent to our country, it put millions of Americans out of work, our businesses are still closed and now being ravaged by the #BidenRiots. America wants to know where is the $1.5 Billion dollars that was paid by China to your son, Hunter? (September 5, 2020)

The findings add support to prior research that social media act as an open-access platform to disseminate misinformation, racism, and xenophobia (Croucher et al., 2020; Gover et al., 2020; Ziems et al., 2020), as Dhanani and Franz (2021) found that exposure to stigmatizing language blaming China for the coronavirus has increased anti-Asian prejudice and discrimination. On the other hand, results indicated term #ChineseVirus appearing on Facebook pages to inform anti-Asian bias gets more interactions in comparison with posts that express hate or other purposes. The finding suggested that social media may also function as a nurturing ground to help combat anti-Asian prejudice and bigotry (Fan et al., 2021; Robert, 2021).

Third, data analyses revealed that the media types and emotional reaction of shock (wow face) positively predict the presence of #ChineseVirus messaging. Video has become the dominant form for Facebook pages sharing information containing racist hashtags. The number of #ChineseVirus messages varied depending on how many Wow reactions were received, as results indicated users were more likely to apply the Wow reactions when they were exposed to Facebook pages containing #ChineseVirus. In other words, the Facebook reaction of Wow acted as an antecedent of social media messages containing racist hashtags. Because Facebook only allows each viewer one type of emoji to represent emotions when communicating online (Wilkerson et al., 2021), further examination on the emotional appeal of racist hashtags is critical. Especially, Facebook whistleblower Frances Haugen noted that more controversial emotions and provocative content were privileged in their algorithmic structure (Perrigo, 2021), and the study showed that posts that sparked Wow reaction emoji were more likely to include the term #ChineseVirus.

Practical Implications

By analyzing the use of the racist hashtags on Facebook pages, this study contributes to the ongoing public controversy calling the coronavirus "Chinese Virus." Consistent with preexisting research (Hswen et al., 2021; Tahmasbi et al., 2021), the current study suggests that social media are employed for spreading detrimental information, including conspiracy theories and hateful speech against Asian minorities. Attribution and fairness theory posits that when threatened by negative events outside the locus of control, people develop a cognitive tendency to seek external blame. In the case of the COVID-19 pandemic, Asian people were subjected to scapegoating, one important factor driving racism (Tahmasbi et al., 2021). The study unveiled some key characteristics of the Facebook posts containing racist hashtags, while exploring how the presence of #ChineseVirus messages differed in generating engagement, having implications for social media platforms to regulate and moderate racist posts targeting Asian Americans.

First, the surge of anti-Asian sentiment on social media has amplified racist and xenophobic attacks against Asian Americans (Alba, 2021). Likewise, this study finds that racist hashtags are used to blame China and spread hate speech, misinformation, and conspiracies, which may seed the idea that the public should be suspicious of or blame Asians. While major social media platforms have been urged to tackle the coronavirus-related misinformation spreading on their platforms (Molina, 2021), they should also create coordinated strategies in response to the rise of racist hashtags, hate speech, and other forms of discrimination that perpetuate structural racism.

Second, public health agencies should coordinate with policymakers, communication experts, and media outlets to avoid words that carry pejorative connotations or prejudices. It is necessary for public health agencies to design counter-messaging strategies to alleviate the harm already inflicted on Asian communities (Hswen et al., 2021, p. 962). As hate crimes and discrimination acts against Asian communities are increasing in the wake of COVID-19, both policymakers and media professionals can provide resources to marginalized populations who greatly suffer from stereotypes and discriminations, dismiss misinformation and inaccurate coronavirus claims, act swiftly to enact policies, and shape public discourse to support marginalized groups who are especially vulnerable during the pandemic.

Limitations

Like all research, this study has its share of limitations. First, the study examined the Facebook pages with U.S.-based administrators who published posts containing racist hashtags rather than every Facebook page. Future research could expand the scope to examine the influence of racist hashtags in other countries. Second, the study solely focused on one single social media platform, Facebook. Future research may expand the analysis of racist hashtags to other social media platforms such as Instagram, Twitter (X), or TikTok. Third, the collected posts were compiled from third-party data which raises questions regarding the reliability of the archived data (Lomborg & Bechmann, 2014). Therefore, the findings from this study may not be generalized across other social media platforms but should be interpreted within the specific realm of Facebook. Despite these limitations, the study shows that racist hashtags were used not only to express hatred of Asian ethnic groups, blame, and criticize the Chinese Communist Party and the Chinese government, but also to disseminate conspiracy stories and created anti-Asian bias to get more interactions, which indicates controversial content with racist hashtags were pervasive on Facebook pages and such content earned more attention and engagement. Counter-messaging interventions are needed to mitigate the rise of anti-Asian bias on social media.

Discussion Questions

Social media have noted a rise in prejudicial attitudes and discrimination against Asian Americans in the United States in relation to COVID-19. A rise in negative racial attitudes and racial bias can have significant social, economic, mental, and physical health impacts. Based on this chapter, we provide a few questions to help facilitate discussion on this topic.

1. Discuss how societal inequities are highlighted and perpetuated by the impact of the coronavirus.
2. Discuss your understanding of how the coronavirus pandemic has led to increased racism against people who are of Chinese or Asian descent, and how to combat violence and racism against Asian Americans.
3. The fear and anxiety around the coronavirus are having an impact on schools and communities and resulting in misinformation and scapegoating. Discuss how policymakers and public officials can take steps to mitigate the spread of racism and xenophobia, preventing further misinformation.

Resources

1. Stop AAPI Hate is a nonprofit organization that runs the Stop AAPI Hate Reporting Center, which tracks incidents of hate and discrimination against Asian Americans and Pacific Islanders in the United States. https://stopaapihate.org/
2. Anti-Racism Resources for Asian Americans: https://docs.google.com/document/d/1FuUbVNesdSCnK6M4iAWWMWCDsSVgfPKt8RuPvFh3-mg/edit
3. Asian Americans Advancing Justice (AAJC): https://www.advancingjustice-aajc.org/
4. Asian American Racial Justice Toolkit: https://www.asianamtoolkit.org/

References

Alba, D. (2021, March 19). How anti-Asian activity online set the stage for real-world violence. *The New York Times.* https://www.nytimes.com/2021/03/19/technology/how-anti-asian-activity-online-set-the-stage-for-real-world-violence.html

Alicke, Mark. (2000). Culpable control and psychology of blame. *Psychological Bulletin, 126,* 556–574. https://doi.org/10.1037/0033-2909.126.4.556

Anderson, M., Barthel, M., Perrin, A., & Vogels, E.A. (2020, June 10). *#BlackLivesMatter surges on Twitter after George Floyd's death.* Pew Research Center. https://www.pewresearch.org/fact-tank/2020/06/10/blacklivesmatter-surges-on-twitter-after-george-floyds-death/

Associated Press, The. (2021, August 12). *More than 9,000 anti-Asian incidents have been reported since the Pandemic began.* NPR. https://www.npr.org/2021/08/12/1027236499/anti-asian-hate-crimes-assaults-pandemic-incidents-aapi

BBC. (2021, May 21). *Covid "hate crimes" against Asian Americans on rise.* BBC News. https://www.bbc.com/news/world-us-canada-56218684

Bleakley, W. (2021). *About Us: Learn more about CrowdTangle.* https://help.crowdtangle.com/en/articles/4201940-about-us

Bostcok, B. (2020). *A GOP senator keeps pushing a thoroughly debunked theory that the Wuhan coronavirus is a leaked Chinese biological weapon gone wrong.* Business Insider. https://www.businessinsider.com/coronavirus-bioweapon-tom-cotton-conspiracy-theory-china-warfare-leak-2020-2

Bruns, A., & Burgess, J.E. (2011). The use of Twitter hashtags in the formation of ad hoc publics. In *Proceedings of the 6th European Consortium for Political Research (ECPR) General Conference.* https://eprints.qut.edu.au/46515/1/The_Use_of_Twitter_Hashtags_in_the_Formation_of_Ad_Hoc_Publics_(final).pdf

Budhwani, H., & Sun, R. (2020). Creating COVID-19 stigma by referencing the novel coronavirus as the "Chinese virus" on Twitter: Quantitative analysis of social media data. *Journal of Medical Internet Research, 22*(5), Article e19301. https://doi.org/10.2196/19301

CBS News. (2021). *Researchers found that those who used the hashtag #chinesevirus were significantly more likely to use other overtly racist hashtags.* Facebook. https://www.facebook.com/131459315949/posts/10158978721195950

Centers for Disease Control and Prevention. (June 11, 2020). *Reducing stigma.* https://www.cdc.gov/coronavirus/2019-ncov/daily-life-coping/reducing-stigma.html?CDC_AA_refVal=https%3A%2F%2Fwww.cdc.gov%2Fcoronavirus%2F2019-ncov%2Fsymptoms-testing%2Freducing-stigma.html

Chappell, B., & Jones, D. (2021, March 18). *"Enough is enough": Atlanta-Area spa shootings spur debate over hate crime label.* NPR. https://www.npr.org/2021/03/18/978680316/atlanta-spa-shootings-expose-frustration-and-debate-over-hate-crime-label

Cho, H., Li, W., Cannon, J., Lopez, R., & Song, C. (2021). Testing three explanations for stigmatization of people of Asian descent during COVID-19: Maladaptive coping, biased media use, or racial prejudice?. *Ethnicity & Health, 26*(1), 94–109. https://doi.org/10.1080/13557858.2020.1830035

Chong, M., & Chen, H. (2021). Racist Framing through Stigmatized Naming: A Topical and Geo-locational Analysis of# Chinavirus and# Chinesevirus on Twitter. *Proceedings of the Association for Information Science and Technology, 58*(1), 70–79. https://doi.org/10.1002/pra2.437

Coombs, W.T. (2007). Attribution theory as a guide for post-crisis communication research. *Public Relations Review, 33*(2), 135–139. https://doi.org/10.1016/j.pubrev.2006.11.016

Criss, S., Michaels, E.K., Solomon, K., Allen, A.M., & Nguyen, T.T. (2020). Twitter fingers and echo chambers: Exploring expressions and experiences of online racism using Twitter. *Journal of Racial and Ethnic Health Disparities*, 1–10. https://doi.org/10.1007/s40615-020-00894-5

Cropanzano, R., Byrne, Z.S., Bobocel, D.R., & Rupp, D.E. (2001). Moral virtues, fairness heuristics, social entities, and other denizens of organizational justice. *Journal of Vocational Behavior, 58*(2), 164–209. https://doi.org/10.1006/jvbe.2001.1791

Croucher, S.M., Nguyen, T., & Rahmani, D. (2020). Prejudice toward Asian Americans in the COVID-19 pandemic: The effects of social media use in the United States. *Frontiers in Communication, 5*, 39. https://doi.org/10.3389/fcomm.2020.00039

Darling-Hammond, S., Michaels, E.K., Allen, A.M., Chae, D.H., Thomas, M.D., Nguyen, T.T., Mujahid, M.M., & Johnson, R.C. (2020). After "The China Virus" went viral: Racially charged coronavirus coverage and trends in bias against Asian Americans. *Health Education & Behavior, 47*(6), 870–879. https://doi.org/10.1177/1090198120957949

Depoux, A., Martin, S., Karafillakis, E., Preet, R., Wilder-Smith, A., & Larson, H. (2020). The pandemic of social media panic travels faster than the COVID-19 outbreak. *Journal of Travel Medicine*, 1–4. https://doi.org/10.1093/jtm/taaa031

Dhanani, L.Y., & Franz, B. (2021). Why public health framing matters: An experimental study of the effects of COVID-19 framing on prejudice and xenophobia in the United States. *Social Science & Medicine, 269*, 113572–113579. https://doi.org/10.1016/j.socscimed.2020.113572

Doubek, J. (2021, June 1). *A video shows a man suddenly hitting an Asian woman in NYC's Chinatown*. NPR. https://www.npr.org/2021/06/01/1002170719/unprovoked-a-man-hits-an-asian-woman-in-new-york-city

Fan, L., Yu, H., & Gilliland, A.J. (2021). # StopAsianHate: Archiving and analyzing Twitter discourse in the wake of the 2021 Atlanta Spa shootings. *Proceedings of the Association for Information Science and Technology*, 58(1), 440–444. https://doi.org/10.1002/pra2.475

Fedushko, S., Syerov, Y., & Kolos, S. (2019). Hashtag as a way of archiving and distributing information on the internet. In *CEUR workshop proceedings* (pp. 274–286). https://ceur-ws.org/Vol-2386/paper20.pdf

Folger, R., & Cropanzano, R. (2001). Fairness theory: Justice as accountability. In J. Greenberg & R. Cropanzano (Eds.), *Advances in organization justice* (pp. 1–55). Stanford University Press.

Gonçalves, J. (2018). Aggression in news comments: How context and article topic shape user-generated content. *Journal of Applied Communication Research*, 46(5), 604–620. https://doi.org/10.1080/00909882.2018.1529419

Gover, A.R., Harper, S.B., & Langton, L. (2020). Anti-Asian hate crime during the COVID-19 pandemic: Exploring the reproduction of inequality. *American Journal of Criminal Justice*, 45(4), 647–667. https://doi.org/10.1007/s12103-020-09545-1

Holt, L.F., Kjærvik, S.L., & Bushman, B.J. (2022). Harm and shaming through naming: Examining why calling the coronavirus, "COVID-19 Virus," to the "Chinese Virus," matters. *Media Psychology*, 1–14. https://doi.org/10.1080/15213269.2022.2034021

Hsueh, M., Yogeeswaran, K., & Malinen, S. (2015). "Leave your comment below": Can biased online comments influence our own prejudicial attitudes and behaviors? Online comments on prejudice expression. *Human Communication Research*, 41(4), 557–576. https://doi.org/10.1111/hcre.12059

Hswen, Y., Xu, X., Hing, A., Hawkins, J.B., Brownstein, J.S., & Gee, G.C. (2021). Association of "# Covid19" Versus "# Chinesevirus" with anti-Asian sentiments on Twitter: March 9–23, 2020. *American Journal of Public Health*, 111(5), 956–964. https://doi.org/10.2105/AJPH.2021.306154

Ipsos. (2020, April 28). *New center for public integrity/Ipsos poll finds most Americans say the coronavirus pandemic is a natural disaster*. https://www.ipsos.com/en-us/news-polls/center-for-public-integrity-poll-2020

Ittefaq, M., Abwao, M., Baines, A., Belmas, G., Kamboh, S.A., & Figueroa, E.J. (2022). A pandemic of hate: Social representations of COVID-19 in the media. *Analyses of Social Issues and Public Policy*, 1–28. https://doi.org/10.1111/asap.12300

Jones, D.A., & Skarlicki, D.P. (2013). How perceptions of fairness can change: A dynamic model of organizational justice. *Organizational Psychology Review*, 3(2), 138–160. https://doi.org/10.1177/2041386612461665

Kandil, C.Y. (2020, March 26). *Asian Americans report over 650 racist acts over last week, new data say*. NBC News. https://www.nbcnews.com/news/asian-america/asian-americans-report-nearly-500-racist-acts-over-last-week-n1169821?cid=sm_npd_nn_fb_ma&fbclid=IwAR2XLCuG6RUEq8RLTBy4RqbYAfV9z7U19vzb82XiIh1n_ZamoH1pkuJHIHI

Kantamneni, N. (2020). The impact of the COVID-19 pandemic on marginalized populations in the United States: A research agenda. *Journal of Vocational Behavior, 119*, 1–4. https://doi.org/10.1016/j.jvb.2020.103439

LIGHT. (2020). Rising levels of hate speech & online toxicity during this time of crisis. https://l1ght.com/Toxicity_during_coronavirus_Report-L1ght.pdf

Lin, S., & Pham, H.L. (2020, April 22). Who's playing the blame game? An analysis of media framing of China and COVID-19 in The New York Times. HCA Graduate Blog. https://hcagrads.hypotheses.org/2966

Lomborg, S., & Bechmann, A. (2014). Using APIs for data collection on social media. *The Information Society, 30*(4), 256–265. https://doi.org/10.1080/01972243.2014.915276

McComas, K.A., Besley, J.C., & Yang, Z. (2008). Risky business: Perceived behavior of local scientists and community support for their research. *Risk Analysis: An International Journal, 28*(6), 1539–1552. https://doi.org/10.1111/j.1539-6924.2008.01129.x

Molina, B. (2021, July 23). Who's responsible for COVID-19 misinformation? Lawmakers introduce bill to hold Facebook, Twitter accountable. USA Today. https://www.usatoday.com/story/tech/2021/07/23/facebook-twitter-targeted-new-bill-covid-misinformation-fight/8067701002/

Müller, K., & Schwarz, C. (2020). From hashtag to hate crime: Twitter and anti-minority sentiment. Available at *SSRN, 3149103*. http://dx.doi.org/10.2139/ssrn.3149103

Ozturk, A. (2021). "Stigmatization spreads faster than the virus. Viruses do not discriminate, and neither should we." Combatting the stigmatization surrounding coronavirus disease (COVID-19) pandemic. *Perspectives in Psychiatric Care, 57*(4), 2030–2034. https://doi.org/10.1111/ppc.12815

Pei, X., & Mehta, D. (2020). # Coronavirus or# Chinesevirus?!: Understanding the negative sentiment reflected in Tweets with racist hashtags across the development of COVID-19. *arXiv preprint arXiv:2005.08224*. https://doi.org/10.48550/arXiv.2005.08224

Perrigo, B. (2021, October 5). Here's how to fix Facebook, according to former employees and leading critics. Time. https://time.com/6103793/how-to-fix-facebook/

Reja, M. (2021, March 18). Trump's "Chinese Virus" tweet helped lead to rise in racist anti-Asian Twitter content: Study. ABC News. https://abcnews.go.com/Health/trumps-chinese-virus-tweet-helped-lead-rise-racist/story?id=76530148

Reny, T.T., & Barreto, M.A. (2020). Xenophobia in the time of pandemic: Othering, anti-Asian attitudes, and COVID-19. *Politics, Groups, and Identities*, 1–24. https://doi.org/10.1080/21565503.2020.1769693

Riecheman, D., & Tang, T. (2020, March 18). President Trump dubs COVID-19 the "Chinese virus"—despite hate crime risks, rise in virus-related discrimination reports. *Chicago Tribune*. https://www.chicagotribune.com/coronavirus/ct-nw-chinese-coronavirus-hate-speech-20200318-y5d5ti6qmjemjg3fosehxihhnu-story.html

Riffe, D., Lacy, S., Watson, B., & Fico, F. (2019). *Analyzing media messages: Using quantitative content analysis in research*. Routledge.

Robert, Y. (2021, March 23). AAPI Voices are taking to social media to spread awareness to #StopAAPIHate. *Forbes.* https://www.forbes.com/sites/yolarobert1/2021/03/23/aapi-voices-are-taking-to-social-media-to-spread-awareness-to-stopaapihate/?sh=449839881f6e

Roh, S. (2017). Examining the paracrisis online: The effects of message source, response strategies and social vigilantism on public responses. *Public Relations Review, 43*(3), 587–596. https://doi.org/10.1016/j.pubrev.2017.03.004

Rovetta, A., & Bhagavathula, A.S. (2020). COVID-19-related web search behaviors and infodemic attitudes in Italy: Infodemiological study. *JMIR Public Health and Surveillance, 6*(2), Article e19374. https://doi.org/10.2196/19374

Rubin, D.I., & Wilson, F.A. (2021). Blame China: Trump and anti-Asian sentiment during COVID-19. In D.I. Rubin & F.A. Wilson (Eds.), *A time of Covidiocy: Media, politics, and social upheaval* (pp. 10–31). BRILL.

Ruiz, N.G., Edwards, K., & Lopez, M.H. (2021, April 21). *One-third of Asian Americans fear threats, physical attacks and most say violence against them is rising.* Pew Research Center. https://www.pewresearch.org/fact-tank/2021/04/21/one-third-of-asian-americans-fear-threats-physical-attacks-and-most-say-violence-against-them-is-rising/

Shah, S. (2020, March 7). The pandemic of xenophobia and scapegoating. *TIME.* https://time.com/5776279/pandemic-xenophobia-scapegoating/

Stop AAPI Hate. (2021, March 16). *2020–2021 National Report.* https://stopaapihate.org/wp-content/uploads/2021/05/Stop-AAPI-Hate-Report-National-210316.pdf

Tahmasbi, F., Schild, L., Ling, C., Blackburn, J., Stringhini, G., Zhang, Y., & Zannettou, S. (2021, April). "Go eat a bat, Chang!": On the Emergence of sinophobic behavior on web communities in the face of COVID-19. In *Proceedings of the web conference 2021* (pp. 1122–1133). https://doi.org/10.1145/3442381.3450024

Velásquez, N., Leahy, R., Restrepo, N.J., Lupu, Y., Sear, R., Gabriel, N., Jha, O., Goldberg, N.F., & Johnson, N.F. (2020). Hate multiverse spreads malicious COVID-19 content online beyond individual platform control. *arXiv preprint arXiv:2004.00673.* https://doi.org/10.48550/arXiv.2004.00673

von Sikorski, C., & Hänelt, M. (2016). Scandal 2.0: How valenced reader comments affect recipients' perception of scandalized individuals and the journalistic quality of online news. *Journalism & Mass Communication Quarterly, 93*(3), 551–571. https://doi.org/10.1177/1077699016628822

Weiner, B. (1985). An attributional theory of achievement motivation and emotion. *Psychological Review, 92*(4), 548–573. https://doi.org/10.1037/0033-295X.92.4.548

Wilkerson, H.S., Riedl, M.J., & Whipple, K.N. (2021). Affective affordances: Exploring Facebook reactions as emotional responses to hyperpartisan political news. *Digital Journalism,* 1–22. https://doi.org/10.1080/21670811.2021.1899011

Wu, C., Qian, Y., & Wilkes, R. (2021). Anti-Asian discrimination and the Asian-white mental health gap during COVID-19. *Ethnic and Racial Studies, 44*(5), 819–835. https://doi.org/10.1080/01419870.2020.1851739

Yam, K. (2020, March 16). *Trump tweets about coronavirus using term "Chinese Virus."* NBC News. https://www.nbcnews.com/news/asian-america/trump-tweets-about-coronavirus-using-term-chinese-virus-n1161161

Yam, K., & Venkatraman, S. (2021). *Asians in the US are the fastest-growing racial group. What's behind the rise.* NBC News. https://www.nbcnews.com/news/asian-america/asians-us-are-fastest-growing-racial-group-rise-rcna1680

Ziems, C., He, B., Soni, S., & Kumar, S. (2020). Racism is a virus: Anti-Asian hate and counter-hate in social media during the COVID-19 crisis. *arXiv preprint arXiv:2005.12423.* https://doi.org/10.1145/3487351.3488324

· 19 ·

CRISIS COMMUNICATION DURING THE COVID-19 PANDEMIC: A COMPARATIVE PERSPECTIVE FROM THE ONLINE COMMUNICATION OF PUBLIC HEALTH AGENCIES IN ITALY, SWEDEN, AND THE UNITED STATES

Kaila Witkowski, Frederike Albrecht, N. Emel Ganapati, Serena Tagliacozzo, & Derrick Boakye Boadu

In 2020, people across the world who observe the Christian holiday Easter experienced a very different holiday celebration. In Italy, citizens watched the Pope deliver his Easter message to an empty St. Peter's Basilica while they remained on a nationwide lockdown (Renzulli, 2020). In Sweden, the public health agency urged citizens to rethink travel plans but relied mostly on voluntary adherence (Savage, 2020). In the United States, most citizens attended virtual and drive-by church services, but some churches remained open citing constitutional liberties (Goldberg & Whitcomb, 2020). The differences in how these countries approached the COVID-19 pandemic during Easter demonstrate the importance of not only the response strategies during this crisis but also the way public organizations communicated these responses to the public.

On March 11, 2020, just one month before Easter, the World Health Organization (WHO) declared the spread of COVID-19 a worldwide pandemic with

54,962 cases and 2,382 deaths worldwide (WHO, 2020, 2021). Just four months later, the case count rose to 1,567,892 with 40,239 deaths (WHO, 2021). The sheer magnitude of the pandemic coupled with uncertain and seemingly changing disease trends challenged crisis communication channels in new and unpredictable ways. This led researchers and practitioners all over the world to question traditional communication avenues in an effort to better respond to the next pandemic.

Communication challenges have long plagued public and non-governmental organizations charged with responding to these crisis events. During crisis events, organizations have to not only communicate information (facts associated with the crisis) but must also manage meanings (people's perceptions or interpretations) (Coombs, 2015; Wendling et al., 2013). Each of these tasks has its own specific challenges. For example, there is a degree of uncertainty surrounding all crisis events which means that information may change throughout the crisis (Fearnley et al., 2017; Hale et al., 2005). People also have differing levels of knowledge and values associated with these events. This means that strategies associated with response (i.e., evacuation orders, etc.) need to have some understanding of the values of different stakeholders (Coombs, 2015).

The advent of social media created a whole new set of challenges for organizations. On the one hand, social media allowed organizations to communicate with the public and answer questions in real time, as the crisis occurred (Lindsay, 2011; Reuter et al., 2018; Veil et al., 2011). However, it also had an "amplifier effect" (Maal & Wilson-North, 2019) which brought a loss of control, ever-increasing stakeholder groups, and created a breeding ground for misinformation (Lindsay, 2011; Stewart & Wilson, 2016).

These traditional communication challenges were heightened during the COVID-19 pandemic. Unlike more traditional crisis events (e.g., hurricane, flu epidemic), the COVID-19 pandemic was described as a "creeping crisis" (Boin et al., 2020) which was characterized as having vague and unpredictable crisis phases. It was also considered a "long wave event" meaning that the crisis phases took place over an extended period causing widespread social and economic impacts (Jung et al., 2021). These two unique characteristics exacerbated the communication challenges associated with this pandemic. According to Uncertainty Reduction Theory, people will attempt to acquire information about events and people in order to reduce unpredictability and uncertainty (Berger & Calabrese, 1975). Due to the high level of uncertainty surrounding the COVID-19 pandemic, the need to acquire information in both traditional and nontraditional communication channels increased, making the need to study and understand these forms of communication during this crisis much more important.

While much is known on the challenges associated with crisis communication, there is limited guidance on the appropriate use of social media and online communication during crisis events (Lindsay, 2011). There is even less from a comparative perspective, which is ultimately needed given the worldwide impact of the COVID-19 pandemic. To fill this gap, this chapter draws on research that examines the online communication of three national public health agencies: the National Institute of Health in Italy, the Public Health Agency in Sweden, and the Centers for Disease Control and Prevention (CDC) in the United States. Using this comparative perspective, we highlight seven recommended strategies that address the unique challenges of social media crisis communication during the COVID-19 pandemic.

Research Methods and Context

This book chapter uses data collected from online communication (i.e., tweets and press releases) from three public health organizations: The Italian National Institute of Health (Istituto Superiore di Sanità; ISS), the Swedish Public Health Agency (Folkhälsomyndigheten; FoHM), and the United States's Center for Disease Control and Prevention (CDC). These three countries were chosen due to their differences in pandemic impact and crisis response strategies. Italy became one of the initial epicenters of the pandemic in March 2020, making up around 14% of the worldwide COVID-19 cases and having one of the largest cumulative case counts at the time (WHO, 2020). Italy also had one of the strictest crisis response strategies which included country-wide mandated lockdowns, among other things. On the other hand, the United States emerged as an epicenter as the pandemic progressed, making up 25% of the worldwide cases by February 2021(Johns Hopkins University, 2021), and had a more decentralized and varied approach led by state and local public agencies. Although Sweden was not considered an epicenter, the country's lax management of the crisis received global attention. While cultural and political differences exist between these three countries, these cases provide an opportunity to examine differences in public health agencies' online communication strategies, providing valuable insight on what works and what doesn't work within the context of a public health crisis.

Tweets were used as the primary data source and the press releases provided additional contextual information to analyze Twitter (X) data. Tweets were chosen as the primary data source as they have been identified as an important tool in crisis communication (Panagiotopoulos et al., 2016). Online communication data was collected from the official Twitter (X) handles and government websites for all three countries. To evaluate the same stages of crisis response, data was collected for a three-month period after the date of initial community spread and thus, varies per country—Italy includes February 21, 2020 to May 21, 2020 (123 tweets), Sweden includes March 10, 2020 to June 10, 2020 (124 tweets), and the United States includes February 26, 2020 to March 26, 2020 (609 tweets). Figure 19.1 depicts the daily tweet count for each country showing the United States with the greatest number of tweets per day and increasing variability per day, perhaps indicating the reactive nature of crisis communication during this time.

This chapter draws on the empirical results from three separate empirical studies conducted as standalone studies. For all of these studies, authors used content analysis to capture how these three public organizations utilized online communication during the ongoing COVID-19 pandemic. The quantitative analysis included the frequency of tweets containing the following concepts: tweets mentioning other actors/organizations, retweets from other organizations, tweets containing joint communication, or targeting messaging for specific organizations/groups (Tagliacozzo et al., 2021). The qualitative content analysis examined communication ecologies, communication objectives (e.g., the main purpose of tweet), communication styles (e.g., agentic, communal), and leadership styles (e.g., transformation, transaction, servant). The quantitative content analysis was carried out by multiple coders utilizing a detailed codebook and discussing any unclear cases among all coders. The empirical studies with qualitative content analysis were coded by a single coder after collectively agreeing on and testing detailed coding instructions to avoid issues related to low intercoder reliability. Table 19.1 provides a description of main themes studied in the empirical analyses. The results of the empirical studies served as the basis for developing the recommendations included within this chapter.

CRISIS COMMUNICATION DURING THE COVID-19 PANDEMIC 359

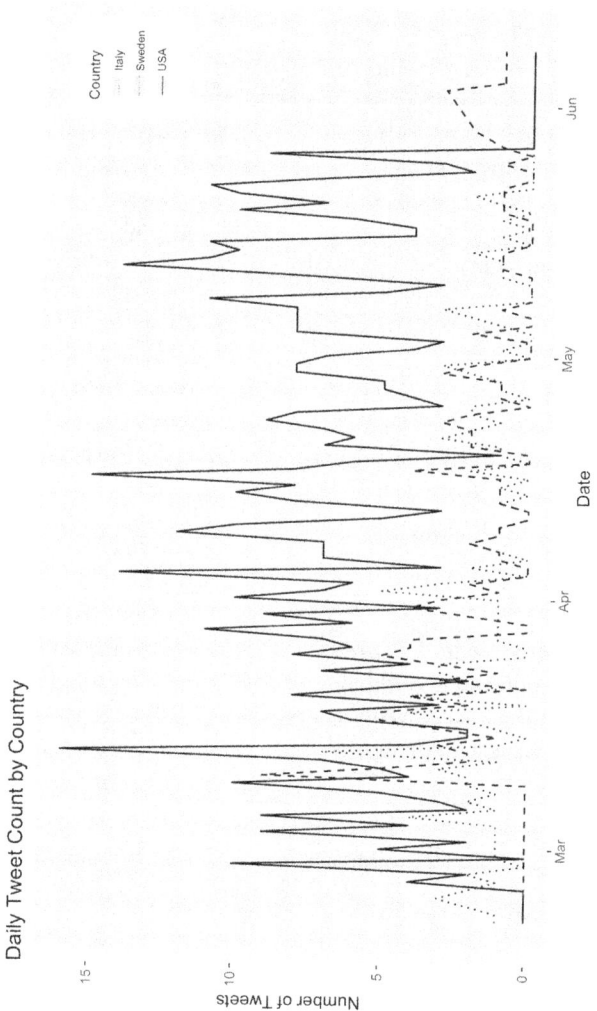

Figure 19.1. Daily Tweet Country by Country

Table 19.1. Coding Scheme in Previous Empirical Studies

Themes in Empirical Studies	Description of Codes	Recommendations
Communication Ecologies	Engagement in a communication network by mentioning other actors, (re)sharing information and collaborative efforts. Targeting specific organizations or social groups with communication.	Communicating with vulnerable groups and the organizations that serve them; communicating with workplaces that are the most impacted; showing partnerships with other organizations; making target audiences explicit.
Communication Objectives	Instructive (guiding others on how to behave), adjustive (assist others in psychosocial needs), reputational (strengthening the organization's reputation) messages.	Communicating with vulnerable groups and the organizations that serve them; communicating with workplaces that are the most impacted; achieving the right balance between different communication styles and objectives.
Communication Styles	Agentic (task-oriented and assertive communication) and communal (social and community-oriented communication).	Showing partnerships with other organizations; making target audiences explicit; achieving the right balance between different communication styles and objectives.
Leadership Styles	Transactional leadership (focusing on rewards and punishments), transformation (creating a vision to guide change).	Assuming the leadership role.

Note: Main coding themes examined in the empirical studies are on the left-hand side of the table. Communication ecologies based on Broad and colleagues (2013). Communication objectives based on Sturges (1994). Communication styles based on work by Abele and Wojciszke (2014) and Carli and Eagly (2001). Leadership styles based on Bass (1997) and Burns (1978).

Recommended Strategies for the Next Pandemic

Acknowledge the Trends

Providing timely and accurate information to the public is of utmost importance in times of emergencies (Sutton & Kuligowski, 2019). Without such information, the public may not be able to assess the level of threat surrounding the emergency and determine how best to protect themselves. For a public health emergency like the COVID-19 pandemic, our recommendations on providing such information are threefold:

1. *Acknowledge the community spread immediately.*

The agencies in Italy and Sweden acknowledged the start of community spread in their respective countries on the day of the first non-travel–related COVID case via Twitter (X). Alternatively, the CDC chose to showcase contradicting messaging. While their messages acknowledged the "transmissible" nature of the disease, they also presented the disease as "not as feared as we thought." Additionally, one of these videos started with a discussion on the mixed COVID messaging coming from the White House and the CDC: the former indicating that the disease is "tightly contained" and the latter saying that "the spread is inevitable." It took the CDC about a month to acknowledge the community spread in the United States. Failing to explicitly reveal the beginning of community spread and posting contradicting videos could have contributed to the communication challenges experienced within the United States during this pandemic.

2. *Disclose the changes in disease trends.*

Disclosing the changes in disease trends is equally important for public health agencies as the public may reconceptualize the level of threat and review their protective actions in light of these changes. Public health agencies could inform the public by mentioning both upward and downward trends. Their trend-focused messages can be combined with messages to inform the public about what needs to be done to stop an upward trend or to thank the public for helping slow down the spread of the disease. Here is an example from the CDC:

The latest CDC #COVIDView report shows the percentage of visits to doctor's offices and ERs for illnesses with symptoms likely related to #COVID19 are declining nationally, thanks in part a result of widespread efforts to slow the spread of #COVID19: https://t.co/zP4VYlo0Pb https://t.co/Ulvwbr7FG5. (May 23, 2020)

3. *Explain who is more likely to be impacted.*

Public health agencies also need to tailor their messages about disease trends to those who are more likely to be impacted. The COVID-19 pandemic affected everyone's life, but some social groups were more vulnerable than others: the elderly, those with pre-conditions, homeless persons, and those who were socio-economically disadvantaged (Panthaky, 2020). These groups need to have access to timely, specific, and relevant information about their health-related vulnerabilities so that they can better prepare for the emergency. ISS's tweet below is an example of a disease trend tweet targeting a vulnerable group:

ISS study reports that out of 105 #Covid19 positive deaths, the average age is 81 years and two-thirds of the cases reported pre-existing conditions. (March 5, 2020)

Showing Partnerships with Other Organizations

Organizational communication is no easy task for public health agencies in times of a pandemic. In addition to timely and accurate information, there are expectations for consistent messaging that outlines the steps needed to prevent the spread of the disease. Providing such messaging, however, is a challenge for public health agencies as a myriad of organizations compete for public attention (Hall & Wolf, 2021). Hence, it is critical for organizations to demonstrate partnership with other governmental and non-governmental agencies at the international, national, state, and local levels (Tagliacozzo et al., 2021). Our research suggests three recommendations for this purpose:

1. *Reiterate important messaging for broader impact.*

Studies suggest that information is better absorbed and acted upon in times of a crisis through redundant messaging, that is, the same message being repeated by multiple sources (Stephens et al., 2013). Such messaging could help address misinformation and inconsistencies surrounding the crisis. Hence, it is important for public health agencies to collaborate with trusted partners at all levels and echo important messages, either through direct quotes or through reposts. This tweet from CDC is an example:

> Know the facts about #COVID19. Don't share rumors & unintentionally spread misinformation. Federal, state & local governments are posting current and accurate information. For help in distinguishing rumor from fact, see @FEMA Coronavirus Rumor Control: https://t.co/Hi5AF1waWk https://t.co/AkbQjOM2xw. (March 23, 2020)

2. Build on the potential of external research institutions.

Our findings indicate these public health agencies relied heavily on internal scientific expertise in their online COVID-19 communication. We attributed such reliance to these agencies' inward-oriented organizational culture (Grönroos, 2019; Waterhouse & Lewis, 2004) and desire to use scientific primary data (Tagliacozzo et al., 2021). There was limited engagement with external research institutions (e.g., academic universities). These institutions, however, played important roles during the pandemic, including educating the public on the virus, tracking COVID-19 data, and conducting disease projections. Hence, public health agencies need to exhibit greater partnership with these institutions in their online communication. One way to do this is by sharing relevant data from trusted partners in responses to questions, as shown in FoHM's example below:

> @krisinformation Hi. Here you can read about a study on blood plasma at the Karolinska Institute: https://t.co/2CNKgJu6ZE. (June 3, 2020)

3. Steer clear of political actors.

By their mandates, public health agencies are science-focused agencies. In line with these mandates, their engagement with political officials (e.g., Prime Ministers, etc.) was relatively limited across the three countries in the early days of the pandemic. The tweets that mentioned political officials typically announced their press conferences or re-used information on the measures that are being undertaken (e.g., testing efforts). Some clarified the discretion of political officials in times of a pandemic. However, there were also a few tweets that emphasized how the public is listening to political officials. We argue that such tweets need to be avoided especially in contexts where the crisis might be politicized and used for ideological interests.

Making Target Audiences Explicit

Public health agencies tailor their social media messages to different target audiences. In some cases, these audiences are other government agencies, non-profit agencies, or private sector actors. In other cases, target audiences are social groups or the public in general. Tailoring messages to different audiences promotes an inclusive communication environment (Tagliacozzo et al., 2021). This is important for addressing the undue burden placed on some social groups as a result of the pandemic. Our recommendations on how to tailor messages effectively are threefold:

1. *Make target audiences explicit.*

Social media messages may not be perceived well or acted upon if it is not clear who the message targets. Hence, our suggestion is for public health agencies to indicate clearly who they are targeting at the beginning of their message. Here is an example of such a tweet by the CDC:

> #Parents, do you have a young child at home? It's important now more than ever to ensure your child is up to date on recommended childhood vaccinations. Learn how to protect your child from vaccine-preventable diseases. https://t.co/AR7356h iGP https://t.co/MnXaxB6tmo. (May 15, 2020)

2. *Customize the language but do it in plain language.*

Bean et al. (2016) suggest that information will be more credible if it is presented without the use of abbreviations. However, most online communication utilizes abbreviations in the form of hashtags or acronyms to meet the word limit. When these abbreviations are recognized and easily identified, they can be useful. When they are not, the message could be dismissed completely. Hence, we suggest the use of plain language that is free of jargon and easily recognizable by anyone during an ongoing epidemic. An example of a CDC message which may be dismissed is the following:

> #HCPs: COCA Call on Tuesday, May 19th, at 2 pm ET can also be found on COCA's Facebook profile via Facebook Live. Topic: Multisystem Inflammatory Syndrome in Children (MIS-C) Associated with Coronavirus Disease 2019 (#COVID19). Learn more: https://t.co/C1jAiruh8t. https://t.co/g1eVOdZc7b. (May 18, 2020)
>
> [HCP: Health Care Professionals; COCA: Clinician Outreach and Communication Activity]

3. *Using the right medium.*

While some audiences may be more active in one medium, others may prefer different mediums (e.g., press releases, YouTube). Hence, public health agencies first need to conduct studies on which outlet(s) are more effective in terms of reaching particular audiences. For example, the CDC does not have a Spanish Twitter (X) account, but it does have a YouTube channel in Spanish.

Communicating with Vulnerable Groups and the Organizations That Serve Them

In recent years, scholars and policymakers have been increasingly called upon to design disaster risk reduction (DRR) policies that are inclusive and avoid sidelining marginalized groups. In 2020, UN Women launched the Progress Tracker for Inclusive DRR Policies which exposed the mismatch between the calls for inclusiveness and their translation into policies and practices. Crisis communication during the COVID-19 pandemic has not been an exception in this respect. A comparative study on the health agencies' online messages in Italy, Sweden, and the United States revealed that less than 2% of the communications targeted groups such as migrants, pregnant women, or people with disabilities (Tagliacozzo et al., 2021). Here, we suggest some practical steps to achieve a more inclusive risk and crisis communication:

1. *Adopting a communication with communities (CwC) approach.*

As opposed to the traditional one-way crisis communication, a CwC approach is based on the principle that communication is a form of aid and that crisis response requires the deployment of an ad-hoc team to gather data on the information demands of crisis-affected communities (CDAC Network, 2014; Tagliacozzo & Magni, 2016). The approach is now widely adopted by many UN agencies and other humanitarian organizations, but it has been mostly neglected by government agencies. A CwC working group should be included in the emergency management agencies at all government levels to respond adequately to the information needs that will arise.

2. *Partnering with civil society.*

Vulnerable groups are the hardest to reach when it comes to providing aid during and after a crisis. For this reason, it is crucial to know and team up with the organizations that routinely serve them, such as faith-based institutions, nonprofits, and community centers (Clark-Ginsberg & Petrun Sayers, 2020).

Partnering with these entities would allow government agencies to overcome distrust and wariness as well as elaborate on official COVID-related information. Unfortunately, government agencies have rarely delivered official communications in collaboration with NGOs and other civil society organizations during the COVID pandemic (Tagliacozzo et al., 2021). Government agencies should consider these organizations as trusted partners and co-design messages together. For example, the Italian Institute of Health developed an online questionnaire in collaboration with the Italian Federation of Rare Diseases to collect data on the needs of patients with rare conditions during the pandemic:

> Online at https://t.co/VIZUtDV6xx and https://t.co/SZ0uYTRkWx #questionnaire to find out the #needs of #rarepatients during the #emergency from #Covid19. Joint initiative ISS and @uniamofimronlus. https://t.co/BELIZNBlDJ @MinistryofHealth @TVMR_CNMR @uniamofimronlus @DTaruscio. (March 23, 2020)

3. *Knowing how individual and social vulnerabilities translate into communication-related vulnerability.*

Recent conceptual shifts in DRR highlight that vulnerability is not a static concept but derives from the intersection of several variables within a given context (Hansson et al., 2020). Elderly people and persons with comorbidities were identified as particularly at risk and this made them a relevant target of many COVID-related communications. However, there is the need to understand how other types of vulnerabilities (e.g., race/ethnicity, migrant status, etc.) produce information inequalities concerning, for example, reduced ability to access, understand, and act upon crisis messages (Hansson et al., 2020). Our research highlighted this vulnerability. Although some messages contained links with information in other languages, all original tweets were written in the official language of the country. This could make it more difficult for non-native speakers to access information during the pandemic. An example from the CDC is below:

> Need #COVID19 information in a different language? Check out CDC's COVID-19 web pages in Spanish, simplified Chinese, Vietnamese, and Korean: https://t.co/tt4 9zOn1hf. https://t.co/tpX4Z3l9xr. (April 5, 2020)

Communicating with Workplaces That Are the Most Impacted

The COVID-19 pandemic has unevenly impacted private and public businesses and services, bringing to light the different needs of individuals in terms of information and support. Specifically, our research showed a vast number of differences between the number of tweets targeting workplaces and the stringency of lockdowns with Sweden (who did not enforce strict lockdown measures) having more messages of this type. For the next pandemic, we suggest public health agencies tailor crisis and risk messages for workplaces based on three main aspects.

1. Differentiate between essential and non-essential services and businesses.

Depending on the stringency of the national lockdown measures, many services and businesses were forced to shut down partially or completely. As a result, employees of essential businesses and services such as grocery stores, logistic and food production, and processing companies found themselves highly exposed to possible COVID-19 infection and in need of information about how to minimize the risk of infection at their workplaces. While much of this information may have been provided by the employers, government, and public health agencies should not put the responsibility to provide risk information solely in private employers' hands. Additionally, our research revealed that most of the online messages targeted healthcare workers or those working from home, providing limited advice for other essential workers (i.e., grocery store attendants), or non-essential workers that cannot work from home (i.e., restaurant workers). Moreover, employees and owners of non-essential services may be more in need of information on the resources available to cope with the hardships caused by the pandemic. These were important aspects missing from the online communication of public health agencies.

2. Differentiate between large and small businesses.

Academic literature shows that large and established firms perform better and recover faster and more easily in times of crisis (Alekseev et al., 2020; Zhang et al., 2009). Apart from size, other important factors include longevity and the gender of the owner, with male-owned businesses being more resilient and able to recover more quickly (Alekseev et al., 2020). This finding calls for a differentiated approach in terms of communication between larger businesses and small, family-run ones. Within our research, the CDC was the only health organization to have targeted messaging toward small businesses. An example is below:

> Are you a small business owner? @CDCgov's new factsheet can help you prepare your business for disruption during the #COVID19 outbreak and protect your employees' health: https://t.co/aLzrQP91sM. (May 8, 2020)

3. *Community and cultural institutions should not be overlooked.*

In a public health emergency, attention is given predominantly to health facilities, such as hospitals and nursing homes. However, governments must not forget that responding to an emergency means much more than just guaranteeing the physical survival of the people—it also means preserving the values and cultural institutions that give meaning to society. In fact, maintaining a community's social capital and well-being are two critical components of long-term resilience. In this respect, the CDC dedicated an entire section of their website to offer information on how to stay safe in community settings (https://www.cdc.gov/coronavirus/2019-ncov/community/index.html). The CDC also directed messaging toward community events and services. We suggest that organizations build off of this example below:

> CDC has new info to help camps, youth sports, K12 schools & higher ed, and restaurants & bars operate during #COVID19. These materials emphasize the importance of working w/ local health officials to make decisions & help prevent spread of COVID-19 See https://t.co/qbIZmiuPwQ https://t.co/x1QMkvWVJ9. (May 21, 2020)

Achieving the Right Balance Between Different Communication Styles and Objectives

Government organizations are responsible for providing relevant and reliable information during crises. In the case of Italy, Sweden, and the United States, these agencies tended to pursue different communication strategies that emphasized certain communication objectives or styles. We argue for three relevant lessons for public organizations' communication strategies.

1. *Provide clear instructions to the public.*

During crises, accurate and clear guidance is essential. During the COVID-19 pandemic, misinformation and disinformation challenged agency communication, particularly on social media (Cinelli et al., 2020; Shibli et al., 2021). Therefore, it is essential that public organizations actively seek to disseminate clear and accurate guidance on social media to proactively reduce the risk of misinformation campaigns. Since social media outlets are major sources when seeking information on ongoing crises (Austin et al., 2012), public organizations should aim to provide comprehensive and clear instructions that can be easily accessed, understood, and shared by other organizations and members of the public. An example of clear instructions can be found in FoHM's communication:

> People over 70 should limit social contact until further notice—Public Health Agency (March 16, 2020).

2. Support the public in adjusting when facing adversity.

During a crisis, people may be forced to adjust their lifestyles. Messages that assisted the public in adjusting to adversity were overall less frequent than, for example, instructions on how to respond. An illustrative supportive message from the CDC is below:

> It can be difficult to cope with fear & anxiety, changing daily routines, and a general sense of uncertainty about #COVID19. Although people respond to stressful situations in different ways, taking steps can help you manage stress. Visit https://t.co/U4L8e9kivh for more info. (April 1, 2020)

Psychosocial support is essential during crises in general and in the case of COVID-19 in particular (Hugelius et al., 2021). Thus, crisis communication by public organizations should consider the public's need to cope with anxiety and use supportive messages to create empathy or boost morale (Coombs, 2020). Therefore, public organizations should actively and frequently provide information that can help members of the public adjust to and cope with experienced challenges.

3. Adapt your communication style to the purpose of the message.

Providing instructions to the public and assisting them in adjusting to a crisis demands the careful use of different communication styles. An agentic communication style to disseminate instructions can be useful to provide clarity and express the reliability of agency information. An illustrative example of agentic communication combined with instructions can be found in ISS's communication:

> With the evolution of the #coronavirus epidemic, those who experience symptoms and think they have been infected must call 112. Here is the update of the decalogue on good behavior https://t.co/Zl3xbrStTq. (February 23, 2020)

In contrast, adjusting to the new situation calls for more communal communication styles that take the psychosocial needs of the targeted audience into consideration. Communal communication can establish the necessary moral and emotional connection to provide support. The CDC made use of communal communication combined with supportive messages:

> We know #COVID19 is causing anxiety for many of us. #BeKindToYourMind during these challenging times. CDC and @Google are partnering to share reliable, trusted information about ways to cope with stress. Learn more: https://t.co/GKZV8vsPCV. (May 10, 2020)

Of course, the right balance between agentic and communal communication styles may depend on cultural backgrounds and communication traditions. However, using different communication styles, depending on the message's purpose, may be best suited to provide the public with relevant and relatable information.

Assuming the Leadership Role

Public health agencies in Italy, Sweden, and the United States have assumed leadership roles in the context of the COVID-19 pandemic. They had to make sense of the unfolding crisis, make critical decisions, and communicate these decisions with diverse target audiences. These audiences looked to their public health agencies to respond to and provide leadership during this unprecedented time.

In this book chapter, we focus on transactional, transformational, and servant leadership styles. By the term transactional leadership, we refer to a process whereby the leader influences the followers to successfully complete a task to avoid punishment or obtain a reward (Van Eeden et al., 2008). The focus of a transformational leader, on the other hand, is on acknowledging the self-worth of the followers and motivating them for the benefit of the organization (Bass, 1997; Burns, 1978). There is also servant leadership, which involves the leader serving the followers by putting their interests first (Stone et al., 2004).

In light of our work on leadership styles, we present three recommendations that public health agencies should consider in their online pandemic-focused communication:

1. *Exhibit the right type of leadership for the policy context.*

Agencies need to make sure that their leadership style, as presented in their online communication, is consistent with the policy context within which they operate. Transactional leadership style, for instance, is more appropriate in contexts where there is a need for strict measures that require higher levels of public compliance (e.g., lockdown measures). Transformational leadership is helpful when there are limited mandatory measures and preventive actions are mainly based on the public's will alone. The below ISS (the first) and CDC (the second) tweets are examples of transactional and transformative messaging:

> How to get proper information about # COVID19 in the #socialnetwork era
> just follow the institutional sources
> think before sharing the news
> always check the publication date
> read the advice of the ISS https://t.co/H7F7vmeipu. (April 3, 2020)

> #COVID19 is the most serious health threat that has faced this country in more than 100 years. Thank you to those who have embraced social distancing. Stay motivated: think about a neighbor, grandmother, or co-worker who are vulnerable. https://t.co/oX9V0qGaJF @LarsLarsonShow. (March 28, 2020)

2. Keep the employees in mind.

Due to limited agency resources, longer shifts, and changing work-life balance, public health agency employees may experience work-related burnout and secondary traumatic stress. Hence, public health agencies need to go beyond targeting other agencies, businesses, and the broader public in their online communication; they also need to reach their employees. For this purpose, both transformational and servant leadership styles may be helpful. The CDC tweet below is an example of a servant leadership style:

> Dr. Vikram Krishnasamy, a CDC medical officer and #diseasedetective, was deployed to the field twice to support the #COVID19 response. Read more about his work and what inspired him to work in public health: https://t.co/4c5J4TPsBJ. https://t.co/rsO9WxBVt6. (May 22, 2020)

3. Acknowledge the mistakes.

There have been many unknowns of COVID-19, especially in the early days of the pandemic. More than a year and a half into the pandemic, these unknowns continue, in part due to new variants. Hence, it is understandable for agencies to make mistakes. However, organizations cannot learn from their mistakes until they admit that they have made one and they take ownership of it. Admitting mistakes is also important for building confidence in leadership. The tweet from FoHM demonstrates how public health agencies acknowledge their mistakes:

We have found errors in the report and now the authors go through the material again. We publish the report again as soon as this is done. (April 22, 2020)

Conclusion

Communication challenges have long plagued organizations charged with responding to crises. While online communication and the unprecedented nature of the COVID-19 pandemic magnified these challenges, this chapter outlines best practices and recommended strategies aimed to address and overcome these challenges. Utilizing data collected from the Twitter (X) accounts and press releases from three public health organizations in the United States, Sweden, and Italy, we developed seven recommendations to improve online communication during the COVID-19 pandemic. As citizens were faced with uncertainty due to the nature of the COVID-19 pandemic and the spread of misinformation, they looked to non-partisan, scientific organizations, like a country's health department, in order to reduce that uncertainty and improve their understanding of the crisis event. Therefore, these recommendations highlight a growing need to effectively utilize social media and Twitter (X) during crisis events.

Within each of these recommendations, we include three specific strategies on how to implement these recommendations. While these recommendations may not be possible to implement within every tweet or press release an organization puts out, we believe that achieving a balance between uniform and targeted messaging is important. Some of the recommendations such as *acknowledging community spread*, *reiterating important messages*, and *providing clear instructions* focus on providing uniform messaging to guide the public on appropriate actions. Such recommendations are important to limit the spread of misinformation and provide actionable steps during a crisis. However, other recommendations such as *customizing language*, *involving communities with vulnerable groups*, and *adapting the communication style* focus on targeted messaging to provide details needed for specific segments of the public or specific purposes. While they may seem at odds, both are needed in times of crisis to ensure equitable and effective online communication. As public health epidemics become more common, strategies like the ones outlined in this chapter will become more important. We hope that organizations, academics, and students will take these outlined strategies and build a better communication infrastructure for the next epidemic.

Discussion Questions

With social media becoming an ever-important channel to relaying information during crises, appropriate and effective use of the tool is becoming crucial to successful response efforts. Based on this chapter, we outline a few questions to help spark discussion on this topic.

1. What are some effective and ineffective ways that public health agencies in the United States, Sweden, or Italy utilized their online communication during the COVID-19 pandemic?
2. A subtheme of the chapter focused on uniform messaging to limit miscommunication but also targeted messaging to help specific vulnerable populations during the COVID-19 pandemic. Although these may seem contradictory, why are both needed for online communication?
3. If you had an opportunity to write a brief memo to advise one of the public health agencies studied within the chapter, what advice would you give and why?

Resources

Books and Articles:

1. Lin, X., Spence, P.R., Sellnow, T.L., & Lachlan, K.A. (2016). Crisis communication, learning and responding: Best practices in social media. *Computers in human behavior, 65,* 601–605.
2. Sutton, J., & Kuligowski, E.D. (2019). Alerts and warnings on short messaging channels: Guidance from an expert panel process. *Natural Hazards Review, 20*(2), Article 04019002.
3. White, C.M. (2011). *Social media, crisis communication, and emergency management: Leveraging Web 2.0 technologies.* CRC Press.

Online Training:

4. National Disaster Preparedness Training Center at the University of Hawai'i. Social Media Platforms for Disaster Management. *NDPTC.* https://ndptc.hawaii.edu/training/catalog/31/

References

Abele, A.E., & Wojciszke, B. (2014). Communal and agentic content in social cognition: A dual perspective model. In *Advances in experimental social psychology* (Vol. 50, pp. 195–255). Academic Press.

Alekseev, G., Amer, S., Gopal, M., Kuchler, T., Schneider, J.W., Stroebel, J., & Wernerfelt, N.C. (2020). *The effects of COVID-19 on U.S. small businesses: Evidence from owners, managers, and employees* (No. w27833). National Bureau of Economic Research.

Austin, L., Fisher Liu, B., & Jin, Y. (2012). How audiences seek out crisis information: Exploring the social-mediated crisis communication model. *Journal of Applied Communication Research, 40*(2), 188-207.

Bass, B.M. (1997). Does the transactional–transformational leadership paradigm transcend organizational and national boundaries?. *American Psychologist, 52*(2), 130. https://psycnet.apa.org/doi/10.1037/0003-066X.52.2.130

Bean, H., Liu, B. F., Madden, S., Sutton, J., Wood, M. M., & Mileti, D. S. (2016). Disaster warnings in your pocket: How audiences interpret mobile alerts for an unfamiliar hazard. *Journal of Contingencies and Crisis Management, 24*(3), 136-147.

Boin, A., Lodge, M., & Luesink, M. (2020). Learning from the COVID-19 crisis: An initial analysis of national responses. *Policy Design and Practice, 3*(3), 189–204. https://doi.org/10.1080/25741292.2020.1823670

Broad, G.M., Ball-Rokeach, S.J., Ognyanova, K., Stokes, B., Picasso, T., & Villanueva, G. (2013). Understanding communication ecologies to bridge communication research and community action. *Journal of Applied Communication Research, 41*(4), 325–345. https://doi.org/10.1080/00909882.2013.844848

Burns, J.M. (1978). *Leadership*. Harper and Row Publishers.

Carli, L.L., & Eagly, A.H. (2001). Gender, hierarchy, and leadership: An introduction. *Journal of Social Issues, 57*(4), 629–636. https://doi.org/10.1111/0022-4537.00232

CDAC Network. (2014). *CDAC Network Typhoon Haiyan learning review case study: Consolidating community feedback through CwC and AAP technical working groups in the Philippines.* CDAC Network. http://www.cdacnetwork.org/contentAsset/raw-data/7561706b-cf63-4754-8c2e-aa342de580c8/attachedFile

Cinelli, M., Quattrociocchi, W., Galeazzi, A., Valensise, C.A., Brugnoli, E., Schmidt, A.L., Zola, P., Zollo, F., & Scala, A. (2020). The COVID-19 social media infodemic. *Nature Scientific Reports, 10*, 16598. https://link.springer.com/content/pdf/10.1038/s41598-020-73510-5.pdf

Clark-Ginsberg, A., & Petrun Sayers, E.L. (2020). Communication missteps during COVID-19 hurt those already most at risk. *Journal of Contingencies and Crisis Management, 28*(4), 482–484. https://doi.org/10.1111/1468-5973.12304

Coombs, W.T. (2015). The value of communication during a crisis: Insights from strategic communication research. *Business Horizons, 58*(2), 141–148. https://doi.org/10.1016/j.bushor.2014.10.003

Coombs, W.T. (2020). Public sector crises: Realizations from Covid-19 for crisis communication. *PACO, 13*(2), 990–1001. https://doi.org/10.1285/i20356609v13i2p990

Fearnley, C., Winson, A.E.G., Pallister, J., & Tilling, R. (2017). Volcano crisis communication: Challenges and solutions in the 21st century. In C.J. Fearnley et al. (Eds.), *Observing the volcano world* (pp. 3–21). Springer.

Goldberg, B., & Whitcomb, D. (2020, April 12). Americans spend grim Easter Sunday at home as COVID-19 deaths near 22,000. *Reuters*. https://www.reuters.com/article/us-health-coronavirus-usa/americans-spend-grim-easter-sunday-at-home-as-covid-19-deaths-near-22000-idUSKCN21U0KN

Grönroos, C. (2019). Reforming public services: Does service logic have anything to offer? *Public Management Review, 21*(5), 775–788. https://doi.org/10.1080/14719037.2018.1529879

Hale, J.E., Dulek, R.E., & Hale, D.P. (2005). Crisis response communication challenges: Building theory from qualitative data. *The Journal of Business Communication (1973), 42*(2), 112–134. https://doi.org/10.1177/0021943605274751

Hall, K., & Wolf, M. (2021). Whose crisis? Pandemic flu, "communication disasters" and the struggle for hegemony. *Health, 25*(3), 322–338. https://doi.org/10.1177/1363459319886112

Hansson, S., Orru, K., Siibak, A., Bäck, A., Krüger, M., Gabel, F., & Morsut, C. (2020). Communication-related vulnerability to disasters: A heuristic framework. *International Journal of Disaster Risk Reduction, 51*(101931). https://doi.org/10.1016/j.ijdrr.2020.101931

Hugelius, K., Johansson, S., & Sjölin, H. (2021). "We Thought We Were Prepared, but We Were Not": Experiences from the management of the psychosocial support response during the COVID-19 pandemic in Sweden. A mixed-methods study. *International Journal of Environmental Research and Public Health, 18*(17), 9079. https://doi.org/10.3390/ijerph18179079

Johns Hopkins University & Medicine. (2021). *COVID-19 dashboard by the Center for Systems Science and Engineering*. Johnson Hopkins University. https://coronavirus.jhu.edu/map.html

Jung et al., 2021 and add Jung, S. M., Endo, A., Kinoshita, R., & Nishiura, H. (2021). Projecting a second wave of COVID-19 in Japan with variable interventions in high-risk settings. *Royal Society Open Science, 8*(3), 202169.

Lindsay, B.R. (2011, September 6). *Social media and disasters: Current uses, future options, and policy considerations*. Congressional Research Service. https://nsi.org/ReferenceLibrary/983.pdf

Maal, M., & Wilson-North, M. (2019). Social media in crisis communication—the "do's" and "don'ts." *International Journal of Disaster Resilience in the Built Environment*. https://www.emerald.com/insight/content/doi/10.1108/IJDRBE-06-2014-0044/full/html

Panagiotopoulos, P., Barnett, J., Bigdeli, A.Z., & Sams, S. (2016). Social media in emergency management: Twitter as a tool for communicating risks to the public. *Technological Forecasting and Social Change, 111*, 86–96. https://doi.org/10.1016/j.techfore.2016.06.010

Panthaky, P. (2020). Redefining vulnerability in the era of COVID-19. *Lancet (London, England), 395*(10230), 1089. https://doi.org/10.1016/S0140-6736(20)30757-1

Renzulli, M. (2020, December 22). *Coronavirus in Italy: Timeline of the COVID-19 pandemic in Italy 2020*. Italofile. https://www.italofile.com/coronavirus-in-italy/#Update_12_April_2020

Reuter, C., Hughes, A.L., & Kaufhold, M.A. (2018). Social media in crisis management: An evaluation and analysis of crisis informatics research. *International Journal of Human–Computer Interaction, 34*(4), 280–294. https://doi.org/10.1080/10447318.2018.1427832

Savage, M. (2020, April 25). *Coronavirus: Has Sweden got its science right?* BBC News. https://www.bbc.com/news/world-europe-52395866

Shibli, R., Kouzi, S., & El-Amine, B. A. (2021). Digital skills as a pathway to decent digital work?. *Digital refugee livelihoods and decent work, 28*.

Stephens, K.K., Barrett, A.K., & Mahometa, M.J. (2013). Organizational communication in emergencies: Using multiple channels and sources to combat noise and capture attention. *Human Communication Research, 39*(2), 230–251. https://doi.org/10.1111/hcre.12002

Stewart, M.C., & Wilson, B.G. (2016). The dynamic role of social media during Hurricane# Sandy: An introduction of the STREMII model to weather the storm of the crisis lifecycle. *Computers in Human Behavior, 54*, 639–646. https://doi.org/10.1016/j.chb.2015.07.009

Stone, A.G., Russell, R.F., & Patterson, K. (2004). Transformational versus servant leadership: A difference in leader focus. *Leadership & Organization Development Journal*. https://www.emerald.com/insight/content/doi/10.1108/01437730410538671/full/html

Sturges, D.L. (1994). Communicating through crisis: A strategy for organizational survival. *Management Communication Quarterly, 7*(3), 297–316. https://doi.org/10.1177/0893318994007003004

Sutton, J., & Kuligowski, E.D. (2019). Alerts and warnings on short messaging channels: Guidance from an expert panel process. *Natural Hazards Review, 20*(2), Article 04019002. https://ascelibrary.org/doi/abs/10.1061/(ASCE)NH.1527-6996.0000324

Tagliacozzo, S., & Magni, M. (2016). Communicating with communities (CwC) during post-disaster reconstruction: An initial analysis. *Natural Hazards, 84*(3), 2225–2242. https://doi.org/10.1007/s11069-016-2550-3

Tagliacozzo, S., Albrecht, F., & Ganapati, N.E. (2021). International perspectives on COVID-19 communication ecologies: Public health agencies' online communication in Italy, Sweden, and the United States. *American Behavioral Scientist, 65*(7), 934–955.

Van Eeden, R., Cilliers, F., & Van Deventer, V. (2008). Leadership styles and associated personality traits: Support for the conceptualisation of transactional and transformational leadership. *South African Journal of Psychology, 38*(2), 253–267. https://hdl.handle.net/10520/EJC98493

Veil, S.R., Buehner, T., & Palenchar, M.J. (2011). A work-in-process literature review: Incorporating social media in risk and crisis communication. *Journal of Contingencies and Crisis Management, 19*(2), 110–122. https://doi.org/10.1111/j.1468-5973.2011.00639.x

Waterhouse, J., & Lewis, D. (2004). Communicating culture change: HRM implications for public sector organizations. *Public Management Review, 6*(3), 353–376. https://doi.org/10.1080/1471903042000256538

Wendling, C., Radisch, J., & Jacobzone, S. (2013). The use of social media in risk and crisis communication. *OECD Working Papers on Public Governance, 24*, 1–42. https://doi.org/10.1787/19934351

World Health Organization. (2020, March 11). *WHO Director-General's opening remarks at the media briefing on COVID-19—11 March 2020.* https://www.who.int/director-general/speeches/detail/who-director-general-s-opening-remarks-at-the-media-briefing-on-covid-19---11-march-2020

World Health Organization. (2021, September 20). *WHO coronavirus dashboard.* https://covid19.who.int

Zhang, Y., Lindell, M.K., & Prater, C.S. (2009). Vulnerability of community businesses to environmental disasters. *Disasters, 33*(1), 38–57. https://doi.org/10.1111/j.1467-7717.2008.01061.x

· 2 0 ·

IN THE END, COVID-19 GOES ON AND ON

Mildred Perreault & Sarah Smith-Frigerio

Years into the pandemic, it almost feels trite to discuss the myriad of ways in which COVID-19 has changed nearly every aspect of our lives, including our communication practices. While scholars and practitioners often focus attention on crisis response, crises are rarely about response, but rather mitigation and preparation efforts. Many argue that COVID-19 highlighted a certain level of hubris about what we thought we knew. Others maintain we need to rethink all crisis communication strategies given what we have learned. The status quo of responding rather than planning for a crisis appears to still dominate.

Even in early 2023, we are seeing news articles critical of Congress and other governmental agencies in the United States, as well as other international governments and agencies and how they handled the pandemic. Many organizations are still not adequately prepared for a large-scale crisis or disaster like the COVID-19 pandemic. For example, one editorial opinion recently published in The Washington Post states:

> Neither the outgoing Congress nor (President) Biden rose to the occasion to create a national bipartisan commission on the pandemic similar to the 9/11 commission. After the death of 1 million Americans, such an investigation would have highlighted lessons learned from the chaotic pandemic response, shown the way forward on future threats and helped unravel the mystery of the virus's origins. As it now

stands, separate probes are planned in Congress's more partisan and divisive atmosphere. (Editorial Board, *The Washington Post*, January 8, 2023)

This book encourages us to think back to those lessons we learned, and the modifications we made, in real time, to the ways we communicated about and within the contexts of the pandemic. The communication ecology approach demonstrates that, on multiple levels, we reorganized and rethought our personal and professional communicative actions, but also our limitations and resourcefulness.

These chapters provide insights into a prolonged, complex, and compounded crisis. The case studies contributed to this volume provide important snapshots into the many challenges that presented themselves throughout the first two years of the pandemic. While other crises and disasters have certainly tested our communication systems and practices before COVID-19, the pandemic shone a spotlight on our communication systems at the individual, organizational, community, and even national and international levels in a way that many laypersons, and even practitioners, may have never experienced before.

Overall, the perspectives we have gained span different levels of communication from the individual and family level, to the organizational, the community and regional level, and national and international level. There are often many things taking place when a crisis occurs that conflate or confound the crisis communication response. COVID-19 showed us that communication efforts were impacted at every level. Media and communication scholars and practitioners, like everyone else, have to figure out ways to communicate effectively and with empathy.

Contributions to the Field

Throughout the chapters in this volume, our contributors have discussed how crisis communication and responses to COVID-19 varied at different levels. But they have also provided a platform for rich discussion around those practices and the places where communication efforts within these levels intersect with one another. We can learn much from crises, as they often present an opportunity to recognize our shortcomings as communicators and improve upon established practices.

Additionally, many of our contributors also chose to shine a light on the compounding crises that individuals and practitioners had to contend with while managing risk involved with COVID-19. Throughout these chapters, we see references to ecological disasters exacerbated by climate change and the additional strain placed on institutions, such as education and healthcare, which were already facing significant pressures. We also see economic impacts, supply chain issues and material shortages. We see the impacts of misinformation and disinformation campaigns on public health, as well as increasing—and for many, unexpected—political polarization surrounding the COVID-19 response.

We see the difficulties of isolation and mental health concerns experienced by many during the pandemic. We see how COVID-19 can—and did—exacerbate issues regarding systemic and overt racism, and posed complications toward advocacy and activism efforts focused on confronting racism. A serious, prolonged crisis often has the capability to uncover structural issues within communities and societies. The COVID-19 pandemic has been no different.

Where Do We Go from Here?

Beyond a snapshot of the issues faced during the first two years of the pandemic, what does this volume provide to readers? As a reader, you may have been practicing in the fields we described within this text at the time of the pandemic, or you are now dealing with the long-term implications of those challenges. Crises end but can create new crises. The cyclical nature of crisis communication is one we can learn from, and reflection and evaluation of existing practices can create new ways to address future crises and improve resiliency. As communication scholars and practitioners, many of us focus on what we can do to change outcomes, alleviate pressures, save lives, and save money. Communication is integral to all those processes.

The value of these chapters also lies in the way that case studies can help us reflect and create new approaches and solutions. Case studies have the capacity to piece together a range of perspectives, creating a richer view of the challenges that are created in crisis situations across varying levels. By including studies with content analysis, interviews, observations, and survey data, the contributors and editors provide a platform for readers to dive deeper and rethink how crisis communication practices impact more than the field of public relations as well as multiple levels within the communication ecology framework simultaneously.

Our older assumptions no longer suffice. Public relations is not the only area in which risk and crisis communication occur, health communication is no longer something we can limit to health promotion, and social media is the first line communication tactic for many individuals and organizations today. Our ability to see beyond the mistakes and missteps during a pandemic is what helps us to rethink our current practices. It helps us to tailor best practices and the foundations of future success.

Practical Implications

Additional answers for readers are also found within the practical and scholarly implications of each chapter. What can and should public health officials do to reduce uncertainty and mitigate damages from misinformation and disinformation campaigns (especially as we confront additional health crises, such as monkeypox, the reappearance of polio across the globe, and the potential of human-to-human transmission of H5N1 highly pathogenic avian influenza)? Even since 2020, issues of biosecurity, climate change, and other challenges involving food poverty, immigration, and disaster management have become more challenging. The problem of misinformation and disinformation, or simply unequal access to accurate and accessible information, becomes central to how all people respond.

Crises do not exist in a single sector or level, and therefore involve an extensive communication ecology, involving exchanges of public information at a variety of levels. There are professional practices which can mitigate, and, in some cases, eliminate long-term implications of these crises. Understanding the roles of journalists, public relations professionals, government officials, and even individuals in this web of communication can provide a stronger network of public communication. The more robust that network, the more equipped it is to respond to a variety of crises and disasters.

The leveled approach we present in this text has been suggested by scholars who use CERC and other frameworks to evaluate crises; that said, this text is one of the first to have the capacity to examine individual, organizational, community and regional, and national and international levels of a crisis. COVID-19 will most likely not be the last major crisis we face, and therefore provides a solid case study for how we should evaluate crises with a multi-level approach in the future.

The chapters contributed to this volume not only provide a snapshot of what we experienced during the first two years of COVID-19 but also provide a springboard for future scholarly research and changes to the way we strategically communicate and craft messages to a wide variety of audiences. How can employers better communicate with and support working parents who must navigate their children's health and educational disruptions with the utmost flexibility and resilience? How do organizations effectively and accurately communicate and mitigate health risks with their stakeholders? What have journalists learned about covering health crises and environmental disasters that can improve the understanding and efficacy of individuals within their communities? How can we better foster individual and community resilience within the helping professions, but also, communities as a whole? How can we combat disaster fatigue as the pandemic and other crises drag on? In fact, it is likely that we will be conducting research on the effects of COVID-19, and changing our communicative practices due to the issues that arose during the pandemic for many years to come.

Key takeaways from this text:

1. What is newsworthy is often what is timely, but crises like COVID-19 and the compounding issues around it merit more examination. Media and communication professionals must keep tabs on how agencies and organizations rethink their professional practices in light of crises that have longer, prolonged impacts.
2. An organization cannot remove itself from the environment in which it is situated. There are often outside forces that affect a person or organization's ability to communicate more widely in a crisis. These external and internal issues extend beyond the control of one person, organization, or even community.
3. The COVID-19 crisis has become part of the culture. That said, over time people forget about the challenges and real-time impacts of a crisis. COVID-19 will not be the last crisis of this scale. People need to continue to talk about it and include pandemics, and crises with similar impacts, in their crisis communication planning and strategies.
4. Social media and digital communication were dominant forms of communication in the pandemic, but they created additional challenges and problems. Social media and digital communication can never entirely replace other means of communication, including quality journalism, public information and interpersonal communication.
5. Policy and strategy are not just made by political figures. Corporations, schools, and families have power to change the narrative around a crisis or disaster. Grassroots movements can help people and communities

communicate about a crisis, build resilience, and create a more vibrant crisis and disaster communication ecology.

In the introductory chapter, we spoke of our goal to be helpful not only to communication and journalism scholars but also to undergraduate and graduate students, as well as to communication practitioners. It is no easy feat to provide beneficial tools and insight to such a wide audience. We sincerely hope that we—along with our gracious contributors—have achieved that goal, and we look forward to the research and applications that result from this work and many other scholars' work on the COVID-19 pandemic.

Reference

Editorial Board. (2023, January 8). Opinion: Congress has not stepped up to fight COVID-19—or the next pandemic. *The Washington Post.* https://www.washingtonpost.com/opinions/2023/01/08/covid-19-pandemic-congress-funding/

EDITORS

Mildred F. "Mimi" Perreault (Ph.D., University of Missouri) is an Assistant Professor in the Zimmerman School of Advertising and Mass Communication at the University of South Florida. Perreault has researched public relations, local journalism, and disaster communication. Previously, Perreault was an Assistant Professor of Media and Communication at East Tennessee State University.

Sarah Smith-Frigerio (Ph.D., University of Missouri) is an Assistant Professor of Public Relations in the Department of Communication at The University of Tampa. She focuses on health and crisis communication, particularly how individuals use digital media for peer support and health advocacy when facing health concerns.

CONTRIBUTORS

Jeanette Abrahamsen (M.A., University of South Florida) is an instructor at the Zimmerman School of Advertising & Mass Communications at the University of South Florida. Abrahamsen earned her master's degree in digital journalism and design in 2015.

Bipul Adhikari (Ph.D., University of Canterbury) has nearly 7 years' experience in journalism and public relations in Nepal, and holds a PhD in disaster communication. Adhikari works with local government in New Zealand concerning policy formation, diversity, and inclusion.

Frederike Albrecht (Ph.D., Uppsala University) is a researcher and Senior Lecturer at the Department of Political Science at the Swedish Defence University. She is also a Research Fellow at the Centre of Natural Hazards and Disaster Science (CNDS), Sweden.

Janelle Applequist (Ph.D., Pennsylvania State University) is an Associate Professor of Advertising and Public Relations at the Zimmerman School of Advertising and Mass Communications at the University of South Florida. She is the author of two books and many articles in the field of advertising and health communication.

Jennifer Anderson (Ph.D., Michigan State University) is an Associate Professor in the School of Communication & Journalism at South Dakota State

University. Anderson is a prolific health communication scholar with over 40 articles in journals including *Health Communication, Journal of Health Communication, International Journal of Communication and Health*.

Cristina L. Azocar (Ph.D., University of Michigan) is a citizen of the Upper Mattaponi Tribe and Professor of Journalism at San Francisco State University. Azocar's research focuses on the intersection of race and journalistic practice, particularly in the area of news coverage of Indigenous people.

Nazanin Bani Amerian (Ph.D., University of Southern Mississippi) is a Postdoctoral Fellow at Northeastern University. Amerian was born and raised in Tehran, Iran and holds a PhD in communication studies, and a master's degree in mass communication and media from the University of Central Florida. Amerian's research focuses on intercultural, health, risk, and crisis communication.

Brandon Boatwright (Ph.D., University of Tennessee) is an Assistant Professor of Sports Communication at Clemson University. He has a BA and MA from Clemson and completed his Ph.D. at the University of Tennessee, Knoxville in Communication and Information with an emphasis in Advertising and Public Relations. His research examines the intersection of sports, social media, and opinion leadership.

Ashleigh Bunn (M.A., East Tennessee State University) With a decade and a half of examining digital marketing data and driving insights, Bunn currently shapes the strategy of Digital Marketing at Duke Health as the Director of Digital Analytics and Marketing Strategy.

Derrick Boakye Boadu (MSc. Development & International Cooperation Sciences from Sapienza University of Rome, Italy) is a Ph.D. student at Florida International University studying in the Department of Public Administration. His research interests are emergency management, organizational leadership, public & nonprofit management, performance management, and diversity management.

Candi Carter Olson (Ph.D., University of Pittsburgh, Pennsylvania) is an Associate Professor of Media and Society in the Department of Journalism and Communication at Utah State University. She's also an affiliate faculty member for American Studies and serves as a faculty contact for American Studies students interested in media courses.

Amnee Elkhalid (Ph.D., University of Missouri) is an Assistant Professor of Communication at the University of Arkansas. Elkhalid researches identity, diversity, and adversity with interest in how messages influence identity development, identity management, and relationships. Elkhalid's recent work includes parent–child communication, family involvement and education, narrative sense-making, stigmatizing communication.

Jessica Elton (Ph.D., Purdue University, Indiana) is a Professor in the School of Communication, Media & Theatre Arts at Eastern Michigan University. She holds a Ph.D. in Health Communication from Purdue University, an M.A. in Intercultural Communication from the University of Denver, and a B.A. in English from the University of Nevada, Reno.

Jessica Freeman (Ph.D., University of Missouri) is a faculty member in the Department of Communication at the University of Tennessee at Chattanooga. Originally from Fort Worth, Texas, Freeman obtained her Ph.D. from the School of Journalism at the University of Missouri. Her research investigates how relationships are socially constructed and defined through both interpersonal and mass communication.

N. Emel Ganapati (Ph.D., University of Southern California) is a Professor in Public Policy and Administration at Florida International University. She holds a M.A. in Planning from the University of Pennsylvania and a Ph.D. degree in Planning from the School of Policy, Planning and Development.

Ella Hackett (B.A., Appalachian State University) is a graduate student at the University of South Florida Zimmerman School of Advertising and Mass Communciations. She has also published in *Journalism & Mass Communication Quarterly*.

Alexis Handler (B.A., Appalachian State University) is a postgraduate student focusing on international and intercultural communication. She holds a B.S. in Public Relations with a dual minor in Spanish, and Hospitality and Tourism Management.

Virginia S. Harrison (Ph.D., Pennsylvania State University) is an Assistant Professor in the Department of Communication at Clemson University's College of Behavioral, Social and Health Sciences. She spent seven years in public relations and fundraising practice before earning her Ph.D. from the Bellisario College of Communications at Penn State University.

J. Brian Houston (Ph.D., University of Oklahoma) is Professor and Chair in the Department of Communication and the Department of Public Health at the University of Missouri and is Director of the Disaster and Community Crisis Center (DCC) at the University of Missouri. Houston's research focuses on communication at all phases of disasters and the mental health effects and political consequences of community crises.

Joel Iverson (Ph.D., Arizona State University) is a Professor in the Department of Communication Studies at the University of Montana. Iverson's work is in organizational communication, nonprofit studies, knowledge management, risk and crisis communication, and health communication. Iverson has been published in more than 20 journal articles and authored a number of book chapters in organizational communication.

Kayleigh Jackson (M.A., Clemson University, South Carolina) graduated from the Clemson University Master of Arts in Communications, Technology, and Society program in spring 2023. Her research interests lie in sports communication, particularly via social media, and the intersection of digital activism with sporting corporations.

Lauren J. Johnsen (Ph.D., University of Missouri) is an Assistant Professor in the English, Philosophy and Communication Studies Department at the University of Wisconsin-Stout. She studies interpersonal, family, and health communication in the context of maternal health. Her work has been published in *Southern Communication Journal* and the *Kentucky Journal of Communication*.

Benjamin R. LaPoe II (Ph.D., Louisiana State University) is an Assistant Professor in the School of Communication Studies at Ohio University, teaching political communication and race. He currently serves as the director of the Political Communication certificate and is the adviser for Ohio University's Political Communication Student Group.

Victoria LaPoe (Ph.D., Louisiana State University) is an Associate Professor in the School of Communication Studies at Ohio University. LaPoe's work focuses on media diversity, digital media and marketing strategy of media. Previously, she served as broadcasting and film coordinator and Assistant Professor at Western Kentucky University's School of Journalism and Broadcasting.

Juan Liu (Ph.D., Wayne State University) is an Assistant Professor in the Department of Mass Communication at Towson University. Her research focuses on corporate social advocacy, strategic communication, social media, and political misinformation.

Monique Luisi (Ph.D., University of Kansas) is an Assistant Professor of Strategic Communication in the School of Journalism at the University of Missouri. Her research focuses on the ways people and media communicate about health and disease prevention, and how identity influences this communication. She researches communication about disease and prevention through new media, improving health & science communication accessibility, and communication about marginalized groups (e.g., race and sexuality) in entertainment media.

Mia Moody-Ramirez (Ph.D., University of Texas at Austin) is Professor and Chair of the Baylor University Department of Journalism, Public Relations and New Media. Her research emphasizes media framing of people of color, women, and other underrepresented groups. The author or co-author of four books, Moody-Ramirez has also been widely published in a variety of academic and industry journals.

Jensen Moore (Ph.D., University of Missouri) is an Associate Professor of Public Relations in the Gaylord College of Mass Communication at the University of Oklahoma. She teaches public relations principles, origins, and practice, crisis communication, social media strategies, public relations campaigns, and contemporary issues in public relations.

Greg Perreault (Ph.D., University of Missouri) is a scholar of digital journalism. Perreault is an Associate Professor of Digital Literacy and Analytics at the University of South Florida, and was previously an Associate Professor at Appalachian State University. He is also the Reviews Editor for *Journalism & Mass Communication Quarterly*.

Joel Lansing Reed (Ph.D., University of Missouri) is an Assistant Professor in the School of Journalism and Strategic Media at the University of Arkansas. He specializes in public relations and strategic political communication. He is especially interested in political moderates and the role of identity cross pressures in political messaging.

Carrie Reif-Stice (Ph.D., University of Southern Mississippi) is an Assistant Professor at Augusta University. Her research agenda concentrates on risk and crisis communication and health communication. She is published in several academic journals, including *Journalism and Mass Communication Educator* and her work is featured in several edited volumes.

Melanie B. Richards (Ph.D., Georgia State University) is the Associate Chair of the East Tennessee State University Department of Media & Communication and leads the department's Advertising and Public Relations program.

She has been working in the research, analytics, and account planning world for over 20 years.

Erika Schneider (Ph.D., University of Missouri) is an Assistant Professor of Public Relations in the S.I. Newhouse School of Public Communications at Syracuse University. Schneider is a public relations researcher who specializes in strategic communication with an emphasis on risk and crisis communication.

Serena Tagliacozzo (Ph.D., University College London) is specialized in disaster communication with a focus on long-term post-disaster recovery. She is currently an Associate Editor of the Journal Frontiers in Disaster Communication.

Anna Valiavska (Ph.D., University of Missouri) is an independent researcher who writes about race, workplace communication, and organizational identity management. She works as a researcher and consultant in areas of innovation and workplace equity. Valiavska teaches Organizational Communication courses at the University of Puget Sound.

Steven Venette (Ph.D., North Dakota State University) is a Professor in the School of Media and Communication at the University of Southern Mississippi. Topic areas of his research include risk communication, crisis communication, public relations, organizational communication, and health communication.

Kaila Witkowski (Ph.D., M.P.A., Florida International University) is an Assistant Professor of Sustainability and Disaster Management at Florida Atlantic University. Witkowski also has a MSW from the University of Maryland. Her research focuses on the intersection of public health, public administration and emergency management.

Carla White (M.A. Clemson University, South Carolina) is a Ph.D. student at the Tombras School of Advertising and Public Relations at the University of Tennessee, Knoxville. She graduated from the Clemson University M.A. in Communications, Technology, and Society program in Spring 2022.

Jayne Yerrick (M.A. Stony Brook University) is a Sociology Ph.D. student at Stony Brook University. Her main research interests include gender, inequality, and media. As an undergraduate student, Yerrick studied Journalism, minored in Sociology, and earned a certificate in Political Communication.

INDEX

advertising 2, 3, 4, 5 6, 135, 136, 137, 138, 139, 140, 141, 143, 145, 147, 148, 167, 177
air pollution 278
anti-Asian 336, 337, 338, 339, 341, 342, 343, 345, 346, 347, 358
attribution theory 337, 339, 342

Black Lives Matter 9, 141, 321, 322, 323, 333, 324, 325, 327, 328, 329, 330, 331
Branding 115, 117, 119, 122, 125, 127, 330

#ChineseVirus 9, 335, 336, 337, 338, 339, 341, 342, 343, 344, 345 346, 347, 354
celebrity advertising 142, 143, 146, 147
community 355, 358, 377
community resilience 1, 7, 8, 260, 261, 262, 263, 265, 266, 267, 268, 269, 270, 271, 319, 383
comparative perspective 355, 357
compounding crisis 304

conflicting crises 276, 280, 281, 288, 289, 290, 291, 292
convergence behavior archetypes 82
coping 4, 41, 44, 46, 49, 50, 53, 110, 182, 183, 268, 269, 259, 301, 302
crisis communication 302, 312, 314, 342, 356, 357, 358, 365, 367, 369, 379, 380, 381, 383
critical race theory 9, 324

disaster communication ecology 301, 384
disaster response 282, 300, 303, 304, 313
disease prevention 189, 203, 204, 393

earthquake 298, 300, 302, 306, 311
environmental 92, 251, 275, 287, 288, 301, 306, 308, 309, 312, 383

Facebook 219, 223, 224, 225, 227, 261, 321, 322, 335, 337, 339, 341, 342, 343, 344, 345, 346, 347, 348, 364

394　INDEX

fairness theory 337, 340, 341, 347, 337, 340, 341, 345, 347
fenceline communities 276, 279, 282, 283, 284, 285, 287, 288, 289, 290, 291
field theory 7, 172, 176, 184

generational differences 216, 218, 219, 224, 227, 228
grief 5, 11, 79, 80, 81, 83, 84, 85, 87, 88, 89, 90, 92, 93, 94

hashtag campaigns 55
healthcare 79, 83, 139, 191, 195, 201, 207, 216, 224, 225, 226, 227, 259, 260, 261, 264, 265, 266, 270, 271, 275, 277, 278, 282, 285, 288, 304, 310
health communication 14, 31, 33, 34, 146, 202, 208, 209, 381
health system 41, 189, 269, 311
higher education 66, 73, 99, 105, 107
hurricane/*typhoon 10, 93, *298, 300, 302, 311, 312, 356

identity 104, 116, 122, 125, 128, 156, 165, 166, 180, 184, 235, 241, 280
Indigenous communities 7, 8, 234, 235, 236, 237, 238, 239, 241, 250, 251
individual resilience 260, 262, 269, 270
infodemic 4, 13, 15, 16, 190
integrated marketing communications 6, 120, 136

journalistic *habitus* 184

marketing 43, 115, 116, 117, 119, 120, 121, 122, 123, 124, 125, 126, 127, 128, 136
media usage 7, 215, 216, 218, 219, 220, 227
meme 46, 322, 324, 325, 326, 328, 329, 330, 331
mental health 4, 11, 27, 30, 40, 41, 42, 43, 44, 45, 46, 47, 48, 49, 50, 51, 52, 53, 54, 63, 64, 66, 67, 68, 69, 70, 71 72, 73, 80, 94, 242, 259, 266, 270, 304, 308, 381, 392

misinformation 3, 4, 13, 14, 15, 16, 17, 25, 31, 33, 34, 35, 36, 42, 49, 172, 175, 181, 182, 183, 227, 262, 263, 267, 306, 308, 321, 336, 337, 338, 346, 347, 356, 362, 363, 368, 369, 372, 381, 382

Native peoples 233, 235, 236, 237, 238, 239, 240, 241
news media 83, 144, 181, 182, 194, 217, 219, 238, 239, 259, 267, 335, 338, 339, 345
NFL 6, 135, 142, 153, 154, 155, 156, 157, 158, 159, 160, 161, 162, 163, 164, 165, 166, 167
nurses 8, 90, 259 260, 261, 263, 264, 265, 266, 267, 268, 269, 270, 271, 277

parenting 4, 63, 64, 65, 66, 68, 69, 70, 71, 72, 73, 74, 75
patient 68, 83, 194, 202, 203, 204, 205, 206, 207, 210, 264, 265, 278, 282, 285, 289, 297, 366
political communication 2, 281, 288, 289
political rhetoric 8, 9, 275, 276, 279
Politics 20, 55, 107, 205, 234, 236, 242, 249, 277, 285, 288, 306, 326
public health 7, 14, 15, 17, 19, 40, 41, 42, 46, 92, 100, 108, 115, 135, 136, 137, 142, 147, 174, 180, 191, 193, 194, 205, 210, 216, 227, 262, 266, 275, 276, 278, 279, 281, 282, 284, 287, 288, 289, 299, 304, 313, 323, 345, 347, 355, 357, 361, 362, 363, 364, 365, 367, 368, 369, 370, 371, 372, 373, 381, 382
public relations 2, 5, 11, 55, 91, 115, 116, 128, 146, 155, 303, 304, 381, 382

reddit 91, 224, 266, 321, 322, 324, 325, 326, 329, 330, 331
renewal 100, 101, 102, 109, 110, 111, 156
reporting 14, 16, 20, 28, 34, 158, 171, 173, 174, 175, 177, 179, 238, 251, 297, 298, 309, 313, 314

situational crisis communication theory 6, 155
social media 3, 4, 5, 7, 8, 14, 16, 19, 21, 22, 23, 24, 30, 34, 36, 40, 42, 43, 44, 54, 55, 56, 80, 81, 82, 83, 84, 85, 86, 87, 88, 89, 90, 91, 92, 93, 102, 117, 118, 120, 121, 123, 127, 129, 136, 137, 138, 143, 144, 145, 147, 148, 154, 155, 156, 157, 165, 166, 167, 172, 173, 174, 181, 18, 183, 194, 195, 196, 197, 201, 202, 203, 205, 206, 207, 208, 209, 210, 215, 216, 219, 224, 225, 227, 228, 233, 237, 239, 240, 241, 242, 243, 244, 246, 247, 248, 249, 250, 251, 252, 259, 261, 262, 263, 267, 271, 286, 302, 314, 321, 322, 324, 325, 330, 331, 336, 337, 338, 339, 340, 341, 342, 346, 347, 348, 356, 357, 364, 368, 372, 373, 382, 383
social media mourning 5, 79, 80, 81, 82, 83, 88, 89, 91, 92, 93
social support 3, 40, 44, 45, 46, 47, 49, 52, 54, 259, 260, 261, 264, 265, 266, 269, 270, 369
spontaneous memorials 89, 90, 91
sport 62, 135, 142, 143, 153, 155, 156, 157, 165, 167, 172, 176, 177, 182, 368
sport fans 142, 153, 154, 156, 157, 158, 161, 162, 164, 165, 166, 167
sterilization 275, 276, 277, 278, 279, 281, 282, 284, 285, 286, 287, 289, 291
systemic racism 280, 322, 330

TikTok 8, 42, 56, 223, 225, 226, 227, 237, 241, 242, 243, 246, 249, 250, 251, 259, 261, 262, 263, 264, 265, 267, 268, 271, 272, 348
Twitter (X) 40, 42, 43, 44, 45, 53, 54, 56, 64, 82, 83, 84, 85, 86, 87, 90, 92, 122, 126, 129, 154, 156, 157, 158, 159, 164, 165, 166, 195, 209, 235, 261, 271, 322, 323, 325, 327, 328, 330, 331, 337, 338, 339, 342, 348, 358, 361, 365, 372

uncertainty 4, 7, 10, 13, 15, 16, 26, 28, 31, 32, 33, 34, 35, 40, 44, 64, 74, 91, 101, 106, 156, 162, 167, 180, 216, 217, 219, 356, 369, 372, 382

vaccine 6, 14, 17, 20, 28, 29, 30, 31, 33, 34, 35, 39, 84, 85, 87, 93, 107, 135, 137, 139, 140, 142, 143, 144, 145, 146, 148, 176, 190, 191, 194, 201, 202, 205, 206, 208, 210, 218, 222, 239, 245, 246, 247, 248, 249, 250, 266, 267, 304, 311, 327, 329, 364

wildfire/brushfire 280, 297, 298, 299, 301, 302, 306, 307, 308
women 8, 62, 66, 69, 71, 72, 147, 167, 233, 234, 235, 236, 237, 243, 252, 279, 336, 365, 393
work-life balance 62, 64, 66, 73, 260, 270, 317

 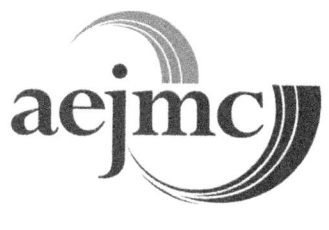

AEJMC–PETER LANG SCHOLARSOURCING SERIES

Launched in 2014, Scholarsourcing is a joint book publishing venture of the Association for Education in Journalism and Mass Communication (AEJMC) and Peter Lang Publishing that has redefined how scholarly books are proposed, peer-reviewed, and approved for contract. An initiative of 2013–2014 AEJMC President Paula Poindexter, Scholarsourcing is based on the concept of crowdsourcing, with AEJMC members proposing books which are then voted on by the association's membership. Authors of top proposals are invited to write full book proposals that are then reviewed by the Scholarsourcing Series editorial board, with the goal of offering at least one book contract annually.

A very special thanks goes to all who have contributed to the success of Scholarsourcing. These include AEJMC Executive Director Jennifer McGill; Peter Lang Publishing, particularly editor Kathryn Harrison and founding editor Mary Savigar; Founding Series Editor Jane B. Singer; founding editorial board members Carolyn Bronstein, David Perlmutter, Paula Poindexter and Richard Waters; and the hundreds of AEJMC members who have contributed ideas and input, along with a rich supply of wonderful book proposals.

To order books, please contact our Customer Service Department at:

peterlang@presswarehouse.com (within the U.S.)
orders@peterlang.com (outside the U.S.)

Or browse online by series at www.peterlang.com

Made in the USA
Monee, IL
03 May 2026

49437795R00233